ACCA

PAPER P6

ADVANCED TAXATION (UK)
FAs 2015

P R A C T I C E & R E V I S I O N K I T

BPP LEARNING MEDIA

FOR EXAMS IN SEPTEMBER 2016, DECEMBER 2016 AND MARCH 2017

First edition 2007
Tenth edition February 2016

ISBN 9781 4727 4447 0
(previous ISBN 9781 4727 2242 3)

e-ISBN 9781 4727 4647 4

British Library Cataloguing-in-Publication Data
A catalogue record for this book
is available from the British Library

Published by

BPP Learning Media Ltd
BPP House, Aldine Place
London W12 8AA

www.bpp.com/learningmedia

Printed by Polestar Wheatons
Hennock Road
Marsh Barton
Exeter
EX2 8RP

Your learning materials, published by BPP Learning Media Ltd, are printed on paper obtained from traceable, sustainable sources.

The contents of this book are intended as a guide and not professional advice. Although every effort has been made to ensure that the contents of this book are correct at the time of going to press, BPP Learning Media makes no warranty that the information in this book is accurate or complete and accepts no liability for any loss or damage suffered by any person acting or refraining from acting as a result of the material in this book.

We are grateful to the Association of Chartered Certified Accountants for permission to reproduce past examination questions. The suggested solutions in the Practice & Revision Kit have been prepared by BPP Learning Media Ltd, except where otherwise stated.

Contents

Question index

The headings in this checklist/index indicate the main topics of questions, but questions are expected to cover several different topics.

Mock exam 1

Mock exam 2

Mock exam 3 (ACCA September/December 2015 Exam)

Topic index

Listed below are the key Paper P6 syllabus topics and the numbers of the questions in this Kit covering those topics. If you need to concentrate your practice and revision on certain topics you will find this index useful.

ME1 is Mock Exam 1, ME2 is Mock Exam 2 and ME3 is Mock Exam 3.

Helping you with your revision

BPP Learning Media – Approved Content Provider

As an ACCA **Approved Content Provider**, BPP Learning Media gives you the **opportunity** to use revision materials reviewed by the ACCA examination team. By incorporating the ACCA examination team's comments and suggestions regarding the depth and breadth of syllabus coverage, the BPP Learning Media Practice & Revision Kit provides excellent, **ACCA-approved** support for your revision.

Tackling revision and the exam

Using feedback obtained from the ACCA examination team review:

- We look at the dos and don'ts of revising for, and taking, ACCA exams

- We focus on Paper P6; we discuss revising the syllabus, what to do (and what not to do) in the exam, how to approach different types of question and ways of obtaining easy marks

Selecting questions

We provide signposts to help you plan your revision.

- A full **question index**

- A **topic index** listing all the questions that cover key topics, so that you can locate the questions that provide practice on these topics, and see the different ways in which they might be examined

Making the most of question practice

At BPP Learning Media we realise that you need more than just questions and model answers to get the most from your question practice.

- Our **Top tips** included for certain questions provide essential advice on tackling questions, presenting answers and the key points that answers need to include

- We show you how you can pick up **Easy marks** on some questions, as we know that picking up all readily available marks often can make the difference between passing and failing

- We include **marking guides** to show you what the examination team rewards

- We include **comments from the examination team** to show you where students struggled or performed well in the actual exam

- We refer to the **Finance Acts 2015 BPP Study Text** for exams in September 2016, December 2016 and March 2017 for detailed coverage of the topics covered in questions

Attempting mock exams

There are three mock exams that provide practice at coping with the pressures of the exam day. We strongly recommend that you attempt them under exam conditions. **Mock exams 1 and 2** reflect the question styles and syllabus coverage of the exam.

Mock exam 3 is the ACCA September/December 2015 exam paper. This exam is compiled from questions selected by the examination team from the September 2015 and December 2015 exams. They do not reflect the entire September or December exams but contain questions most appropriate for students to practice.

Revising P6

Firstly we must emphasise that you will need a good knowledge of the **whole syllabus**. This means **learning/memorising the rules** in order to be able to answer questions. The examination team has commented that it is a **lack of precise knowledge** that causes many candidates problems in the exam.

Any part of the syllabus could be tested within compulsory Section A. Having to choose two out of three optional questions in Section B does not really represent much choice if there are areas of the syllabus you are keen to avoid. That said, there are certain topics which are **particularly important**:

- The **calculation of income tax payable**, including the **restriction of the personal allowance** and **income tax credits**

- **Personal pension schemes**, in particular the **annual allowance** and the **annual allowance charge**

- The **basis of assessment for unincorporated businesses**, including rules on commencement and cessation. Don't neglect the **impact of losses** in these situations

- The **calculation of benefits from employment** so that you can make sensible comparisons between **remuneration packages**. Make sure you can advise on **tax free benefits** too. The rules for **share schemes** and on **termination payments** should be known very well

- The **structure and mechanics** of **inheritance tax** (eg types of transfer, nil rate band, seven year cumulation)

- The **exemptions** and **reliefs available for the different taxes**, in particular **for capital gains tax** (eg entrepreneurs' relief, gift relief, rollover relief) and **inheritance tax** (eg spouse exemption, business property relief). **Exemptions and reliefs** are the **foundation of any tax planning**

- The **computation of corporation tax**, including dealing with **loan relationships**, **intangible assets**, and **research and development expenditure**

- **Close companies** including the position of **participators**

- All aspects of **corporation tax groups** including the impact of related 51% group companies, loss relief, chargeable gains groups, the effect of group VAT registration and stamp taxes groups. You should pay particular attention to the impact on **corporate restructuring**

- For **value added tax**, the **rules on land and buildings**, the **capital goods scheme**, **special VAT schemes** available for small businesses so that you can advise if and when they might be appropriate, and the **partial exemption rules**

- **Overseas aspects** of income tax, CGT, IHT, corporation tax and VAT

- **Tax administration**, including filing dates, penalties and interest for all taxes

- **Ethical considerations** when acting for clients

You should use the Passcards and any brief notes you have to revise these topics, but you mustn't spend all your revision time passively reading. **Question practice is vital**; doing as many questions as you can in full will help develop your ability to analyse scenarios and produce relevant discussion and recommendations.

You should make sure you leave yourself enough time during your revision to practise Section A questions as you cannot avoid them, and the scenarios and requirements of Section A questions are more complex than Section B questions. You should also leave yourself enough time to do the three mock exams.

Passing the P6 exam

Displaying the right qualities

The examination team expects students to display the following qualities.

Qualities required	
Knowledge development	Basic knowledge of the core taxes from Paper F6 is key, extended to encompass further overseas aspects of taxation, additional aspects of CGT and IHT, trusts, stamp taxes and additional exemptions and reliefs.
Knowledge application	You must be able to apply your knowledge to the issues commonly encountered by individuals and businesses. You will be expected to consider more than one tax at any one time and to identify planning issues and areas of interaction of the taxes.
Skill development	Paper P6 seeks to develop the skills of analysis and interpretation. You must be able to interpret and analyse the information provided in the question, keeping your answers focused and as accurate as possible, while avoiding waffle.
Communication skills	Paper P6 also seeks to develop the skill of communication. It is no good having the knowledge but not being able to communicate it effectively, so ensure you keep your communication appropriate to the intended audience. Practise using the appropriate terminology in your answers: you will need to be more technical when communicating with a tax manager (eg using technical terms for loss relief) and less so when speaking to a client (who may not understand 'early years loss relief'!)
Keeping current	The examination team expects you to advise using established tax planning methods in the exam. Fortunately they do not expect you to invent new ones. However, you must be aware of current issues in taxation.
Computation skills	Computations are not the focus of the P6 exam. However they may be required in support of explanations. It is therefore essential that you can complete calculations of tax liabilities speedily and without difficulty to provide numerical evidence for your tax advice.

You will not always produce the exact same solution as we have in our answer section. This does not necessarily mean that you have failed the question, as marks are often available for any other relevant key points you make.

Avoiding weaknesses

We give details of the examination team's comments and criticisms at various points throughout this Kit. These reports always emphasise the need to demonstrate a fairly wide syllabus knowledge, but also to identify and justify the availability (or non-availability) of particular reliefs and exemptions. There are various things you can do on the day of the exam to enhance your chances. Although these all sound basic, the examination team has commented that scripts show:

- A failure to read the question and requirements properly and answer the question set, instead churning out irrelevant 'set pieces'

- Clear evidence of poor time management

- Tendency to confuse CGT and IHT and even personal and corporation tax issues

Make sure you attempt only four questions (as only four will be marked) and start each question on a new page, clearly labelled.

Finally, never ever cross your workings out. These may be correct and you will not be given credit if you have crossed the working out.

Choosing which questions to answer first

You will need to answer the two compulsory questions in Section A and two out of the three optional questions in Section B, with a larger number of marks awarded for the first two questions (60 marks in total).

- We recommend that you spend time at the beginning of your exam carefully reading through all of the questions in the paper, and each of their requirements. Once you feel familiar with your exam paper we then recommend that you attempt the optional questions first.

- The optional questions will be for 20 marks each. Answer the question on your most comfortable topic but be strict with timing. It is all too tempting to write everything you know about your favourite topic. Don't!

- The reason for attempting the optional questions first is, in the examination team's words:

  'The majority of…candidates appeared to attempt the compulsory questions first, and overrun the time allocation, which they may have regretted later when they reached some relatively straightforward areas in the Section B questions, but didn't have time to have a reasonable attempt at them.'

- Doing the optional questions first should mean that you can manage your time more effectively and not run out of time answering the longer compulsory questions. Attempting the easier questions first means that you will have been generating ideas and remembering facts for the more difficult questions.

- In Section A there will be 35 marks for question 1 (including 4 professional marks) and 25 marks for question 2. Many students prefer to answer question 1 with the larger number of allocated marks first. Others again prefer to answer a question on their most comfortable topic. Usually one question will be a personal tax question and one question a business tax question.

- Whatever the order, make sure you leave yourself **sufficient time** to tackle all the questions. Don't get bogged down in the more difficult areas, or re-write your answer two or three times. Instead move on and try the rest of the question as there may be an easier part. You do not want to be in a position where you have to rush the rest of the paper.

- Allocate your time carefully between different question parts. If a question is split into a number of requirements, use the number of marks available for each to allocate your time effectively. Remember also that small overruns of time during the first half of the exam can add up to leave you very short of time towards the end.

Tackling questions

You'll improve your chances by following a step-by-step approach along the following lines.

Step 1   Identify the requirements of the question

Identify the knowledge areas being tested and see precisely what the examination team wants you to do. This will help you focus on what's important in the question.

In Section B questions, this means reading the requirement of the question. However, in Section A questions, you will usually need to look also at the more detailed instructions within the body of the question to find out exactly what is required. Look for key phrases in the question such as 'I need the following ….' or 'Please prepare the following for me…'.

Step 2   Check the mark allocation

This helps you allocate time.

Step 3   Read the question actively

You will already know which knowledge area(s) are being tested from having identified the requirements so whilst you read through the question underline or highlight key words and figures as you read. This will mean you are thinking about the question rather than just looking at the words blankly, and will allow you to identify relevant information for use in your advice and supporting calculations.

Step 4   Plan your answer

You may only spend five minutes planning your answer but it will be five minutes well spent. Identify the supporting calculations (and appropriate proformas) you will need to do, if any. Plan the structure of your written answer, even if it is only a series of bullet points, or maybe a spider diagram, using suitable headings and sub headings. Determine whether you can you use bullet points in your answer or if you need a more formal format.

Step 5   Write your answer

Stick carefully to the time allocation for each question, and for each part of each question.

Gaining the easy marks

There are two main ways to obtain easy marks in the P6 exam.

Providing supporting computations

Although computations will not normally be required in isolation in Paper P6 as the focus is on written explanations and advice, there will always be marks available for calculating figures which will support your recommendations. Often you cannot provide any sensible advice until you know the tax cost of a course of action so make sure you can readily set out proformas and fill in the numbers from the question. Make it easy for yourself to pick up the easy marks.

Answering the question

If you need to consider alternative planning strategies in a question and provide advice on which is the most suitable, do exactly that. If you do not advise on the most suitable plan you'll be losing easy marks. Similarly, if you are asked to consider CGT and IHT in a requirement, don't think that by including some income tax considerations you will pick up extra marks – you won't. Show the examining team you have read the question and requirements carefully and have attempted to answer them as expected – not how you would like to.

Exam information

Format of the exam

Time allowed: 3 hours 15 minutes

Tax rates and allowances and information on certain reliefs will be provided in the examination paper.

Paper P6 is split into sections A and B each comprising scenario based questions which will usually involve consideration of more than one tax, together with some elements of planning and the interaction of taxes. The focus is on explanations and advice rather than computations.

Section A contains two compulsory questions. Question 1 has 35 marks (including 4 professional marks) and question 2 has 25 marks.

Section B consists of three questions, two of which must be answered. Each Section B question has 20 marks.

The exams set before 2013 had a slightly different allocation of marks. Section A questions varied in length between 25 and 37 marks and Section B questions varied between 16 and 20 marks. The time allocation for each mark was the same as for the current exam format. We have therefore retained the original marking structure for questions in the main part of this Kit. The marks for Mock Exams 1 and 2 have been adjusted for the fixed mark structure, where appropriate, and these exams have been reviewed by the examination team.

Examiner's general comments

If you are preparing to sit Paper P6 you should pay particular attention to the following in order to maximise your chances of success.

1   *Know your stuff*

- Successful candidates are able to demonstrate sufficient, precise knowledge of the UK tax system. This knowledge must be up to date. Candidates sitting the exam from 1 September 2016 to 31 March 2017 must familiarise themselves with changes introduced by Finance Act 2015 and Finance (No. 2) Act 2015 as summarised in the Finance Acts article published in Student Accountant magazine and on the website.

- This includes knowledge brought forward from the F6 (UK) syllabus.

2   *Question practice*

- Practise questions from past exams with the aim of adopting the style of the model answers. In particular, candidates should practise the often more intellectually demanding Section A style questions.

3   *Address the requirement*

- Read the requirement carefully – in the Section A questions the detailed tasks that you are to perform may be set out in one of the documents. It may be helpful to tick off the tasks as you address them. Marks are awarded for satisfying the requirements and not for other information even if it is technically correct.

- The requirement of each question is carefully worded in order to provide you with guidance as regards the style and content of your answers. You should note the command words within the requirement (calculate, explain etc), any matters which are not to be covered and the precise issues you have been asked to address.

- You should also note any guidance given in the question or in any notes following the requirement regarding the approach you should take when answering the question.

- Pay attention to the number of marks available – this provides you with a clear indication of the amount of time you should spend on each question part.

4   *Don't provide general explanations or long introductions*

- If you are asked to calculate, there is no need to explain what you are going to do before you do it; just get on with it – only provide explanations when you are asked to.

- Think before you write. Then write whatever is necessary to satisfy the requirement.

- Apply your knowledge to the facts by reference to the requirement.

5   *Think before you start and manage your time*

- Ensure that you allow the correct amount of time for each question.

- Before you start writing, think about the issues and identify all of the points you intend to address and/or any strategy you intend to adopt to solve the problem set.

Resitting P6

If you are preparing to resit the exam, think about the number of additional marks you need and identify a strategy to earn them. For example:

- Identify those areas of the syllabus where you are weakest and work to improve your knowledge in those areas. This should include any technical areas brought forward from F6 (UK) where necessary.

- Ask yourself whether you could improve the way you manage your time in the exam and whether you address all of the parts of all four questions or whether you waste time addressing issues which have not been asked for.

- Make sure that you earn the professional skills marks and that you are prepared to address the ethical issues that may be examined.

Marks available in respect of professional skills

In order to earn marks for professional skills such as report writing, candidates first have to satisfy the requirement in relation to the format of the document requested. Further marks are then available for the clarity of the answer, including the ease with which it can be marked and the degree to which the conclusions reached follow logically from the explanations and calculations provided. These latter marks are more likely to be earned by those candidates who think about the manner in which they intend to satisfy the requirement such that there is a sense of purpose and a coherency to their answers.

Analysis of past papers

The table below provides details of when each element of the syllabus has been examined and the question number and section in which each element appeared.

With the introduction of the four exam sessions, ACCA will continue to publish the same number of exams, two per year, and at the same times, after the December and June exam sessions. These exams will be compiled from questions selected from the two preceding sessions. The first of this kind was published in December 2015, compiled from September 2015 and December 2015 exams, and this has been included in the analysis below.

Covered in Text chapter		Sept/ Dec 2015	June 2015	Dec 2014	June 2014	Dec 2013	June 2013	Dec 2012	June 2012	Dec 2011	June 2011
	INCOME TAX										
1	Principles of income tax	1(a), 2(b), 5(a)	3(b), 5(a)	1(b)	1(a), 4(a), 5(c)	5(a)	3(a)	2(a)	4(c)	2(a)	1(a)
2	Pensions and other tax efficient investment products	5(a), 5(b)				3(b)	3(a)		4(c)		4(b)
3	Property and other investment income	4(b)	4(b)		4(a)	5(a)					
4	Employment income	1(a), 4(a)	5(a)		3(a), 5(c)	4(c)	3(a), 5(b)	2(a)	3(b), 3(c)	3(b)	1(a), 2(a)
5	Employment income: additional aspects			5(b)	3(b), 3(c)	5(b)	5(b)	1(a), 2(a)	4(a)	3(a)	
6	Trade profits	1(a)	5(b)	4(a)	1(a)			2(a)	3(b), 4(b)	2(a)	3(a)
7	Capital allowances		3(a)	2(a)	1(a), 5(b)	1(b)	4(b)	1(a)	5(c)		
8	Trading losses	1(a)	1(b)	1(b)			5(a)	2(a)		2(a)	3(b)
9	Partnerships and limited liability partnerships								4(b)		3(b)
10	Overseas aspects of income tax		1(a)	4(b)			3(b)			2(b)	
	CAPITAL GAINS TAX										
11	Chargeable gains: an outline		4(a)	1(a), 3(d)	1(a)	1(b), 3(b), 5(a)	2(b)	4(a)	1(a)	2(a)	1(a)
12	Shares and securities					3(b)					4(c)
13	Chargeable gains: reliefs	2(b)	1(c), 4(b)	3(c)	1(a), 5(b)	1(b), 3(b), 5(a)	2(b)	2(b), 4(a)	1(a)	2(a)	1(a)
14	Chargeable gains: additional aspects	1(c), 3(a), 5(c)	3(d)	4(b)			2(a)	4(a)		2(a), (b)	
	TAX ADMINISTRATION FOR INDIVIDUALS										
15	Self assessment for individuals and partnerships			1(b)				4(c), 5(a), 5(b)	1(b)		
	INHERITANCE TAX										
16	An introduction to	5(b)	4(b)	1(a),	1(b)	1(b),	2(b)	2(b), 5(c)	1(a)	4(b)	1(b), 4(a)

Covered in Text chapter		Sept/Dec 2015	June 2015	Dec 2014	June 2014	Dec 2013	June 2013	Dec 2012	June 2012	Dec 2011	June 2011
	inheritance tax			3(a)		3(a)					
17	Inheritance tax: valuation, reliefs and the death estate	1(b)	4(c)	3(b)	1(b)	3(a)	2(b)	5(c)	1(a)	4(b)	1(b)
18	Inheritance tax: additional aspects		1(d), 4(c)	3(c)	4(c)	1(b), 3(c)		5(c)	1(a)	2(b), 4(a), 4(b)	1(b)
	STAMP TAXES										
19	Stamp taxes		2(a)				2(b)		1(a)		1(a)
	CORPORATION TAX										
20	Computing taxable total profits	2(a), 3(a), 4(b)	2(b)	2(a), 2(b)		2(a), 2(b)		1(a)	2(b), 5(c)		
21	Chargeable gains for companies	2(b), 3(b)	2(a), 2(c)	2(a)	2(b)	2(a)	4(a)	1(a)	2(b), 2(c)		2(b), 5(c)
22	Computing corporation tax payable	2(a)		5(a)		2(a)	1(a)		2(d), 3(b), 5(a), 5(b)	1(a)	2(a)
23	Administration, winding up, purchase of own shares						1(c)	3(a)			
24	Losses and deficits on non-trading loan relationships		2(b)	2(a)					2(a)	1(a), 5(b)	
25	Close companies and investment companies		3(a)		5(c)	2(b)		3(a), 3(b)		1(a)	
26	Groups and consortia	2(b), 3(a), 3(c)	2(a), 2(c)	2(a)	2(a)	2(a)	1(a)	1(a)	2(a), 5(c)	1(a), 5(a)	
27	Overseas aspects of corporate tax			5(c)		4(b)		3(b)			5(a), (b)
	VALUE ADDED TAX										
28	Value added tax 1	2(b), 2(c)	1(d)	1(d)			4(c)	4(b)		2(b), 5(c)	2(a), (b)
29	Value added tax 2	4(c)	3(c)	2(c)	1(a), 5(a)	2(c), 4(a)	1(b)	1(a)	2(b), (c)	1(a), 5(c)	2(a), (b)
	IMPACT OF TAXES AND TAX PLANNING										
30	Impact of taxes and tax planning	1(a)	2(d)	1(c)	1(a), 2(c)	1(a), 5(a)	1(a), 1(c), 1(d), 3(a)	1(b)	1(b), 3(a)	1(b)	2(b)

IMPORTANT!

The table above gives a broad idea of how frequently major topics in the syllabus are examined. It should not be used to question spot and predict for example that Topic X will not be examined because it came up two sittings ago. The examiner's reports indicate that the examination team is well aware some students try to question spot. Examiners avoid predictable patterns and may, for example, examine the same topic two sittings in a row.

Useful websites

The websites below provide additional sources of information of relevance to your studies for *P6 Advanced Taxation.*

- www.accaglobal.com

  ACCA's website. The students' section of the website is invaluable for detailed information about the qualification, past issues of Student Accountant (including technical articles) and even interviews with the examiners.

- www.bpp.com

  Our website provides information about BPP products and services, with a link to the ACCA website.

- www.gov.uk/government/organisations/hm-revenue-customs

  HM Revenue and Customs official site. The section for tax agents and advisors is particularly relevant.

Questions

INCOME TAX AND NATIONAL INSURANCE CONTRIBUTIONS

Questions 1 to 11 focus on income tax and national insurance contributions. These are the subject of Chapters 1 to 10 in the BPP Study Text.

1 Styrax   53 mins

You should assume that today's date is 15 March 2016.

You have recently been approached to act as an accountant for Styrax who is self-employed. The following information has been extracted from client files and from meetings with Styrax.

Styrax:

- Annual trading profits have been fairly constant at approximately £20,000 for the last few years.

- Has building society savings amounting to around £35,000 which generate gross annual interest of approximately £1,000.

- Wife, Salvia is expecting their first child and has recently given up employed work.

- The couple has no other sources of income.

- Disposable income is about £3,000 pa after paying their mortgage and living expenses.

Investment strategy:

- Neither Styrax nor his wife have made, and for the present do not wish to start making, any pension provision.

- Risk averse

Stryax's brother, Taxus:

- Single.

- Prepared to take medium to high risk in his investments.

- Considering investing in the Enterprise Investment Scheme (EIS), the Seed Enterprise Investment Scheme (SEIS), and in Venture Capital Trusts (VCTs). He has not previously made any investments under any of these Schemes.

Required

(a)   (i)   Prepare notes for a meeting with Styrax setting out any measures that could be undertaken by the couple in order to reduce their income tax and national insurance liabilities following Salvia leaving her employment.

You should assume that Styrax does not wish to incorporate his business, that Salvia does not wish to join him in partnership and that Styrax already has two employees such that the employment allowance is already utilised against the secondary Class 1 national insurance contributions for these employees.

Detailed income tax computations are not required in this part of the question.   **(8 marks)**

(ii)   Explain the options open to the couple regarding making future pension provision.   **(3 marks)**

You should assume that the tax rates and allowances for 2015/16 apply throughout.

(b)   Write a memorandum to Taxus setting out the income tax consequences of investing in the EIS, the SEIS, and VCTs. You should include details of the risk and taxation implications of each type of investment.

(16 marks)

(Total = 27 marks)

2 Spike (ATAX 06/13)

39 mins

Spike requires advice on the loss relief available following the cessation of his business and on the tax implications of share options and a relocation payment provided by his new employer.

Spike:

- Ceased to trade and sold his unincorporated business to an unrelated individual on 30 September 2015.
- Sold his house, 'Sea View', on 1 March 2016 for £125,000 more than he had paid for it.
- Began working for Set Ltd on 1 May 2016.
- Has no income or capital gains other than the amounts referred to in the information below.

Spike's unincorporated business:

- There are overlap profits from the commencement of the business of £8,300.
- The sale of the business resulted in net capital gains of £78,000.
- The tax adjusted profits/(loss) of the business have been:

		£
Year ended 31 December 2011	Profit	52,500
Year ended 31 December 2012	Profit	68,000
Year ended 31 December 2013	Profit	54,000
Year ended 31 December 2014	Profit	24,995
Nine months ending 30 September 2015	Loss	(13,500)

Remuneration from Set Ltd:

- Spike is being paid a salary of £65,000 per year.
- On 1 May 2016, Spike was granted an option to purchase ordinary shares in Set Ltd.
- On 1 July 2016, Set Ltd will pay Spike a relocation payment of £33,500.

The option to purchase ordinary shares in Set Ltd:

- Spike paid £3,500 for an option to purchase 7,000 ordinary shares, representing a 3.5% shareholding.

- The option is exercisable on 1 May 2020 at £4.00 per share.

- An ordinary share in Set Ltd was worth £5.00 on 1 May 2016 and is expected to be worth £8.00 on 1 May 2020.

- Set Ltd does not have any tax advantaged share option schemes.

The relocation payment of £33,500:

- Spike sold 'Sea View', and purchased a new house, in order to live near the premises of Set Ltd.
- £22,000 of the payment is to compensate Spike for having to sell his house at short notice at a low price.
- £11,500 of the payment is in respect of the costs incurred by Spike in relation to moving house.

Required

(a) (i) Calculate the trading loss for the tax year 2015/16, and the terminal loss, on the cessation of Spike's unincorporated business. **(4 marks)**

(ii) Explain the reliefs available in respect of the losses calculated in part (i) and quantify the potential tax savings for each of them. **(10 marks)**

(b) (i) Explain all of the income tax and capital gains tax liabilities arising on Spike in respect of the grant and the exercise of the share options and the eventual sale of the shares in Set Ltd. **(4 marks)**

(ii) Explain the income tax implications for Spike of the relocation payment. **(2 marks)**

Notes

1   You should assume that the tax rates and allowances for the tax year 2015/16 apply to all tax years.
2   Ignore national insurance contributions throughout this question.

(Total = 20 marks)

3 Piquet and Buraco (ATAX 12/14)

39 mins

Your firm has been asked to provide advice to two unrelated clients, Piquet and Buraco. Piquet, an unincorporated sole trader, requires advice on a proposed change to the date to which he prepares his accounts. Buraco requires advice on his residence status and the remittance basis.

(a) **Piquet:**

- Began trading as an unincorporated sole trader on 1 January 2009.
- Has always prepared accounts to 31 October.
- Has overlap profits of £15,000 for a five-month overlap period.
- Is planning to change his accounting date to 28 February 2017.

Actual and budgeted tax adjusted trading profit of Piquet's business:

	Profit per month £	Profit for the period £
Year ended 31 October 2015	4,500	54,000
16 months ending 28 February 2017	5,875	94,000
Year ending 28 February 2018	7,333	88,000
Year ending 28 February 2019	9,000	108,000

Alternative choice of accounting date:

- Piquet is also considering a year end of 30 April.

- To achieve this, Piquet would prepare accounts for the 18 months ending 30 April 2017 and annually thereafter.

Required

(i) On the assumption that Piquet changes his accounting date to 28 February, state the date by which he should notify HM Revenue and Customs of the change, and calculate the taxable trading profit for each tax years 2016/17 and 2017/18. **(3 marks)**

(ii) On the assumption that Piquet changes his accounting date to 30 April, state the basis periods for the tax years 2016/17 and 2017/18 and the effect of this change on Piquet's overlap profits. **(3 marks)**

(iii) Identify and explain TWO advantages for Piquet of using a year end of 30 April rather than 28 February. **(4 marks)**

(b) **Buraco's links with the country of Canasta:**

- Buraco is domiciled in Canasta.
- Buraco owns a home in the country of Canasta.
- Buraco's only income is in respect of investment properties in Canasta.
- Buraco frequently buys and sells properties in Canasta.

Buraco's links with the UK:

- Buraco's ex-wife and their 12-year-old daughter moved to the UK on 1 May 2015.
- Buraco first visited the UK in the tax year 2015/16 but was not UK resident in that year.
- Buraco did not own a house in the UK until he purchased one on 6 April 2016.
- Buraco expects to live in the UK house for between 100 and 150 days in the tax year 2016/17.

Required

(i) Explain why Buraco will not satisfy any of the automatic overseas residence tests for the tax year 2016/17, and, on the assumption that he does not satisfy any of the automatic UK residence tests, explain how his residence status will be determined for that tax year. **(7 marks)**

(ii) On the assumption that Buraco is resident in the UK in the tax year 2016/17, state the tax implications for him of claiming the remittance basis for that year and explain whether or not there would be a remittance basis charge. **(3 marks)**

(Total = 20 marks)

4 Jodie (ATAX 06/15)

68 mins

Your manager has received a letter from Jodie in connection with her proposed emigration from the UK. Extracts from the letter and from an email from your manager are set out below.

Extract from the letter from Jodie

> I have always lived in the UK. I plan to leave the UK and move to the country of Riviera on 5 April 2017. My intention is to move to Riviera permanently and acquire a new home there. However, if my children are not happy there after four years, we will return to the UK.
>
> My husband died three years ago. My brother lives in Riviera and is the only close family I have apart from my children. I will not have any sources of income in the UK after 5 April 2017.
>
> I intend to work part-time in Riviera so that I can look after my children. In the tax year 2017/18, I will return to the UK for a holiday and stay with friends for 60 days; for the rest of the tax year I will live in my new home in Riviera.
>
> **My unincorporated business**
>
> I prepared accounts to 31 December every year until 31 December 2015. I then ceased trading on 31 May 2016. I made a tax adjusted trading loss in my final period of trading of £18,000.
>
> I attach an appendix setting out the information you requested in relation to the business.
>
> I was unable to sell my business as a going concern due to the decline in its profitability. Accordingly, on 31 May 2016 I sold my business premises for £190,000. I paid £135,000 for these premises on 1 June 2003. I also sold various items of computer equipment, which I had used in my business, for a total of £2,000. This equipment cost me a total of £5,000. I retained the remaining inventory, valued at £3,500, for my own personal use.
>
> My taxable income for the last five tax years is set out below. There is no property income in the 2016/17 tax year because I sold my rental property in May 2015.
>
> | | 2012/13 | 2013/14 | 2014/15 | 2015/16 | 2016/17 |
> |---|---|---|---|---|---|
> | | £ | £ | £ | £ | £ |
> | Trading income | 64,000 | 67,000 | 2,000 | 3,000 | Nil |
> | Property income | 15,000 | 13,000 | 14,000 | 2,500 | Nil |
> | Bank interest | 2,000 | 2,000 | 3,000 | 3,500 | 8,000 (est.) |
>
> **Other matters**
>
> On 30 April 2016 I sold my house, which is built on a one hectare plot, for £400,000. I purchased the house for £140,000 in March 1995 and lived in it throughout my period of ownership. I have been living in a rented house in the UK since 1 May 2016. My tenancy of this rented house will end on 5 April 2017.
>
> When we spoke, you mentioned that you wanted details of any gifts I have received. The only item of significance is 2,000 ordinary shares in Butterfly Ltd which my mother gave to me on 14 May 2014 when the shares were worth £60,000. Butterfly Ltd is a UK resident trading company.
>
> My mother and I submitted a joint claim for capital gains tax holdover relief on the gift of these Butterfly Ltd shares, such that no capital gains tax was payable. I recently received an offer of £68,000 for these shares, but I decided not to sell them. My mother had inherited the shares from her brother on 18 December 2002 when they were worth £37,000. Neither I nor my mother have ever worked for Butterfly Ltd.

Extract from an email from your manager

Additional information

- Jodie's business has always been registered for the purposes of value added tax (VAT). The sales proceeds respect of the business assets are stated net of VAT.

- Jodie has overlap profits from the commencement of her business of £6,500.

Please prepare paragraphs for inclusion in a letter from me to Jodie addressing the following issues.

(a)   UK tax residence status and liability to UK income tax

- Assuming Jodie leaves the UK in accordance with her plans, explain how her residence status for the tax year 2017/18 will be determined and conclude on her likely residence status for that year. To help, I have already concluded that Jodie will **not** be regarded as non-UK resident using the automatic overseas tests so there is no need to consider these tests.

- State how becoming non-UK resident will affect Jodie's liability to UK income tax.

(b)   Relief available in respect of the trading loss

- Calculate the income tax relief which Jodie would obtain if she were to claim terminal loss relief in respect of her trading loss. You should **not** consider any other ways in which the loss could be relieved.

- There is no need to calculate Jodie's tax liabilities for each of the years concerned; just calculate the tax which will be saved due to the offset of the loss and explain how you have determined this figure.

(c)   Capital gains tax

Assuming that Jodie becomes non-UK resident from 6 April 2017 and does not return to the UK for at least four tax years:

- Explain how this will affect her liability to UK capital gains tax in the tax year 2017/18 and future years and in 2016/17 (the tax year prior to departure); and

- Calculate her capital gains tax liability for the tax year 2016/17. You should include explanations of the chargeable gains which have arisen or may arise in that year and the tax rate(s) which will be charged.

(d)   Other matters

- Explain how leaving the UK will affect the UK inheritance tax liability on any gifts Jodie may make in the future.

- Explain the matters which Jodie should be aware of in relation to VAT in respect of the cessation of her business. I have already checked that Jodie charged the correct amount of VAT when she sold the business premises and the computer equipment.

Tax manager

Required

Prepare the paragraphs for inclusion in a letter from your manager to Jodie as requested in the email from your manager. The following marks are available:

(a)	UK tax residence status and liability to UK income tax	**(7 marks)**
(b)	Relief available in respect of the trading loss	**(8 marks)**
(c)	Capital gains tax	**(11 marks)**
(d)	Other matters	**(5 marks)**

Professional marks will be awarded for following the manager's instructions, the clarity of the explanations and calculations, the effectiveness with which the information is communicated, and the overall presentation.

(4 marks)

Notes

1.   You should assume that the tax rates and allowances for the tax year 2015/16 apply to all tax years.

2.   Ignore national insurance contributions throughout this question.

(Total = 35 marks)

5 John and Maureen (ATAX 06/08)

You have received the following memorandum from your manager.

To: Tax senior
From: Tax manager
Date: 2 June 2018
Subject: John and Maureen

I had a meeting with John and his wife Maureen yesterday. They have two children; Will, aged seven and Penny, aged nine. John and Maureen have made a number of errors in their income tax returns and Maureen requires advice in connection with her business.

Errors in income tax returns

John inherited a portfolio of quoted shares, an investment property and a large sum of cash in May 2015. Whilst completing his tax return for 2015/16 he decided to 'give' all the income arising from the shares, property and cash deposits to his wife for tax purposes. Accordingly, he omitted the income from his own tax return and included it in that of his wife. He did the same thing in 2016/17.

John has since realised that such a 'gift' has no effect for tax purposes and has decided to notify HM Revenue and Customs (HMRC) of his mistake.

In January 2016 John gave the investment property to Maureen who sold it a week later. The gift to Maureen was the subject of a legitimate legal conveyance but, after the sale, Maureen gave the sales proceeds to John in accordance with an agreement they had made prior to the gift. Maureen declared the capital gain of £13,870 in her 2015/16 income tax return. John used his annual exempt amount for 2015/16 on a disposal in September 2015.

John has asked us to calculate the additional tax payable as a result of his mistaken declaration to HMRC. A schedule prepared by John summarising the family's income for the two years 2015/16 and 2016/17 together with details of the investment property is on your desk. The gain on the sale of the investment property was the couple's only capital gain in the last four years, other than the disposal in September 2015.

Maureen's business

Maureen began in business as a sole trader on 1 November 2015. She registered for value added tax (VAT) immediately and prepared her first accounts to 30 September 2016. A schedule prepared by Maureen summarising the results of the business is also on your desk.

All of Maureen's customers are registered for VAT. The business has recoverable input tax of approximately £300 per quarter. Despite accounting for VAT on an annual basis, Maureen is finding the administration of the tax very time consuming and is considering deregistering unless the amount of administration can be reduced.

Please prepare the following for me.

(a)   A calculation of the additional taxes payable by John in respect of the tax years 2015/16 and 2016/17 as a result of disclosing to HMRC the errors in his tax returns.

There's quite a bit to do here; please ensure that your calculations are clear and logical so that they are easy to follow. You'll need to work out the extra tax payable by John on the investment income and compare it with the tax paid by Maureen (probably a fairly small amount as most if not all of her income will have fallen into her basic rate band).

Please **do not** address the issue of interest and penalties for the moment.

(b)   Advice for Maureen on her ability to deregister for the purposes of VAT together with the procedure she should follow and implications of deregistration. Include details of any alternative strategy that might solve her problem.

I do not want you to write a letter or to prepare illustrative calculations; just write the necessary paragraphs for me to incorporate in a letter that will cover a number of other issues.

Thank you

Irwin

The schedule summarising all of the family's income, with the exception of that relating to Maureen's business, is set out below.

John and Maureen – Income received in tax years 2015/16 and 2016/17			
	Notes	2015/16 £	2016/17 £
Income arising on inherited assets:			
Dividend income received in respect of share portfolio		8,856	9,108
Rental income in respect of investment property		2,550	–
Bank interest income received in respect of cash deposits		2,424	2,576
John – other income:			
Salary		30,294	31,066
Company car	1		
Trust income received	2	660	715
Maureen – other income:			
Unincorporated business	3		
Will – bank deposit interest received	4	Nil	88
Penny – bank deposit interest received	4	Nil	144

Notes

1   I have had use of the car since 1 August 2015 for both business and private use. I also receive free petrol in respect of all of my mileage. The car had a list price when new of £17,400 and has a CO_2 emission rate of 147 grams per kilometre.

2   The trust is a discretionary trust established by my uncle.

3   Maureen will provide you with a summary of the results of her business.

4   I transferred cash from my bank account to two new accounts for the children on 1 June 2016. The interest is credited gross as there is no tax liability on the children's income.

The schedule summarising the result of Maureen's business is set out below.

Maureen – Sole trader business

–   Began trading on 1 November 2015

–   Purchased a computer and other equipment for £22,917 (excluding value added tax (VAT)) in November 2015 and a car (CO_2 emissions of 120 g/km) for £6,010 (excluding VAT) in December 2015 which is used wholly for business purposes

–   Tax adjusted trading profits, before deduction of capital allowances

Period ended 30 September 2016	£54,456
Year ended 30 September 2017	£32,139

Required

(a)   Prepare a calculation of the additional taxes payable by John and Maureen in respect of the tax years 2015/16 and 2016/17 as a result of disclosing to HMRC the errors in their tax returns.   **(26 marks)**

Additional marks will be awarded for the clarity with which the information is presented and the extent to which the calculations are structured in a logical manner.   **(2 marks)**

(b)   Advise Maureen on deregistration for the purposes of value added tax (VAT) and any possible alternative strategy.   **(8 marks)**

An additional mark will be awarded for the effectiveness with which the information is communicated.   **(1 mark)**

Assume that the tax rates and allowances for 2015/16 apply to subsequent years.

(Total = 37 marks)

6 Monisha and Horner (ATAX 12/13)

39 mins

Your firm has been asked to advise two unrelated clients, Monisha and Horner. The advice relates to furnished holiday accommodation, tax planning for a married couple, and the personal service company (IR 35) rules.

(a) **Monisha:**

- Is married to Asmat.
- Earns a salary of £80,000 per year and realises chargeable gains of £6,000 per year.
- Owns a UK investment property, which is let to short-term tenants.

Asmat:

- Looks after the couple's children and has no income or chargeable gains.
- Expects to return to work on 6 April 2022 on an annual salary of £18,000.

The UK investment property owned by Monisha:

- The property cost £270,000 and is currently worth £300,000.
- The letting does not qualify as a commercial letting of furnished holiday accommodation.
- Annual income and expenditure:

	£
Rental income	20,000
Repairs and maintenance	1,600
Council tax	1,200
Agent's fees	2,000

- Monisha claims the wear and tear allowance in respect of this property.
- The property will be sold on 5 April 2023 and is expected to create a chargeable gain of £100,000.

Proposals to reduce the couple's total tax liability:

- Monisha will give a 20% interest in the investment property to Asmat on 1 April 2017.

- The couple will ensure that, from 6 April 2017, the letting of the investment property will qualify as a commercial letting of furnished holiday accommodation.

- From the tax year 2017/18 onwards, Monisha will claim annual capital allowances equal to the current annual wear and tear allowance.

Required

(i) State the conditions which must be satisfied in order for the letting of a UK furnished property to qualify as a commercial letting of furnished holiday accommodation. **(3 marks)**

(ii) Calculate the total tax saving in the six tax years 2017/18 to 2022/23 if ALL of the proposals to reduce the couple's tax liabilities are carried out. In respect of the second proposal, you should assume that the letting will qualify as a commercial letting of furnished holiday accommodation for the whole of the period of joint ownership and that all beneficial reliefs are claimed.

Note. You should ignore inheritance tax. **(10 marks)**

(b) **Horner:**

- Horner owns all of the shares of Otmar Ltd.

- Horner is the sole employee of Otmar Ltd.

- All of the income of Otmar Ltd is subject to the personal service company (IR 35) rules.

- Budgeted figures for Otmar Ltd for the year ending 5 April 2017 are set out below. Where applicable, these amounts are stated exclusive of value added tax (VAT).

	£
Income in respect of relevant engagements carried out by Horner	85,000
Costs of administering the company	3,900
Horner's annual salary	50,000
Dividend paid to Horner	15,000
Contributions paid into an occupational pension scheme in respect of Horner	2,000

Required

(i)   Outline the circumstances in which the personal service company (IR 35) rules apply.   **(3 marks)**

(ii) Calculate the deemed employment income of Horner for the year ending 5 April 2017.   **(4 marks)**

(Total = 20 marks)

7 Cate and Ravi (ATAX 06/15)   39 mins

Cate requires advice on the after-tax cost of taking on a part-time employee and the tax implications of starting to sell items via the internet. Cate's husband, Ravi, requires advice in relation to capital gains tax on the disposal of an overseas asset.

Cate:

- Is resident and domiciled in the UK.
- Is married to Ravi.
- Runs a successful unincorporated business, D-Designs.
- Receives dividends of £28,080 each year.
- Wants to sell some second-hand books online.

D-Designs business:

- Was set up by Cate in 2009.
- Is now making a taxable profit of £90,000 per annum.
- Operates a number of dress shops and already employs six full-time staff.
- Requires an additional part-time employee.

Part-time employee – proposed remuneration package:

- Salary of £12,000 per annum.

- Qualifying childcare vouchers of £25 per week for 52 weeks a year.

- Mileage allowance of 50 pence per mile for the 62-mile round trip required each week to redistribute stock between the shops. This will be for 48 weeks in the year.

- This employment will be the employee's only source of taxable income.

Sale of second-hand books:

- Cate inherited a collection of books from her mother in December 2014.
- Cate intends to sell these books via the internet.
- Some of the books are in a damaged state and Cate will get them rebound before selling them.

Ravi:

- Is domiciled in the country of Goland.

- Has been resident in the UK since his marriage to Cate in February 2008.

- Has UK taxable income of £125,000 in the tax year 2015/16.

- Realises chargeable gains each year from disposals of UK assets equal to the capital gains tax annual exempt amount.

- Sold an investment property in Goland in February 2016 for £130,000, realising a chargeable gain of £70,000. None of the proceeds from the sale of this property have been remitted to the UK.

Required

(a) Calculate the annual cost for Cate, after income tax and national insurance contributions, of D-Designs employing the part-time employee. **(9 marks)**

(b) Discuss whether the profit from Cate's proposed sale of books via the internet will be liable to either income tax or capital gains tax. **(5 marks)**

(c) Advise Ravi on the options available to him for calculating his UK capital gains for 2015/16. Provide supporting calculations of the tax payable by him in each case. **(6 marks)**

(Total = 20 marks)

8 Simone (ATAX 06/09)   35 mins

Simone is a partner in the firm Ellington and Co. She is seeking advice on the tax efficient use of her share of the partnership's loss for the year ended 5 April 2016. Simone intends to establish a new business and is considering the need to register for the purposes of value added tax (VAT).

The following information has been obtained from a meeting with Simone.

Simone's income and capital gains:

*   Dividends received of £12,600 in the tax year 2014/15, £10,800 in the tax year 2015/16 and £nil in subsequent years. In years prior to this, she had received dividends of £9,000 per annum.

*   Share of profits from Ellington and Co for the year ended 5 April 2015 of £48,615.

*   Capital gains of £94,000 on the sale of a portfolio of quoted shares on 1 February 2016.

Ellington and Co:

*   Has been trading for many years.
*   Has two partners; Ellington and Simone. A third partner, Basie, retired on 28 February 2016.
*   Made a loss in the year ended 5 April 2016.
*   Is budgeted to make tax adjusted trading profits of no more than £25,000 per year for the next few years.
*   Is registered for the purposes of VAT.

Ellington and Co – results for the year ended 5 April 2016:

*   The firm made a tax adjusted trading loss, before deduction of capital allowances, of £90,000.
*   The firm purchased office equipment on 1 December 2015 for £21,200 exclusive of VAT.
*   The balance on the capital allowances main pool as at 5 April 2015 was £700.

Ellington and Co – profit sharing arrangements:

*   From 6 April 2015 until 28 February 2016

	Ellington	Simone	Basie
Annual salaries	£15,000	£11,500	£13,000
Profit sharing ratio	3 :	2 :	2

*   From 1 March 2016

	Ellington	Simone
Annual salaries	£14,000	£14,000
Profit sharing ratio	1 :	1

Simone's new business:

*   Simone intends to start trading on 1 September 2016.
*   Taxable trading profit is budgeted to be approximately £1,550 per month.
*   Taxable supplies are expected to be between £80,000 and £100,000 in the first year.
*   Simone does not wish to register voluntarily for VAT.

Required

(a) (i) Calculate Simone's share of the tax adjusted trading loss for the year ended 5 April 2016. **(5 marks)**

(ii) State the alternative strategies available to Simone in respect of her share of the taxable trading loss for the year ended 5 April 2016. **(3 marks)**

(iii) Explain, using supporting calculations where necessary, which of the strategies will save the most tax and calculate the total tax saved via the operation of this strategy.

Note. Your calculations should be based on the assumption that the tax rates and allowances for the year 2015/16 apply to all relevant years. **(7 marks)**

(b) Explain when Simone would be required to register and to start charging her customers VAT and, in relation to this, comment on the relevance of Ellington and Co being VAT registered.

Note. You are not required to prepare calculations for part (b) of this question. **(3 marks)**

(Total = 18 marks)

9 Morice (ATAX 12/11)   33 mins

Morice is the finance director of Babeen plc. Babeen plc is a non-close quoted trading company. Morice wants to provide information to the company's employees on a proposed Schedule 3 Save As You Earn (SAYE) share option scheme, a medical care scheme and payments to employees for driving their own cars on business journeys.

The following information has been obtained from a telephone conversation with Morice.

Proposed Schedule 3 SAYE scheme rules:

- Employees will invest in the scheme for five years.

- The scheme will permit monthly investments of between £5 and £750.

- The scheme will be open to all employees and directors who are at least 21 years old and have worked full-time for the company for at least three years.

- The share options granted under the scheme will enable employees to purchase shares for £2.48 each.

Detailed explanations, with supporting calculations, requested by Morice:

- Whether or not **each** of the proposed rules will be acceptable for a Schedule 3 SAYE scheme.

- The tax and national insurance liabilities for the employee in the illustrative example below in respect of the grant and exercise of the share options, the receipt of the bonus and the sale of the shares on the assumption that the scheme referred to meets all of the conditions for approval.

Illustrative example – SAYE scheme compliant with Schedule 3:

- The share options will be granted on 1 January 2017 to purchase shares at £2.48 each.

- The employee will invest £250 each month for five years.

- A bonus equal to 90% of a single monthly payment will be paid at the end of the five-year period.

- The amount invested, together with the bonus, will be used to exercise share options.

- The share options will be exercised on 31 December 2021 and the shares will be sold on the same day.

- The employee's interest in the employing company will be less than 1%.

- A share in the employing company will be worth: £3.00 on 1 January 2017
                                        £4.00 on 31 December 2021

Medical care scheme:

- Babeen plc is to offer free private health insurance to its employees.

- The health insurance will cost the company £470 annually per employee.

- The insurance would cost each employee £590 if they were to purchase it personally.

- Employees who decline the offer will be able to borrow up to £12,500 from Babeen plc to pay for medical treatment.

- The loans will be interest-free and repayable over four years.

Payments to employees for driving their own cars on business journeys:

- For each mile driven – 36 pence
- For each mile driven whilst carrying a passenger – an additional 3 pence

Required

(a)   Prepare the DETAILED explanations, with supporting calculations, as requested by Morice in respect of the proposed SAYE scheme.   **(10 marks)**

(b)   Explain the income tax and national insurance implications for the employees of Babeen plc of:

    (i)   The medical care scheme
    (ii)   The payments for driving their own cars on business journeys

The following mark allocation is provided as guidance for this requirement:

    (i)   3 marks
    (ii)   4 marks   **(7 marks)**

You may assume that the tax rules and rates for 2015/16 will continue to apply for the foreseeable future.

(Total = 17 marks)

10 Banda (ATAX 12/07)   64 mins

You have received the following email from your manager.

From:	Tax Manager
Date:	3 December 2016
To:	Tax senior
Subject:	Banda

I've put a copy of a letter from a potential new client, Banda, on your desk. I've arranged a meeting with Banda for Friday this week to discuss the most appropriate structure for her new business, 'Aral'.

I spoke to Banda yesterday and obtained the following additional information.

- Banda has owned the whole of the ordinary share capital of Flores Ltd since 1 January 2013.
- Flores Ltd pays Banda a salary of £15,825 per annum and pays dividends to her of £20,250 on 31 July each year.
- Banda does not intend to take any income from Aral until the tax year 2019/20 at the earliest.
- Flores Ltd is Banda's only source of income.

Banda also mentioned that Flores Ltd made some sort of 'informal loan' to her in 2013 of £21,000 to pay for improvements to her house. I decided not to press her about this over the phone but I need to discuss with her what she meant by 'informal' and whether or not the loan has been disclosed to HM Revenue and Customs.

Please prepare the following schedules for me to use as a basis for our discussions. I will give Banda copies of schedules (a) and (b) but not schedule (c), as some of its contents may be sensitive.

(a)   Calculations of the anticipated tax adjusted trading profit/loss of Aral for its first three trading periods.

(b)   Explanations, together with relevant supporting calculations, of the tax relief available in respect of the anticipated trading losses depending on whether the business is run as a sole trader or a limited company. When considering the use of a limited company, don't forget that it could be owned by Banda or by Flores Ltd.

    Please include a recommendation based on your figures but do not address any other issues regarding the differences between trading as a sole trader and as a company; I just want to focus on the losses for the moment.

(c)   Explanatory notes of the tax implications of there being a loan from Flores Ltd to Banda and whether or not such a loan might affect our willingness to provide her with tax advice.

BPP
LEARNING MEDIA

Take some time to think about your approach to this before you start; I want you to avoid preparing any unnecessary calculations and to keep the schedules brief.

Thank you

Kara

The letter referred to in Kara's email is set out below.

Dear Kara

Aral business

I am the managing director of Flores Ltd, a company that manufactures waterskiing equipment. I am looking for a tax adviser to help me with my next business venture.

When I began the Flores business in 2011 it was expected to make losses for the first year or so. I was advised not to form a company but to trade as a sole trader and to offset the losses against my income of earlier years. I followed that advice and transferred the business to Flores Ltd on 1 January 2013, once it had become profitable.

Flores Ltd has made taxable trading profits of approximately £120,000 each year since it was formed. It prepares accounts to 30 June each year.

For the past few months I have been researching the windsurfing market. I must have spent at least £6,000 travelling around the UK visiting retailers and windsurfing clubs (half of which was spent on buying people lunch!).

However, it was all worth while as on 1 January 2017 I intend to start a new business, 'Aral', manufacturing windsurfing equipment.

The budgeted results for the first three trading periods of the Aral business are set out below:

		£
6 months ending 30 June 2017	Trading loss	(25,500)
Year ending 30 June 2018	Trading loss	(13,000)
Year ending 30 June 2019	Trading profit	77,000

The figures above have been adjusted for tax purposes but take no account of the tax relief available in respect of the equipment to be acquired in January each year.

The business will purchase equipment (machinery, computers, shelving etc) in January 2017 at a cost of £11,500. Further equipment will be purchased in January 2018 at a cost of £1,500 and in January 2019 at a cost of £1,200.

The next decision I need to make is whether the new business should trade as a company or as an unincorporated entity. It would make more sense commercially to form a company immediately but I would be willing to use the same approach as I used when establishing the Flores business if this maximises the relief obtained in respect of the trading losses. I want to obtain relief for the losses now; I do not want the losses carried forward for relief in the future unless there are no other options available.

Yours sincerely

Banda

Required

Prepare the schedules requested by Kara.

Marks are available for the three schedules as follows:

(a) Tax adjusted trading profit/loss of the new business (Aral) for its first three trading periods. **(4 marks)**

(b) The tax relief available in respect of the anticipated trading losses, together with supporting calculations and a recommended structure for the business. **(16 marks)**

(c) Explanatory notes, together with relevant supporting calculations, in connection with the loan. **(10 marks)**

Additional marks will be awarded for the appropriateness of the format and presentation of the schedules, the effectiveness with which the information is communicated and the extent to which the schedules are structured in a logical manner. **(3 marks)**

Notes

1   You should assume that the rules, rates and allowances for the tax year 2015/16 and for the Financial Year to 31 March 2016 apply throughout the question.

2   You should ignore value added tax (VAT).

(Total = 33 marks)

11 Shuttelle (ATAX 06/13)   39 mins

Your firm has been asked to provide advice to Shuttelle in connection with personal pension contributions and to three non-UK domiciled individuals in connection with the remittance basis of taxation for overseas income and gains.

(a)   **Personal pension contributions:**

- Shuttelle has been the production director of Din Ltd since 1 February 2003.
- Shuttelle joined a registered personal pension scheme on 6 April 2013.

Shuttelle's tax position for the tax year 2015/16:

- Shuttelle's only source of income is her remuneration from Din Ltd.
- Shuttelle's annual salary is £203,910.
- Shuttelle lived in a house owned by Din Ltd for a period of time during the tax year 2015/16.

The house provided by Din Ltd for Shuttelle's use:

- Was purchased by Din Ltd on 1 January 2003 for £635,000 and has an annual value of £7,200.
- Shuttelle lived in the house from 1 February 2003 until 30 June 2015.
- The house had a market value of £870,000 on 6 April 2015.

Contributions to Shuttelle's personal pension scheme:

- Shuttelle has made the following gross contributions.

    6 April 2013 – £19,000
    6 April 2014 – £38,000
    6 April 2015 – £120,000

- Din Ltd contributes £4,000 to the scheme in each tax year.

Required

(i)   Calculate Shuttelle's income tax liability for the tax year 2015/16.   **(8 marks)**

(ii)   Calculate the amount of tax relief obtained by Shuttelle as a consequence of the gross personal pension contributions of £120,000 she made on 6 April 2015.   **(3 marks)**

(b)   The remittance basis of taxation:

- Advice is to be provided to three non-UK domiciled individuals.
- Each of the three individuals is more than 18 years old.

Details of the three individuals:

Name	Lin	Nan	Yu
Tax year in which the individual became UK resident	2005/06	2000/01	2005/06
Tax year in which the individual ceased to be UK resident	Still resident	2014/15	Still resident
Overseas income and gains for the tax year 2015/16	£39,200	£68,300	£130,700
Overseas income and gains remitted to the UK for the tax year 2015/16	£38,500	Nil	£1,400

Required

(i)   In respect of each of the three individuals for the tax year 2015/16:

    (1)   Explain whether or not the remittance basis is available.

    (2)   On the assumption that the remittance basis is available to ALL three individuals, state, with reasons, the remittance basis charge (if any) that they would have to pay in order for their overseas income and gains to be taxed on the remittance basis.

The following mark allocation is provided as guidance for this requirement:

    (1)   3 marks
    (2)   4 marks   **(7 marks)**

(ii) Give TWO examples of actions that would be regarded as remittances other than simply bringing cash into the UK.   **(2 marks)**

(Total = 20 marks)

Questions 12 to 23 focus on capital gains tax, tax administration for individuals, inheritance tax and stamp taxes. These are the subject of Chapters 11 to 19 in the BPP Study Text.

12 Ava (ATAX 12/09) 39 mins

Ava has not yet submitted her income tax return for the tax year 2015/16. She also requires advice on the capital gains tax and inheritance tax implications of making a gift of a farm to her nephew.

The following information has been obtained from a letter from Ava and from her client file.

Ava's personal circumstances:

- Ava is 84 years old.
- Ava's husband, Burt, died on 1 November 2017 after a long and serious illness.
- Ava has no children.

Ava's income tax reporting:

- Burt had always looked after Ava's tax affairs as well as his own.
- Ava has recently realised that her income tax return for the tax year 2015/16 has not been submitted.
- The notice to file the income tax return for the tax year 2015/16 was sent to Ava on 1 May 2016.

Burt's will and lifetime gifts:

- Burt made no transfers for the purposes of inheritance tax during his lifetime.
- Burt left quoted shares worth £293,000 to his sister.
- Burt left 'Hayworth', a small farm, and the residue of his estate to Ava.
- Consequently, his chargeable death estate was less than his nil rate band.

Ava's lifetime gifts:

- Ava made a gift of quoted company shares (all minority holdings) worth £251,000 to her niece on 1 December 2016.
- Ava intends to gift Hayworth Farm to her nephew on 1 February 2018.
- Capital gains tax gift relief will not be claimed in respect of the intended gift.
- Ava is a higher rate taxpayer.

Hayworth Farm:

- Is situated in the UK.
- Was purchased by Burt on 1 January 2008 for £330,000.
- Was leased to tenant farmers on 1 January 2009 and was never farmed by Burt.
- Will continue to be leased to and farmed by the tenant farmers in the future.

Hayworth Farm – Valuations of farm buildings and surrounding land:

	1 November 2017 £	1 February 2018 £
Market value	494,000	650,000
Agricultural value	300,000	445,000

- It can be assumed that both values will increase by 5% per year from 1 February 2018.

Required

(a) State by when Ava's 2015/16 income tax return should have been submitted and list the consequences of submitting the return, together with Ava's outstanding income tax liability, on 15 December 2017.

Note. You are not required to prepare calculations for part (a) of this question. **(4 marks)**

(b)   (i)   Provide a reasoned explanation for the availability or non-availability of agricultural property relief and business property relief in respect of the intended gift of Hayworth Farm by Ava.   **(4 marks)**

   (ii)   Calculate the capital gains tax and the inheritance tax payable in respect of the gift of Hayworth Farm on the assumption that Ava dies on 1 January 2022. State the due dates for the payment of the tax liabilities (on the assumption that they are not paid in instalments), the date on which any beneficial claim(s) need to be submitted and any assumptions made.   **(12 marks)**

(Total = 20 marks)

You should assume that the tax rates and allowances for the tax year 2015/16 will continue to apply for the foreseeable future.

13 Brad (ATAX 06/13)   49 mins

Your manager has had a meeting with Brad, a client of your firm. Extracts from your manager's meeting notes together with an email from your manager are set out below.

Extracts from meeting notes

Personal details

Brad is 69 years old. He is married to Laura and they have a daughter, Dani, who is 38 years old.

Brad had lived in the UK for the whole of his life until he moved with his wife to the country of Keirinia on 1 January 2013. He returned to live permanently in the UK on 30 April 2016. Therefore, he was non-UK resident for the years 2013/14 to 2015/16 inclusive but otherwise UK resident. The split year treatment did not apply in either 2012/13 or 2016/17. He has always been domiciled in the UK. Brad has significant investment income and has been a higher rate taxpayer for many years.

Capital gains

Whilst living in the country of Keirinia, Brad sold various assets as set out below. He has not made any other disposals since 5 April 2012.

Asset	Date of sale	Proceeds £	Date of purchase	Cost £
Quoted shares	1 February 2013	18,900	1 October 2011	14,000
Painting	1 June 2015	36,400	1 May 2011	15,000
Antique bed	1 March 2016	9,400	1 May 2013	7,300
Motor car	1 April 2016	11,000	1 February 2012	8,500

I explained that, although Brad was non-UK resident for several tax years, these disposals may still be subject to UK capital gains tax because he will be regarded as only temporarily non-UK resident. There is no capital gains tax in the country of Keirinia.

Inheritance tax planning

Brad's estate is worth approximately £5 million. He has not made any lifetime gifts and, in his will, he intends to leave half of his estate to his daughter, Dani, and the other half to his wife, Laura. I pointed out that it may be advantageous to make a lifetime gift to Dani. Brad agreed to consider giving Dani 1,500 of his shares in Omnium Ltd and has asked for a general summary of the inheritance tax advantages of making lifetime gifts to individuals.

Omnium Ltd is an unquoted manufacturing company which also owns a number of investment properties. Brad was given his shares in the company by his wife on 1 January 2012. The ownership of the share capital of Omnium Ltd is set out below.

	Shares
Laura (Brad's wife)	4,500
Brad	3,000
Vic (Laura's brother)	1,500
Christine (friend of Laura)	1,000
	10,000

The current estimated value of a share in Omnium Ltd is set out below.

Shareholding	Value per share
	£
Up to 25%	190
26% to 50%	205
51% to 60%	240
61% to 74%	255
75% to 80%	290
More than 80%	300

Email from your manager

In preparation for my next meeting with Brad, please prepare the following:

(a) **Capital gains tax**

An explanation, with supporting calculations, of the UK capital gains tax liability in respect of the disposals made by Brad whilst living in the country of Keirinia. Your explanation should include the precise reasons for Brad being regarded as only temporarily non-UK resident and a statement of when the tax was/will be payable.

(b) **Inheritance tax**

(i) An explanation of the inheritance tax advantages of making lifetime gifts to individuals, in general.

(ii) In respect of the possible gift of 1,500 shares in Omnium Ltd to Dani:

– A calculation of the fall in value of Brad's estate which will result from the gift

– A detailed explanation of whether or not business property relief would be available in respect of the gift and, on the assumption that it would be available, the manner in which it would be calculated

– A **brief** statement of any other tax issues arising from the gift, which will need to be considered at a later date

Tax manager

Required

Carry out the work required as requested in the email from your manager. The following marks are available.

(a) Capital gains tax   **(8 marks)**

(b) Inheritance tax

(i) Explanation of the inheritance tax advantages of making lifetime gifts to individuals   **(7 marks)**

(ii) In respect of the possible gift of 1,500 shares in Omnium Ltd to Dani   **(10 marks)**

You should assume that the 2015/16 tax rules (including the statutory residence test) and rates apply in all years.

(Total = 25 marks)

BPP note. This question has been rewritten by BPP for the statutory residence test in Finance Act 2013 and reviewed by the P6 examination team.

14 Sushi (ATAX 12/10)

An extract from an email from your manager regarding a meeting with a client, Sushi, together with an email from Sushi are set out below.

Email from your manager

I have just had a meeting with Sushi who has been a client of the firm since she moved to the UK from the country of Zakuskia in May 2002. Sushi was born in the country of Zakuskia in 1959. Her father died in 2009 and, as you will see from her email, her mother died in October 2016. Her father and mother were both domiciled and resident in the country of Zakuskia throughout their lives. Zakuskian inheritance tax is charged at the rate of 24% on all land and buildings situated within the country that are owned by an individual at the time of death. There is no capital gains tax in the country of Zakuskia. There is no double tax treaty between the UK and the country of Zakuskia.

Until the death of her mother, Sushi's only assets consisted of her house in the UK, a number of investment properties also situated in the UK, and cash in UK bank accounts. Her total UK assets are worth approximately £3 million. Sushi has taxable income of £34,000 each year and realises taxable capital gains of more than £20,000 each year. She has made significant cash gifts to her son in the past and, therefore, does not require an explanation of the taxation of potentially exempt transfers or the accumulation principle. Sushi is resident in the UK.

I want you to write a letter to Sushi addressing the points below:

(a) **UK inheritance tax and the statue**

An explanation of:

- The UK inheritance tax implications of the death of Sushi's mother.

- Which of Sushi's assets will be subject to UK inheritance tax when she dies. This will require some careful and detailed consideration of her domicile position both now and in the future.

- The manner in which UK inheritance tax would be calculated, if due, on any land and buildings situated in the country of Zakuskia that are owned by Sushi when she dies.

- Why the gift of the statue to her son, as referred to in her email, will be a potentially exempt transfer, and how this treatment could be avoided.

The statue has not increased in value since the death of Sushi's mother. Accordingly, the proposed gift of the statue to Sushi's son will not give rise to a capital gain.

(b) **The Zakuskian income**

The Zakuskian income will be subject to tax in the UK because Sushi is UK resident. Accordingly, we need to think about whether or not Sushi should claim the remittance basis. In order to do this I want you to prepare calculations of the increase in her UK tax liability due to the Zakuskian income on the assumption that the remittance basis is not available and then on the assumption that it is available. You should assume that Sushi remits £30,000 (gross) to the UK each year in accordance with her plans.

In relation to the taxation of the Zakuskian income, the letter should include explanations of the meaning of the terms 'remittance basis' and 'remittance', and whether or not the remittance basis is available to Sushi, together with your conclusions based on your calculations but no other narrative. You should include brief footnotes to your calculations where necessary to aid understanding of the figures.

There is no need to consider the implication of capital gains on overseas assets as Sushi does not intend to dispose of any of her Zakuskian assets, apart from the statue, for the time being.

Thank you

Tax manager

Email from Sushi

My mother died on 1 October 2016 and left me the whole of her estate. I inherited the following assets.

The family home in the country of Zakuskia
Investment properties in the country of Zakuskia
Cash in Zakuskian bank accounts
Paintings and other works of art in the country of Zakuskia

The works of art include a statue that has been owned by my family for many years. I intend to bring the statue to the UK in December 2016 and give it to my son on his birthday on 1 July 2017. The statue was valued recently at £390,000.

The assets inherited from my mother will generate gross annual income of up to £55,000 before tax, all of which is subject to 10% Zakuskian income tax. I intend to bring £30,000 (gross) of this income into the UK each year. The balance will remain in a bank account in Zakuskia.

I would like to meet with you to discuss these matters.

Thank you for your help.

Sushi

Required

Prepare the letter to Sushi requested in the email from your manager. The following marks are available.

(a)   UK inheritance tax and the statue   **(12 marks)**
(b)   The Zakuskian income   **(12 marks)**

Professional marks will be awarded in this question for the appropriateness of the format of the letter, the degree to which the calculations are approached in a logical manner, and the effectiveness with which the information is communicated.   **(3 marks)**

(Total = 27 marks)

You should assume that the tax rates and allowances of the tax year 2015/16 will continue to apply for the foreseeable future.

15 Surfe (ATAX 12/11)   **33 mins**

Surfe has requested advice on the tax implications of the creation of a discretionary trust and a calculation of the estimated inheritance tax liability on her death. The following information was obtained at a meeting with Surfe.

Surfe:
- Is a 63-year-old widow who has two adult nephews.
- Intends to create a trust on 1 January 2017.

Death of Surfe's husband:
- Surfe's husband, Flud, died on 1 February 2008. He had made no gifts during his lifetime.
- In his will, Flud left £148,000 in cash to his sister and the remainder of his estate to Surfe.

The trust:
- The trust will be a discretionary (relevant property) trust for the benefit of Surfe's nephews.
- Surfe will give 200 of her ordinary shares in Leat Ltd and £100,000 in cash to the trustees of the trust on 1 January 2017.
- The inheritance tax due on the gift will be paid by Surfe.
- The trustees will invest the cash in quoted shares.

Leat Ltd:
- Leat Ltd has an issued share capital of 1,000 ordinary shares.
- Surfe owns 650 of the company's ordinary shares.
- The remaining 350 of its ordinary shares are owned by 'Kanal', a UK registered charity.
- Leat Ltd is a property investment company such that business property relief is not available.

Leat Ltd – value of an ordinary share:

- As at

	1 January 2017	1 July 2019
	£	£
As part of a holding of 75% or more	2,000	2,400
As part of a holding of more than 50% but less than 75%	1,000	1,200
As part of a holding of 50% or less	800	1,000

Surfe – lifetime gifts:

- 1 February 2005   Surfe gave 350 ordinary shares in Leat Ltd to 'Kanal', a UK registered charity.
- 1 October 2016   Surfe gave £85,000 in cash to each of her two nephews.

Surfe's death:

- It should be assumed that Surfe will die on 1 July 2019.
- Her death estate will consist of the house in which she lives, worth £1,400,000, quoted shares worth £600,000 and her remaining shares in Leat Ltd.
- Her will divides her entire estate between her two nephews and their children.

Required

(a)   Outline BRIEFLY:

    (i)   The capital gains tax implications of:

        (1)   The proposed gift of shares to the trustees of the discretionary trust.

        (2)   Any future sale of the quoted shares by the trustees.

        (3)   The future transfer of trust assets to Surfe's nephews.

    (ii)   The inheritance tax charges that may be payable in the future by the trustees of the discretionary trust.

        Note. You are not required to prepare calculations for part (a) of this question.

        The following mark allocation is provided as guidance for this requirement:

        (i)   4 marks

        (ii)   2 marks   **(6 marks)**

(b)   Calculate the inheritance tax liabilities arising as a result of Surfe's death on 1 July 2019.   **(11 marks)**

You may assume that the tax rules and rates for 2015/16 will continue to apply for the foreseeable future.

(Total = 17 marks)

16 Una (ATAX 06/12)

60 mins

Your manager has sent you an email, together with an attachment in respect of a new client called Una. The email and the attachment are set out below.

Email from your manager

I have had a meeting with Una, a new client of the firm. Una was born in 1942 and is a widow. She has a son, Won, who was born in 1967.

Una is resident and domiciled in the UK. Her annual taxable income is approximately £90,000. She makes sufficient capital gains every year to use her annual exempt amount.

Una made a gift of cash of £40,000 to Won in May 2012. This is the only transfer she has made for the purposes of inheritance tax in the last seven years. Una has left the whole of her estate to Won in her will. Her estate is expected to be worth more than £3 million at the time of her death.

For the purposes of this work I want you to assume that Una will die on 31 December 2021.

Gift to son

Una is considering making a gift to Won of either some farmland situated in England or a villa situated in the country of Soloria. Una has prepared a schedule setting out the details of the farmland and the villa. The schedule is attached to this email. Una will make the gift to Won on his birthday on 18 November 2016; she is not prepared to delay the gift, even if it would be advantageous to do so.

The tax system in the country of Soloria

Capital gains tax   There is no capital gains tax in Soloria.

Inheritance tax   If Una still owns the villa at her death on 31 December 2021, the inheritance tax liability in Soloria would be £170,000.

If Una gifts the villa to Won on 18 November 2016 and dies on 31 December 2021, the inheritance tax liability in Soloria would be £34,000, all of which would be payable following Una's death.

The Double Taxation Agreement between the UK and the country of Soloria includes an exemption clause whereby assets situated in one of the countries that is party to the agreement are subject to inheritance tax in that country only and not in the other country.

Gift to granddaughter

Una's granddaughter, Alona, will begin a three-year university course in September 2016. Una has agreed to pay Alona's rent of £450 per month while she is at university.

Undeclared income

Una purchased a luxury motor car for her own use in 2012, but found that many of her friends wanted to borrow it for weddings. In June 2013, she began charging £200 per day for the use of the car but is of the opinion that the income received cannot be subject to income tax as she only charges a fee 'to help cover the car's running costs'. However, I have considered the situation and concluded that the hiring out of the car has resulted in taxable profits.

I want you to prepare the following:

(a)   **Gifts to son and granddaughter**

A **memorandum** for the client file that addresses the following issues.

(i)   In respect of the gift to Won:

- Calculations of the potential reduction in the inheritance tax payable on Una's death as a result of each of the possible gifts to Won. The farmland will not qualify for business property relief, but you will need to consider the availability of agricultural property relief.

- Calculations of the capital gains tax liability in respect of each of the possible gifts.

- Explanations where the calculations are not self-explanatory, particularly in relation to the availability of reliefs, and a note of any assumptions made.

- A concise summary of your calculations in relation to these capital taxes in order to assist Una in making her decision as to which asset to give to Won.

- Any other tax and financial implications in respect of the gifts of which Una should be aware before she makes her decision.

(ii)   In respect of the payment of Alona's rent:

- The conditions that would need to be satisfied in order for the payments to be exempt for the purposes of inheritance tax.

(b)   **Undeclared income**

A **brief letter** to be sent from me to Una in relation to the luxury motor car.

The letter should explain the implications for Una and our firm of failing to declare the income to HM Revenue and Customs and the implications for Una of not having declared the income sooner.

Tax manager

Attachment – Schedule from Una – Details of the farmland and villa

	Notes	Date acquired	Cost	Estimated value 18 November 2016	Estimated value 31 December 2021
			£	£	£
Farmland	1	September 2013	720,000	900,000	1,100,000
Villa	2	August 2002	510,000	745,000	920,000

Notes

1   The agricultural value of the farmland is approximately 35% of its market value. The farmland has always been rented out to tenant farmers.

2   I inherited the villa when my husband died on 14 January 2006. Its market value at that date was £600,000. The villa has never been my principal private residence. It is situated in the country of Soloria and rented out to long-term tenants. The income is subject to Solorian tax at the rate of 50%. I do not own any other assets situated in Soloria.

3   The whole of my husband's nil rate band was used at the time of his death.

Required

(a)   Prepare the memorandum requested in the email from your manager.

Note. For guidance, the calculations in part (a) of this question are worth no more than half of the total marks available.   **(21 marks)**

Professional marks will be awarded in part (a) for the overall presentation of the memorandum and the effectiveness with which the information is communicated.   **(3 marks)**

(b)   Prepare the letter requested in the email from your manager.   **(6 marks)**

A professional mark will be awarded in part (b) for the overall presentation of the letter.   **(1 mark)**

You should assume that the tax rates and allowances for the tax year 2015/16 will continue to apply for the foreseeable future.

(Total = 31 marks)

17 Kantar (ATAX 12/14)   68 mins

Your manager has had a meeting with Kantar. Kantar recently appointed your firm to be his tax advisers. Extracts from the memorandum recording the matters discussed at the meeting and from an email from your manager are set out below.

Extract from the memorandum

Kantar is resident and domiciled in the UK.

Kantar has owned and operated his unincorporated business since 2003. In February 2016 Kantar disposed of some land. He used the proceeds to purchase equipment and vans on 1 May 2016 in order to expand his business.

Kantar's only other income consists of UK property business income of £5,000 per year.

Capital transactions

1 November 2014	Kantar inherited eight acres of land from his uncle. Kantar's uncle had purchased the land for £70,000 in 1998. At the time of the uncle's death, the land was worth £200,000.
5 November 2014	Kantar gave £400 to each of his three nephews.
1 February 2016	On this date, when the eight acres of land were worth £290,000, Kantar gave two acres, valued by an independent expert at £100,000, to his son. Capital gains tax gift relief was not available in respect of this gift.
2 February 2016	Kantar sold the remaining six acres of land at auction for £170,000.

Kantar has not made any disposals for the purposes of capital gains tax other than those set out above.

Kantar has not made any transfers of value for the purposes of inheritance tax other than those set out above.

Kantar's business

Kantar's business provides delivery services. The majority of its customers are members of the public. Kantar is not registered for the purposes of value added tax (VAT).

The recent actual and budgeted results of the business are set out below.

| | Year ended 31 March | | |
	Actual 2015 £	Actual 2016 £	Budgeted 2017 £
Sales	48,000	65,000	96,000
Expenses	(6,000)	(8,000)	(13,000)
Profit per the accounts	42,000	57,000	83,000
Adjustment for tax purposes	2,000	1,000	4,000
Capital allowances	(1,000)	(1,000)	(155,000)
Tax adjusted profit/(loss)	43,000	57,000	(68,000)
Income tax liability for the tax year	8,827	14,203	Nil

In the year ending 31 March 2018, no capital allowances will be available to Kantar. With the exception of capital allowances, the results for the year ending 31 March 2018 are expected to be the same as those for the year ended 31 March 2017.

Extract from an email from your manager

Additional information

- The income tax liabilities in the memorandum take account of Kantar's UK property business income as well as his trading income and are correct.

- Kantar pays all of his tax liabilities on or before the due dates.

Please prepare notes for use in a meeting with Kantar. The notes should address the following issues:

(a) **Capital transactions**

   (i) **Inheritance tax**

   - The availability of the small gifts exemption in respect of Kantar's gifts to his nephews.

   - A calculation of the potentially exempt transfer on 1 February 2016 after deduction of any available exemptions.

   (ii) A calculation of Kantar's chargeable gains and capital gains tax liability for the tax year 2015/16.

(b) **Budgeted trading loss for the year ending 31 March 2017**

   (i) Calculations, with **brief** supporting explanations where necessary, of the tax which would be saved in respect of the offset of the trading loss for the tax year 2016/17 if:

   (1) The loss is relieved as soon as possible.
   (2) The loss is carried forward for relief in the future.

   A brief evaluation of your findings and the relevance to Kantar of the £50,000 restriction on the offset of trading losses.

   (ii) On the assumptions that the trading loss is carried forward and that Kantar wishes to maximise his cash flow position, prepare a schedule of the dates and amounts of the payments on account and balancing payments Kantar would expect to make, post 1 January 2017, in respect of his tax liabilities for 2015/16, 2016/17 and 2017/18. Include brief explanations of the payments on account amounts.

(c) **Reporting of chargeable gains**

   Kantar does not intend to report his chargeable gains on his income tax return as he believes that the tax authorities should be able to obtain this information from other sources. Explain the implications for Kantar, and our firm, of Kantar failing to report the chargeable gains to HM Revenue and Customs.

(d)   **Value added tax (VAT)**

Explain, without performing any calculations, Kantar's obligation to compulsorily register for VAT; and state Kantar's ability, following registration, to recover the input tax incurred prior to registering.

Tax manager

Required

Prepare the meeting notes requested in the email from your manager. The following marks are available:

(a)   Capital transactions.

      (i)   Inheritance tax   **(4 marks)**

      (ii)   Capital gains tax   **(4 marks)**

(b)   Budgeted trading loss for the year ending 31 March 2017.

      (i)   Offset of the trading loss   **(10 marks)**

      (ii)   Further tax payments if the loss is carried forward

             Note. Ignore national insurance contributions and value added tax (VAT).   **(5 marks)**

(c)   Reporting of chargeable gains   **(4 marks)**

(d)   Value added tax (VAT)   **(4 marks)**

Professional marks will be awarded for the clarity of the calculations, analysis of the situation, the effectiveness with which the information is communicated, and the quality of the overall presentation.   **(4 marks)**

(Total = 35 marks)

18 Kesme and Soba (ATAX 06/14)   39 mins

Assume today's date is 6 June 2016.

Kesme and Soba, a married couple, require advice on Kesme's taxable income and rent a room relief, the capital gain on a future sale of the family home, and the assets which will be received by Soba under Kesme's will.

Kesme:

- Is UK resident and UK domiciled.
- Is married to Soba.
- Has not made any lifetime gifts for the purposes of inheritance tax.

Soba:

- Is UK resident but non-UK domiciled.
- Has elected to be treated as UK domiciled for the purposes of inheritance tax.

Kesme's income for the tax year 2015/16:

- State retirement pension of £7,900 (gross)
- A pension from a former employer of £24,515 (gross)
- Rental income in respect of furnished rooms in the family home
- Interest in respect of 8% loan stock in Ramen plc

Rental income in respect of furnished rooms in the family home:

- Kesme and Soba purchased the family home on 1 July 1992 and have lived there since that date.
- Three furnished rooms have been rented out to an individual tenant since 6 April 2015.
- The tenant does not share Kesme and Soba's living accommodation or take meals with them.
- The three rooms represent 30% of the property.
- The annual rent is £14,400 and there are allowable expenses of £1,600 per year.

8% loan stock in Ramen plc:

- Kesme purchased £18,000 of 8% loan stock on 1 May 2009.
- Interest is payable on 31 May and 30 November annually.
- Kesme sold the 8% loan stock on 30 September 2015 cum interest.

Kesme's estate and his will:

- Kesme's share of the family home, a plot of land and chattels are worth £1,280,000 in total.
- The plot of land is worth £370,000 and is situated in the UK.
- Kesme has left the plot of land to his daughter.
- Kesme has left the residue of his estate to his wife, Soba.

Required

(a) Explain the availability and operation of rent a room relief in relation to Kesme and calculate his taxable income for the tax year 2015/16 on the assumption that the relief is claimed. **(8 marks)**

(b) Explain the effect of renting out the furnished rooms on the amount of the taxable capital gain on a future sale of the family home. **(6 marks)**

(c) Explain the implications of the election made by Soba to be treated as UK domiciled for the purposes of inheritance tax, and calculate the value of the residue of the estate which she would receive under Kesme's will if he were to die today. **(6 marks)**

(Total = 20 marks)

19 Pescara (ATAX 12/13) 39 mins

Pescara requires advice on the inheritance tax payable on death and on the gift of a property, and on the capital gains tax due on a disposal of shares, together with the relief available in respect of the purchase of enterprise investment scheme shares.

Pescara and her parents:

- Pescara is a higher rate taxpayer who is resident and domiciled in the UK.
- Pescara's father, Galvez, died on 1 June 2007.
- Pescara's mother, Marina, died on 1 October 2016.
- Both Galvez and Marina were resident and domiciled in the UK.

Galvez – lifetime gifts and gifts on death:

- Galvez had not made any lifetime gifts.
- In his will, Galvez left cash of £80,000 to Pescara and a further £80,000 to Pescara's brother.
- Galvez left the remainder of his estate to his wife, Marina.

Marina – lifetime gifts:

- On 1 February 2012, Marina gave Pescara 375,000 shares in Sepang plc.
- Marina had made no other lifetime gifts.

Marina – gift of 375,000 shares in Sepang plc to Pescara:

- 1 January 2009 – Marina purchased 375,000 shares for £420,000.
- 1 February 2012 – Marina gave all of the shares to Pescara.
  The shares were quoted at £1.84 – £1.88.
  Assume that the valuation rules for gifts of quoted shares applicable in the tax year 2015/16 also applied in the tax year 2011/12.
- The shares did not qualify for business property relief or capital gains tax gift relief.

Acquisition of Sepang plc by Zolder plc and subsequent bonus issue:

- 1 January 2014 – Zolder plc acquired the whole of the ordinary share capital of Sepang plc.
  Pescara received 30 pence and two ordinary shares in Zolder plc, worth £1 each, for each share in Sepang plc.
  The takeover was for genuine commercial reasons and not for the avoidance of tax.
- 1 July 2015 – Zolder plc declared a 2 for 1 bonus issue.

Pescara's actual and intended capital transactions in the tax year 2016/17:

			£
15 November 2016	Sale	1,000,000 shares in Zolder plc	445,000
1 April 2017	Purchase	Qualifying enterprise investment scheme (EIS) shares	50,000

Pescara – gift of a UK property:

- Pescara intends to give a UK property to her son on 1 October 2017.
  Pescara intends to continue to use this property, rent-free, such that this gift will be a gift with reservation.

Required

(a) Calculate the inheritance tax payable in respect of Marina's gift of the shares in Sepang plc, as a result of her death. **(7 marks)**

(b) (i) Calculate Pescara's capital gains tax liability for the tax year 2016/17 on the assumption that enterprise investment scheme (EIS) relief is claimed in respect of the shares to be purchased on 1 April 2017 and that entrepreneurs' relief is not available. **(6 marks)**

   (ii) State the capital gains tax implications of Pescara selling the EIS shares at some point in the future. **(3 marks)**

(c) Explain how the proposed gift of the UK property will be treated for the purposes of calculating the inheritance tax due on Pescara's death. **(4 marks)**

(Total = 20 marks)

20 Mirtoon (ATAX 12/11)   70 mins

Your manager has sent you an email, together with an attachment, in respect of a client called Mirtoon. The email and the attachment are set out below.

Email from your manager

Mirtoon intends to leave the UK on 15 January 2017 in order to live in the country of Koro. He has entered into a full-time contract of employment for a fixed term of four years starting on that date but he may stay in Koro for as long as ten years. He will buy a house in Koro and will not make any return trips to the UK whilst he is living in Koro.

Mirtoon will sell his house in the UK and cease his business prior to his departure. Details of these proposals, together with information regarding agricultural land owned by Mirtoon, are set out in the attached extract from his email.

Background information

Mirtoon is divorced. He has always been resident and domiciled in the UK. He will continue to be UK domiciled whilst living in the country of Koro.

He does not own any buildings other than his home. He receives bank interest in respect of UK bank deposits of £25,728 per year. He will continue to hold these bank deposits whilst living in the country of Koro.

Mirtoon has not made any disposals for the purposes of capital gains tax in the tax year 2016/17. He has capital losses brought forward as at 5 April 2016 of £4,000.

Mirtoon is self employed. He has overlap profits brought forward in respect of his business of £7,600. He is registered for value added tax (VAT) and makes standard rated supplies only. He has never made any claims in respect of entrepreneurs' relief.

I want you to prepare the following:

(a) **Mirtoon's financial position**

   Mirtoon wants to know how his plans to dispose of assets and his departure from the UK will affect his financial position. The details of his plans are in the following attachment. He has asked us to prepare a calculation of the total of the following amounts:

   - The after tax proceeds from the sale of his home and business assets.
   - The tax saving in respect of the offset of his trading losses
     The trading losses should be offset against the total income of the tax year 2015/16; there is no need to consider any other loss reliefs.

In order to accurately determine the tax effect of the relief available, you should prepare calculations of Mirtoon's income tax liability for 2015/16 both before and after the offset of the losses.

- Any other tax liabilities arising as a result of Mirtoon's plans to leave the UK

    You should include explanatory notes where this is necessary to assist Mirtoon's understanding of the calculations. This may be particularly useful in relation to the availability of any reliefs and allowances and the tax relief available in respect of the offset of the trading losses.

(b) **A letter to be sent from me to Mirtoon that addresses the following matters**

    (i)   VAT: The VAT implications of the cessation of the business and the sale of the business assets.

    (ii)   Income tax and capital gains tax: Whether or not Mirtoon will be liable to UK income tax and capital gains tax whilst he is living in the country of Koro by reference to his residence and domicile status. You should include specific reference to the capital gains tax implications of the proposed sale of the agricultural land in June 2018. There is no double tax treaty between the UK and the country of Koro.

    (iii)   Inheritance tax: Mirtoon has asked me to discuss some ideas he has had in relation to reducing the potential inheritance tax liability on his death. To help me with this, please include a summary of the rules relating to associated operations and gifts with reservation in the letter.

Tax manager

Attachment – Extract from an email from Mirtoon

Sale of house

I will sell my house on 31 December 2016 for £850,000. I purchased the house for £540,000 on 1 July 2006 and I have lived there ever since that date. Two rooms, representing 20% of the property, have always been used exclusively for the purposes of my business.

Sale of business assets

My business made a tax adjusted profit in the year ended 30 June 2015 of £90,000. However, in the year ended 30 June 2016 it made a tax adjusted loss of £20,000. I have not been able to find a buyer for the business and will therefore cease trading on 31 December 2016. I will then sell any remaining business assets.

I expect to be able to sell the business assets, consisting of machinery and inventory, for £14,000, with no asset being sold for more than cost. The business will make a tax adjusted loss of £17,000 in the six months ending 31 December 2016 after taking account of the sale of the business assets.

Agricultural land

In May 2012 my father gave me 230 acres of agricultural land situated in the UK. A capital gain of £72,900 arose in respect of this gift and my father and I submitted a joint claim for gift relief. I expect the value of the land to increase considerably in 2017 and I intend to sell it in June 2018.

Required

(a) The calculations showing how Mirtoon's disposal of assets and subsequent departure from the UK will affect his financial position as requested in the email from your manager.

    Note. Ignore national insurance contributions.   **(17 marks)**

(b) Prepare the letter to Mirtoon requested in the email from your manager. The following marks are available.

    (i)   Value added tax (VAT)   **(3 marks)**
    (ii)   Income tax and capital gains tax   **(7 marks)**
    (iii)   Inheritance tax   **(6 marks)**

Professional marks will be awarded in this question for the extent to which the calculations are approached in a logical manner in part (a) and the effectiveness with which the information is communicated in part (b). **(3 marks)**

You may assume that the tax rules and rates for 2015/16 will continue to apply for the foreseeable future.

                                                        (Total = 36 marks)

21 Cada (ATAX 12/14)

39 mins

Your firm has been asked to provide advice in connection with inheritance tax and capital gains tax following the death of Cada. The advice relates to the implications of making lifetime gifts, making gifts to charity, varying the terms of a will and other aspects of capital gains tax planning.

Cada and her family:

- Cada, who was UK domiciled, died on 20 November 2016.
- Cada is survived by two daughters: Raymer and Yang.
- Raymer has an adult son.
- Yang has no children.

Cada – Lifetime gifts and available nil rate band:

- Cada had not made any lifetime gifts since 30 November 2012.
- Cada's nil rate band available at the date of her death was £220,000.

Cada's death estate and the details of her will:

- Cada owned assets valued at £1,000,000 at the time of her death.
- Cada left her house, valued at £500,000, to Raymer.
- Cada left cash of £60,000 to a UK national charity.
- Cada left her remaining assets (including a portfolio of shares) valued at £440,000, to Yang.
- None of the remaining assets qualified for any inheritance tax reliefs.

Raymer:

- Is not an accountant, but has some knowledge of the UK tax system.
- Has made four observations regarding her mother's estate and her inheritance.

Raymer's four observations:

- 'My mother should have made additional gifts in her lifetime.'
- 'The tax rate on the chargeable estate should be less than 40% due to the gift to charity.'
- 'I do not intend to live in the house but will give it to my son on 1 July 2017.'
- 'My mother paid capital gains tax every year. However, when she died, some of her shareholdings had a value of less than cost.'

Cada's shareholdings at the time of her death:

- Quoted shares in JW plc valued at more than cost.
- Quoted shares in FR plc valued at less than cost.
- Unquoted shares in KZ Ltd valued at £nil.

Required

(a) Explain the inheritance tax advantages, other than lifetime exemptions, which could have been obtained if Cada had made additional lifetime gifts of quoted shares between 1 December 2012 and her death.

(4 marks)

(b) Calculate the increase in the legacy to the charity which would be necessary in order for the reduced rate of inheritance tax to apply and quantify the reduction in the inheritance tax liability which would result.

(5 marks)

(c) Explain the capital gains tax and inheritance tax advantages which could be obtained by varying the terms of Cada's will and set out the procedures required in order to achieve a tax-effective variation. **(6 marks)**

(d) In relation to capital gains tax, explain what beneficial actions Cada could have carried out in the tax year of her death in respect of her shareholdings. **(5 marks)**

(Total = 20 marks)

22 Claudia

Claudia requires advice on employee shareholder shares and the tax implications of investing through the Seed Enterprise Investment Scheme (SEIS).

The following information has been obtained from discussions with Claudia.

Claudia:

- Is married to Nigel and has one adult daughter, Joanne.
- Has been offered employment by Noble plc.
- Has been offered 'employee shareholder' shares by Noble plc as part of a remuneration package.
- Has never owned any shares in Noble plc and will not acquire any further shares in Noble plc.
- Made a gain of £42,000 on the sale of a plot of land in June 2015.
- Will have an income tax liability (before any SEIS relief) of £50,000 in the tax year 2015/16.

Noble plc:

- Does not have a parent company.
- Is listed on the London Stock Exchange.

Investment by Claudia in Petite Ltd:

- Subscribed for £60,000 £1 ordinary shares at par value in January 2016.
- Investment qualifies for SEIS income tax relief.
- Claudia intends to dispose of her shares in Petite Ltd in December 2017.

Required

(a) (i) Explain what is meant by the term 'employee shareholder' and outline the conditions that must be satisfied for Claudia to be an employee shareholder. **(4 marks)**

   (ii) Assuming that Claudia takes up employment with Noble plc and is issued with employee shareholder shares worth £5,000, explain the income tax and national insurance consequences for Claudia of the issue of the shares. **(2 marks)**

   (iii) State the capital gains tax consequence of a disposal by Claudia of the employee shareholder shares in Noble plc in the following circumstances:

   1   Sale to an unconnected buyer

   2   Sale to Nigel

   3   Takeover of Noble plc by Token plc and Claudia receives shares in Token plc in exchange for her shares in Noble plc **(4 marks)**

(b) (i) State the tax reducer to which Claudia is entitled for the tax year 2015/16 in respect of her investment in Petite Ltd. **(1 mark)**

   (ii) State the maximum amount of SEIS reinvestment relief that Claudia can claim for the tax year 2015/16 and state how the relief operates. **(2 marks)**

   (iii) Explain the income tax and capital gains tax implications of the proposed disposal of Petite Ltd shares by Claudia in December 2017 if she:

   1   Gives the shares to Joanne
   2   Sells them to an unconnected buyer for their market value of £45,000 **(3 marks)**

   (Total = 16 marks)

23 Robert, Meredith and Adrian 35 mins

Robert is a non-UK resident who requires advice about two residential properties situated in the UK. Meredith is a UK-resident who has recently acquired assets situated outside the UK. Adrian requires advice on the capital gains tax liability on incorporation of his sole trader business.

The following information has been obtained from discussions with each of the individuals.

Robert:

- Was UK resident until 5 April 2015.
- Will not be UK resident in 2015/16 or any future year.
- Owns two residential properties in the UK, a house (Redacre) and a holiday cottage (Bluesky).
- Used Redacre as his main residence from its purchase on 6 April 2005 for £150,000.
- Had Redacre valued on 5 April 2015 at £325,000.
- Stays in Redacre during his visits to the UK which do not exceed 30 days in a tax year.
- Will sell Redacre on 5 October 2018 for net proceeds of £450,000.
- Has always rented out Bluesky as a furnished holiday letting.
- Is considering gifting Bluesky to his daughter Emily who is also non-UK resident.

Meredith:

- Has always been UK resident.
- Recently inherited assets situated outside the UK.
- Has not yet reported income arising from those assets to HM Revenue and Customs (HMRC).
- Is considering deliberately not informing HMRC of the income arising from the assets.

Adrian:

- Has run his sole trader business for five years.

- Has decided to incorporate his trading business by selling the assets of his business to a new company, Better Ltd, in exchange for loan notes (so incorporation relief is not available).

- Will be the sole director and shareholder of Better Ltd.

- Will sell two chargeable assets to Better Ltd which are a freehold shop (gain on sale £50,000) and goodwill (gain on sale £42,000).

- Has no other chargeable assets and is a higher rate taxpayer.

Required

(a) (i) Advise Robert, with supporting calculations, of the taxable gain that will arise on the sale of Redacre, assuming any relevant elections are made and that this is the only disposal that Robert will make in the tax year 2018/19. **(6 marks)**

(ii) Advise Robert whether or not he can claim gift (holdover) relief on the proposed gift of Bluesky to Emily. **(2 marks)**

(b) Outline the penalty for error that might be imposed on Meredith if she deliberately omits to inform HMRC of the offshore income and the circumstances in which a further penalty that might be imposed. You should assume that the error will be treated as deliberate but not concealed. **(5 marks)**

(c) Advise Adrian of the capital gains tax liability that will arise on the sale of his business to Better Ltd. **(5 marks)**

(Total = 18 marks)

CORPORATION TAX

Questions 24 to 32 cover the taxation of companies. This is the subject of Chapters 20 to 27 of the BPP Study Text.

24 Klubb plc (ATAX 12/14)   39 mins

Klubb plc, a client of your firm, requires advice on the penalty in respect of the late filing of a corporation tax return, the establishment of a tax-advantaged share scheme, and its shareholding in an overseas-resident company.

Klubb plc:

- Is a UK resident trading company.
- Has been charged a penalty in respect of the late filing of corporation tax return.
- Intends to establish a tax-advantaged share plan.
- Purchased 30% of the ordinary share capital of Hartz Co from Mr Deck on 1 April 2016.

Late filing of corporation tax returns:

- Klubb plc prepared accounts for the 16-month period ended 31 March 2015.
- The corporation tax returns for this period were filed on 31 May 2016.

Tax-advantaged share plan:

- The plan will be either a Schedule 2 share incentive plan (SIP) or a Schedule 4 company share option plan (CSOP).

- If a SIP, the shares would be held within the plan for five years.

- If a SIP, members will not be permitted to reinvest dividends in order to purchase further shares.

- If a CSOP, the options would be exercised within five years of being granted.

- In both cases it can be assumed that the plan members would sell the shares immediately after acquiring them.

Klubb plc wants the share plan to be flexible in terms of:

- The employees who can be included in the plan.
- The number or value of shares which can be acquired by each plan member.

Hartz Co:

- Is resident in the country of Suta.
- Mr Deck continues to own 25% of the company's ordinary share capital.
- Kort Co, a company resident in the country of Suta, owns the remaining 45%.

Budgeted results of Hartz Co for the year ending 31 March 2017:

- Trading profits of £330,000
- Chargeable gains of £70,000
- All of Hartz Co's profits have been artificially diverted from the UK.
- Hartz Co will pay corporation tax at the rate of 11% in the country of Suta.
- Hartz Co will not pay a dividend for the year ending 31 March 2017.

Required

(a) State the corporation tax returns required from Klubb plc in respect of the 16-month period ended 31 March 2015 and the due dates for filing them. Explain the penalties which may be charged in respect of the late filing of these returns. **(4 marks)**

(b)   Compare and contrast a Schedule 2 share incentive plan with a Schedule 4 company share option plan in relation to:

- The flexibility desired by Klubb plc regarding the employees included in the plan and the number or value of shares which can be acquired by each plan member.

- The income tax and capital gains tax implications of acquiring and selling the shares under each plan.
  (9 marks)

(c)   (i)   Explain whether or not Hartz Co will be regarded as a controlled foreign company (CFC) for the year ending 31 March 2017 and the availability or otherwise of the low profits exemption.   **(4 marks)**

(ii)   On the assumption that Hartz Co is a CFC, and that no CFC exemptions are available, calculate the budgeted CFC charge for Klubb plc based on the budgeted results of Hartz Co for the year ending 31 March 2017.   **(3 marks)**

(Total = 20 marks)

25 Sank Ltd and Kurt Ltd (ATAX 06/12)   35 mins

Sank Ltd and Kurt Ltd are two unrelated clients of your firm. Sank Ltd requires advice in connection with the payment of its corporation tax liability and the validity of a compliance check enquiry it has received from HM Revenue and Customs. Kurt Ltd requires advice in connection with the purchase of machinery and expenditure on research and development.

(a)   **Sank Ltd:**

- Has been a large company for the purposes of payment of corporation tax for many years.
- Has had two related 51% group companies for many years.
- Will prepared its next accounts for the 11 months ending 30 September 2016.
- Has received a compliance check notice from HM Revenue and Customs.

Taxable total profits for the 11 months ending 30 September 2016:

- Figures prepared on 31 March 2016 indicated taxable total profits for this 11-month period of £640,000.

- As at 1 June 2016, taxable total profits for this 11-month period are expected to be £750,000.

The compliance check notice from HM Revenue and Customs:

- HM Revenue and Customs gave notice of the compliance check on 31 May 2016.
- It relates to Sank Ltd's corporation tax return for the year ended 31 October 2013.
- No amendments have been made to the corporation tax return since it was submitted.

Required

In relation to Sank Ltd:

(i)   Explain, with supporting calculations, the payment(s) required in respect of the company's corporation tax liability for the 11 months ended 30 September 2016 and the implications of the increase in the expected taxable total profits.   **(7 marks)**

(ii)   In relation to the date on which the compliance check into the corporation tax computation for the year ended 31 October 2013 was notified, explain the circumstances necessary for the notice to be regarded as valid. You should assume that Sank Ltd has not been fraudulent or negligent.   **(3 marks)**

(b)   **Kurt Ltd:**

- Was incorporated and began to trade on 1 August 2015.
- Is owned by Mr Quinn, who also owns three other trading companies.
- Has made a tax adjusted trading loss in the eight months ending 31 March 2016.
- Has no other income or chargeable gains in the eight months ending 31 March 2016.
- Is expected to be profitable in future years.
- Is a small enterprise for the purposes of research and development.

Expenditure in the period ending 31 March 2016:

- Machinery for use in its manufacturing activities – £510,000
- The cost of staff carrying out qualifying scientific research in connection with its business – £28,000

Required

In relation to Kurt Ltd, explain the tax deductions and/or credits available in the period ending 31 March 2016 in respect of the expenditure on machinery and scientific research and comment on any choices available to the company.

(8 marks)

(Total = 18 marks)

26 Opus Ltd group (ATAX 06/14)   49 mins

Your manager is due to attend a meeting with the finance director of Opus Ltd. A schedule of information obtained from the client files and an email from your manager in connection with the Opus Ltd group are set out below.

Schedule of information

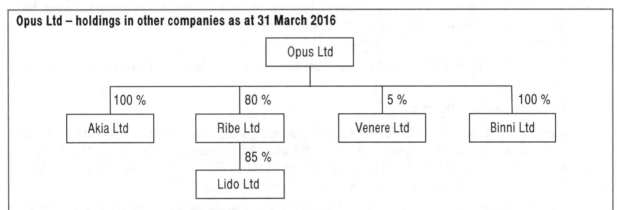

Opus Ltd – holdings in other companies as at 31 March 2016

Results for the period ended 31 March 2016

	Opus Ltd £	Akia Ltd £	Ribe Ltd £	Lido Ltd £	Venere Ltd £	Binni Ltd £
Trading profit/(loss)	10,000	(93,000)	41,000	75,000	160,000	78,000
Property income	8,000	–	–	–	–	–
Chargeable gain	Note 3	6,000	–	21,000	–	–

Notes

Holdings in other companies

1   All of the companies are UK resident trading companies.

2   All of the companies, including Binni Ltd, have always paid corporation tax by instalments.

3   Opus Ltd – acquisition of the holdings in other companies:

- Opus Ltd acquired Akia Ltd and the shareholding in Ribe Ltd (together with its subsidiary Lido Ltd) on 1 January 2001.

- Venere Ltd has an issued share capital of 1,000,000 ordinary shares. Opus Ltd acquired 170,000 ordinary shares in Venere Ltd on 1 July 2006 for £65,000. It sold 120,000 of these shares on 1 October 2015 for £150,000. Assume the indexation factor from July 2006 to October 2015 is 0.304.

- Opus Ltd acquired Binni Ltd on 1 December 2015.

4   The minority interests in Ribe Ltd and Lido Ltd are owned by individuals.

5   Venere Ltd is a 75% subsidiary of Jarrah Ltd, a company with no connections to the Opus Ltd group.

Results for the period ended 31 March 2016

6   All of the companies, with the exception of Binni Ltd, have prepared accounts for the year ended 31 March 2016. Binni Ltd has prepared accounts for the ten months ended 31 March 2016.

7   Where necessary, the results shown above have been adjusted for tax purposes.

8   Akia Ltd's trading loss includes writing down allowances in the main pool of £35,000.

9   Akia Ltd is not expected to return to profitability for a number of years.

10   Ribe Ltd has trading losses brought forward of £68,000 as at 1 April 2015.

Email from your manager

Please carry out the following work in preparation for the Opus Ltd meeting.

(a)   Relieving the trading losses of Akia Ltd and Ribe Ltd

The objective of the group is to relieve all losses as soon as possible.

Prepare calculations, together with supporting explanations, to show how the group's objective can best be achieved, clearly identifying any losses to be carried forward as at 31 March 2016 and any further information which may need to be obtained.

There may be some interesting planning possibilities here; you should think carefully about the tax position of each company.

(b)   Sale of the shares in Venere Ltd

Opus Ltd has received an offer of £80,000 for its remaining 50,000 ordinary shares in Venere Ltd. If the sale were to go ahead, it would take place on 30 June 2016. However, the management of Opus Ltd are of the opinion that the results of Venere Ltd for the year ending 31 March 2017 will be such that the shares could be worth as much as £100,000 if the sale were to be delayed until 30 April 2017.

Set out the matters which the management of Opus Ltd should consider in order to decide on which of the two dates it would be more financially advantageous to sell the shares in Venere Ltd. When calculating the indexation allowance, use an approximate indexation factor of 0.400 for the period from 1 July 2006 until the date of sale.

(c)   Error in the corporation tax return of Binni Ltd

A detailed review of the results of Binni Ltd for the year ended 31 May 2014 has revealed that no adjustment was made in respect of an amount of disallowable expenditure. As a result of this, the company's corporation tax liability for the year was understated by £8,660. I have told the company that there may be interest and penalties in respect of this error.

Explain how the interest on the underpaid tax will be calculated and state the matters which would need to be considered if the company were unwilling to disclose the error to HM Revenue and Customs.

Tax manager

Required

Carry out the work required as set out in the email from your manager. The following marks are available:

(a)   Relieving the trading losses of Akia Ltd and Ribe Ltd.   **(14 marks)**

(b)   Sale of the shares in Venere Ltd.   **(5 marks)**

(c)   Error in the corporation tax return of Binni Ltd.

Note. You are not required to calculate the amount of interest payable or to consider any penalty which may be charged.   **(6 marks)**

(Total = 25 marks)

27 Helm Ltd group (ATAX 06/15)

49 mins

Your manager has had a number of telephone conversations with Gomez, a potential new client. Gomez owns the whole of the ordinary share capital of Helm Ltd. Extracts from the memorandum prepared by your manager setting out the matters discussed and an email from your manager in connection with the Helm Ltd group are set out below.

Extracts from the memorandum

Helm Ltd

The past and present members of the Helm Ltd group are set out below.

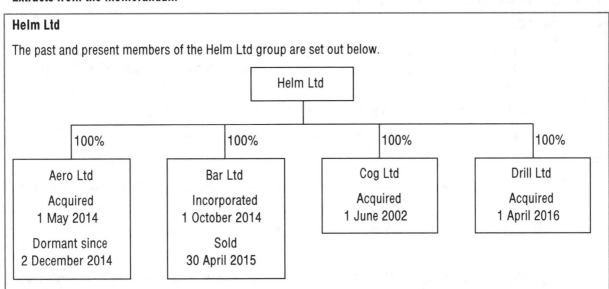

Year ended 31 March 2016

Sale of Bar Ltd

The whole of the ordinary share capital of Bar Ltd was sold to an unconnected party on 30 April 2015 for £1,200,000. Bar Ltd was incorporated on 1 October 2014, when Helm Ltd subscribed £1,000,000 for 200,000 ordinary shares.

Bar Ltd was formed to purchase the entire trade and assets of Aero Ltd for £1,000,000. This purchase occurred on 1 December 2014. The assets consisted of a building located in England valued at £830,000, inventory and receivables. The building had cost Aero Ltd £425,000 on 1 July 1995 and was valued at £880,000 on 30 April 2015 when it was still owned by Bar Ltd.

Year ended 31 March 2017

Purchase of Drill Ltd

Helm Ltd purchased the whole of the ordinary share capital of Drill Ltd on 1 April 2016. Drill Ltd has capital losses to carry forward as at 31 March 2016 of £74,000.

The business of Drill Ltd is to be expanded in the year ending 31 March 2017.

- Drill Ltd intends to borrow £1,350,000 in order to finance the purchase of a building and to provide additional working capital. Drill Ltd will be required to pay an arrangement fee of £35,000 in order to obtain this loan.

- The building will cost Drill Ltd £1,200,000. To begin with, this building will be larger than Drill Ltd requires. One quarter of the building will be rented out to a third party until Drill Ltd needs the additional space.

Cog Ltd

On 1 May 2016, Cog Ltd sold a warehouse for £470,000. Cog Ltd had owned the warehouse for almost two years and had rented it to a tenant throughout this period. Cog Ltd had always intended to bring the warehouse into use in its trade at some point in the future, but before this could happen, it sold the warehouse and realised a chargeable gain of £82,000.

Email from your manager

Additional information

1.   All of the companies are UK resident trading companies.

2.   All of the companies are profitable and prepare accounts to 31 March each year.

Please carry out the following work in preparation for a meeting with Gomez.

(a)   Sale of Bar Ltd

- Calculate the chargeable gain resulting from the sale of the shareholding in Bar Ltd assuming the substantial shareholding exemption is not available. Explain any significant matter(s) which affect this calculation.

- Explain whether or not the substantial shareholding exemption will be available.

- Explain the implications of the sale in relation to stamp duty land tax.

(b)   Drill Ltd

Explain how tax relief may be obtained in respect of the arrangement fee and the interest payable on the loan of £1,350,000 (you should be aware that Drill Ltd receives less than £50 of interest income each year).

(c)   Cog Ltd – chargeable gain on the sale of the warehouse

Explain:

- whether or not the chargeable gain on the sale of the warehouse can be relieved by rollover relief; and

- how Drill Ltd's capital losses can be relieved; in particular, whether or not they can be offset against the chargeable gain made on the sale of the warehouse by Cog Ltd.

(d)   Becoming tax advisers to Gomez and the Helm Ltd group of companies

Prepare a summary of the information we require, and any actions which we should take before we agree to become tax advisers to Gomez and the Helm Ltd group of companies.

Tax manager

Required

Carry out the work required as requested in the email from your manager. The following marks are available:

(a)   Sale of Bar Ltd.   **(11 marks)**

Note: The following figures from the Retail Prices Index should be used, where necessary.
July 1995	149.1
October 2014	257.7
December 2014	257.5
April 2015	257.8

(b)   Drill Ltd.   **(5 marks)**

(c)   Cog Ltd – chargeable gain on the sale of the warehouse.   **(4 marks)**

(d)   Becoming tax advisers to Gomez and the Helm Ltd group of companies.   **(5 marks)**

(Total = 25 marks)

28 Bond Ltd group (ATAX 12/14)

49 mins

You have received an email with an attachment from your manager relating to a new client of your firm.

The attachment is a memorandum prepared by the client, Mr Stone, who owns the whole of the ordinary share capital of Bond Ltd. The email from your manager contains further information in relation to the Bond Ltd group of companies and sets out the work you are to perform. The attachment and the email are set out below.

Attachment – Memorandum from Mr Stone

Bond Ltd group of companies

Formation of the group

The Bond Ltd group consists of Bond Ltd, Ungar Ltd and Madison Ltd.

1 April 2014	I purchased the whole of the ordinary share capital of Bond Ltd.
1 December 2014	Bond Ltd purchased the whole of the ordinary share capital of Ungar Ltd.
1 October 2016	Madison Ltd was incorporated on 1 October 2016. Bond Ltd acquired 65% of the ordinary share capital of Madison Ltd on that date.

Bond Ltd – Results for the six months ended 30 September 2016

	£	Notes
Trading losses brought forward	(20,000)	1
Tax adjusted trading income for the period	470,000	2, 3
Chargeable gain	180,000	4

Notes

1. On 31 March 2014, Bond Ltd had trading losses to carry forward of £170,000. The company's total taxable trading income for the two years ended 31 March 2016 was only £150,000, such that on 31 March 2016 it had trading losses to carry forward of £20,000.

2. Bond Ltd's trade consists of baking and selling bread and other baked products. Up to 31 March 2016, its main product had always been low-cost bread which was sold to schools, hospitals and prisons. In April 2016, Bond Ltd introduced a new range of high quality breads and cakes. This new range is sold to supermarkets and independent retailers and, for the six months ended 30 September 2016 represents 65% of the company's turnover and 90% of its profits.

3. In order to produce the new product range, Bond Ltd invested £285,000 in plant and machinery in April 2016. The tax adjusted trading income is after deducting capital allowances of £285,000, ie 100% of the cost of the plant and machinery.

   The tax written down value brought forward on the company's main pool as at 1 April 2016 was zero and there were no other additions or disposals of plant and machinery in the period.

4. The chargeable gain arose on the sale of a plot of land on 1 May 2016 for proceeds of £350,000. The land had always been used in the company's business but was no longer required.

Ungar Ltd

The trade of Ungar Ltd consists of baking high quality cakes. Ungar Ltd trades from premises purchased on 1 July 2015 for £310,000.

Ungar Ltd also develops new baking processes and techniques which it has patented. It uses these processes and techniques itself and licenses the patents to other manufacturers.

Madison Ltd

Madison Ltd purchased a building for £400,000 (plus 20% value added tax (VAT)) and machinery for £300,000 (plus 20% VAT) and began to trade on 1 October 2016.

Madison Ltd is partially exempt for the purposes of VAT. In the year ending 30 September 2017, its VAT recovery percentage is expected to be 80%. However, I expect this percentage to fall slightly in future years.

Email from your manager

Additional information

- Bond Ltd, Ungar Ltd and Madison Ltd are all resident in the UK.

- Bond Ltd and Ungar Ltd had always prepared accounts to 31 March. However, in 2016 it was decided to change the group's year end to 30 September and accounts have been prepared for the six months ended 30 September 2016.

- The original cost of the land sold by Bond Ltd on 1 May 2016 was £150,000. The chargeable gain of £180,000 is after the deduction of indexation allowance and is correct.

Please carry out the following work:

(a)   Corporation tax liability of Bond Ltd

Calculate the corporation tax liability of Bond Ltd for the six months ended 30 September 2016 based on the information provided by Mr Stone. You should review Mr Stone's capital allowances figure of £285,000 and assume the company will claim the maximum possible rollover relief.

Include notes on the following matters.

(i)   The capital allowances available.

(ii)   The use of Bond Ltd's trading losses brought forward bearing in mind that Mr Stone only recently acquired the company.

(iii)   The availability of rollover relief in respect of the chargeable gain on the land.

You should **ignore VAT** when carrying out this work.

We will need to do further work in order to finalise this computation. In the meantime, make a note of any assumptions you have made in order to complete the computation as far as possible for now.

(b)   Ungar Ltd – Patent box regime

State, giving reasons, whether or not the patent box regime is available to Ungar Ltd and briefly describe the operation of the regime.

(c)   Madison Ltd – Recovery of input tax

Explain how much of the input tax in respect of the purchase of the building and machinery can be recovered by Madison Ltd in the year ending 30 September 2017 and how this may be adjusted in future years. Include an example of a possible adjustment in the year ending 30 September 2018.

Tax manager

Required

Carry out the work required as requested in the email from your manager. The following marks are available:

(a)   Corporation tax liability of Bond Ltd

     Note. For guidance, approximately two-thirds of the available marks relate to the written notes.   **(16 marks)**

(b)   Ungar Ltd – Patent box regime   **(5 marks)**

(c)   Madison Ltd – Recovery of input tax   **(4 marks)**

                                                      (Total = 25 marks)

29 Trifles Ltd (ATAX 12/10)

33 mins

Trifles Ltd intends to carry out a purchase of its own shares. The shareholders from whom the shares are to be purchased require advice on their tax position. Trifles Ltd also intends to loan a motorcycle to one of the shareholders.

The following information has been obtained from the shareholders in Trifles Ltd.

Trifles Ltd:

- Is an unquoted company specialising in the delivery of small, high value items.

- Was incorporated and began trading on 1 February 2009.

- Has an issued share capital of 10,000 ordinary shares subscribed for at £2 per share.

- Has four unrelated shareholders: Torte, Baklava, Victoria and Melba.

- Intends to purchase some of its own shares from Victoria and Melba.

- Victoria and Melba have been directors of the company since they acquired their shares but will resign immediately after the purchase of their shares.

The purchase by Trifles Ltd of its own shares:

- Will take place on 28 February 2017 for Victoria's shares, and on 31 March 2017 for Melba's shares at an agreed price of £30 per share.

- Will consist of the purchase of all of Victoria's shares and 450 shares from Melba.

Victoria:

- Is resident in the UK.
- Has taxable income of £40,000 in 2016/17.
- Will make no other capital disposals in the tax year 2016/17.
- Has a capital loss carried forward as at 5 April 2016 of £3,300.
- Will have no link with Trifles Ltd following the purchase of her shares.
- Inherited her holding of 1,500 ordinary shares on the death of her husband, Brownie, on 1 February 2015.
- Brownie paid £16,500 for the shares on 1 February 2013.
- The probate value of the 1,500 ordinary shares was £16,000 on 1 February 2015.

Melba:

- Is resident in the UK.

- Has taxable income of £40,000 in 2016/17 and 2017/18.

- Acquired her holding of 1,700 ordinary shares when Trifles Ltd was incorporated.

- Following the purchase of her shares Melba's only link with Trifles Ltd will be her remaining ordinary shareholding and the use of a motorcycle belonging to the company.

The motorcycle:

- Will be purchased by Trifles Ltd for £9,000 on 1 April 2017.
- Will be made available on loan to Melba for the whole of the tax year 2017/18.
- Melba will pay Trifles Ltd £30 per month for the use of the motorcycle.

Required

(a) Explain whether or not Victoria and/or Melba satisfy the conditions relating to period of ownership and reduction in level of shareholding such that the amount received from Trifles Ltd on the purchase of own shares may be treated as capital. **(6 marks)**

(b) Calculate Victoria's after tax proceeds from the purchase of her shares:

- If the amount received is treated as capital.
- If the amount received is treated as income. **(6 marks)**

(c)   Explain, with supporting calculations where necessary, the tax implications of the purchase and loan of the motorcycle for both Melba and Trifles Ltd.   **(5 marks)**

Note. Ignore value added tax (VAT).

You should assume that the tax rates and allowances of the tax year 2015/16 and for the financial year to 31 March 2016 will continue to apply for the foreseeable future.

(Total = 17 marks)

30 Bamburg Ltd (ATAX 06/14)   39 mins

Charlotte is the owner of Bamburg Ltd. She requires advice on the value added tax (VAT) flat rate scheme, the sale of a substantial item of machinery, and the alternative methods by which she can extract additional funds from the company.

Charlotte:

- Is UK resident and UK domiciled.

- Owns 100% of the ordinary share capital of Bamburg Ltd.

- Earns an annual salary from Bamburg Ltd of £46,000 and has no other income.

- Has two ideas to generate additional cash in Bamburg Ltd.

- Wants to receive an additional £14,000 (after the payment of all personal taxes) from Bamburg Ltd on 30 June 2016.

Bamburg Ltd:

- Is a UK resident trading company.
- Is registered for VAT.
- Has budgeted sales revenue for the year ending 31 March 2017 of £120,000 excluding VAT.
- Makes wholly standard rated supplies apart from £6,000 of exempt supplies.
- Has a nil tax written down value on its main pool as at 31 March 2016.
- Will not purchase any plant and machinery in the year ending 31 March 2017.

Charlotte's ideas to generate additional cash in Bamburg Ltd:

- 'Bamburg Ltd should join the VAT flat rate scheme in order to save money.'
- 'Bamburg Ltd should sell the 'Cara' machine and offset the resulting loss against its profits.'

The 'Cara' machine:

- Was purchased on 1 January 2014 for £94,000.
- Rollover relief was claimed in respect of this purchase to defer a chargeable gain of £13,000.
- The 'Cara' machine is currently worth £80,000.
- Following the sale of the 'Cara' machine, Bamburg Ltd will rent a replacement machine.

Alternative methods of extracting an additional £14,000 from Bamburg Ltd:

- Bamburg Ltd to pay Charlotte a bonus.
- Bamburg Ltd to pay Charlotte a dividend.
- Bamburg Ltd to make an interest-free loan of £14,000 to Charlotte.

Required

(a)   Explain, with reference to the information provided, whether or not Bamburg Ltd would be permitted to join the value added tax (VAT) flat rate scheme and set out the matters which would need to be considered in order to determine whether or not it would be financially beneficial for the company to do so.   **(5 marks)**

(b)   Explain the tax and financial implications of Bamburg Ltd selling the 'Cara' machine during the year ending 31 March 2017.   **(5 marks)**

(c) (i) Prepare calculations to determine whether it would be cheaper for Bamburg Ltd to pay Charlotte a bonus or a dividend, such that she would receive £14,000 after the payment of all personal taxes.

(5 marks)

(ii) Explain the immediate tax implications for Bamburg Ltd and Charlotte of Bamburg Ltd making an interest-free loan of £14,000 to Charlotte. **(5 marks)**

(Total = 20 marks)

31 Liza (ATAX 06/13)   39 mins

Liza requires detailed advice on rollover relief, capital allowances and group registration for the purposes of value added tax (VAT).

Liza's business interests:

* Liza's business interests, which have not changed for many years, are set out below.

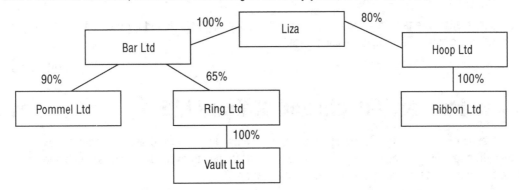

* All six companies are UK resident trading companies with a 31 March year end.
* All of the minority holdings are owned by individuals, none of whom is connected with Liza or with each other.

A building ('Building I') sold by Bar Ltd:

* Bar Ltd sold Building I on 31 May 2016 for £860,000.
* Bar Ltd had purchased the building on 1 June 2010 for £315,000 plus legal fees of £9,000.
* On 5 June 2010, Bar Ltd had carried out work on the building's roof at a cost of £38,000 in order to make the building fit for use.
* On 1 July 2015, Bar Ltd spent £14,000 repainting the building.
* Bar Ltd used Building I for trading purposes apart from the period from 1 January 2012 to 30 June 2013.
* It is intended that the chargeable gain on the sale will be rolled over to the extent that this is possible.

A replacement building ('Building II') purchased by Bar Ltd:

* Bar Ltd purchased Building II, new and unused, for £720,000 on 1 May 2016.
* Bar Ltd uses two thirds of this building for trading purposes; the remaining one-third is rented out.

The trading activities of the Bar Ltd and Hoop Ltd groups of companies:

* The number of transactions between the Bar Ltd group and the Hoop Ltd group is increasing.
* Vault Ltd makes zero rated supplies; all of the other five companies make standard rated supplies.

Required

(a) (i) Calculate the chargeable gain on the sale of Building I, ignoring any potential claim for rollover relief.

(3 marks)

(ii) In relation to claiming rollover relief in respect of the disposal of Building I, explain which of the companies in the Bar Ltd and Hoop Ltd groups are, and are not, able to purchase qualifying replacement assets, and state the period within which such assets must be acquired. **(4 marks)**

(iii) Explain, with the aid of supporting calculations, the additional amount that would need to be spent on qualifying assets in order for the maximum amount of the gain on Building I to be relieved by rollover relief. **(4 marks)**

Notes

1   You should ignore value added tax (VAT) when answering part (a) of this question.
2   The following figures from the Retail Prices Index should be used, where necessary.

June 2010   224.1
July 2015   258.2 (assumed)
May 2016   260.8 (assumed)

(b) Explain the capital allowances that are available in respect of the electrical, water and heating systems that were acquired as part of Building II. **(2 marks)**

(c) Explain which of the companies in the Bar Ltd and Hoop Ltd groups would be able to register as a single group for the purposes of value added tax (VAT) and discuss the potential advantages and disadvantages of registering them as a single VAT group. **(7 marks)**

You should assume that the tax rates and allowances of the tax year 2015/16 and for the Financial Year to 31 March 2016 will continue to apply for the foreseeable future.

(Total = 20 marks)

32 Drake Ltd, Gosling plc and Mallard Ltd   39 mins

Drake Ltd, Gosling plc and Mallard Ltd are three unrelated clients of your firm. Drake Ltd requires advice in connection with goodwill. Gosling plc requires advice in connection with expenditure on research and development. Mallard Ltd requires advice in connection with disincorporation.

(a) **Drake Ltd:**

- Acquired the assets of the business of another company, including goodwill, on 1 September 2015.
- Will amortise the goodwill in the company's accounts.
- May sell the goodwill in a few years' time.

Required

Explain the tax treatment of the goodwill while owned by Drake Ltd and on sale. **(4 marks)**

(b) **Gosling plc:**

- Is a large company for the purposes of research and development (R&D).
- In the year to 31 March 2016 spent £500,000 on qualifying R&D.
- Has taxable total profits, before taking into account R&D expenditure, of £4,500,000.

Required

In relation to Gosling plc, calculate the corporation tax payable for the year ended 31 March 2016 if the company claims:

(i)   R&D deduction relief.   **(2 marks)**
(ii) Above the Line tax credit for R&D expenditure.   **(3 marks)**

(c) **Mallard Ltd:**

- Carries on a trade of computer repairs.
- Owns a freehold shop and a motor car.
- Has goodwill built up since incorporation in 2007.
- Has inventory of computer spare parts.

Nathan:

- Is the sole shareholder of Mallard Ltd, acquiring his shares on incorporation.

- Wishes to disincorporate Mallard Ltd in 2016, acquiring ownership of all its assets, and thereafter will carry on the computer repair business as a sole trade.

Required

In relation to Mallard Ltd:

(i)   Explain the conditions for an election for disincorporation relief to be made, identifying any further
      information required.   **(4 marks)**

(ii) State who must enter into the election for disincorporation relief and the date by which it must be
      submitted to HM Revenue and Customs.   **(2 marks)**

(iii) Outline the effect of disincorporation relief.   **(3 marks)**

(iv) Explain the effect of any other reliefs which may be relevant on the disincorporation of Mallard Ltd.
                                                                                                 (2 marks)

                                                                                        (Total = 20 marks)

VALUE ADDED TAX

Questions 33 to 35 cover value added tax (VAT). This is the subject of Chapters 28 and 29 in the BPP Study Text.

33 Jerome (ATAX 06/12)

35 mins

Jerome is an unincorporated sole trader who is about to sell his business to a company. He requires advice on the value added tax (VAT) implications of the sale of the business, whether a new lease in respect of a motor car for use by him should be entered into by him or by the company and the payment of travel expenses in respect of the family of an employee working overseas.

Jerome's business:

- Has annual taxable profits of £75,000 and is growing.

- Is registered for the purposes of VAT.

- Jerome leases a motor car in which he drives 20,000 miles per year of which 14,000 miles are on business. He anticipates that this level and pattern of mileage will continue in the future.

- The assets of the business include a building that was completed in 2014 and purchased by Jerome in April 2014 for £320,000.

The sale of Jerome's business to Tricycle Ltd:

- The business will be sold to Tricycle Ltd on 1 August 2016.

- Jerome will own the whole of the share capital of Tricycle Ltd.

- Tricycle Ltd will not change the nature of the business but will look to expand it by exporting its products to Italy.

The lease of the motor car:

- The existing lease will end on 31 July 2016.
- A new lease will be entered into on 1 August 2016 by either Jerome or Tricycle Ltd.
- The annual leasing costs of the new car will be £4,400.

The motor car to be leased on 1 August 2016:

- Will be diesel powered and have a list price when new of £31,000.
- Will have CO_2 emissions of 147 grams per kilometre.
- Will have annual running costs, including fuel, of £5,000 in addition to the leasing costs.

Remuneration to be paid by Tricycle Ltd to Jerome:

- A salary of £4,000 per month.

- If Tricycle Ltd leases the motor car, Jerome will use it for business and private purposes and will be provided with fuel for all his motoring.

- If Jerome leases the motor car, he will be paid 50 pence per mile for driving it on business journeys.

Expansion into Europe:

- An employee of Tricycle Ltd will work for up to three months in Italy between April and July 2017.

- The employee will continue to be resident and domiciled in the UK.

- Tricycle Ltd will pay the travel costs of the employee's wife and three-year-old child when they visit him in June 2017.

- The travel costs will be taxable in the hands of the employee as employment income.

Required

(a) Explain the value added tax (VAT) implications of the sale of Jerome's business to Tricycle Ltd. **(6 marks)**

(b) Prepare calculations for the 12-month period to show the total tax cost, for Tricycle Ltd and Jerome, of the car being leased by:

(i) Tricycle Ltd
(ii) Jerome

Note. Ignore VAT for part (b) of this question. **(10 marks)**

(c) State the conditions that must be satisfied for a deduction for the travel costs paid by Tricycle Ltd to be given against the employee's total employment income. **(2 marks)**

You should assume that the tax rates and allowances for the tax year 2015/16 and for the Financial Year to 31 March 2016 will continue to apply for the foreseeable future.

(Total = 18 marks)

34 Spetz Ltd group (ATAX 12/13) 39 mins

The management of the Spetz Ltd group requires advice on the value added tax (VAT) annual adjustment for a partially exempt company, the tax position of a company incorporated and trading overseas, and the income tax treatment of the costs relating to an employee working abroad.

Spetz Ltd group of companies:

- Novak Ltd and Kraus Co are two 100% subsidiaries of Spetz Ltd.
- Novak Ltd has a VAT year end of 30 September.
- Spetz Ltd acquired Kraus Co on 1 October 2015.
- Meyer, an employee of Spetz Ltd, has been seconded to work for Kraus Co.

Novak Ltd – Figures for the year ended 30 September 2016:

		£
Taxable supplies (excluding VAT)		1,190,000
Exempt supplies		430,000
Input tax:	attributed to taxable supplies	12,200
	attributed to exempt supplies	4,900
	unattributed	16,100
	recovered on the four quarterly returns prior to the annual adjustment	23,200

Kraus Co:

- Is incorporated in, and trades through, a permanent establishment in the country of Mersano.

- Has no taxable income or chargeable gains apart from trading profits.

- Has taxable trading profits for the year ended 30 September 2016 of £520,000, all of which arose in Mersano.

- It has been determined that no charge would arise within the controlled foreign company (CFC) regime in respect of Kraus Co.

- Has not made an election to exempt its overseas trading profits from UK tax.

The tax system in the country of Mersano:

- It can be assumed that the tax system in the country of Mersano is the same as that in the UK.
- However, the rate of corporation tax is 17%.
- There is no double tax treaty between the UK and Mersano.

Meyer:

- Will work for Kraus Co in the country of Mersano from 15 December 2016 to 31 March 2017.
- Will continue to be employed by Spetz Ltd.
- Will continue to be resident and domiciled in the UK.

The costs relating to Meyer's secondment to Kraus Co:

- Meyer will be reimbursed for the cost of the flights at the start and end of the contract.

- Meyer will return to the UK for a holiday in February 2017, and will pay his own transport costs.

- Meyer will be reimbursed for the cost of laundry and telephone calls home.

- Spetz Ltd does not have a Form P11D dispensation (PAYE dispensation) in place with HM Revenue and Customs.

Required

(a)   Calculate the value added tax (VAT) partial exemption annual adjustment for Novak Ltd for the year ended 30 September 2016 and state when it must be reported to HM Revenue and Customs. You should state, with reasons, whether or not each of the three *de minimis* tests is satisfied.   **(7 marks)**

(b)   (i)   Explain how to determine whether or not Kraus Co is resident in the UK.   **(3 marks)**

      (ii)   Explain, with supporting calculations, the UK corporation tax liability of Kraus Co for the year ended 30 September 2016 on the assumption that it is resident in the UK, and discuss the advantages and disadvantages of making an election to exempt its overseas profits from UK tax.   **(5 marks)**

(c)   Explain the UK income tax implications for Meyer of the costs relating to his secondment to Kraus Co.   **(5 marks)**

(Total = 20 marks)

35 Nocturne Ltd (ATAX 06/15)   39 mins

Nocturne Ltd, a partially exempt company for the purposes of value added tax (VAT), requires advice on the corporation tax implications of providing an asset to one of its shareholders; the income tax implications for another shareholder of making a loan to the company; and simplifying the way in which it accounts for VAT.

Nocturne Ltd:

- Is a UK resident trading company.

- Prepares accounts to 31 March annually.

- Has four shareholders, each of whom owns 25% of the company's ordinary share capital.

- Owns a laptop computer, which it purchased in October 2013 for £1,200, and which has a current market value of £150.

- Has purchased no other plant and machinery for several years and the tax written down value of its main pool at 31 March 2016 was £nil.

Provision of a laptop computer to one of Nocturne Ltd's shareholders:

- Nocturne Ltd is considering two alternative ways of providing a laptop computer in the year ending 31 March 2017 for the personal use of one of its shareholders, Jed.

- Jed is neither a director nor an employee of Nocturne Ltd.

- Option1: Nocturne Ltd will buy a new laptop computer for £1,800 and give it immediately to Jed.

- Option 2: Nocturne Ltd will gift its existing laptop to Jed and will purchase a replacement for use in the company for £1,800.

Loan from Siglio:

- Siglio will loan £60,000 to Nocturne Ltd on 1 October 2016 to facilitate the purchase of new equipment.
- Siglio is both a shareholder of Nocturne Ltd and the company's managing director.
- Nocturne Ltd will pay interest at a commercial rate on the loan from Siglio.
- Siglio will borrow the full amount of the loan from his bank on normal commercial terms.

VAT – partial exemption:

- Nocturne Ltd is partially exempt for the purposes of VAT.

- Nocturne Ltd's turnover for the year ended 31 March 2016 was £240,000 (VAT exclusive).

- Nocturne Ltd's turnover for the year as a whole for VAT purposes comprised 86% taxable supplies and 14% exempt supplies.

- The input VAT suffered by Nocturne Ltd on expenditure during the year ended 31 March 2016 was:

	£
Wholly attributable to taxable supplies	7,920
Wholly attributable to exempt supplies	1,062
Unattributable	4,150

- Nocturne Ltd expects its turnover and expenditure figures to increase by approximately 25% next year.

- Siglio has heard about an annual test for computing the amount of recoverable input VAT during an accounting period and would like more information about this.

Required

(a) Explain, with the aid of supporting calculations, which of the two proposed methods of providing the laptop computer to Jed would result in the lower after-tax cost for Nocturne Ltd.

Note: You should ignore value added tax (VAT) for part (a) of this question. **(7 marks)**

(b) Explain the income tax implications for Siglio of providing the loan to Nocturne Ltd. **(4 marks)**

(c) (i) Determine, by reference to the *de minimis* tests 1 and 2, Nocturne Ltd's recoverable input VAT for the year ended 31 March 2016. **(4 marks)**

  (ii) Advise Siglio of Nocturne Ltd's eligibility for the annual test for computing the amount of recoverable input VAT for the year ending 31 March 2017 and the potential benefits to be gained from its use. **(5 marks)**

(Total = 20 marks)

IMPACT OF TAXES AND TAX PLANNING

Questions 36 to 42 cover impact of taxes and tax planning. These are the subject of Chapter 30 in the BPP Study Text.

36 Desiree (ATAX 06/10)

31 mins

Desiree requires advice on whether she should run her new business as an unincorporated sole trader or via a company together with the financial implications of registering voluntarily for value added tax (VAT).

The following information has been obtained from a meeting with Desiree.

Desiree:

- Resigned from her job with Chip plc on 31 May 2016.
- Had been employed by Chip plc on an annual salary of £72,000 since January 2013.
- Has no other income apart from bank interest received of less than £1,000 per year.
- Intends to start a new business, to be called Duchess, on 1 September 2016.

The Duchess business:

- The business will sell kitchen equipment and utensils.
- Market research consultants have estimated that 80% of its sales will be to commercial customers.
- The consultants were paid fees in November 2015 and March 2016.

Budgeted results of the Duchess business:

- The budgeted tax-adjusted trading profit/(loss) for the first three trading periods are:

	£
Ten months ending 30 June 2017	(46,000)
Year ending 30 June 2018	22,000
Year ending 30 June 2019	64,000

- The fees paid to the market research consultants have been deducted in arriving at the loss of the first period.

Desiree's financial position:

- Desiree has not yet decided whether to run the business as an unincorporated sole trader or via a company.

- Her primary objective when deciding whether or not to operate the business via a company is the most beneficial use of the loss.

Registration for VAT:

- The turnover of the business is expected to exceed the VAT registration limit in January 2017.
- Desiree would consider registering for VAT earlier if it were financially advantageous to do so.

Required

(a) (i) Calculate the taxable trading profit or allowable trading loss of the business for each of the first three taxable periods for the following alternative structures:

  – The business is unincorporated.
  – The business is operated via a company. **(4 marks)**

  (ii) Provide Desiree with a thorough and detailed explanation of the manner in which the budgeted trading loss could be used depending on whether she runs the business as an unincorporated sole trader or via a company and state which business structure would best satisfy her primary objective.

  Note. You are not required to prepare detailed calculations for part (ii) of this part of this question or to consider non-taxation issues. **(8 marks)**

(b)   Explain in detail the financial advantages and disadvantages of Desiree registering voluntarily for VAT on 1 September 2016. **(4 marks)**

You may assume that the tax rules and rates for 2015/16 will continue to apply for the foreseeable future.

(Total = 16 marks)

37 Poblano (ATAX 06/10)   72 mins

Your manager has had a meeting with Poblano. Poblano is the Finance Director of Capsicum Ltd, a subsidiary of Scoville plc. He is a higher rate taxpayer earning £60,000 per year with no other income. Scoville plc together with its subsidiaries and its directors have been clients of your firm for many years. The memorandum recording the matters discussed at the meeting and an extract from an email from your manager detailing the tasks for you to perform are set out below.

Memorandum recording matters discussed at meeting with Poblano

To	The files
From	Tax manager
Date	4 June 2016
Subject	Poblano

I had a meeting with Poblano on 3 June 2016.

(a)   **Working in Manchester**

Poblano currently lives and works in Birmingham. However, Capsicum Ltd has recently acquired the Manchester operations of the group from a fellow subsidiary of Scoville plc. As a result of this, Poblano is going to be based in Manchester from 1 August 2016 for a period of at least five years. He will be paid an additional £15,000 per year during this period.

Poblano does not want to relocate his family to Manchester for personal reasons. He has been offered the use of a furnished flat in Manchester belonging to Capsicum Ltd to live in during the week. He will drive home each weekend. Details of the company's flat are set out below.

	£
Current market value	555,000
Purchase price (1 June 2013)	415,000
Annual value	9,300
Monthly contribution required from Poblano	200

Alternatively, if he does not live in the flat, Capsicum Ltd will pay him a mileage allowance of 50 pence per mile to cover the cost of travelling to Manchester every Monday and returning home every Friday. During the week, whilst he is in Manchester, Poblano will stay with his aunt, paying her rent of £325 per month

Poblano estimates that he will drive 9,200 miles per year travelling to Manchester each week and that he will spend £1,400 per year on petrol. There would also be additional depreciation in respect of his car of approximately £1,500 per year. Capsicum Ltd has a policy of not providing its employees with company cars.

Poblano expects to be better off due to the increase in his salary. He wants to know how much better off he will be depending on whether he lives in the company flat or receives the mileage allowance and stays with his aunt.

(b)   **Financial accounting problems in Manchester**

Poblano is aware that there are rules relating to the responsibility of senior accounting officers for taxation matters of a company. He asked me for a brief summary of the rules and whether or not they could apply to him in the future.

Poblano's interest in the new rules has been prompted by the review he has performed on the results of the Manchester operation for the year ended 30 September 2015. During that review Poblano identified a number of expenditure classification errors including capital expenditure in respect of improvements to the factory roof that had been classified as plant and machinery in the corporation tax return submitted to HM Revenue and Customs.

(c) **Father's property in the country of Chilaca**

Paprikash (Poblano's father) owns a property in the country of Chilaca that he uses for holidays. It has always been intended that the property would be left to Poblano in his father's will. However, Paprikash has recently agreed to give the property to Poblano now, if to do so would make sense from a tax point of view. Paprikash may still wish to use the property occasionally in the future.

The property is currently worth £600,000. However, due to the economic situation in the country of Chilaca, it is possible that this figure could either rise or fall over the next few years.

Paprikash is domiciled in the UK and is a higher rate taxpayer. He is in poor health and is not expected to live for more than a further five years. His total assets, including the property in the country of Chilaca, are worth £2 million. Paprikash makes gifts on 1 May each year in order to use his annual exemption. His only other gift in the last seven years was to a trust on 1 June 2015. The gift consisted of a number of minority holdings of quoted shares valued at £290,000 in total. The trust is for the benefit of Poblano's daughter, Piri. It can be assumed that Paprikash will not make any further lifetime gifts.

There is no capital gains tax or inheritance tax in the country of Chilaca.

(d) **Trust created for the benefit of Poblano's daughter**

The trust was created on 1 June 2015 as noted above. Poblano's daughter, Piri, received income from the trust for the first time in March 2016. Poblano did not have any further information on the trust and agreed to bring the relevant documentation to our next meeting. Piri's only other income is an annual salary of approximately £35,000.

Tax manager

Email from your manager

I want you to prepare notes for a meeting that we will both attend with Poblano. You will be leading the meeting. Set out the information so that it is easy for you to find what you need as we go through the various issues. Include the briefest possible notes where the numbers are not self-explanatory. The meeting notes need to include:

(a) **Working in Manchester**

- Calculations showing how much better (or worse) off Poblano will be under each of the alternatives as compared to his current position. If he is worse off under either of the alternatives, include a calculation of the amount of salary he would have to be paid, in addition to the £15,000, so that he is not out of pocket.

- An explanation of the tax treatment for the recipients of the mileage allowance to be paid to Poblano and the rent to be paid to his aunt.

- Any further information required and the effect it could have on the calculations you have prepared

(b) **Financial accounting problems in Manchester**

- The information requested by Poblano.

- The further action required by the company and, potentially, ourselves in respect of the classification errors.

(c) **Father's property in the country of Chilaca**

- Calculations of the inheritance tax liability that will become due in respect of the property in the country of Chilaca depending on whether the property is gifted to Poblano on 1 August 2016 or via his father's will. You should assume the following:

  - His father, Paprikash, will die on either 31 December 2018 or 31 December 2020.

  - The property will be worth £600,000 on 1 August 2016.

  - Three possible values of the property at the date of Paprikash's death: £450,000, £600,000 and £900,000.

You should calculate the inheritance tax for each of the 12 possible situations on the property only assuming that Paprikash does not use the property after the date of the gift. You should start by calculating the tax on a lifetime gift with Paprikash's death on 31 December 2018. If you then think about the relationships between the different situations you should find that the calculations do not take too long. In order for the calculations to be comparable, when calculating the tax on the gift via Paprikash's will, you should assume that any available nil band is deductible from the property.

- Conclusions drawn from the calculations.

- Any other issues that we should draw to Poblano's attention.

(d) **Trust created for the benefit of Poblano's daughter**

- A summary of the tax treatment of the income received by Poblano's daughter Piri, as beneficiary, depending on the nature of the trust. I understand from Poblano that the only income of the trust is dividend income.

Required

Prepare the meeting notes requested in the email from your manager. The following marks are available.

(a)	Working in Manchester	**(10 marks)**
(b)	Financial accounting problems in Manchester	**(7 marks)**
(c)	Father's property in the country of Chilaca	**(12 marks)**
(d)	Trust created for the benefit of Poblano's daughter	**(6 marks)**

Professional marks will be awarded in this question for the appropriateness of the format and presentation of the notes and the effectiveness with which the information is communicated. **(2 marks)**

You may assume that the tax rules and rates for 2015/16 will continue to apply for the foreseeable future.

(Total = 37 marks)

38 Ziti (ATAX 06/14)   68 mins

Your manager has received a letter from Ziti. Ziti owns and runs an unincorporated business which was given to him by his father, Ravi. Extracts from the letter and from an email from your manager are set out below.

Extract from the letter from Ziti

I have decided that, due to my father's serious illness, I want to be able to look after him on a full-time basis. Accordingly, I am going to sell my business and use the proceeds to buy a house nearer to where he lives.

My father started the business in 2001 when he purchased the building referred to in the business assets below. He gave the business (consisting of the goodwill, the building and the equipment) to me on 1 July 2012 and we submitted a joint claim for gift relief, such that no capital gains tax was payable. I have no sources of income other than this business.

I have identified two possible methods of disposal.

(i) My preferred approach would be to close the business down. I would do this by selling the building and the equipment on 31 January 2017 at which point I would cease trading.

(ii) My father would like to see the business carry on after I sell it. For this to occur, I would have to continue trading until 30 April 2017 and then sell the business to someone who would continue to operate it.

In each case I would prepare accounts for the year ending 30 April 2016 and then to the date of cessation or disposal.

I attach an appendix setting out the information you requested in relation to the business.

Sadly, I have been told that my father is unlikely to live for more than three years. Please let me know whether his death could result in an inheritance tax liability for me in respect of the gift of the business.

My father's only lifetime gift, apart from the business given to me, was of quoted shares to a discretionary (relevant property) trust on 1 May 2008. The shares had a market value of £190,000 at the date of the gift and did not qualify for business property relief.

Appendix

Business assets (all figures exclude value added tax (VAT))

	Goodwill	Building	Equipment
	£	£	£
Original cost of the business assets	Nil	60,000	18,000
Market value at the time of my father's gift on 1 July 2012	40,000	300,000	9,000
Expected market value as at 31 January 2017 and 30 April 2017	40,000	330,000	10,000

Financial position of the business

The tax adjusted trading profits for the year ended 30 April 2015 were £55,000.

From 1 May 2015, it can be assumed that the business generates trading profits of £5,000 per month. The only tax adjustment required to this figure is in respect of capital allowances.

The tax written down value of the main pool as at 30 April 2015 was nil. I purchased business equipment for £6,000 on 1 August 2015. There have been no disposals of equipment since 30 April 2015.

Extract from an email from your manager

Additional background information

- Ziti and Ravi are both resident and domiciled in the UK.
- Ziti has overlap profits from when he took over the business of £9,000.
- All of the equipment is moveable and no item has a cost or market value of more than £6,000.
- The business is registered for the purposes of VAT.
- No election has been made in respect of the building in relation to VAT.

Please prepare notes, which we can use in a meeting with Ziti, which address the following issues:

(a) **Sale of the business**

    (i)   Calculations to enable Ziti to compare the financial implications of the two possible methods of disposal.

        You will need to calculate:

- Ziti's taxable trading profits from 1 May 2015 onwards and the income tax thereon.
- Any capital gains tax (CGT) payable.

        You should include:

- Explanations of the availability of any CGT reliefs.
- A summary of the post-tax cash position.
- Any necessary assumptions.

    (ii)   Explanations of whether or not VAT would need to be charged on either or both of the alternative disposals.

(b) **Inheritance tax**

    Calculations of the amount of inheritance tax which would be payable by Ziti for all possible dates of his father's death between 7 June 2016 and 30 June 2019. You should include an explanation of the availability of any inheritance tax reliefs.

    When calculating these potential inheritance tax liabilities you should assume that Ziti will sell the business on 30 April 2017.

    The best way for you to approach this is to identify the particular dates on which the inheritance tax liability will change.

Tax manager

Required

Prepare the meeting notes requested in the email from your manager. The following marks are available.

(a)   Sale of the business.

    (i)   Comparison of the financial implications of the alternative methods for disposing of the business. **Note.** Ignore national insurance contributions.   **(17 marks)**

    (ii)   Value added tax (VAT).   **(5 marks)**

(b)   Inheritance tax.   **(9 marks)**

Professional marks will be awarded for adopting a logical approach to problem solving, the clarity of the calculations, the effectiveness with which the information is communicated, and the overall presentation of the notes.   **(4 marks)**

(Total = 35 marks)

39 Dokham (ATAX 06/10)   31 mins

Dokham requires advice on his pension position at retirement, the rules relating to enterprise management incentive (EMI) schemes and the tax implications of his mother helping to pay his children's school fees.

The following information has been obtained from a telephone conversation with Dokham.

Dokham:

- Is married with two children.
- Is domiciled and resident in the UK.
- Has been offered a job by Criollo plc.
- His mother, Virginia, has offered to contribute towards Dokham's children's school fees.

The job offer from Criollo plc:

- Dokham's salary will be £70,000 per year.
- Criollo plc will make annual contributions of £8,000 into Dokham's personal pension scheme.
- Criollo plc will invite Dokham to join the company's EMI scheme.

Dokham's pension arrangements:

- Dokham has not made any pension contributions to date and has not been a member of a pension scheme.
- Dokham intends to make gross annual contributions of £11,000 into a registered personal pension scheme.

The EMI scheme:

- The scheme will have five members including Dokham.

- Criollo plc will grant Dokham an option to purchase 26,185 shares at a price of £9.00 per share. This will represent a holding of less than 1% of the company.

- The option can be exercised at any time until 31 December 2021.

- Criollo plc's current share price is £9.53.

Dokham has requested explanations of the following in respect of the job offer from Criollo plc:

- What would be the difference for me, from a tax point of view, if Criollo plc increased my salary by £8,000 instead of contributing into my personal pension scheme and I made additional gross annual pension contributions of £8,000?

- When can I start to receive benefits from the pension scheme and how does 'flexible access drawdown' work?

- Why might Criollo plc have told me that it is 'not possible' to increase the number of shares I can purchase within the EMI scheme?

- What are the tax implications for me when I exercise my EMI share option and when I sell the shares? I hope to continue to work for Criollo plc even after selling my shares.

Virginia:

- Is domiciled and resident in the UK.
- Has taxable income of more than £120,000 per year.
- Owns a portfolio of quoted shares that is worth more than £500,000.
- Uses her capital gains tax annual exempt amount and inheritance tax annual exemption every year.
- Is considering three alternative ways of contributing towards Dokham's children's school fees.

The three alternative ways of contributing towards the children's school fees:

- Make a one-off gift to Dokham of £54,000 in cash.

- Make a one-off gift to Dokham of 9,800 shares (a holding of less than 1%) in Panatella plc, a quoted company, worth £54,000.

- Make a gift to Dokham of £8,000 in cash every year for the next seven years.

Required

(a)   Provide the information requested by Dokham in respect of the job offer from Criollo plc as set out above.

(9 marks)

(b)   Explain in detail the possible tax liabilities that could result from the three alternative ways proposed by Virginia to contribute towards the children's school fees.   **(7 marks)**

You may assume that the tax rules and rates for 2015/16 will continue to apply for the foreseeable future.

(Total = 16 marks)

40 King (ATAX 06/15)   39 mins

King, a wealthy client of your firm with a significant property portfolio, requires advice on the sale of some unquoted shares and on the capital gains tax and inheritance tax implications of transferring assets to a trust and to his two children.

King:

- Is resident and domiciled in the UK.
- Is an additional rate taxpayer.
- Has used his capital gains tax annual exempt amount for the tax year 2016/17.
- Has made one previous lifetime gift of £25,000 to his daughter, Florentyna, on 1 June 2015.
- It should be assumed that King will die on 1 May 2018.

King's family:

- King's daughter, Florentyna, is 34 years old and has two young children.

- Florentyna will have income from part-time employment of £10,600 in the tax year 2016/17. This is her only source of taxable income.

- King's son, Axel, is 40 years old and has an 18-year-old daughter, who is a university student.

King's plans:

- On 1 September 2016, King will sell some of his shares in Wye Ltd.

- On 1 October 2016, King will put a cottage he owns in Newtown and the after-tax cash proceeds from the sale of the shares in Wye Ltd into an interest in possession trust for Florentyna and her children.

- On 1 March 2017, King will gift his share of a flat in Unicity to Axel.

Sale of shares in Wye Ltd:

- Wye Ltd is an unquoted investment company.
- King acquired 5,000 shares in Wye Ltd on 1 June 2003 at a cost of £5 each.
- These shares will be worth £45 each on 1 September 2016.
- King will sell sufficient shares to generate after-tax proceeds of £30,000.

Cottage in Newtown:

- This property is wholly owned by King.
- It is expected to have a value of £315,000 on 1 October 2016.

Creation of the interest in possession trust:

- King will pay any inheritance tax arising as a result of the gifts made to the trust.

- Florentyna will be the life tenant and her two young children will be the remaindermen of the trust.

- Florentyna will live in the cottage in Newtown and the trustees will invest the cash in quoted shares which will generate annual dividends of £3,000.

Flat in Unicity:

- The flat in Unicity is jointly owned by King and his wife, Joy, in the proportions: King 75% and Joy 25%.

- King and Joy have recently signed a contract with Axel's daughter to rent the flat to her for three years starting on 1 September 2016.

- The rental agreement is on a commercial basis.

- King has obtained the following expected valuations for the flat as at 1 March 2017:

	With vacant possession £	Without vacant possession £
Value of a 25% share	60,000	40,000
Value of a 75% share	220,000	160,000
Value of the whole property	340,000	250,000

Required

(a) Calculate the minimum number of shares in Wye Ltd which King must sell to generate after-tax proceeds of £30,000. **(3 marks)**

(b) (i) Advise King, with the aid of supporting calculations, of the capital gains tax and immediate inheritance tax implications of the proposed gift of assets into the interest in possession trust on 1 October 2016. **(6 marks)**

    (ii) Explain how Florentyna will be taxed on the income arising in the trust and calculate the additional income tax, if any, payable by her in respect of this income for the tax year 2016/17. **(4 marks)**

(c) Explain, with the aid of supporting calculations, why the disposal of the flat in Unicity may be caught by the associated operations rules and the increase in the inheritance tax liability which would arise on King's death on 1 May 2018 if these rules were to apply. **(7 marks)**

(Total = 20 marks)

41 Robusto Ltd (ATAX 12/10)   33 mins

Robusto Ltd, a partially exempt company for the purposes of value added tax (VAT), requires advice on the cost of purchasing services from various suppliers and an explanation of the implications if the relationship between the company and the person providing the services is one of employer and employee.

The following information was obtained during a meeting with the managing director of Robusto Ltd.

Robusto Ltd – Budgeted results for the year ending 31 March 2017:

- Turnover (exclusive of VAT):

	£
Standard rated	850,000
Exempt	330,000
Zero rated	120,000

- The irrecoverable VAT for the year will exceed the *de minimis* limits.

- Robusto Ltd is growing quickly and intends to purchase market analysis services relating to all aspects of its business.

Potential providers of market analysis services:

- There are three potential service providers: Cognac Ltd, Fonseca Inc and Pisco.
- Robusto Ltd will use the provider that results in the lowest cost to the company.
- Alternatively, Robusto Ltd will take on a new employee to carry out the market analysis.

Cognac Ltd:

- Cognac Ltd is a UK resident company wholly owned by Offley, a UK resident individual.
- Offley is the company's only employee.
- Offley would be contractually obliged to perform all of the market analysis services provided by Cognac Ltd.
- Cognac Ltd would charge a fixed fee of £28,500 plus VAT.

Fonseca Inc:

- Fonseca Inc is a company resident in the country of Parejo.
- The country of Parejo is not a member of the European Union.
- Fonseca Inc would charge a fixed fee of £29,000.

Pisco:

- Pisco is a UK resident unincorporated sole trader who is not registered for VAT.
- Pisco would charge a fixed fee of £29,500.

Required

(a)   In respect of the market analysis services:

- Explain, with the aid of supporting calculations, which service provider would result in the lowest cost to Robusto Ltd.

- Calculate the maximum salary that could be paid by Robusto Ltd to an employee such that the total cost would be no more than that of the cheapest service provider. You should assume that Robusto Ltd has other employees such that the employment allowance is already utilised against the secondary Class 1 national insurance contributions for these employees.   **(9 marks)**

(b)   On the assumption that the services are purchased from Pisco, give **three** examples of specific contractual arrangements that would assist HM Revenue and Customs in arguing that the relationship between Robusto Ltd and Pisco is that of employer and employee.   **(3 marks)**

(c)   On the assumption that HM Revenue and Customs could successfully argue that the relationship between Robusto Ltd and the individual carrying out the market analysis services, Offley or Pisco, is one of employer and employee:

- Explain the tax implications for Robusto Ltd and Cognac Ltd if the services are purchased from Cognac Ltd.

- Explain why Robusto Ltd might prefer to offer the contract to Cognac Ltd rather than to Pisco.

Note. You are not required to prepare any calculations for part (c) of this question or to describe in detail how any deemed salary payment would be calculated.   **(5 marks)**

You should assume that the tax rates and allowances of the tax year 2015/16 and for the Financial Year to 31 March 2016 will continue to apply for the foreseeable future.

(Total = 17 marks)

42 FL Partnership (ATAX 12/13)

68 mins

Your manager has had a meeting with Farina and Lauda, potential new clients, who are partners in the FL Partnership. The memorandum recording the matters discussed, together with an email from your manager, is set out below.

Memorandum

To: The Files
From: Tax manager
Date: 5 December 2016
Subject: FL Partnership

Background

Farina and Lauda began trading as the FL Partnership on 1 May 2011. Accounts have always been prepared to 31 March each year. They are each entitled to 50% of the revenue profits and capital profits of the business.

On 1 March 2017, the whole of the FL Partnership business will be sold as a going concern to JH plc, a quoted trading company which is not a close company. The consideration for the sale will be a mixture of cash and shares. Capital gains tax relief on the transfer of a business to a company (incorporation relief) will be available in respect of the sale.

Farina and Lauda will both pay income tax at the additional rate in the tax year 2016/17 and anticipate continuing to do so in future years. They are very wealthy individuals, who use their capital gains tax annual exempt amounts every year. Both of them are resident and domiciled in the UK.

The sale of the business on 1 March 2017

The assets of the FL Partnership business have been valued as set out below. All of the equipment qualified for capital allowances.

	Value £	Cost £
Goodwill	1,300,000	Nil
Inventory and receivables	30,000	30,000
Equipment (no item to be sold for more than cost)	150,000	200,000
Total	1,480,000	

The total value of the consideration will be equal to the value of the assets sold. Farina and Lauda will each receive consideration of £740,000; £140,000 in cash and 200,000 shares in JH plc. Following the purchase of the FL Partnership, JH plc will have an issued share capital of 8,400,000 shares.

Future transactions

Farina:

On 1 August 2017, Farina will make a gift of 15,000 of her shares in JH plc to the trustees of a discretionary (relevant property) trust for the benefit of her nieces and nephews. Farina will pay any inheritance tax liability in respect of this gift. The trustees will transfer the shares to the beneficiaries over the life of the trust.

Lauda:

On 1 June 2018, Lauda will give 40,000 of her shares in JH plc to her son.

For the purposes of giving our advice, the value of a share in JH plc can be assumed to be:

	£
On 1 March 2017	3
On 1 August 2017	4
On 1 June 2018	5

Email from your manager

I want you to prepare a memorandum for the client file in respect of the following:

(i)   **Capital allowances**

A DETAILED explanation of the calculation of the capital allowances of the FL Partnership for its final trading period ending with the sale of its equipment to JH plc for £150,000 on 1 March 2017.

(ii)   **Farina**

BRIEF explanations of:

(1)   The manner in which any inheritance tax payable by Farina in her lifetime in respect of the gift of the shares to the trustees of the discretionary (relevant property) trust will be calculated and the date on which the tax would be payable.

(2)   The availability of capital gains tax gift relief in respect of the transfer of the shares to the trustees of the discretionary (relevant property) trust and the subsequent transfers of shares from the trustees to the beneficiaries.

(iii)   **Lauda**

A review of whether or not Lauda should disclaim incorporation relief.

The review should encompass the sale of the FL Partnership business, the gift of the shares to Lauda's son and the effect of incorporation relief on the base cost of the remaining shares owned by Lauda, as she intends to sell all of her shares in JH plc in the next few years.

It is important that you include a summary of your calculations and a statement of the key issues for me to discuss with Lauda. You should also include BRIEF explanations of the amount of incorporation relief available, the availability of any additional or alternative reliefs, and the date(s) on which any capital gains tax will be payable.

Tax manager

Required

(a)   It is anticipated that Farina and Lauda will require some highly sophisticated and specialised tax planning work in the future.

Prepare a summary of the information which would be required, together with any action(s) which should be taken by the firm before it agrees to become the tax advisers to Farina and Lauda.   **(5 marks)**

(b)   Prepare the memorandum requested in the email from your manager. The following marks are available:

(i)   Capital allowances   **(5 marks)**
(ii)   Farina   **(7 marks)**
(iii)   Lauda   **(14 marks)**

Note. Ignore value added tax (VAT).

Professional marks will be awarded in part (b) for the overall presentation of the memorandum, the provision of relevant advice and the effectiveness with which the information is communicated.   **(4 marks)**

(Total = 35 marks)

Answers

1 Styrax

Marking scheme

				Marks
(a)	(i)	Salvia's PA wasted	1	
		Transferable allowance	1	
		Styrax needs to transfer income	1	
		Employment of Salvia	1	
		Tax savings	2	
		Use of ISAs and savings starting rate band	2	
		Tax savings	1	
		Max		8
	(ii)	Personal pension provision	1	
		Maximum contributions	1	
		Occupational scheme	1	
		Suitability	1	
		Max		3
(b)		*Enterprise Investment Scheme*		
		Aim of scheme	1	
		Income tax reducer	2	
		Carry back	1	
		Withdrawal of relief	1	
		Risk	1	
		Seed Enterprise Investment Scheme		
		Aim of scheme	1	
		Income tax reducer	2	
		Withdrawal of relief	1	
		Risk	1	
		Venture Capital Scheme		
		Aim of scheme	1	
		Income tax reducer	1	
		Dividends	1	
		Withdrawal of relief	1	
		Risk	1	
				16
				27

(a) (i) **Notes for meeting with Styrax**

Use of Salvia's personal allowance

Now that Salvia has given up employed work, she does not have any source of income. This means that her personal allowance (£10,600) is being wasted. It is only possible for Salvia to elect to transfer £1,060 of her personal allowance to Styrax resulting in a tax reduction to him of £212.

Styrax needs to transfer some of his income to Salvia in order for her to utilise her personal allowance in full. Styrax could do this by employing Salvia in his business (the question states that she does not want to be a partner so this is not considered).

Salvia's salary must be commercially justifiable for the work that she will do. Styrax will then be able to deduct the salary from his trading profits. This will save income tax at 20% and also reduce his Class 4 NICs at 9%.

A salary up to the remaining income tax personal allowance of £9,540 (after transfer of £1,060 of the personal allowance) will be free of income tax and a salary up to the primary national insurance contributions threshold of £8,060 will also be free of Class 1 NICs for both Salvia as employee and Styrax as employer. A salary of up to £8,060 will therefore save tax and NICs of 29%.

If Styrax were to pay anything above the level of the remaining personal allowance to Salvia, this would be subject to 20% income tax and 12% employee Class 1 NICs in the hands of Salvia. Styrax will also have to pay 13.8% employer Class 1 NICs. Therefore the overall tax rate is 45.8%. However, Styrax would also save income tax and NICs at approximately the rate of 33% (income tax of 20%, Class 4 NICs at 9%, and income tax and Class 4 NICs on the employer's Class 1 contributions which would be 13.8% × (20% + 9%) = 4%). Therefore, it would not be advantageous to pay this additional amount as the overall additional tax is more than the tax saving.

Therefore if the salary exceeded the remaining personal allowance for Salvia, this would not be tax efficient as both Styrax and Salvia would be basic rate tax payers and the Class 1 NIC costs would outweigh the tax saving for Styrax.

Savings income

Styrax could give Salvia the £35,000 cash which she could invest in an interest bearing account. The interest will be covered by her starting rate savings band of £5,000 on which tax is payable at 0% thus saving income tax of £1,000 × 20% = £200.

Alternatively, the couple could take advantage of Individual Savings Accounts. Each of them can invest up to £15,240 per tax year in cash, stocks and shares, or a combination of each. The income generated by the accounts is tax free as are any gains on shares. Since the couple are risk adverse, shares are not a suitable investment for them. Each of them should open a cash ISA and invest the maximum amount allowable in cash. (Styrax would need to transfer £15,240 to Salvia.) This would save income tax on their interest income of £30,480/35,000 × £1,000 × 20% = £174.

(ii) **Future pension provision**

Styrax and Salvia could both start personal pensions.

The maximum tax relievable contributions that Styrax could make would be the higher of:

(1) £3,600
(2) The amount of his earnings

Salvia could make contributions up to £3,600 even though she has no earnings (unless she becomes employed by Styrax).

Alternatively, if Salvia becomes an employee of Styrax, she could join a workplace pension scheme.

Since the couple only have disposable income of £3,000 per year, they would probably not wish to spend all of it on pension provision. Possibly both of them could try to invest a small amount per month (say £50).

Tutorial note

Salvia would not earn enough to trigger automatic enrolment into a workplace pension as an employee of Styrax. However, she would be entitled to opt into such a workplace pension scheme since her earnings will be more than the lower threshold. However, you are not required to know this level of detail about workplace pensions for the P6(UK) exam.

(b) **Memorandum**

Enterprise Investment Scheme

The Enterprise Investment Scheme (EIS) is designed to promote enterprise and investment. It helps such high-risk, unlisted trading companies raise finance by issuing new shares (usually ordinary shares) to unconnected individuals.

If you subscribe for EIS shares you can claim a tax reduction of the lower of:

(i) 30% of the amount subscribed for qualifying investments (maximum qualifying investments are £1,000,000 in 2015/16)

(ii) Your tax liability for the year after deducting VCT relief (described below)

For example, if you subscribed the maximum of £1,000,000, you could claim a tax reduction of £1,000,000 × 30% = £300,000. However, if your tax liability is less than £300,000, you can only bring that liability down to nil.

You can also claim to treat all or any of the shares as being issued in 2014/15, instead of 2015/16 and thus claim a tax reducer in 2014/15 instead of 2015/16.

You must hold the shares for at least three years if the income tax relief is not to be withdrawn or reduced. The main reason for the withdrawal of relief will be the sale of the shares by you within the three year period mentioned above.

EIS investments are high risk because there is total exposure to unquoted companies engaged in risky trades.

Seed Enterprise Investment Scheme (SEIS)

This is similar to the EIS but is designed to encourage investment into small early stage companies.

If you subscribe for SEIS shares you can claim a tax reduction of the lower of:

(i) 50% of the amount subscribed for qualifying investments (maximum qualifying investments are £100,000 in 2015/16)

(ii) Your tax liability for the year after deducting VCT relief and EIS relief

The maximum tax reducer under the SEIS is therefore £100,000 × 50% = £50,000.

You can also claim to treat all or any of the shares as being issued in 2014/15, instead of 2015/16 and thus claim a tax reducer in 2014/15 instead of 2015/16.

The same rules apply to SEIS as for EIS concerning the three year holding period to avoid withdrawal or reduction of the relief.

SEIS investments are even more high risk than EIS investments as the companies in which investments are made are small, start up companies.

Venture capital trusts (VCTs)

Venture capital trusts (VCTs) are listed companies which invest in unquoted trading companies and meet certain conditions.

If you invest in a VCT, you will obtain the following income tax benefits on a maximum qualifying investment of £200,000 in 2015/16:

(i) A tax reduction of 30% of the amount invested

(ii) Dividends received are tax-free income

BPP
LEARNING MEDIA

You must hold the shares for at least five years if the income tax relief is not to be withdrawn or reduced. The main reason for the withdrawal of relief will be the sale of the shares by you within five years of acquisition.

The VCT scheme differs from EIS or SEIS in that you can spread your risk over a number of higher-risk, unquoted companies. However, it is still a moderately high risk investment.

2 Spike (ATAX 06/13)

Text references. Loss relief is covered in Chapter 8. Chargeable gains, including the rates of CGT, are to be found in Chapter 11. Share options are dealt with in Chapter 5. Employment income is the subject of Chapter 4.

Top tips. It is important to realise that the trading loss which can be relieved against general income (and gains) is computed differently from the terminal loss.

Easy marks. There were some easy marks in part (b)(i) for explaining the gain on the disposal of the shares and also in part (b)(ii) in respect of the relocation expenses.

Examiner's comments. Part (a) concerned losses realised on a cessation of trade and was in two parts. Part (a)(i) was short and direct; it was intended to ensure that all candidates attempting this question addressed the two possibilities that needed to be considered when they went on to part (a)(ii) and had to explain the reliefs available in respect of the loss. In part (a)(i) candidates were required to calculate the trading loss in the year of cessation and the terminal loss of the last 12 months. Very few candidates made a reasonable job of this; the majority of candidates simply did not know the rules. Accordingly, many candidates simply did not appreciate the difference between the loss of the tax year and the terminal loss. Of those candidates who were aware that the terminal loss is calculated in its own particular way, very few knew how to do it. In addition, many candidates deducted the overlap profits from the loss rather than using them to increase the loss. In part (a)(ii) things did not really improve. Although many candidates were aware that there was the possibility of carrying back a loss on cessation to the three years prior to the loss, there was a general lack of precision as regards the rules and a confused approach to the figures. When dealing with losses, there are only really two things that need to be known: the years in which the losses can be offset and the type of income or gains that the losses can be offset against. Marks were available in part (a)(ii) for knowing these fundamental rules but they were not awarded as frequently as one might have expected. The approach of most candidates to part (a)(ii) was not as measured or considered as was necessary. Candidates would have benefited from clearly defining the possibilities in their minds and then writing brief, precise points that addressed each of the possibilities. Instead, most candidates wrote too much that was confused and often contradictory. In addition, because they did not give themselves sufficient time to consider the possibilities, many candidates did not consider the possibility of relieving the capital gains. Those that did often did so in general terms as opposed to addressing the particular gains in the question.

Part (b) was in two parts and concerned share options and a relocation payment. It was done reasonably well. Part (b)(i) concerned the tax implications of the grant and exercise of a non-tax advantaged option to purchase shares and the eventual sale of the shares. The question made it clear that the option was not part of a tax advantaged scheme and it was important that candidates identified this point. There were many satisfactory answers to this question but also many unsatisfactory ones. The candidates who did well tended to be those who were better organised and were methodical in their approach. In particular, the requirement listed the three matters to address: the grant, exercise and sale of the shares. Some candidates did not address all three of these matters, making it much more difficult to pass this part of the question. Part (b)(ii) concerned the £8,000 exemption available in respect of relocation costs and was answered well.

				Marks
(a)	(i)	Loss for the tax year 2015/16	1	
		Terminal loss	3	
				4
	(ii)	Relief of the loss for the tax year 2015/16		
		The reliefs available	2	
		Tax savings 2015/16		
		Business assets	1½	
		House	2	
		Tax savings 2014/15	1	
		Relief of the terminal loss		
		The reliefs available	3	
		Tax savings – terminal loss	1	
		Tax savings – excess of trading loss over terminal loss	1½	
		Max		10
(b)	(i)	Grant	1	
		Exercise	2	
		Sale of shares	2	
		Max		4
	(ii)	Relocation payment		2
				20

(a)   (i)   **Loss relief available on the cessation of the trade**

Trading loss for the tax year 2015/16

	£
Loss for the period from 1 January 2015 to 30 September 2015	13,500
Add overlap profits	8,300
Trading loss 2015/16	21,800

Tutorial note

The basis period for the tax year 2015/16 runs from 1 January 2015 (the end of the basis period for the previous year) until 30 September 2015 (the cessation of trade).

Terminal loss

	£	£
6 April 2015 to 30 September 2015		
Loss £13,500 × 6/9		9,000
Add: overlap profits		8,300
		17,300
1 October 2014 to 5 April 2015		
1 October 2014 to 31 December 2014		
Profit £24,995 × 3/12	6,249	
1 January 2015 to 5 April 2015		
Loss £13,500 × 3/9	(4,500)	
Net profit ignored for the purposes of terminal loss	1,749	
		0
Terminal loss		17,300

(ii) **The reliefs available in respect of the trading loss and the terminal loss**

Relief of the loss for the tax year 2015/16

The loss for the tax year 2015/16 can be offset against Spike's general income of 2015/16 and/or 2014/15.

Once the loss has been offset against the general income of a particular tax year, it can also be offset against the capital gains of that same year.

Spike has no general income in the tax year 2015/16. But, a claim can be made for the whole of the loss to be relieved against his 2015/16 capital gains. Relieving the loss against the gains on the sale of the business assets would save capital gains tax at the rate of 10% due to the availability of entrepreneurs' relief. The tax saved would be £21,800 × 10% = £2,180.

Spike's sale of his house will be an exempt disposal of his principal private residence if he has always occupied it, or is deemed to have always occupied it. If part of the gain on the house is taxable, capital gains tax will be payable at 28% because the gains on the business assets will have used the basic rate band. Accordingly, if this is the case, the loss should be offset against any gain on the house in priority to the gain on the business assets.

In the tax year 2014/15, the loss would be offset against the general income of £24,995. The claim cannot be restricted in order to obtain relief for the personal allowance of that year. The tax saved would be £(24,995 – 10,600) = £14,395 × 20% = £2,879.

Relief of the terminal loss

The terminal loss can be offset against the trading profit of the business for 2015/16 and the three preceding tax years, starting with the latest year.

The trading profit in the tax year 2015/16 is nil, such that the terminal loss will be relieved in the tax year 2014/15. This would save tax of £(24,995 – 10,600) = £14,395 × 20% = £2,879.

The excess of the trading loss of 2015/16 over the terminal loss is £(21,800 – 17,300) = £4,500. This amount can be offset against general income and capital gains in 2015/16 and 2014/15 as set out above. However, once the terminal loss has been relieved in the tax year 2014/15, Spike's remaining general income of £(24,995 – 17,300) = £7,695 is less than the personal allowance, thus there is no taxable income and, therefore, no further tax saving to be achieved in either of the two relevant years. Accordingly, the remaining loss should be relieved against the capital gains of 2015/16. This would save tax of £4,500 × 10% = £450 if the loss is relieved against the gains on the sale of the business, or £4,500 × 28% = £1,260 if it is relieved against a non-exempt gain arising on the sale of the house.

(b) (i) **The option to purchase ordinary shares in Set Ltd**

There will be no tax liability in respect of the grant of the option.

When Spike exercises the option and acquires the shares, he will be subject to income tax on the excess of the market value of the shares at that time over the price paid for the option and the shares, ie £(8.00 – 0.50 – 4.00) = £3.50 per share. Accordingly, there will be an income tax liability of 7,000 × £3.50 × 40% = £9,800 when the option is exercised on the assumption that Spike continues to be a higher rate taxpayer.

On the sale of the shares, the excess of the sales proceeds per share over £8.00 (the market value of the shares when the option was exercised) will be taxed as a capital gain. The capital gain, less the annual exempt amount, will be subject to capital gains tax at 28% on the assumption that Spike continues to be a higher rate taxpayer. Entrepreneurs' relief will not be available unless Spike has acquired more shares, such that he owns at least 5% of the company's share capital.

(ii) **The relocation payment**

The compensation in respect of the sale of the house at short notice at a low price will be regarded as having been derived from employment, such that it will be taxable in full. £8,000 of the payment in respect of the costs of moving house will be exempt; the remaining £(11,500 – 8,000) = £3,500 of the payment will be taxable.

3 Piquet and Buraco (ATAX 12/14)

Text references. Change of accounting date is dealt with in Chapter 6. Overseas aspects of income tax are the subject of Chapter 10.

Top tips. In part (a)(i) it is important to identify the tax year of change of the accounting date as this will affect both the treatment of the long period of account and the date of notification to HM Revenue and Customs.

Easy marks. The accounting date change to 28 February in part (a)(i) was reasonable straightforward. The implications of claiming the remittance basis in part (b)(ii) should have been well known.

Examiner's comments. The calculations in parts (a)(i) and (a)(ii) would have been straight forward for those candidates who knew the rules and had practised applying them. Unfortunately, most candidates who attempted this question did not know the rules, such that very few scored well on these parts of the question. Part (a)(iii) required candidates to identify two advantages of using a 30 April year end as opposed to a year end of 28 February. Many candidates were able to identify one advantage but few were able to come up with two. This was disappointing as the choice of year end is a basic aspect of tax planning for the unincorporated trader and one that candidates should be confident of. Candidates should recognise that change of accounting date is not part of the Paper F6 (UK) syllabus and must therefore be regarded as an area that will be examined regularly in future Paper P6 (UK) exams.

Part (b)(i) required candidates to explain certain aspects of an individual's residency position by reference to the facts provided in the question. Candidates' appeared to be well-prepared for a question on this area of the syllabus with good levels of knowledge. However, it was important for candidates to realise that this was a question that required their knowledge to be applied to the specific facts and that it was not enough to simply set down everything they knew on the topic. For example, candidates should have realised that, depending on the number of days spent in the UK (which was left imprecise in the question) the relevant number of ties was either two or three. Then, it was not sufficient to list the ties, it was necessary to state whether or not they were met by the individual concerned. It was then good exam technique to draw the various aspects of the explanation together into a form of summary or conclusion. The other common mistake made by candidates when answering this question was to include irrelevant information in their answers. A significant number of candidates explained the automatic UK residency tests despite the wording of the requirement. Such explanations would not have scored any marks as they were irrelevant to the requirement and thus such candidates put themselves under unnecessary time pressure as a result. Part (b)(ii) was answered well by many candidates. There were only two matters to note here. Firstly, some candidates' knowledge of the rules governing the remittance basis charge was somewhat imprecise. Secondly, a minority of candidates set out the rules but did not apply them to the individual concerned.

Marking scheme

				Marks
(a)	(i)	Date for notification to HMRC	1	
		Calculations of taxable trading profits	2	
				3
	(ii)	Basis periods for two tax years	1½	
		Creation of overlap profits	1½	
				3
	(iii)	Identification of issue – one mark each	2	
		Explanation of issue – one mark each	2	
				4

				Marks
(b)	(i)	Automatic overseas tests	1	
		Days in UK and UK ties	2½	
		Work, family and available accommodation ties	3	
		90 day tie	1½	
		Conclusion	1	
		Max		7
	(ii)	UK tax on overseas income and gains	1	
		Personal allowance and annual exempt amount	1	
		No remittance basis charge	2	
		Max		3
				20

(a)   (i)   **Accounting date changed to 28 February**

If Piquet changes his accounting date to 28 February, the year of change is 2016/17 so he must notify HMRC of the change by 31 January following the end of the tax year (ie 31 January 2018).

Taxable trading profits

	£
2016/17 (year of change)	
16 months ended 28 February 2017 (long period of account ending in year)	94,000
Less relief for overlap profits £15,000 × 4/5	(12,000)
Taxable trading profits	82,000
2017/18	
Year ended 28 February 2018 (current year basis)	88,000

(ii)   **30 April year end – Basis periods and overlap profits**

The basis period for 2016/17 is the 12 months to the new accounting date which would have fallen in that tax year which is 30 April 2016.

This will create additional overlap profits as profits for the period 1 May 2015 to 31 October 2015 have already been taxed in the tax year 2015/16. These overlap profits are £4,500 × 6 = £27,000.

The basis period for the tax year 2017/18 is the 12 months ended 30 April 2017.

Tutorial note

If accounts are prepared for the 18 month period to 30 April 2017, there will be no period of account ending in the tax year 2016/17. A basis period for 2016/17 must be manufactured by taking the actual new accounting date of 30 April 2017 and deducting one year.

(iii)   **Advantages of 30 April year end**

As Piquet's profits are rising, a date early in the tax year, such as 30 April, delays the time when rising accounts profits feed through into rising taxable profits, whereas a date late in the tax year, such as 28 February, accelerates the taxation of rising profits. This is because with an accounting date of 30 April, the taxable profits for each tax year are mainly the profits earned in the previous tax year. With an accounting date of 28 February the taxable profits are almost entirely profits earned in the current year.

An accounting date of 30 April gives the maximum interval between earning profits and paying the related tax liability. For example if Piquet prepares accounts to 30 April 2018, this falls into the tax year 2018/19 with payments on account being due on 31 January 2019 and 31 July 2019, and a balancing payment due on 31 January 2020. If he prepares accounts to 28 February 2018, this falls in the tax year 2017/18 and the payments will be due one year earlier (ie on 31 January 2018, 31 July 2018 and 31 January 2019).

Knowing profits well in advance of the end of the tax year makes tax planning much easier. For example, if Piquet wants to make personal pension contributions and prepares accounts to 30 April 2018 (2018/19), he can make contributions up to 5 April 2019 based on those relevant earnings. If he prepares accounts to 28 February 2018, he will probably not know the amount of his relevant earnings until after the end of the tax year 2017/18, too late to adjust his pension contributions for that tax year.

Note

Only TWO advantages were required.

Tutorial note

Credit would also be given to students who explained the effect of a trader's year end on the basis period in the tax year of cessation (although this may be a disadvantage since, with an accounting date of 30 April, the assessment for the year of cessation could be based on up to 23 months of profits).

(b)   (i)   **Residence status for the tax year 2016/17**

Automatic overseas residence tests

Buraco does not satisfy the only relevant automatic overseas residence test for the tax year 2016/17 as he will spend 46 days or more in the UK in that tax year.

Tutorial note

As Buraco does not work full-time overseas, the spending less than 91 days in the UK test is not relevant.

Residence status for tax year 2016/17

As Buraco meets none of the automatic overseas tests and (as stated in the question) none of the automatic UK tests, the 'sufficient ties' test must be considered to decide if he is UK resident for the tax year 2016/17.

As Buraco was not UK resident in any of the previous three tax years, the relevant ties are:

- UK resident close family: Buraco has a minor child who is UK resident so this is a tie.

- Substantive UK work: Buroco does not work in the UK so this is not a tie.

- Available UK accommodation: Buraco has accommodation available him for a consecutive period of 91 days or more in the tax year and in which he spends one or more nights during the tax year so this is a tie.

- 90 day tie: if Buraco spent more than 90 days spent in the UK in either or both of the previous two tax years (in this case only 2015/16 is relevant based on the information in the question) this would be a tie. More information is needed on this point.

Buraco therefore has two definite UK ties and one possible UK tie.

As Buraco was not previously resident in the UK in any of the previous three tax years, if he has two ties he will be UK resident for the tax year 2016/17 if he spends between 121 days and 150 days in the UK, but not UK resident if he spends between 100 days and 120 days in the UK.

If, however, it is found that Buraco has three UK ties, he will be UK resident for the tax year 2016/17 based on any number of his expected days in the UK since the minimum number of days for this test is 91 days.

(ii)   **Tax implications of claiming remittance basis**

If Buraco claims the remittance basis for the tax year 2016/17, he will be liable to UK tax on overseas income and gains arising in that tax year only to the extent that they are remitted to the UK.

Buraco would not be entitled to the personal allowance for income tax or the annual exempt amount for capital gains tax for the tax year 2016/17.

The remittance basis charge would not apply in the tax year 2016/17 as Buraco has not been UK resident for at least seven of the nine tax years preceding that tax year.

4 Jodie (ATAX 06/15)

Text references. Overseas aspects of income tax are dealt with in Chapter 10. Trading losses are covered in Chapter 8. The calculation of gains and capital gains tax liability are dealt with in Chapter 11. Gift relief will be found in Chapter 13 and principal private residence relief and overseas aspects of capital gains tax in Chapter 14. Overseas aspects of inheritance tax are covered in Chapter 18. Value added tax deregistration is dealt with in Chapter 28.

Top tips. It is really important to attempt all the requirements of the question. For example, in part (d) you needed to discuss both the inheritance tax aspects of Jodie leaving the UK and the value added tax aspects of ceasing to trade.

Easy marks. There were some easy marks in part (a) for explaining the statutory residence tests. However, it was important to apply the rules to the particular scenario rather than just state all the tests.

Examiner's comments. Part (a) was generally answered well, with many candidates demonstrating a strong knowledge of these aspects of the syllabus. In particular, candidates knew how to determine the number of ties that needed to be satisfied and were able to describe the ties and relate them to the facts of the question. Unfortunately, many candidates failed to consider the automatic UK residence tests and were unable to state clearly the income tax implications of being non-UK resident, ie not being subject to UK income tax on overseas income. This latter point was part of an overall lack of clarity among many candidates in relation to the overseas aspects of personal tax. Candidates were vague about the implications or wasted time providing significant amounts of information on the remittance basis.

Part (b) was generally answered well. This was a marked change in the performance in this area when compared with that in recent exams. In particular, many candidates were able to calculate the terminal loss reasonably accurately and to calculate the tax saving at the margin without preparing detailed income tax computations. Those candidates who performed less strongly had two main problems. Firstly, they did not know the detailed process necessary to calculate a terminal loss, such that they simply used the loss of the final trading period. Secondly, they prepared various detailed income tax computations in the hope that this would eventually lead to the tax saving required by the question. The problem with this approach was that it was very time consuming and, on the whole, it did not produce an acceptable answer. Well prepared candidates scored well in this part and were able to do so in a sensible amount of time.

Part (c) was perhaps more challenging than part (b), but there were still plenty of very accessible marks, such that a well prepared candidate should have no issue achieving a reasonable number of marks. The first requirement was the more challenging aspect of this part of the question and required candidates to state the basic rule in relation to residency and capital gains tax and to highlight the possible issue of temporary non-residence. The temporary non-resident rule was relevant due to the statement in the question that Jodie would return to the UK after four years (ie within five years) if her children were not happy overseas. This was only answered well by a minority of candidates. The main problem related to something which came up throughout this exam which was a lack of clarity as regards the overseas aspects of personal taxation. Some candidates thought that being non-resident was only relevant in relation to assets situated overseas whilst others wrote at length about the remittance basis and the importance of either remitting or not remitting gains made but did so by reference to Jodie's non-resident status as opposed to her domicile status.

There were a number of tasks to carry out in order to satisfy the second requirement of part (c) and those candidates who kept moving and tried to address all of the aspects of the question were able to score well. The gains on the business assets and the availability of entrepreneurs' relief were tackled well by the majority of candidates. The availability of the relief in respect of the principal private residence was identified by most candidates but only a minority considered the relevance of the size of the plot of land on which the property stood. The more challenging aspect of the question related to the charging of the heldover gain on the Butterfly Ltd shares as a result of Jodie leaving the UK within six years of the gift. This was, perhaps not surprisingly, missed by many candidates although it was picked up by some.

The final part of the question related to other aspects of Jodie leaving the UK and concerned inheritance tax and VAT. The inheritance tax aspects were not done particularly well with only a minority of candidates stating clearly the implications of Jodie's departure from the point of view of inheritance tax. In particular, candidates should have stated the relevance of domicile to inheritance tax and referred to the relevance of deemed domicile. The VAT aspects were handled better but still very few candidates were able to pick up all of the available marks here.

Marking scheme

			Marks
(a)	Automatic UK residence test	2	
	Sufficient ties test		
	Number of ties relevant for 60 day period	1	
	Consideration of each tie (1 mark each – maximum 4 marks)	4	
	Conclusion	1	
	Tax implications	1	
	Max		7
(b)	Calculation of terminal loss	4	
	Relief available		
	Calculation	2	
	Explanations	3	
	Max		8
(c)	Becoming non-UK resident		
	Future liability to capital gains tax	3	
	Shares in Butterfly Ltd	3	
	Disposals		
	Business assets	3	
	Home	2	
	Liability	2	
	Max		11
(d)	Inheritance tax		
	Cessation of UK domicile	1	
	Deemed domicile	1	
	Liability to UK inheritance tax	1	
	Value added tax		
	Notify HM Revenue and Customs	1	
	Business assets retained	2	
	Max		5
	Followed instructions	1	
	Clarity of explanations and calculations	1	
	Effectiveness of communication	1	
	Overall presentation and style	1	
			4
			35

Notes for meeting

Client: Jodie
Prepared by: Tax senior
Date: 5 June 2016

(a) **UK tax residence and liability to UK income tax**

It has already been concluded that you will not be non-UK resident in the tax year 2017/18 under the automatic overseas residence tests.

It is therefore necessary to consider whether you will be UK resident in the tax year 2017/18 under the automatic UK residence tests. You will be UK resident under the automatic UK resident tests if, during 2017/18:

- You spend **183 days or more in the UK**; or
- You have a **home in the UK** and **no home overseas**; or
- You **work full-time in the UK**.

Since none of these tests will be met during 2017/18, you will not be UK resident under the automatic UK resident tests.

There is a further set of tests which will be used to determine whether you are UK resident in the tax year 2017/18. These are the 'sufficient ties' tests which consider the number of days you spend in the UK and the number of connection factors or 'ties' you have to the UK. Since you have been UK resident in at least one of the previous three tax years and want to spend between 46 and 90 days in the UK during 2017/18, you will be UK resident for that year if you have three or more ties.

The ties are as follows:

- You have **UK resident close family** (spouse/civil partner, child under the age of 18) during the tax year
- You do **substantive UK work** (40 days or more) during the tax year
- There is **UK accommodation available to you** for a consecutive period of 91 days or more during the tax year
- You spent **90 days or more in the UK** in either or both of the previous two tax years
- You are **in the UK for the same or more days in that tax year than in any other country**

Since the only tie that you have with the UK for 2017/18 is the 90 day tie, you will not be UK resident for that tax year under your current plans. However, if you change your plans, for example you spend more days in the UK during that tax year, it will be necessary to reconsider your residence status.

As a non-UK resident, you will only be liable to UK income tax on your UK source income and not on your overseas income, even if you remit that income to the UK.

(b) **Terminal loss relief**

Your terminal trading loss for the final 12 months of trading is £22,750 (see Appendix 1). This loss can be relieved against your taxable trading profits for tax year of cessation (2016/17 – but in your case there are no trading profits in that year) and the preceding three tax years, relieving later years before earlier years.

The total income tax saved is £7,500 (see Appendix 1).

(c) **Capital gains tax**

Non-UK residence in the tax year 2017/18

You will not be subject to UK capital gains tax in 2017/18 under general rules if you are non-UK resident in that tax year nor in any subsequent year when you are non-UK resident.

However, if you are non-UK resident for a temporary period (five years or less), there is a special charging rule which applies to you because you were UK resident for at least four out of the seven tax years immediately preceding 2017/18. This rule states that gains made by you in the non-UK resident period on assets which you owned before you became non-resident, such as the shares in Butterfly Ltd, will be chargeable in the tax year you become UK resident again.

Withdrawal of holdover (gift) relief on shares in Butterfly Ltd

Since you will become non-UK resident within six tax years following the year of the transfer of the shares in Butterfly Ltd to you and you still own those shares, the gain held over will become chargeable on you as if it arose immediately before you become non-UK resident (ie on 5 April 2017 so taxable in 2016/17). The gain is £(60,000 – 37,000) = £23,000. It will be taxable at the rate of 28%.

Sale of business

The gain of the sale of your business premises is £(190,000 – 135,000) = £55,000. You can claim entrepreneurs' relief on this disposal so the gain will be taxable at the rate of 10%. This is because the premises were in use for the purposes of a business at the time when the business ceased to be carried on, you carried on the business throughout the period of one year ending with the date of cessation and that cessation date is within three years before the date of the disposal.

There is no chargeable gain on the computer equipment because this is a chattel which was sold for gross proceeds of £6,000 or less. Inventory is not a chargeable asset for capital gains tax.

Sale of your home

The gain arising on the sale of your only or main private residence is exempt from capital gains tax. The exemption covers total grounds of up to half a hectare. The total grounds can exceed half a hectare if the house is large enough to warrant it, but if not, the gain on the excess grounds is taxable.

Since your house stood on a one hectare plot, it will be necessary to investigate whether the extended exemption applies. If it is decided that part of the gain is chargeable, it will be subject to capital gains tax at the rate of 28%.

Capital gains tax liability 2016/17

Your capital gains tax liability for 2016/17 will be at least £8,832 (see Appendix 2). It may be larger if it is determined that part of the gain on the sale of your home is chargeable to capital gains tax.

(d) **Other matters**

Inheritance tax

If you are UK domiciled, or deemed to be UK domiciled, transfers of all your assets, wherever situated, are subject to inheritance tax. Under general law, you are domiciled in the country which you regard as your permanent home. You will be deemed to be UK domiciled for inheritance tax purposes for 36 months after ceasing to be domiciled in the UK under general law. If you are not UK domiciled nor UK deemed domiciled, only transfers of your UK assets are subject to inheritance tax.

You can become non-UK domiciled under general law by severing your ties to the UK and settling permanently in another country. Given your current plans, since you may return to the UK if your children are not happy in Riviera, it is likely that you will still be domiciled in the UK under the general law until it is clear that you have settled permanently in Riviera.

Value added tax (VAT)

You will be subject to compulsory deregistration from VAT because you are no longer making taxable supplies and you must notify HM Revenue and Customs accordingly. Failure to notify within 30 days may lead to a penalty.

On deregistration, VAT is chargeable on all assets on which input tax was claimed and you have retained, since you are making a taxable supply to yourself as a newly unregistered trader. However the VAT chargeable does not exceed £1,000, it need not be paid. Since the only asset retained is the inventory of £3,500, no payment is required.

APPENDIX 1

Terminal loss relief

Calculation of terminal trading loss

	£	£
2016/17 (6 April 2016 to 31 May 2016)		
Loss £18,000 × 2/5		7,200
Overlap relief		6,500
2015/16 (1 June 2015 to 5 April 2016)		
1 June 2015 to 31 December 2015		
Profit £3,000 × 7/12	(1,750)	
1 January 2016 to 5 April 2016		
Loss £18,000 × 3/5	10,800	
		9,050
Terminal loss		22,750

Tax saving using terminal loss relief

	2013/14 £	2014/15 £	2015/16 £	Total £
Trading income	67,000	2,000	3,000	
Loss relief	17,750	2,000	3,000	22,750
Tax saving				
2015/16 (N1)			3,000 @ 0%	0
2014/15 (N2)		2,000 @ 20%		400
2013/14 (N3)	17,750 @ 40%			7,100
Total				7,500

Notes

1   Your income in the tax year 2015/16 will be covered by your personal allowance so no income tax will be saved for that tax year since there was no tax liability.

2   You paid income tax at the basic rate of 20% in the tax year 2014/15 and so the trading loss will save tax at 20%.

3   You paid income tax at the higher rate of 40% in the tax year 2013/14 on your taxable income in excess of the basic rate threshold and so the trading loss will save 40% tax since you had at least £17,750 taxable at the higher rate.

APPENDIX 2

Capital gains tax liability 2016/17

	Qualifying for entrepreneurs' relief £	Not qualifying for entrepreneurs' relief £
Business premises	55,000	
Heldover gain on Butterfly Ltd shares		23,000
Less annual exempt amount		(11,100)
		11,900
Capital gains tax at 10%/28%	5,500	3,332
Total liability £(5,500 + 3,332)		8,832

1   The annual exempt amount will be deducted from the heldover gain as this gain is taxed at a higher rate than that on the business premises.

2   The heldover gain will be taxable at the rate of 28% because the gain on the sale of the business premises will be treated as using up Jodie's basic rate band.

5 John and Maureen (ATAX 06/08)

Text references. Income tax and employment income is covered in Chapter 1 to 5. Trade profits are in Chapter 6. Capital allowances are in Chapter 7. Basic chargeable gains is in Chapter 11. VAT deregistration is covered in Chapter 28 and the flat rate scheme in Chapter 29.

Top tips. Be methodical. You needed to consider the tax liability of each person for both years assuming that the income had been both correctly and incorrectly treated in order to compute the error. Whilst there are a lot of calculations to do they were quick once you got started. A lot of marks could be scored quickly.

Easy marks. Listing out the income tax computations for each year for each person should have been straightforward.

Examiner's comments. Part (a) of this question required candidates to carry out a series of calculations to determine the income tax underpaid where the income of one spouse was incorrectly declared on the tax return of the other. This is an example of a question that tests fundamental tax knowledge (brought forward from Paper F6) in a Paper P6 context.

There was a large number of marks here for dealing with basic aspects of investment income, employment income and trading income and the calculation of income tax liabilities. Most of these matters were handled well by the majority of candidates although knowledge of the trading income opening years rules and capital allowances was noticeably weaker than that relating to other matters.

Further marks were then available for determining the additional tax due on the income declared in the incorrect tax return. This could be handled most efficiently by working at the margin; calculating the tax on the additional income only and comparing it with the tax already paid on that income. However, this approach was not taken by the majority of students who wasted time preparing full income tax computations both with and without the incorrectly declared income.

Part (b) required candidates to explain the implications of deregistration for the purposes of VAT and to identify an alternative strategy that would assist in reducing the administration of VAT. Although the rules regarding deregistration were known by many candidates, a considerable amount of time was wasted by some who went on to describe the advantages and disadvantages of being registered in detail. The identification of an alternative strategy was not done particularly well, with many candidates providing a comprehensive list of VAT schemes rather than identifying the flat rate scheme as the one which would genuinely help the client.

Marks

(a)   The additional income:
        Interest – ½ mark for each year   1
        Dividends – ½ mark for each year   1
        Property income   ½
        Children's interest – identification of issue   1
                             De minimis   1
    John's income tax:
    2015/16
        Car benefit   1
        Fuel benefit   ½
        Trust income   1
        Personal allowance   ½
        Remainder of basic rate band   ½
        Additional tax liability   2
        Tax credits   1
        Comparison with the tax paid by Maureen   ½
    2016/17
        Car   ½
        Fuel benefit   ½
        Trust income   ½
        Personal allowance   ½
        Remainder of basic rate band   ½
        Additional tax liability   2
        Tax credits   1
        Comparison with the tax paid by Maureen ½
    Maureen's income tax:
        Trading income:
        Capital allowances   2
        2015/16 assessment   1
        2016/17 assessment   1½
    Tax on investment income:
        2015/16   2½
        2016/17   2½
    Additional capital gains tax due:
        Annual exempt amount   ½
        Additional tax   1½
    Total additional tax due   ½
                          Max   **26**

    Clarity of presentation and use of headings   1
    Logical structure   1
                                             2

(b)   Conditions for voluntary deregistration   1
    Effective date   ½
    Deemed supply   1
    De minimis limit   1
    Stop charging VAT   ½
    Cannot recover input tax   ½
    Deductible for income tax   ½
    Need to monitor turnover   1
    Suggestion of flat rate scheme   1
    Operation of the scheme   2
    Possible financial advantage   ½
                          Max   **8**

    Effectiveness of communication   **1**
                                            37

(a)   **John and Maureen – Additional tax payable**

Additional income tax payable – 2015/16

	£	£
2,550 × 20% (property income (W1))		510
2,021 × 20% (interest income (W1))		404
4,571 (reminder of basic rate band)		
1,009 × 40% (interest income (£3,030 – £2,021))		404
9,840 × 32.5% (dividend income (W1))		3,198
		4,516
Less tax credits		
£3,030 × 20%		(606)
£9,840 × 10%		(984)
		2,926
Tax paid by Maureen (W3)		(510)
Additional income tax payable		2,416

Additional capital gains tax payable – 2015/16

Additional capital gains tax payable £11,100 × 28% + £(13,870 – 11,100) × 10% (Note)   3,385

Note. The gift of the property to Maureen would not be effective for capital gains tax purposes due to the prior agreement whereby Maureen gave the sales proceeds to John. Therefore an amount equal to Maureen's unused annual exempt amount becomes taxable. The rate of tax is 28% because John is now a higher rate taxpayer. Furthermore Maureen would have paid CGT on her taxable gain of £(13,870 – 11,100) = £2,770 at 18% whereas John's rate of CGT is 28%.

Additional income tax payable – 2016/17

	£
539 × 20% (interest income (W1))	108
539 (remainder of basic rate band(W2))	
2,681 × 40% (interest income (£3,220 – £539))	1,072
144 × 40% (interest income – Penny (W1))	58
10,120 × 32.5% (dividend income (W1))	3,289
	4,527
Less tax credits	
£3,220 × 20%	(644)
£10,120 × 10%	(1,012)
	2,871
Tax paid by Maureen (W4)	(923)
Additional income tax payable	1,948
Total additional tax payable (£2,416 + £3,385 + £1,948)	7,749

Workings

1   John – Additional taxable income

	2015/16	2016/17
	£	£
Arising on inherited assets:		
Property income	2,550	–
Interest income (£2,424/£2,576 × 100/80)	3,030	3,220
Dividend income (£8,856/£9,108 × 100/90)	9,840	10,120
Children's bank accounts:		
Will – below *de minimis* limit of £100	–	–
Penny	–	144

2   John – Reminder of basic rate band

	2015/16	2016/17
	£	£
Salary	30,294	31,066
Car benefit:		
14 + (145 – 95)/5 = 24%		
£17,400 × 24% × 8/12	2,784	
£17,400 × 24%		4,176
Fuel benefit:		
£22,100 × 24% × 8/12	3,536	
£22,100 × 24%		5,304
Trust income (£660/£715 × 100/55)	1,200	1,300
Less personal allowance	(10,600)	(10,600)
Taxable income	27,214	31,246
Basic rate band	(31,785)	(31,785)
Remainder of basic rate band	4,571	539

3   Maureen – Tax paid on investment income 2015/16

	£
Trading income (W5)	13,885
Property income	2,550
Interest income (W1)	3,030
Dividend income (W1)	9,840
	29,305
Less personal allowance	(10,600)
Taxable income	18,705
Tax on property income (Note)	
£2,550 × 20%	510

Note. All of the investment income fell into the basic rate band. The tax liability in respect of the interest and dividend income was covered by the related tax credits. Accordingly, in respect of the income arising on the inherited assets, only the property income gave rise to income tax payable.

4   Maureen – Tax paid on investment income 2016/17

	£
Trading income (W5)	33,150
Interest income (W1)	3,220
Dividend income (W1)	10,120
	46,490
Less personal allowance	(10,600)
Taxable income	35,890
Tax on dividend income in higher rate band (Note)	
£4,105 × 32.5%	1,334
Less tax credit	
£4,105 × 10%	(411)
	923

Note. The tax liability in respect of the investment income that fell into the basic rate band was covered by the related tax credits. Accordingly, income tax was payable in respect of the dividend income that fell into the higher rate band only, ie £4,105 (£35,890 – £31,785).

5　Maureen – Trading income

	Period ended 30 September 2016 £	Year ended 30 September 2017 £
Adjusted trading profit	54,456	32,139
Less capital allowances (W6)	(23,909)	(903)
Taxable trading income	30,547	31,236

2015/16		
1 November 2015 – 5 April 2016		
£30,547 × 5/11	13,885	
2016/17		
1 November 2015 – 31 October 2016		
1 November 2015 – 30 September 2016		30,547
1 October 2016 – 31 October 2016		
£31,236 × 1/12		2,603
		33,150

6　Capital allowances

	AIA £	Main pool £	Allowances £
p/e 30.9.16			
Additions qualifying for AIA			
11.15 Equipment	22,917		
AIA	(22,917)		22,917
Additions not qualifying for AIA			
12.15 Car		6,010	
WDA @ 18% x 11/12		(992)	992
TWDV c/f		5,018	
Allowances			23,909
y/e 30.9.17			
WDA @ 18%		(903)	903
TWDV c/f		4,115	
Allowances			903

(b)　**Advice on Maureen's VAT position**

Deregistration

In order to voluntarily deregister for VAT you must satisfy HMRC that the value of your taxable supplies in the next 12 months will not exceed £80,000. You will then be deregistered with effect from the date of your request or a later date as agreed with HMRC.

On deregistering you are regarded as making a supply of all stocks and equipment in respect of which input tax has been claimed. However, the VAT on this deemed supply need only be paid to HMRC if it exceeds £1,000.

Once you have deregistered, you must no longer charge VAT on your sales. You will also be unable to recover the input tax on the costs incurred by your business. Instead, the VAT you pay on your costs will be allowable when computing your taxable profits.

You should monitor your sales on a monthly basis; if your sales in a 12-month period exceed £82,000 you must notify HMRC within the 30 days following the end of the 12-month period. You will be registered from the end of the month following the end of the 12-month period.

Flat rate scheme

Rather than deregistering you may wish to consider operating the flat rate scheme. This would reduce the amount of administration as you would no longer need to record and claim input tax in respect of the costs incurred by your business.

Under the flat rate scheme you would continue to charge your customers VAT in the way that you do at the moment. You would then pay HMRC a fixed percentage of your VAT inclusive turnover each quarter rather than calculating output tax less input tax. This may be financially advantageous as compared with deregistering; I would be happy to prepare calculations for you if you wish.

6 Monisha and Horner (ATAX 12/13)

Text references. The principles of income tax, including jointly held property, will be found in Chapter 1. Property income is covered in Chapter 3. The basics of chargeable gains are dealt with in Chapter 11 and reliefs in Chapter 13. Personal service companies are covered in Chapter 4.

Top tips. You might want to start with part (b) of this question as it was self-contained and would have taken less time to achieve the available marks than part (a) which needed a bit more thought.

Easy marks. The conditions for FHLs in part (a)(i) should have been known from your F6 studies. The computation of the deemed employment income in part (b) was relatively straightforward.

Examiner's comments. Part (a)(i) required a statement of the conditions that must be satisfied for the letting of a UK furnished property to qualify as furnished holiday accommodation. This was answered very well by the majority of candidates. The only difficulty related to confusion over the meaning of 'longer term accommodation' and the maximum number of days of such occupation permitted in a tax year.

Part (a)(ii) was the more difficult part of the question. It required a calculation of the total tax saving on the transfer of a 20% interest in a rental property from one spouse (Monisha) to the other (Asmat) together with the property being let as furnished holiday accommodation in the future. This was done poorly by many candidates who either did not have a thorough attempt at it or worked very hard but did not pause to think about how to approach the problem. The key was to first calculate the taxable property income in order to identify the amount of taxable income that would be taxed in the hands of Asmat rather than Monisha. It was then necessary to recognise that for the first five years under consideration, Monisha would be a higher rate taxpayer whereas Asmat's income would be covered by his personal allowance, such that no tax would be payable. Accordingly, by working at the margin, it was easy to see that for the first five years the saving would be 40% of the income transferred. In the sixth year, Asmat was expected to be employed, such that the income transferred would be taxed at 20% and the saving would therefore be 20% (40% − 20%) of the income transferred. The problem was that very few candidates chose to work at the margin. Instead, many chose to prepare income tax computations for the two individuals before and after the transfer of the interest in the property in order to quantify the difference in the total liability. This was very time consuming. Some candidates even prepared calculations for each of the five years despite the fact that the figures were the same in each year. Calculating tax liabilities can be very time consuming. Candidates should always stop and think about the most efficient way of approaching a set of calculations before they start writing. The capital gains tax element of this part of the question was not handled particularly well. This was perhaps due to a shortage of time. It required candidates to recognise that an additional annual exempt amount would be available and that tax would be charged at 10%, due to the availability of entrepreneurs' relief, rather than at 28%. Only a minority of candidates were able to quantify the effect of these points.

Part (b)(i) required an outline of the circumstances in which the personal service company rules (IR35) apply. The majority of candidates struggled to satisfy this requirement despite a reasonable knowledge of the rules. It was generally recognised that the rules were in place in order to prevent the avoidance of tax but there was some confusion as to exactly where tax was being avoided. Very few candidates were able to state the commercial relationship between the taxpayer, the personal service company and the client in a clear manner.

Part (ii) required a calculation of the deemed employment income under the rules. This was done well or very well by the majority of candidates. The only common error was a failure to calculate employer's national insurance contributions in respect of the salary paid.

BPP LEARNING MEDIA

					Marks
(a)	(i)	Conditions for FHL – 1 mark each		3	
		Longer term occupation		1	
			Max		3
	(ii)	Income tax			
		Property business income		2	
		Allocated equally		1	
		First five tax years		1½	
		Final tax year		1	
		Capital gains tax			
		No gain, no loss disposal		1	
		CGT if proposals not carried out		1½	
		CGT if proposals are carried out		2½	
		Total tax saving		½	
			Max		10
(b)	(i)	Conditions for IR35 – 1 mark each		4	
		Employment/self employment test reference		1	
			Max		3
	(ii)	95% of income		1½	
		Deductions:			
		Salary and pension contributions		1	
		Employer's NIC on actual salary		1½	
		Employer's NIC on deemed employment income		1	
			Max		4
					20

(a) Monisha

(i) Furnished holiday accommodation in the UK – conditions

- Availability – during the relevant period (usually a tax year), the accommodation is available for commercial letting as holiday accommodation to the public generally for at least 210 days.

- Letting – during the relevant period, the accommodation is commercially let as holiday accommodation to members of the public for at least 105 days (the days let exclude any days that are longer term occupation – below).

- Pattern of occupation – during the relevant period, not more that 155 days fall during periods of longer term occupation. Longer term occupation is defined as a continuous period of more than 31 days during which the accommodation is in the same occupation unless there are abnormal circumstances.

(ii) Total tax saving for six years ending 5 April 2023

Income tax

	£
Income tax saved in first five tax years £6,660 (W) × 40% × 5	13,320
Income tax saved in final tax year £6,660 (W) × 20%	1,332
Total income tax saved	14,652

For the first five tax years, Asmat will not have any other income so that his share of the property income will be covered by his personal allowance thus saving tax at 40%. In the final tax year, Asmat will have employment income so that the property income will be taxed at 20%, saving tax at (40% – 20%) = 20%.

Working – Property business income taxable on Asmat

	£
Rental income	20,000
Less: allowable expenses £(1,600 + £1,200 + £2,000)	(4,800)
capital allowances equal to wear and tear allowance £(20,000 – 1,200) × 10%	(1,880)
Property business income	13,320
Property business income taxable on Asmat £13,320 × ½	6,660

Tutorial note

The income of a jointly held asset is automatically split equally between a married couple, regardless of their actual interests in the property. (Monisha and Asmat could elect to split the income between them in the ratio 80:20, but to do so would not be beneficial in their particular circumstances.) Accordingly, property income of £6,660 will be subject to income tax on Asmat.

Capital gains tax

The gift of the 20% interest in the property will take place on a no gain, no loss basis because Monisha and Asmat are a married couple. The gain on the sale of the property will therefore be allocated between Monisha and Asmat in the ratio 80:20. A gain on the sale of furnished holiday accommodation qualifies for entrepreneurs' relief.

	£
Capital gains tax on sale of property if proposals *not* carried out	
Monisha: £(100,000 – £[11,100 – 6,000]) × 28%	26,572
Capital gains tax on sale of property if proposals *are* carried out	
Monisha: £(80,000 – £[11,100 – 6,000]) × 10% (entrepreneurs' relief)	7,490
Asmat: £(20,000 – 11,100) × 10% (entrepreneurs' relief)	890
Total capital gains tax on sale	8,380
Capital gains tax saved £(26,572 – 8,380)	18,192

Total tax saving

	£
Income tax saving	14,652
Capital gains tax saving	18,192
Total tax saving	32,844

(b) **Horner**

   (i) **Circumstances in which personal service company (IR 35) rules apply**

   • An individual ('the worker') performs, or has an obligation to perform, services for 'a client'.

   • The performance of those services is referable to arrangements involving a third party (eg the personal service company), rather than referable to a contract between the client and the worker.

   • If the services were to be performed by the worker under a contract between himself and the client, the worker would be regarded as employed by the client (using the usual tests which distinguish between employment and self-employment).

   • The worker (alone or with associates) control more than 5% of the ordinary share capital of the company, or are entitled to receive more than 5% of any dividends from the company, or the worker receives, or could receive, payments or benefits from the company which are not salary, but could reasonably be taken to represent payment for the services he provides to clients.

	£	£
Otmar Ltd – 95% of income from relevant engagements		
£85,000 × 95%		80,750
Less: salary paid to Horner		(50,000)
pension contributions		(2,000)
employer's NIC on actual salary		
£(50,000 – 8,112) = £41,888 × 13.8%	5,781	
Less: employment allowance (sole employee)	(2,000)	
		(3,781)
		24,969
Less: employer's NIC on deemed payment		
£24,969 × 13.8/113.8		(3,028)
Deemed employment income		21,941

Tutorial note

The dividend paid to Horner will be treated as exempt to avoid a double charge to tax on the same income.

7 Cate and Ravi (ATAX 06/15)

Text references. Employment income, including national insurance aspects, is the subject of Chapter 4. The income tax computation is covered in Chapter 1. The badges of trade are dealt with in Chapter 6. The chattels exemption and overseas aspects of capital gains tax are covered in Chapter 14.

Top tips. In part (a) it is important to work out the marginal cost of Cate employing the new employee. The key points are that Cate is a higher rate taxpayer and pays some of her Class 4 NICs at 2%. As a result she will save tax and Class 4 NICs of 42% of these costs.

Easy marks. The badges of trade in part (b) should have been familiar from F6(UK). However, it was important to apply the tests to the specific situation given in the question.

Examiner's comments. Part (a) concerned an individual, Cate, running a successful unincorporated business that required an additional part-time employee. The requirement was to calculate the annual cost of employing the part-time employee. The first thing candidates had to do was determine all of the costs that were going to be incurred. On the whole this was done reasonably well, although some candidates confused cost with tax deductibility, and some simply prepared tax computations for Cate, which was not what they had been asked to do. In addition, many candidates failed to consider the employer national insurance contributions aspects which were a key part of the question. Once the costs had been determined, it was simply a case of recognising that Cate was a higher rate tax payer, such that she would save income tax at 40% and class 4 national insurance contributions at 2% as a result of the increased costs. This was not tackled well by the majority of candidates who tried to do before and after calculations rather than working at the margin. In addition, many failed to consider the class 4 national insurance contribution implications altogether. There was a more subtle point in the question in relation to the income tax personal allowance. The reduction in Cate's taxable trading income due to the costs relating to the part-time employee meant that part of her personal allowance would be reinstated, thus reducing the after-tax cost to her of taking on the new employee.

Part (b) required a discussion of the tax treatment of the profit derived from the sale of books on the internet. This required candidates to consider the badges of trade in relation to the specific transactions taking place. This part of the question was done well by many candidates. However, some candidates did not give themselves sufficient thinking time, such that they failed to realise what the question was testing. It was important that candidates tried to reach a conclusion based on the information provided and that they thought about the capital gains tax implications as well as the income tax implications. There was no right answer as such, just a need to think about the relevant issues and to express the implications in a clear manner.

The final part of the question was arguably more challenging. It concerned the capital gains tax position of an individual, Ravi, who was resident in the UK but domiciled overseas and focussed principally on the remittance basis. Although some candidates did reasonably well here, almost all candidates could have scored more marks if they had organised their thoughts before they began writing. There was a mark for making the point that Ravi was liable to UK capital gains tax because he was UK resident and a further mark for recognising that the remittance basis was available because he was domiciled overseas. In order to score these two marks, candidates had to make it clear that the liability to capital gains tax was due to his residence status and the remittance basis was due to his domicile status. Many candidates did not make these two points clearly, such that they only scored one of the two available marks. Candidates were then expected to address the remittance basis charge and the loss of the annual exempt amount. This was done well by the majority of candidates.

Marking scheme

				Marks
(a)	Total additional expenditure		5	
	Income tax and Class 4 NIC saving		2	
	Saving due to personal allowance		2½	
		Max		9
(b)	Trading income or capital gain issue		1	
	Relevant badges of trade factors		3	
	Any reasonable conclusion		1	
	Chattels exemption		1	
		Max		5
(c)	CGT on arising basis as UK resident		2	
	Optional remittance basis as non-UK domiciled		1	
	CGT implications if remittance basis used		2	
	Remittance basis charge		1½	
	Conclusion		½	
		Max		6
				20

(a) **Cate – after-tax cost of taking on part time employee**

	£
Salary	12,000
Childcare vouchers £25 × 52	1,300
Mileage allowance £0.50 × 62 × 48	1,488
Class 1 NI secondary contributions (W1)	558
Total additional expenditure	15,346
Less: income tax higher rate tax saving £15,346 × 40%	(6,138)
Class 4 NIC saving £15,346 × 2%	(307)
income tax personal allowance saving	
£7,673 (W2) × 40%	(3,069)
After-tax cost	5,832

Workings

1   *Class 1 NI secondary contributions*

	£
Salary £(12,000 – 8,112) = £3,888 × 13.8%	537
Mileage allowance £(0.50 – 0.45) = £0.05 × 62 × 48 × 13.8%	21
	558

Tutorial note

The employment allowance would have already been fully used against the Class 1 secondary NI contributions payable in respect of D-Designs' existing employees.

2   *Personal allowance*

	Before £	After £
Basic personal allowance	10,600	10,600
Less: [£90,000 + (£28,080 × 100/90)] = £(121,200 – 100,000) = £21,200 × ½	(10,600)	
Less: £(121,200 – 15,346 – 100,000) = £5,854 × ½		(2,927)
Personal allowance available	0	7,673

Tutorial notes

1   Only the excess mileage over 45p per mile is liable to Class 1 NIC.

2   Childcare vouchers up to £55 per week for a basic rate taxpayer are exempt from Class 1 NIC.

3   Cate's (adjusted) net income before taking on the part time employee was £121,200 so her personal allowance was reduced to nil.

Cate's (adjusted) net income after taking on the part time employee would be reduced by the total additional expenditure of £15,346 to £105,854. She will therefore be entitled to a personal allowance of £7,673.

(b)   **Cate – sale of second hand books**

The tax treatment of the profit from the sale of the books will depend on whether Cate is carrying on the trade of selling books or whether she is selling them as capital assets. If she is carrying on a trade, her profit will be trading income (in the same way as her profit from D-Design) and subject to income tax. If she is selling the books as capital assets (chattels), she may be liable to capital gains tax on the gains.

In order to ascertain whether or not a trade is being carried on, a number of factors known as 'the badges of trade' must be considered. The most relevant factors in this case are:

• *Frequency of transactions*: transactions which may, in isolation, be of a capital nature will be interpreted as trading transactions where their frequency indicates the carrying on of a trade. Cate only intends to sell the books she has inherited from her mother and so this appears to be an isolated transaction and so not a trading transaction.

• *Existence of similar trading transactions or interests*: if there is an existing trade, then a similarity to the transaction which is being considered may point to that transaction having a trading character. Cate's existing trade of running dress shops is not similar to selling books online and again this suggests there is not a trading transaction.

• *Way in which the assets sold were acquired*: if goods are acquired deliberately, trading may be indicated. If goods are acquired unintentionally, for example by gift or inheritance as in this case, their later sale is unlikely to be trading.

• *Supplementary work and marketing*: when work is done to make an asset more marketable, or steps are taken to find purchasers, the courts will be more ready to ascribe a trading motive. Cate will be carrying on supplementary work by having some of the books rebound and this could be considered to point to a trading transaction.

Overall, a consideration of these factors suggests that Cate will not be carrying on a trade by selling the books. She will therefore be making disposals of the books as chattels but these are likely to be exempt disposals as both cost and deemed proceeds are likely to be less than £6,000.

Tutorial note

Marks are available for discussion of *any* relevant factors and for reaching a *sensible* conclusion.

(c)   **Ravi – capital gains tax on overseas property gain**

As Ravi is UK resident, under general principles he will be liable to UK capital gains tax on gains arising from assets situated anywhere in the world.

On the arising basis, the overseas property gain will be subject to CGT at the rate of 28% since Ravi has already used his annual exempt amount for 2015/16 and his income exceeds the basic rate threshold in that year. The CGT payable is therefore £70,000 × 28% = £19,600. If Ravi has paid tax on the gain in Goland, UK double taxation relief will be available either under treaty relief or unilateral credit relief.

Since Ravi is not UK domiciled, he can make a claim for the remittance basis to apply so that his overseas property gain is taxable only to the extent that the proceeds of the disposal are remitted to the UK. As none of the proceeds have been remitted, there will be no liability to CGT on this gain.

If Ravi makes a remittance basis claim, he will not be entitled to annual exempt amount and so he will have an additional CGT liability of £11,100 × 28% = £3,108. In addition, since Ravi has been resident in the UK since February 2008 (at least seven out of the previous nine tax years prior to 2015/16), he will be subject to a remittance basis charge of £30,000. The total amount payable as a result of claiming the remittance basis would therefore be £(30,000 + 3,108) = £33,108.

Ravi should therefore not make a remittance basis claim for 2015/16.

8 Simone (ATAX 06/09)

Text references. Capital allowances are covered in Chapter 7, trading losses in Chapter 8 and partnerships in Chapter 9. VAT registration is covered in Chapter 28.

Top tips. Use a proforma to calculate the share of the loss for each partner.

Easy marks. The calculation of capital allowances should have been an easy marks.

Examiner's comments. In part (a) the calculation of the capital allowances was done well. However, the allocation of the loss between the partners was done poorly with the majority of candidates treating the salaries as employment income rather than as a share of the trading loss. The use of the loss was also problematic. Weaker candidates were confused as to corporate and personal loss offset rules.

Even many stronger candidates lacked the precise knowledge required to score well; a statement of how losses can be used must describe precisely the income against which the loss can be offset, for example, 'against future profits of the same trade' in order to earn all of the marks available. Many candidates ignored the requirement to calculate the total tax saved and simply prepared various income tax computations.

In part (b) weaker candidates wasted time describing the future test in detail despite it not being relevant to this particular question. In addition, many candidates lacked precise knowledge (for example in relation to the date registration comes into effect) such that they did not score as well as would have been expected.

Marking scheme

				Marks
(a)	(i)	Capital allowances	1½	
		6 April 2015 to 28 February 2016	2	
		1 March 2016 to 5 April 2016	2	
		Max		5
	(ii)	Against general income of 2015/16 and/or 2014/15	1	
		Against capital gain in 2015/16	1	
		Against future profits of the same trade	1	
				3

		Marks
(iii)	Evaluation of offset against future profits of the same trade	2
	Evaluation of offset against general income and gains in 2015/16	2
	Evaluation of offset against general income in 2014/15	3
	Calculation of maximum tax saving	½
	Max	7
(b)	Taxable supplies exceed limit in the previous 12 months	1
	Exclude capital assets	½
	Notify within 30 days	½
	Date of effective registration	1
	Relevance of Ellington and Co being VAT registered	1
	Max	3
		18

(a)   (i)   **Share of the taxable trading loss for the year ended 5 April 2016**

	Total £	Ellington £	Simone £	Basie £
Tax adjusted trading loss	(90,000)			
Capital allowances				
Additions in the year within AIA limit	(21,200)			
Writing down allowance (N)	(700)			
Loss available for relief	(111,900)			
6 April 2015 – 28 February 2016				
Loss £(111,900) × 11/12	(102,575)			
Salaries				
£15,000/£11,500/£13,000 × 11/12	(36,209)	13,750	10,542	11,917
Balance 3:2:2	(138,784)	(59,478)	(39,653)	(39,653)
1 March 2016 – 5 April 2016				
£(111,900) × 1/12	(9,325)			
Salaries £14,000 × 1/12	(2,334)	1,167	1,167	0
Balance 1:1	(11,659)	(5,830)	(5,829)	(0)
	(111,900)	(50,391)	(33,773)	(27,736)

Note

As the unrelieved expenditure on the main pool is less than £1,000, a WDA can be claimed equal to this amount.

(ii)   **Alternative strategies**

The following alternative strategies are available to Simone in respect of her share of the taxable trading loss.

Offset against her general income for the current year (2015/16) and/or the previous year (2014/15).

Following a claim against her general income in 2015/16, the remaining loss could be offset against her capital gains of that year.

Any losses not used as set out above will be carried forward for offset against her share of the taxable trading profits of Ellington & Co in the future.

(iii)   **Advice**

Offset against future profits of the same trade

Assuming an annual taxable trading profit of £25,000, Simone's share of the budgeted profit of Ellington and Co in 2016/17 and future years will be £12,500 (£25,000 × 1/2). The profit from her new business is budgeted to be £10,850 (£1,550 × 7) in 2016/17 and £18,600 (£1,550 × 12) in future years. Accordingly, Simone will be a basic rate taxpayer and the total tax saved via the offset of the loss will be £6,755 (£33,773 @ 20%). The tax saved in 2016/17 and in 2017/18 will be £2,500 (£12,500 @ 20%) and the balance of £1,755 (£6,755 − (2 × £2,500)) will be saved in 2018/19.

Offset against general income and capital gains in 2015/16

Simone's only income in 2015/16 is dividend income of £10,800. Offsetting her loss against this income will not save any tax as the dividend tax credit is not repayable.

However, having offset the loss against her general income in 2015/16, Simone would then be able to offset the remaining loss of £21,773 (£33,773 − (£10,800 × 100/90)) against her capital gain. The capital gains tax saved would be £6,096 (£21,773 @ 28% − this is Simone's highest marginal rate on her gains). However, this is not as beneficial as using the loss in 2014/15 (see below) both considering the rate at which tax is saved and the time at which is it saved.

Offset against general income in 2014/15

Simone's original income tax liability in 2014/15 is set out below.

	Non-savings income £	Dividend income £	Total £
Trading income	48,615		
Dividend income £12,600 × 100/90		14,000	
Net income	48,615	14,000	62,615
Less personal allowance	(10,600)		
Taxable income	38,015	14,000	52,015

	£
Tax on non-savings income	
£	
31,785 @ 20%	6,357
6,230 @ 40%	2,492
38,015	
Tax on dividend income	
£14,000 × 32.5%	4,550
Tax liability	13,399
Less dividend tax credit £14,000 @ 10%	(1,400)
Tax payable	11,999

Simone's liability in 2014/15 following the offset of the trading loss is:

	Non-savings income £	Dividend income £	Total £
Trading income	48,615		
Dividend income £12,600 × 100/90		14,000	
Total income	48,615	14,000	62,615
Less trading loss	(33,773)		
Net income	14,842		28,842
Less personal allowance	(10,600)		
Taxable income	4,242	14,000	18,242

	£
Tax on trading income	
£4,242 @ 20%	848
Tax on dividend income	
£14,000 @ 10%	1,400
Tax liability	2,248
Less dividend tax credit £14,000 @ 10%	(1,400)
Tax payable	848

The tax saved via the offset of the trading loss would be £11,151 (£11,999 – 848).

Conclusion

Simone will save the most tax by offsetting the loss against her general income in 2014/15. This claim saves some tax at the higher rate and saves tax at the basic rate at the earliest time.

Note

The use of the loss would also have resulted in a saving of Class 4 NICs which could also have been mentioned.

(b) **VAT registration**

Simone is required to register for VAT when her cumulative taxable supplies (standard and zero rated), excluding supplies of capital assets, exceed £82,000 in the previous 12 months.

Simone must notify HMRC within 30 days of the end of the month in which the limit is exceeded.

Simone will be registered and must charge VAT from the end of the month following the month in which the limit is exceeded, or from an earlier date if she and HMRC agree.

As Simone and Ellington and Co are separate taxable persons, the fact that Ellington and Co is VAT registered is irrelevant when considering Simone's position.

9 Morice (ATAX 12/11)

Text references. SAYE schemes are covered in Chapter 5. Employment income in general is dealt with in Chapter 4.

Top tips. In part (a), it was vital that you provided *detailed* explanations relating to the proposed SAYE scheme. In part (b), you were only required to discuss the implications for the *employees* of the proposed benefits.

Easy marks. There were some easy marks in part (a) for basic details concerning the capital gains tax computation. In part (b), the rates for cars are in the Tax Tables.

Examiner's comments. Part (a) required a detailed knowledge of Save As You Earn share option schemes in order to comment on the acceptability or otherwise of a proposed set of rules and to calculate the income tax and national insurance liabilities in respect of shares acquired. In order to score well it was important for candidates to address each of the detailed rules in the question as opposed to writing generally about share option schemes.

Many candidates who attempted this question were knowledgeable about Save As You Earn schemes but only a minority took a sufficiently disciplined approach to score well. The explanation of the tax liabilities in respect of the shares acquired under the scheme was not done particularly well. Many candidates lacked precise knowledge of this area such that they did not know that no tax would be charged until the shares were sold. In addition, it needed to be recognised that the position of each employee would vary depending on whether or not they had made any other capital gains and on the level of their taxable income; very few candidates considered these matters.

Part (b) concerned the medical care scheme and the payments to employees for driving their own cars on business journeys. The medical care scheme was not handled particularly well in that many candidates incorrectly stated that the provision of health insurance would be an exempt benefit for the employees. However, this was not too important as it was only a minor part of the answer. The provision of an interest free loan was also not dealt with as well as might have been expected. The question stated that the loan would be 'up to £12,500' so it was necessary to point out that loans of no more than £10,000 would be exempt. The explanation of the implications of the payments to employees for driving their own cars was handled well.

The only common error was the failure to recognise that there would be no national insurance implications. The question asked for the tax implications 'for the employees' as opposed to the tax implications generally. Accordingly, it was necessary to consider the national insurance issues for the employees (but not the employer) and there was no need to address the ability of the employer to obtain tax relief for the costs incurred.

Marking scheme

					Marks
(a)	Scheme rules				
		Investment period and investment limits	1½		
		Eligible employees	1½		
		Share price	1½		
	Illustrative example				
		Grant and exercise of option, receipt of bonus	1½		
		Gain	1½		
		Capital gains tax	3		
		National insurance contributions	1		
				Max	10
(b)	(i)	Health insurance	½		
		Interest-free loan	2½		
		National insurance contributions	½		
	(ii)	Driving on company business			
		Income tax	2		
		National insurance contributions	1		
		Carrying passengers	1½		
				Max	7
					17

(a) **Schedule 3 SAYE scheme**

Whether or not the proposed rules will be compliant with Schedule 3

The investment period of five years and the minimum monthly investment limit of £5 are acceptable. The maximum monthly investment limit for a Schedule 3 SAYE scheme is £500.

It is not acceptable to have a minimum age requirement.

It is not acceptable to exclude part-time employees (although it is possible to exclude part-time directors).

It is acceptable to exclude employees who have worked for the company for less than a qualifying period, provided that the period chosen does not exceed five years.

The price at which shares are offered under the scheme must be at least 80% of the market value of the shares at the time the option is granted. Accordingly, the price proposed of £2.48 will only be acceptable if the value of a share on 1 January 2017 is no more than £3.10 (£2.48/80%).

Illustrative example – Schedule 3 compliant SAYE scheme

Grant and exercise of share options

There is no tax liability in respect of the grant and exercise of the share options.

Receipt of the bonus

There is no tax liability in respect of the receipt of the bonus.

Sale of shares

The total amount invested will be £15,225 ((12 x £250 × 5) + (0.9 × £250)). The number of shares purchased will be 6,139 (£15,225/£2.48).

Therefore, there will be a capital gain on the sale of the shares as set out below.

	£
Proceeds 6,139 × £4.00	24,556
Less cost 6,139 × £2.48	(15,225)
Gain	9,331

Entrepreneurs' relief will not be available as the employee will not own 5% of the company's ordinary share capital. The gain will be reduced by the annual exempt amount (currently £11,100). Accordingly, there will be no tax liability where an employee has at least £9,331 of their annual exempt amount available for the tax year 2021/22.

Where the employee has other gains in the tax year such that the total gains exceed the employee's available annual exempt amount, the excess will be subject to capital gains tax. The rate of tax depends on the employee's level of taxable income.

Capital gains tax will be charged at 28% if the individual's taxable income exceeds the income tax basic rate band of £31,785. Where the individual's taxable income is less than £31,785, the amount of the gain that falls within the basic rate band will be taxed at 18% with the balance being taxed at 28%.

National insurance contributions

There are no national insurance implications in respect of a Schedule 3 SAYE scheme.

(b) **Income tax and national insurance implications for the employees of Babeen plc**

(i) *Medical care scheme*

The cost to the company of providing the health insurance of £470 will be a taxable benefit for each P11D employee.

There is no taxable benefit where the total low-interest loans to an employee do not exceed £10,000. Where an employee's total low-interest loans exceed £10,000, there will be a taxable benefit equal to interest at the official rate of 3% on the amount outstanding. The benefit is calculated by reference to the average balance for the tax year but either HM Revenue and Customs or the taxpayer can choose to calculate the benefit by reference to the balance outstanding on a daily basis.

There are no national insurance implications for the employees in respect of the taxable benefits relating to either the health insurance or the loans.

(ii) *Payments to employees for driving their own cars*

The total amount paid to each employee in a tax year for driving on company business will need to be compared to the statutory mileage allowances of 45 pence per mile for the first 10,000 miles and 25 pence per mile thereafter.

- Where the amount paid is more than the statutory amount, the excess is subject to income tax.

- Where the amount paid is less than the statutory amount, the shortfall is an allowable deduction when computing an employee's taxable employment income.

There will be no national insurance implications regardless of the mileage driven as the amount per mile is less than 45 pence.

The amount paid for carrying a passenger will not be subject to income tax or national insurance contributions as it is less than the statutory maximum of 5 pence per mile. The shortfall of 2 pence per mile is not an allowable deduction when computing an employee's taxable employment income.

10 Banda (ATAX 12/07)

Text references. Chapters 6 and 7 deal with computation of trading profits and capital allowances. Losses for a sole trader are covered in Chapter 8. Corporation tax losses are dealt with in Chapter 24 and group relief in Chapter 26. Close companies are covered in Chapter 25 and taxable employment benefits in Chapter 4. Ethics are covered in Chapter 30.

Top tips. It was very important to follow the order of the schedules set out in the question. You needed to calculate the losses available for relief in part (a) first and then apply loss relief in part (b).

Easy marks. The calculation of the losses and profits and the application of basis periods to tax years was knowledge that you should have been familiar with from the F6 syllabus. You should also have been able to state some basic rules on loss relief.

Examiner's comments. Part (b), representing almost half of the question, required candidates to determine the tax relief available in respect of the anticipated trading losses depending on the legal structure of the venture. This necessitated some clear thinking, ideally communicated to the examiner via the use of subheadings, such that a distinction was drawn between operating as an unincorporated trader and operating as a company. In many cases there was little evidence of such thinking taking place.

The majority of candidates either ignored the opening year rules for the unincorporated trader or failed to apply them to the situation. To be fair this was a relatively tricky situation due to the presence of the losses but it did seem as though many candidates had forgotten the basic rules governing the taxation of an unincorporated trader.

In order to calculate the potential tax relief it was necessary to determine the taxpayer's income tax liability for the years in which loss relief was available. Candidates had no problems calculating the income but were unsure how to proceed from there. In particular there was a lack of thought with many candidates performing calculations for all years rather than recognising that the income was the same in each year such that only one calculation was necessary.

Answers improved when considering the position of a company but there was a lack of precision when describing the loss reliefs available. There was also some confusion as to whether group relief would be available if the two companies were owned personally by the individual taxpayer (it wouldn't). Finally, there was a general unwillingness to satisfy the requirement and calculate the 'tax relief available'.

The final part of the question concerned a loan from a close company to a participator. Candidates did well in identifying the tax implications of the loan but many ignored the ethical considerations inherent within the question.

Marking scheme

			Marks
(a)	Pre-trading expenditure	1	
	Capital allowances on plant and machinery	1½	
	Tax adjusted profit/(losses)	1½	
			4
(b)	*Business run as sole trader*		
	Basis periods	1½	
	Losses	2½	
	Available loss reliefs	2	
	Set against general income	1	
	Dividend tax credit not repayable	1	
	Tax saving each year	2	
	Overall tax relief	1	
	Business run as company		
	Allowable losses	1½	
	Loss relief if Aral Ltd owned by Banda	1½	
	Loss relief if Aral Ltd owned by Flores Ltd	2	
	Recommendation	1	
	Max		16

	Marks
(c) *Tax implications of loan*	
Tax payable to HMRC on close company loan	1
Due date	½
Reason for tax being due	1½
Repayment of tax by HMRC if loan ceases	1
Taxable employment benefit	½
Report on P11D	1
Income tax due	1
Interest and penalties	1
Willingness to act for Banda	
Threat to fundamental principles	1
Requirement for full disclosure	1
Deliberate concealment	1

		Marks
	Max	10
Appropriate style and presentation	1	
Effectiveness of communication	1	
Logical structure	1	
		3
		33

(a) **Tax adjusted profit/(loss) of the Aral business**

	Period ending 30 June 2017 £	Year ending 30 June 2018 £	Year ending 30 June 2019 £
Budgeted profit/(loss)	(25,500)	(13,000)	77,000
Less: pre trading expenditure			
(£6,000 × 1/2) (note)	(3,000)		
capital allowances (less than max. AIA)	(11,500)	(1,500)	(1,200)
Tax adjusted profit/(loss)	(40,000)	(14,500)	75,800

Note

Expenditure incurred in the seven years prior to the start of trading is treated as if incurred on the first day of trading. Entertaining expenditure is not allowable.

(b) **Banda**

Tax relief available in respect of the anticipated trading losses

(i) *Business run as a sole trader*

The anticipated allowable losses for the business are set out below.

	Trading income £	Allowable loss £
2016/17 (1 January 2017 to 5 April 2017)		
Allowable loss £40,000 × 3/6	0	(20,000)
2017/18 (1 January 2017 to 31 December 2017)		
Allowable loss £40,000 – £20,000 + (£14,500 × 6/12)	0	(27,250)
2018/19 (Year ending 30 June 2018)		
Allowable loss £14,500 – (£14,500 × 6/12)	0	(7,250)

Banda can use the losses by deducting the losses:

- From her general income in the year of loss and/or the previous year.
- From her general income in the three years preceding the year of loss, starting with the earliest year, under early years trading loss relief.

All of the losses can be used in this way and therefore the possibility of carrying the losses forward has not been considered.

Banda's income throughout the years in which the losses can be relieved (2013/14 to 2018/19) consists of her salary and dividends from Flores Ltd. In any year in which she claims loss relief, she will save the income tax on her employment income only. There will be no saving in respect of her dividend income because Banda is a basic rate taxpayer and the 10% tax credit is not repayable.

The income tax position of Banda before taking account of loss relief is as follows:

	Non-savings income £	Dividend income £	Total £
Salary	15,825		
Dividend income (£20,250 × 100/90)		22,500	
Total/Net income	15,825	22,500	38,325
Less personal allowance	(10,600)		
Taxable income	5,225	22,500	27,725

Tax	£
£5,225 × 20%	1,045
£22,500 × 10%	2,250
Tax liability	3,295
Less tax credit on dividend	(2,250)
Tax payable	1,045

The total tax saved would be £1,045 × 3 = £3,135 as the losses would be set off against non-savings income in preference to dividend income.

The best use of relief would be to use the losses under early years trading loss relief as this would give the earliest tax relief (in 2013/14, 2014/15 and 2015/16).

Tutorial note

The examiner did not expect you to provide any more detailed computations than those shown above, but you might find it easier to understand why the loss relief applies in this way if you look at the following computations.

Banda could use the loss of 2016/17 against general income in 2013/14 as follows:

	Non savings income £	Dividend income £	Total £
Salary	15,825		
Dividend income (£20,250 × 100/90)		22,500	
Total income	15,825	22,500	38,325
Less early years loss relief	(15,825)	(4,175)	(20,000)
Net income	0	18,325	18,325
Less personal allowance	(0)	(10,600)	(10,600)
Taxable income	0	7,725	7,725

Tax	£
£7,725 × 10%	772
Less tax credit on dividend	(772)
Tax payable	0
Tax saved £(1,045 – 0)	£1,045

Banda could use the loss of 2017/18 against general income in 2014/15 as follows:

	Non savings income £	Dividend income £	Total £
Salary	15,825		
Dividend income (£20,250 × 100/90)		22,500	
Total income	15,825	22,500	38,325
Less early years loss relief	(15,825)	(11,425)	(27,250)
Net income	0	11,075	11,075
Less personal allowance	(0)	(10,600)	(10,600)
Taxable income	0	475	475

Tax	£
£475 × 10%	47
Less: tax credit on dividend	(47)
Tax payable	0

Tax saved £(1,045 – 0)	£1,045

Banda could use the loss of 2018/19 against general income in 2015/16 as follows:

	Non savings income £	Dividend income £	Total £
Salary	15,825		
Dividend income (£20,250 × 100/90)		22,500	
Total income	15,825	22,500	38,325
Less early years loss relief	(7,250)	(0)	(7,250)
Net income	8,575	22,500	31,075
Less personal allowance	(8,575)	(2,025)	(10,600)
Taxable income	0	20,475	20,475

Tax	£
£20,475 × 10%	2,047
Less tax credit on dividend	(2,047)
Tax payable	0

Tax saved £(1,045 – 0)	£1,045

(ii) **Business run as a company – Aral Ltd**

The anticipated allowable losses for Aral Ltd are as follows:

	Trading income £	Allowable Loss £
6 months ending 30 June 2017	0	(40,000)
Year ending 30 June 2018	0	(14,500)

Aral Ltd owned by Banda

The losses would have to be carried forward and deducted from the trading profits of the year ending 30 June 2019.

Aral Ltd cannot offset the loss in the current period or carry it back as it has no other income or gains.

Aral Ltd owned by Flores Ltd

The two companies will form a group relief group if Flores Ltd owns at least 75% of the ordinary share capital of Aral Ltd. The trading losses could be surrendered to Flores Ltd in the period ending 30 June 2017 (note) and the year ending 30 June 2018.

The total tax saved would be £(40,000 + 14,500) × 20%   £10,900

Note

The whole of the loss for the period ending 30 June 2017 can be surrendered to Flores Ltd as it is less than that company's profit for the corresponding period, ie £60,000 (£120,000 × 6/12).

Recommended structure

The Aral business should be established in a company owned by Flores Ltd.

This will maximise the relief available in respect of the trading losses and enable relief to be obtained in the period in which the losses are incurred.

(c)   **Tax implications of there being a loan from Flores Ltd to Banda**

Flores Ltd should have paid tax to HMRC equal to 25% of the loan, ie £5,250. The tax should have been paid on the company's normal due date for corporation tax in respect of the accounting period in which the loan was made, which was 1 April following the end of the accounting period.

The tax is due because Flores Ltd is a close company that has made a loan to a participator and that loan is not in the ordinary course of the company's business.

HMRC will repay the tax when the loan is either repaid or written off.

Flores Ltd should also have included the loan on Banda's Form P11D in order to report it to HMRC because it is a taxable benefit as the loan is interest-free.

Banda should have paid income tax on an annual benefit equal to 3% of the amount of loan outstanding during each tax year as follows:

£21,000 × 3% × 20%   £126

Interest and penalties may be charged in respect of the tax underpaid by both Flores Ltd and Banda and in respect of the incorrect returns made to HMRC.

Tutorial note

If the Aral business is carried on as a sole trade, these annual benefits will be covered by early years trading loss relief in part (b)(i) above.

Willingness to act for Banda

We would not wish to be associated with a client who has engaged in deliberate tax evasion as this poses a threat to the fundamental principles of integrity and professional behaviour.

Accordingly, we should refuse to act for Banda unless she is willing to disclose the details regarding the loan to HMRC and pay the ensuing tax liabilities.

Even if full disclosure is made, we should consider whether the loan was deliberately hidden from HMRC or Banda's previous tax adviser and, if so, should refuse to act for her.

11 Shuttelle (ATAX 06/13)

Text references. Employment income is covered in Chapter 4 and pensions in Chapter 2. The income tax computation is dealt with in Chapter 1. Overseas aspects of income tax are the subject of Chapter 10.

Top tips. Although there are no specific marks for presentation in this question, it would be advisable to set out the computations in part (a) neatly to make sure that relevant marks were awarded.

Easy marks. There were some easy marks in part (a) for basic income tax computations. In part (b), the remittance basis charge should have been well known.

Examiner's comments. Part (a) was in two closely related parts. It required candidates to calculate the benefit in respect of accommodation provided by an employer and to appreciate the effect on an individual's income tax liability of making pension contributions in excess of the annual allowance, where contributions of less than the annual allowance had been made in earlier years. Candidates also had to recognise that the pension contributions would affect the personal allowance available and the tax bands. This was a tricky question to get absolutely correct, and very few candidates did so, but there were plenty of marks available to candidates who knew how to put an income tax computation together and were aware of the rules relating to the determination of the annual allowance for a particular year. On the whole candidates scored reasonably well. In particular, most candidates handled the accommodation benefit well and knew that the tax bands needed to be extended. Many candidates were also aware that there was a three-year rule in respect of the annual allowance, although many were not absolutely clear as to how the rule worked. Many candidates missed the fact that the personal allowance would be available in full possibly because they did not pause and think at that stage of the calculation. Tax calculations should be done as a series of small steps with thought at each step in order to ensure that important matters are not missed.

Part (b) concerned the remittance basis and was not done particularly well. The problem here was that candidates did not have a clear set of rules. Instead, they had an awareness of a series of technical terms and time periods that were all confused. This made it very difficult to score well. The first thing candidates had to do was to explain whether or not the remittance basis was available to each of three individuals. This required a statement of the availability of the remittance basis together with a reason. For those who did not know the rules there was a 50:50 chance as regards the availability of the remittance basis. However, the reason for its availability or non-availability caused a lot more problems. Candidates must learn the rules and be able to apply them and state them clearly. In addition, the marks available for giving a reason are only awarded where the whole of the reason given is correct.

For example, the remittance basis was available to Lin because he was UK resident but not UK domiciled. Candidates who stated this together with various time periods of residency could not score the mark for the reason as it was not clear from their answer whether it was his residence and domicile status that was relevant or the time periods. The second thing candidates had to do was to state, with reasons, the remittance basis charge applicable to each of the individuals on the assumption that the remittance basis was available to all of them. Again, this was not done particularly well due to many candidates having a very confused knowledge of the rules. One particular area of confusion related to the automatic applicability of the remittance basis where **unremitted** income and gains are less than £2,000; many candidates thought the rule related to the level of **remitted** income and gains.

					Marks
(a)	(i)		Benefit in respect of accommodation	2	
			Personal allowance	1	
			Tax bands	1½	
			Relevance of employer's pension contribution	1	
			Annual allowance	2	
			Tax on excess pension contributions	1½	
			Max		8
	(ii)		Comparison with original liability	2½	
			Tax relief at source on pension contributions	1	
			Max		3
(b)	(i)	(1)	Availability of remittance basis		
			General rule	1½	
			Application of the rule to the individuals	1½	
		(2)	The remittance basis charge		
			Lin	1	
			Nan	1½	
			Yu	1½	
					7
	(ii)		Example of remittances – one mark each		2
					20

(a) **Shuttelle**

(i) **Income tax liability for the tax year 2015/16**

	£
Salary	203,910
Accommodation (W1)	6,000
Net income	209,910
Less personal allowance (W2)	(10,600)
Taxable income	199,310

Income tax liability

£(31,785 + £120,000) = £151,785 × 20%	30,357
£(199,310 – 151,785) = £47,525 × 40%	19,010
Excess pension contributions £59,000 (W3) × 40%	23,600
Income tax liability	72,967

Tutorial notes

1   The higher rate limit has been increased to £270,000 (£150,000 + £120,000), due to the pension contributions. Accordingly, the excess pension contributions will be taxed at 40%.

2   In the exam, equal credit was given to candidates who included the excess pension contributions within taxable income.

Workings

1   *Benefit in respect of accommodation*

	£
Basic benefit: annual value	7,200
Additional benefit £(635,000 – 75,000) = £560,000 × 3%	16,800
Total benefits for full tax year	24,000
Benefits in 2015/16: £24,000 × 3/12 (available 6.4 to 30.6)	6,000

2   *Personal allowance*

The adjusted net income is as follows:

	£
Net income	209,910
Less gross personal pension contributions	(120,000)
Adjusted net income	89,910

Since the adjusted net income does not exceed the limit of £100,000, the personal allowance is available in full.

3   *Excess pension contributions*

	£
Gross contributions by Shuttelle	120,000
Gross contributions by Din Ltd	4,000
Annual allowance available in 2015/16 (W4)	(65,000)
Excess pension contributions	59,000

4   *Annual allowance available in 2015/16*

	£	£
Annual allowance for 2015/16		40,000
Brought forward from 2013/14		
£(50,000 – 19,000 – 4,000)	27,000	
Less: used in 2014/15		
£(40,000 – 38,000 – 4,000)	(2,000)	
		25,000
Annual allowance available in 2015/16		65,000

(ii)   **Total tax relief in respect of the gross personal pension contributions of £120,000**

	£
Income tax on taxable income of £209,910	
(ie ignoring the pension contributions)	
£31,785 × 20%	6,357
£(150,000 – 31,785) = £118,215 × 40%	47,286
£(209,910 – 150,000) = £59,910 × 45%	26,959
Income tax liability, ignoring the pension contributions	80,602
Less income tax liability, after pension contributions (part (i))	(72,967)
Add tax relief on pension contributions at source £120,000 × 20%	24,000
Total tax relief in respect of pension contributions	31,635

Tutorial notes

1   When calculating the liability ignoring the pension contributions, there would be no personal allowance due to the level of the net income.

2   By charging tax on the excess pension contributions, relief is effectively only given for the balance of the contributions, £61,000 (£120,000 – £59,000), as set out below:

	£
Tax saved in respect of pension contribution of £61,000	
£59,910 × 45%	26,959
£1,090 × 40%	436
Tax saved in respect of PA becoming available	
£10,600 × 40%	4,240
	31,635

(b)   **The three non-UK domiciled individuals**

   (i)   *The availability of the remittance basis and the remittance basis charge*

      (1)   The availability of the remittance basis

         The remittance basis is available to UK resident individuals who are not domiciled in the UK. Accordingly:

         –   The remittance basis is available to Lin and Yu.

         –   The remittance basis is not available to Nan as he is not UK resident (and so his overseas income is not liable to UK income tax and so remittance is irrelevant).

      (2)   The remittance basis charge

         Lin has unremitted overseas income and gains of less than £2,000. Accordingly, the remittance basis will apply automatically, such that there will not be a remittance basis charge.

         Nan has unremitted overseas income and gains of more than £2,000. If Nan were able to make a claim for the remittance basis, he would be liable for the remittance basis charge of £60,000 because Nan has been resident in the UK for 12 of the 14 tax years prior to 2015/16.

         Yu has unremitted overseas income and gains of more than £2,000. If Yu made a claim for the remittance basis, he would be liable for the remittance basis charge of £30,000 because Yu has been resident in the UK for seven of the nine tax years prior to 2015/16.

   (ii)   *Actions that would be regarded as remittances*

      Bringing property into the UK which was purchased out of overseas income/gains.

      Paying for services received in the UK out of overseas income/gains.

      The use of overseas income/gains to pay the interest/capital on a debt where the funds borrowed have been brought into the UK or used to acquire property or services in the UK.

      Tutorial note. Only two examples were required.

12 Ava (ATAX 12/09)

Text references. Income tax administration is covered in Chapter 15. The inheritance tax aspects of this question are dealt with in Chapters 16 and 17.

Top tips. Where you are told that two spouses or civil partners have died, always check to see if the first spouse had a nil rate band which was not fully utilised.

Easy marks. Part (a) covered basic income tax administration and should have produced easy marks.

Examiner's comments. Part (a) required a list of the consequences of the late submission of an income tax return and the late payment of the individual's income tax liability. This was a relatively straightforward requirement and the majority of candidates earned marks for the points they made. However, the list should have included four separate consequences whereas most candidates only included two.

Part (b) concerned the inheritance tax and capital gains tax implications of the gift of a farm and was in two parts.

Part (i) required a reasoned explanation of the availability of both agricultural property relief and business property relief in respect of the gift. This part was answered well with many candidates scoring full marks.

Part (ii) required calculations of the capital gains tax and inheritance tax payable in respect of the gift together with the due dates of payment. Answers to this part varied considerably. Stronger candidates were able to score well with accurate calculations and correct dates. Weaker candidates confused the two taxes and the reliefs and exemptions available by, for example, including agricultural property relief in the capital gains tax computation. They also failed to include the dates asked for. The majority of students missed the fact that a proportion of the husband's nil rate band could be transferred to the widow.

Marks

(a) Submission date for return 1
Penalty for late submission 1
Penalty on overdue tax 1
Interest on overdue tax 1

4

(b) (i) *Agricultural property relief*
Location in EEA ½
Amount of relief 1
Qualifying period 2
Business property relief 1

Max 4

(ii) *Capital gains tax*
Amount payable 2
Due date 1
Inheritance tax
Amount chargeable to IHT 2
Nil rate band 3
IHT due 1½
Due date 1
Date of claim to transfer unused nil rate band 1
Assumption 1

Max 12
20

(a) **Late submission of 2015/16 income tax return**

The latest date for submission of the 2015/16 income tax return was 31 January 2017. The penalty date is the day after the due date.

An immediate penalty of £100 will have arisen because the return was late. As the return was over three months late, HMRC could charge a daily penalty of £10 per day for a maximum of 90 days. A further penalty for submission of the return more than six months but less than twelve months following the penalty date applies being the greater of 5% of the tax liability and £300.

A penalty also arises on the late payment of the balancing payment. The penalty date in this case is 30 days after the due date of 31 January 2017.

A penalty equal to 10% of the outstanding income tax will be levied because the tax will be paid between five months but not more than 11 months after the penalty date.

Interest will be charged on the outstanding income tax from 31 January 2017 until 14 December 2017 at an annual rate of 3%.

(b) (i) **Availability of agricultural property relief and business property relief**

Hayworth Farm is agricultural property situated in the EEA (which includes the UK) and therefore qualifies for agricultural property relief. The relief is given on the agricultural value of the property rather than its market value. 100% relief is available.

Because the farm is farmed by tenants, it must have been owned by Ava and farmed by someone (in this case the tenants) for at least seven years prior to the transfer. Ava is able to satisfy this condition because she inherited the farm from her husband and therefore his period of ownership can be added to hers.

Business property relief is not available in respect of the gift of the farm as it has always been held as an investment and not as a business asset.

(ii)   **Tax payable on gift of Hayworth Farm**

Capital gains tax

	£
Market value (February 2018)	650,000
Less cost (probate value November 2017)	(494,000)
Gain	156,000
Less annual exempt amount (assumed available)	(11,100)
Taxable gain	144,900

	£
Capital gains tax @ 28% (due 31 January 2019)	40,572

Inheritance tax

	£	£
Potentially exempt transfer		
Market value (February 2018)		650,000
Less APR £445,000 @ 100%		(445,000)
Transfer of value		205,000
Less annual exemption 2017/18		(3,000)
Potentially exempt transfer now chargeable		202,000
Nil rate bands available		
Ava's nil rate band	325,000	
Less gift on 1.12.16 £(251,000 – 6,000)	(245,000)	
		(80,000)
Burt's nil rate band	325,000	
Less legacy to sister	(293,000)	
		(32,000)
Amount chargeable to inheritance tax		90,000
Inheritance tax @ 40%		36,000
Less taper relief (3 to 4 years @ 20%)		(7,200)
Inheritance tax payable on PET		28,800

The inheritance tax will be payable on 31 July 2022 (six months after the end of the month of Ava's death).

The claim to transfer Burt's unused nil rate band to Ava must be made by 31 January 2024 (two years from the end of the month of Ava's death).

Assumption: Ava's nephew still owns the farm on 1 January 2022, or has died prior to that date whilst owning it, and so APR is available on the farm when the PET comes into charge on Ava's death.

13 Brad (ATAX 06/13)

Text references. Overseas aspects of capital gains tax are covered in Chapter 14. The basics of inheritance tax are dealt with in Chapter 16. Related property valuation and business property relief are covered in Chapter 17. The basics of chargeable gains are in Chapter 11 and stamp taxes in Chapter 19.

Top tips. It is important to read the question very carefully and produce an answer which covers all of the requirements. For example, in part (a), you were given a very specific brief about what to include in your answer.

Easy marks. There were some easy marks in part (b)(i) for a basic description of inheritance tax advantages of making lifetime gifts to individuals.

Examiner's comments. This question was done well by many candidates. Part (a) required candidates to explain Brad's UK capital gains tax liability and the reasons for him being only temporarily non-UK resident and to state the payment date for the tax due. The majority of candidates had some knowledge of the temporary non-UK resident rules and quite a reasonable knowledge of capital gains tax generally, such that they scored reasonably well. Most candidates knew the five-year rule although a much smaller number stated the four years out of seven rule. A minority of candidates stated a rule correctly in general terms but failed to apply it to the facts of the question. For example, some candidates stated that assets bought and sold during the period of non-residence were not subject to UK capital gains tax but then went on to calculate a gain in respect of the antique bed. Other candidates failed to apply the basics. For example, a minority of candidates omitted the annual exempt amount whilst others either provided an incorrect payment date or failed to provide one at all. When providing a payment date it is important to make it clear which tax year is being addressed. There were three possible relevant tax years in this question so stating a date without a year could not score unless the candidate explained in general terms how the date is determined, ie 31 January after the end of the tax year.

Part (b)(i) was an invitation to candidates to be general rather than specific as it required an explanation of the advantages of lifetime giving. Many candidates did very well but the performance of the majority was unsatisfactory. The advantages of lifetime giving are scattered throughout the inheritance tax system with certain exemptions only being available in respect of lifetime gifts, potentially exempt transfers being exempt once the donor has lived for seven years, taper relief once the donor has lived for at least three years, and the value of a gift being frozen at the time of the gift together with the availability of relief for any fall in value of the assets gifted. Most candidates would have known all of these rules but many did not include them all in their answers. Instead they wrote at length about some of them whilst omitting others. In particular, many candidates did not address the exemptions available in respect of lifetime giving. This is likely to be because candidates simply started writing and kept writing until they felt they had written enough. These candidates would have benefited from thinking their way through the inheritance tax system and noting each of the advantages of lifetime giving before they started writing. Part (b)(ii) concerned a particular gift of shares and required knowledge of the valuation rules and business property relief. The valuation, which involved fall in value together with related property, was done well with many candidates scoring full marks. A minority of candidates were not aware that it is only the spouse's property that is related whilst others failed to appreciate that it is only the donor's property that is valued (the related property is only relevant when determining the valuation). The business property relief was done well with the majority of candidates identifying the two year rule and the relevance of the investments. Fewer candidates stated the need for the donee to continue owning the shares until the death of the donor.

Candidates did not do so well when it came to identifying other tax issues. Most candidates simply repeated the basics of the inheritance tax rules in relation to potentially exempt transfers when what was required here was consideration of capital gains tax and stamp duty.

				Marks
(a)	Conditions		2	
	Antique bed and motor car		1½	
	Quoted shares		3	
	Tax liabilities		3½	
		Max		8
(b)	(i) Seven year rule		1	
	Valuation		2	
	Exemptions		3	
	Taper relief		2	
		Max		7
	(ii) Fall in value		3½	
	Availability of business property relief			
	Business of Omnium Ltd		1½	
	Brad's ownership of the shares		1	
	Circumstances on Brad's death		1	
	Calculation of business property relief			
	Rate of relief		1	
	Excepted assets		2	
	Other tax matters		2½	
		Max		10
				25

(a) **Capital gains tax**

Brad will be regarded as only temporarily non-UK resident whilst living in Keirinia because:

- He was non-UK resident for less than five years.

- Having always lived in the UK prior to moving to Keirinia, he was UK resident for at least four of the seven tax years immediately prior to the tax year of departure.

As a temporary non-UK resident, Brad will be subject to UK capital gains tax on the assets sold whilst he was non-UK resident, which he owned at the date of his departure from the UK. Accordingly, the antique bed is excluded from these rules as it was both bought and sold during the period of temporary non-UK residence. The profit on the sale of the motor car is ignored as motor cars are exempt assets for the purposes of capital gains tax.

The shares were sold in 2012/13, the tax year of departure, so the gain on these shares was subject to tax in that year under general principles, as Brad was UK resident in that year. However, there will have been no tax to pay as the capital gain of £4,900 (£18,900 – £14,000) was covered by the annual exempt amount for 2012/13.

The capital gains tax due on the sale of the painting is calculated as follows:

	£
Capital gain £(36,400 – 15,000)	21,400
Less annual exempt amount	(11,100)
	10,300
Capital gains tax @ 28%	2,884

The gain on the sale of the painting is subject to tax in 2016/17, the tax year in which Brad became UK resident again, and not in the year of sale. Accordingly, the tax is due on 31 January 2018.

(b) **Inheritance tax**

(i) **The inheritance tax advantages of making lifetime gifts to individuals**

A lifetime gift to an individual is a potentially exempt transfer. It will be exempt from inheritance tax if the donor survives the gift by seven years.

If the donor dies within seven years of making the gift, such that the gift is chargeable to inheritance tax, the value used will be the value at the time of the gift and not the value at the time of death. Any increase in the value of the asset will be ignored, although relief will be available if the asset falls in value following the gift.

Certain exemptions are available only in respect of lifetime gifts. These exemptions are:

- Annual exemption of £3,000 each year
- Gifts in consideration of marriage/civil partnership up to certain limits
- Regular gifts out of income that do not affect the donor's standard of living
- Small gifts exemption of £250 per donee per tax year

Any inheritance tax due on the donor's death will be reduced by taper relief if the donor survives the gift by more than three years. The tax due will be reduced by 20% if the donor survives the gift by more than three but less than four years. The percentage reduction will increase by 20% for each additional year that the donor survives the gift.

(ii) **In respect of the possible gift of 1,500 shares in Omnium Ltd to Dani**

Fall in value of Brad's estate

The fall in value of Brad's estate on a gift of 1,500 shares in Omnium Ltd will be calculated as follows:

| | Related property | |
| | Included | Ignored |
	£	£
Value of shares held prior to the gift:		
3,000 × £290 (30% + 45% = 75%)	870,000	
3,000 × £205 (30%)		615,000
Value of shares held after the gift:		
1,500 × £240 (15% + 45% = 60%)	(360,000)	
1,500 × £190 (15%)		(285,000)
Transfer of value	510,000	330,000

The higher fall in value of £510,000, produced by reference to related property, will be used.

Tutorial note

The value of Brad's shares is determined by reference to the shares held by him and his wife under the related property rules.

Business property relief

Business property relief will not be available if the business of Omnium Ltd consists wholly or mainly of dealing in securities, stocks or shares or land and buildings or the making or holding of investments. Accordingly, it will be necessary to determine the significance of the investment properties to the activities of Omnium Ltd as a whole.

Brad must have owned the shares for at least two years at the time of the gift. This condition is satisfied.

Business property relief will not be available unless Dani still owns the shares at the time of Brad's death (or had died whilst owning the shares) and the shares continue to qualify for the relief.

If all of the conditions set out above are satisfied, business property relief will be available at the rate of 100%, because Omnium Ltd is an unquoted company.

However, where there are excepted assets, business property relief will be restricted to:

$$100\% \times \text{the fall in value} \times \frac{\text{Omnium Ltd's non-excepted assets}}{\text{Omnium Ltd's total assets}}$$

Excepted assets are assets that have not been used for the purposes of the company's business in the two years prior to the transfer and are not required for such use in the future. Some or all of Omnium Ltd's investment properties may be classified as excepted assets.

Tutorial note

Business property relief will only be relevant if Brad were to die within seven years of making the gift, such that the potentially exempt transfer became a chargeable transfer. Business property relief would also be available if Dani has disposed of the shares prior to Brad's death and acquired qualifying replacement property within three years of the disposal.

Other tax issues

The gift of shares will be a disposal at market value for the purposes of capital gains tax. Gift relief will be available but will be restricted because of the investment properties owned by Omnium Ltd.

Gifts of shares are not subject to stamp duty.

Tutorial note

The question asked for a brief statement only of the other tax issues.

14 Sushi (ATAX 12/10)

Text references. Inheritance tax overseas aspects and variations are covered in Chapter 18. Overseas aspects of income tax are dealt with in Chapter 10.

Top tips. Remember to use a letter format in your answer – there is a specific mark for this aspect.

Easy marks. The remittance basis is a favourite topic of this examiner and there were some easy marks for basic points.

Examiner's comments. Part (i) concerned inheritance tax and, in particular, the relevance of domicile to an individual's tax position. The level of knowledge here was good with some very strong, thorough answers. However, many candidates who scored well for this part of the question often did so in an inefficient manner which may have left them short of time for the remainder of the exam. As always, there was a need to pause; this time in order to determine the best way to say what needed to be said. Weaker candidates simply kept writing, often repeating themselves, until they finally got to where they wanted to be. Stronger candidates wrote short, precise phrases which earned all of the marks despite using very few words. Candidates should practise explaining areas of taxation making sure that their explanations are concise and clear.

There was a need to address the position of both the mother and the daughter but many candidates simply addressed 'inheritance tax' rather than the situation of the individuals. Candidates will be more successful in the exam if they think in terms of providing advice to individuals and companies rather than addressing technical issues as this will help them to stick to the point and to satisfy the questions' requirements.

A somewhat surprising error made by a significant minority of candidates was to state that the inheritance tax position on the death of Sushi's mother depended on the domicile status of Sushi as opposed to that of her mother. It is, of course, the status of the person whose estate has fallen in value that is relevant.

A final thought on this part of the question is that many candidates wasted time calculating inheritance tax, despite not having sufficient information, whilst others provided a considerable amount of detail regarding the taxation implications of making a potentially exempt transfer, despite being specifically told not to in the question.

Part (ii) concerned overseas income and the remittance basis. The performance of candidates for this part was mixed. To begin with there was much confusion regarding the conditions that must be satisfied in order for the remittance basis to be available with candidates mixing up domicile and residence with the remittance basis charge rules (and the rule for inheritance tax deemed domicile). The application of the £2,000 rule was also misunderstood by many.

Candidates were asked to explain the meaning of 'remittance' and the 'remittance basis'. Most candidates attempted to do this, which was very encouraging, but few had much knowledge beyond the absolute basics. Similarly, most candidates were aware of the remittance basis charge but a significant number were confused as to the situation in which the charge would be levied. On the plus side, the vast majority of candidates provided a conclusion (as requested) and many produced neat and reasonably accurate calculations.

Marks were available for professional skills in this question. In order to earn these marks candidates first had to satisfy the requirement in relation to the format of the document requested. Further marks were then available for providing clear explanations and coherent calculations.

On the whole, the performance of candidates in this area was good with the majority of candidates producing correctly formatted documents in a style that was easy to follow. However, many candidates failed to maintain the correct style of a document throughout their answer such that, for example, the letters written in response to this question often referred to the client correctly as 'you' to begin with but then reverted to using the client's name later in the answer.

Marking scheme

			Marks
(a)	Assets subject to inheritance tax	1½	
	Mother's death	1	
	Sushi's death		
	UK assets	½	
	Foreign assets	½	
	Domicile of origin	1	
	Domicile of choice	1	
	Deemed domicile	2½	
	UK IHT on land and buildings in Zakuskia		
	Valuation	1½	
	UK IHT and double tax relief	2	
	The statue	3½	
	Max		12
(b)	Meaning and availability of remittance basis	1½	
	Meaning of remittance	3	
	Calculations		
	Remittance basis not available	2	
	Remittance basis available		
	Remittance basis charge	1	
	Loss of personal allowance and annual exempt amount	2	
	Tax on remitted income	1	
	Explanatory notes (1 mark per sensible point) – maximum	3	
	Conclusion	1	
	Max		12
	Appropriate style and presentation	1	
	Effectiveness of communication	1	
	Approach to problem solving	1	
	Max		3
			27

Sushi's address
6 December 2016

Dear Sushi

Personal taxation

I set out below my advice in connection with the assets you have inherited from your mother.

(a)   **UK inheritance tax and the statue**

UK inheritance tax is charged on assets situated in the UK. It is also charged on assets situated overseas where the owner is domiciled or deemed domiciled in the UK. A person's domicile is, broadly speaking, the country in which they have their permanent home.

On the death of your mother

Your mother was domiciled in Zakuskia and did not own any UK assets. Accordingly, there will be no UK inheritance tax liability on her estate.

On your death

You now own both UK and Zakuskian assets. On your death, UK inheritance tax will, inevitably, be charged in respect of the UK assets but the treatment of the assets in Zakuskia will depend on your domicile position. When you were born you would have acquired a domicile of origin in Zakuskia as your father was domiciled there. You will have retained this domicile unless you have acquired a domicile of choice in the UK. You will have acquired a domicile of choice in the UK if it can be seen that you have severed all of your ties with Zakuskia with the intention of making the UK your permanent home. You will continue to be domiciled in Zakuskia if we can show that you have retained ties there with the intention of returning there one day.

However, even if you continue to be domiciled in Zakuskia, you will be deemed domiciled in the UK (for the purposes of inheritance tax only) once you have been resident here for 17 of the 20 tax years ending with the year in which any assets are transferred. At the end of the tax year 2016/17 you will have been resident here for 15 years. Accordingly, 2018/19 will be your seventeenth year of UK residence and you will be deemed domiciled in the UK from that year onwards such that your Zakuskian assets, in addition to your UK assets, will then be subject to inheritance tax. Until 2018/19, provided you have not acquired a domicile of choice in the UK, your Zakuskian assets will not be subject to inheritance tax.

UK inheritance tax on land and buildings situated in Zakuskia

Land and buildings situated in Zakuskia but subject to UK inheritance tax will be included in your death estate at the market value in Zakuskia converted into sterling at the UK buying rate as this gives the lowest sterling equivalent. Expenses incurred in Zakuskia in connection with administering and realising the property will be deductible up to a maximum of 5% of the value of the property, so far as those expenses are attributable to the property's location overseas.

Any available nil rate band will be deducted from your death estate and the balance will be subject to UK inheritance tax at 40%. The amount payable in respect of the land and buildings in Zakuskia is calculated by determining the percentage, by reference to market values, of your assets held at death represented by the land and buildings and applying that percentage to the total UK inheritance tax due. The inheritance tax due in Zakuskia will be deductible from the UK liability on these assets but cannot result in a repayment.

The statue

Once you bring the statue into the UK it will become a UK asset and the gift will be a potentially exempt transfer regardless of your country of domicile. However, the gift of the statue will not be a potentially exempt transfer if we are able to demonstrate that you are currently domiciled in Zakuskia (ie you have not acquired a domicile of choice in the UK), and you give the statue to your son whilst it is in Zakuskia. Such a gift would be outside UK inheritance tax as the asset would be overseas and you, the donor, would not be UK domiciled.

If you have already acquired a UK domicile of choice the gift of the statue will be a potentially exempt transfer regardless of where it is situated.

Alternatively, you could make a variation of your inheritance from your mother as if the statue had been left by your mother to your son. The variation must be made by you within two years of your mother's death, in writing and state that it is to have effect for inheritance tax purposes. The result would be that the transfer would be treated as made to your son by your mother on her death of an asset not situated in the UK. Accordingly, there will be no UK inheritance tax liability on this transfer.

(b)   **The Zakuskian income**

If you are domiciled in Zakuskia you can choose to be taxed on the remittance basis such that you will only be taxed on remittances to the UK. If you have acquired a domicile of choice in the UK you will be taxed on all of the Zakuskian income regardless of whether or not it is remitted to the UK.

The most obvious example of a remittance occurs where the overseas income is brought into the UK. However, the definition of remittance is much wider than this. For example, it includes the situation where the overseas income is used to repay an overseas debt where the funds borrowed have been brought into the UK. A remittance would also occur where the overseas income is used to purchase items which are themselves brought into the UK. There are exceptions to this latter rule in respect of: items costing less than £1,000, items for personal use (clothes, watches etc), and items brought into the UK for repair or for no more than 275 days. There are also exceptions where money or property is brought into the UK to acquire shares in or make a loan to a trading company or a member of a trading group or to pay the remittance basis charge.

My calculations are included in the appendix to this letter.

You can see that if you remit £30,000 per annum, it will not be beneficial for you to claim the remittance basis due to the remittance basis charge (at £60,000 since you have been resident in the UK for at least 12 of the 14 tax years preceding 2016/17) and the loss of tax reliefs. The additional UK tax payable in respect of the Zakuskian income will therefore be £16,500 per year on the arising basis.

Please do not hesitate to contact me if I can be of any further assistance.

Yours sincerely

Tax manager

Appendix

Sushi – increase in UK tax liability due to the Zakuskian income

A   *Remittance basis not available*

	£
Zakuskian income gross of Zakuskian tax	55,000
UK income tax at 40% (as non-savings (property) and savings income) (N1)	22,000
Less relief for Zakuskian tax at 10% (lower than UK tax)	(5,500)
Annual increase in UK tax payable	16,500

B   *Remittance basis available and claimed – Remit £30,000 (gross) per annum*

	£
Remittance basis charge (N2)	60,000
Loss of income tax personal allowance (£10,600 × 40%) (N3)	4,240
Loss of capital gains tax annual exempt amount (£11,100 × 28%) (N3)	3,108
Cost of claiming remittance basis	67,348

	£
Zakuskian income remitted to the UK, gross of Zakuskian tax	30,000
UK income tax at 40% (N4)	12,000
Less relief for Zakuskian tax at 10% (lower than UK tax)	(3,000)
UK income tax on remitted income	9,000
Annual increase in UK tax payable £(67,348 + 9,000)	76,348

Notes

1   Your taxable income, before taking into account the Zakuskian income, is £34,000. This amount is after deducting your personal allowance and means that your net income is £(34,000 + 10,600) = £44,600. When the Zakuskian income of £55,000 is added to this, your net income will rise to £99,600 which is below the limit of £100,000 after which the personal allowance is gradually reduced. Therefore the Zakuskian income of £55,000 is taxable at 40% (with no additional tax due to abatement of the personal allowance).

2   The remittance basis will not be available to you automatically because you will have unremitted income of more than £2,000. The remittance basis charge of £60,000 will be payable because you are claiming the remittance basis and you have been resident in the UK for at least 12 of the 14 preceding tax years.

3   On claiming the remittance basis you will no longer be entitled to the income tax personal allowance and the capital gains tax annual exempt amount.

4   Income taxed under the remittance basis is taxed as non-savings income regardless of its true nature. Accordingly, the amount remitted will be taxed at 40%.

15 Surfe (ATAX 12/11)

Text references. Trusts are covered in Chapter 18. Inheritance tax is dealt with in Chapters 16 to 18.

Top tips. Where there is a gift of unquoted shares, watch out for the loss to donor rules when computing the transfer of value. Also, think about the effect of related property.

Easy marks. There were some easy marks relating to inheritance tax exemptions. The calculation of the death estate was also straightforward.

Examiner's comments. Part (a) required an outline of the capital gains tax implications of various transactions relating to the trust and the inheritance tax charges that may be payable in the future by the trustees. It was important for candidates to be methodical in their approach to this question. There were three transactions to be addressed in relation to capital gains tax whereas the inheritance aspects of the question were more open ended.

The majority of candidates knew some of the capital gains tax implications of the transactions but very few knew all of them. In particular, there was a lack of understanding that capital gains would arise when the trustees transfer trust assets to the beneficiaries of the trust. As always, when dealing with capital gains tax, it is vital to consider the availability of reliefs; gift relief is available when assets are transferred to a discretionary trust and again when they are transferred to the beneficiaries.

The inheritance aspects of part (a) were not handled as well as the capital gains tax aspects. The majority of candidates failed to mention the ten-yearly charges and exit charges payable out of the trust's assets.

Part (b) required a calculation of the inheritance tax liability arising on the death of an individual who had made a number of lifetime gifts. This was a fairly straightforward question, albeit with a couple of tricky points within it, but it was not handled particularly well.

There was a lack of appropriate structure to candidates' answers that indicated that, perhaps, there had been insufficient practice of this area. Inheritance tax computations should all look the same, starting with the tax on any chargeable lifetime transfers, followed by the consideration of gifts within seven years of death and ending with the death estate. However, many candidates began with the death estate and worked their way backwards towards the lifetime gifts; a method that was never going to be successful.

There was confusion as to which gift benefited from the annual exemptions and in respect of the utilisation of the nil rate band. There was also a general lack of knowledge of the impact of related property on the valuation of a gift. Other technical errors, made by a minority of candidates, included the treatment of cash as an exempt asset and business property relief being given in respect of the shares owned by the taxpayer.

On the positive side, the majority of candidates identified the availability of the husband's nil rate band and the death estate was handled well.

				Marks
(a)	(i)	Gift of shares	1½	
		Future sale of quoted shares	½	
		Transfer of trust assets to beneficiaries	1½	
		Election details	1	
	(ii)	Inheritance tax	2½	
			Max	6
(b)		Inheritance tax in respect of lifetime gifts		
		Gift to charity	½	
		Gift to nephews	1½	
		Gift to trust		
		Shares – fall in value	2	
		Cash	½	
		Lifetime tax	1½	
		Gross chargeable transfer	½	
		Nil rate band available on death	2½	
		Inheritance tax payable on death	1½	
		Inheritance tax in respect of death estate	1½	
			Max	11
				17

(a) (i) Capital gains tax

A capital gain will arise on the gift of the shares to the trustees by reference to the market value of the shares. Gift relief will be available because the gift is a chargeable lifetime transfer for the purposes of inheritance tax. The gift relief election should be signed by Surfe and submitted by 5 April 2021 (within four years of the end of the tax year of the gift).

Capital gains made by the trustees whilst they are managing the assets of the trust will be subject to capital gains tax. The tax will be paid out of the trust assets.

A capital gain will arise on the transfer of trust assets from the trustees to Surfe's nephews by reference to the market value of the trust assets. Gift relief will be available because the transfer is immediately chargeable to inheritance tax. The gift relief election should be signed by the trustees and the recipient nephew and submitted within four years of the end of the tax year in which the transfer occurs.

Tutorial note. The detailed rules in connection with the calculation of capital gains tax payable by the trustees of a trust are not in the P6 syllabus.

(ii) Inheritance tax

It is assumed in the question that Surfe will die on 1 July 2019, ie within seven years of the gift of the shares and cash to the trust. Accordingly, the trustees will have to pay inheritance tax on the gift at 40% less the lifetime tax paid.

The trust will be subject to an inheritance tax charge every ten years (the 'principal' charge). The maximum charge will be 6% (30% of the lifetime tax rate of 20%) of the value of the trust assets at the time of the charge.

The transfer of trust assets from the trustees to the beneficiaries will also result in an exit charge to inheritance tax. The maximum charge will be 6% (30% of the lifetime tax rate of 20%) of the value of the assets transferred, times 39 quarters out of 40 quarters.

The principal charges are payable by the trustees, out of the trust assets. The trustees may also pay exit charges out of the trust assets.

(b) **Inheritance tax payable on Surfe's death on 1 July 2019**

Gifts in the seven years prior to death

The gift on 1 February 2005 to the charity was an exempt transfer.

The gifts on 1 October 2016 to Surfe's nephews were reduced by the annual exemptions for 2016/17 and 2015/16. The potentially exempt transfer of £164,000 ((£85,000 × 2) − (£3,000 × 2)) will be covered by the nil rate band.

The gift of the shares to the trust on 1 January 2017

	£
Gross chargeable transfer (W1)	543,750
Inheritance tax:	
£325,667 (W2) × 0%	0
£218,083 × 40%	87,233
£543,750	87,233
Less lifetime tax paid (W1)	(43,750)
	43,483

There will be no taper relief as the gift is less than three years prior to death.

Workings

1 *Gift to trust 1 January 2017*

	£
Value of Surfe's holding prior to gift 650 × £2,000 (N)	1,300,000
Less value of Surfe's holding after gift 450 × £2,000 (N)	(900,000)
	400,000
Cash	100,000
Net transfer of value	500,000
Inheritance tax:	
£325,000 × 0%	0
£175,000 × 20/80 (Surfe is paying tax – grossing up required)	43,750
£500,000	43,750
Gross transfer of value £(500,000 + 43,750)	£543,750

Note.

The value per share of Surfe's holding is determined by reference to the number of shares she owns personally and any related property. Related property includes shares given by Surfe to a charity that the charity still owns. Accordingly, Surfe's holding prior to the gift, including related property, will be 100% (65% + 35%). Her holding after the gift, including related property, will be 80% (45% + 35%).

2 *Nil rate band on death*

	£
Nil rate band as at the date of death	325,000
Add: unused nil rate band of Flud adjusted for increase in nil rate	
band £(300,000 − 148,000) = £152,000 × £325,000/£300,000	164,667
	489,667
Less amount utilised by gifts on 1 October 2016	(164,000)
Available nil rate band	325,667

The death estate on 1 July 2019

	£
House	1,400,000
Quoted shares	600,000
Shares in Leat Ltd (450 × £2,400) (N)	1,080,000
Chargeable estate	3,080,000

                                                                              £

   Inheritance tax:
   £3,080,000 × 40% (nil rate band utilised by gifts on 1 January 2017 and
   1 October 2016)   1,232,000

Note.

Surfe's holding, including the related property held by the charity, will be 80% (45% + 35%).

16 Una (ATAX 06/12)

Text references. Inheritance tax is covered in Chapters 16 to 18. Stamp taxes are covered in Chapter 19. Capital gains tax computation is dealt with in Chapter 11 and reliefs in Chapter 13. Income tax administration is in Chapter 15 and ethics in Chapter 30.

Top tips. When you are asked to include 'other tax implications' in your answer as in part (a) of this question, it is a good idea to jot down the main taxes that might be relevant to an individual and then consider whether any points arise from the scenario you have been given. Don't forget stamp duties!

Easy marks. There were some easy marks for the inheritance tax calculations in part (a). The four professional marks should also have been easy to obtain.

Examiner's comments. Part (a) was answered reasonably well. In particular, only a minority of candidates confused the rules of inheritance tax and capital gains tax. Also, many candidates demonstrated strong technical knowledge of the mechanics of inheritance tax and agricultural property relief. Now that inheritance tax has been part of Paper F6 for a while, candidates sitting Paper P6 can expect to see more questions in this style, ie questions which work at the margin rather than requiring complete tax computations.

The one common error in relation to inheritance tax was a failure to realise that the earlier cash gift had no effect on the nil band in respect of the later gift as it was made more than seven years prior to death. Other, less common, errors included deducting taper relief from the value transferred rather than from the inheritance tax liability and deducting the annual exemptions from the death estate.

The capital gains tax elements of the question were not handled as well as inheritance tax. Many candidates did not know the conditions relating to the availability of capital gains tax reliefs and simply assumed, incorrectly, that gift relief would be available. A substantial minority also forgot the fundamental point that there is no capital gains tax on death and calculated liabilities in respect of both lifetime gifts and gifts via Una's will.

However, the main problems experienced by candidates related to exam technique. There were three particular problems; failing to read the question sufficiently carefully, failing to address all of the requirements and running over time.

When reading the question, many candidates failed to identify the relevance of the exemption clause in the Double Taxation Agreement. The effect of the clause was to exempt the overseas villa from UK inheritance tax. This meant that, when dealing with the villa, candidates needed only to consider the tax suffered overseas. Those candidates who failed to appreciate this did not lose many marks but wasted time calculating UK inheritance tax on the villa.

The question required calculations of the 'possible reduction in the inheritance tax payable as a result of Una's death' in respect of each of the possible lifetime gifts. This required candidates to compare the tax arising on a lifetime gift with that arising if the asset passed via Una's will for both of the assets. There was then the need to consider the capital gains tax on the lifetime gift whilst remembering that there would be no capital gains tax if the assets were retained until death. Finally, candidates were asked to provide a concise summary of their calculations 'in order to assist Una in making her decision'. The problem was that many candidates were not sufficiently methodical such that they did not carry out all of the necessary tasks and missed out on easy marks. In particular, many candidates did not provide the final summary.

The final problem in relation to exam technique related to time management: it was evident that some candidates did not have a sufficient sense of urgency when answering this question. This resulted in lengthy explanations of how inheritance tax, and, to a lesser extent, capital gains tax, is calculated together with details of Una's plans.

The question asked for 'explanations where the calculations are not self-explanatory, particularly in relation to the availability of reliefs'. Candidates need to think carefully before providing narrative as writing is very time consuming. They should identify, in advance, the points they are planning to make and should then make each point in as concise a manner as possible. There is likely to be a mark for each relevant point so each one should take no more than two short sentences.

Part (b) was done reasonably well. There were two elements to a good answer: the penalties that could be levied on the taxpayer and the professional issues relating to the firm of accountants. The two elements were indicated clearly in the question which stated that 'the letter should explain the implications for Una and our firm'. Those candidates who failed to address both elements struggled to do well.

			Marks
(a)	Calculations		
	Farmland – inheritance tax		
	Owned at death	2	
	Lifetime gift	4	
	Farmland – capital gains tax	1	
	Villa – inheritance tax (Soloria)	1	
	Villa – capital gains tax (UK)	1½	
	Notes on availability of relevant reliefs – one mark each	3	
	Other relevant tax and financial requirements – one mark each	5	
	Relevant assumption	1	
	Summary of position re capital taxes	2	
	Payment of rent	3	
	Max		21
	Professional marks for the overall presentation of the memorandum and the effectiveness with which the information is communicated		3
(b)	Determination of taxable profit	1	
	The need to disclose	4	
	Interest and penalties	3	
	Max		6
	Professional mark for overall presentation of the letter		1
			31

(a) To   The files
From Tax senior
Date   15 June 2016
Subject Una – Gifts to son and granddaughter

The purpose of this memorandum is to provide advice to Una on the tax implications of a gift to be made to her son, Won, and the payment of rent on behalf of her granddaughter, Alona. For the purposes of this memorandum, it has been assumed that the gift to Won will be made on 18 November 2016 and that Una's death will occur on 31 December 2021.

(i) **Gift to Won**

Inheritance tax

Farmland situated in England

If Una owns the farmland at her death it will be included in her death estate. The inheritance tax on the farmland in the death estate will be as follows.

	£
Market value in death estate	1,100,000
Less APR £1,100,000 × 35% (100% of agricultural value)	(385,000)
Value included in death estate	715,000
Inheritance tax @ 40% (nil rate band used by other assets)	286,000

If Una gifts the farmland to Won – it will be a potentially exempt transfer (N1). The death tax in relation to this gift will be as follows:

	£
Market value (N2)	900,000
Less annual exemptions 2016/17 and 2015/16 b/f	(6,000)
Potentially exempt transfer (PET)	894,000
Inheritance tax on death on 31 December 2021	
£325,000 (N3) @ 0%	0
£569,000 @ 40%	227,600
£894,000	227,600
Less taper relief (death within 5 to 6 years of gift) @ 60%	(136,560)
	91,040
Add additional tax on death estate due to use of nil rate band	
£325,000 @ 40%	130,000
Total death tax arising as a result of lifetime gift of farmland	221,040
Potential saving £(286,000 – 221,040)	64,960

Notes

1   There will be no UK inheritance tax when the gift is made as it will be a potentially exempt transfer.

2   Agricultural property relief will not be available in respect of a gift on 18 November 2016 as Una will not have owned the farm for the requisite seven years. This is on the assumption that the farmland did not replace other agricultural property which, together with this farmland, had been owned for seven out of the previous ten years.

3   The gift to Won in 2012 was initially partially exempt (2 annual exemptions) and the remaining value was a PET. The PET element became an exempt transfer when Una survived until May 2019. Therefore the full nil rate band is available against the PET of the farmland.

Villa situated in Soloria

There will be no UK inheritance tax due to the exemption clause in the UK–Soloria Double Taxation Agreement. There will be no inheritance tax in Soloria until Una's death.

The gift will save inheritance tax in Soloria as set out below.

	£
Liability if Una owns the villa at her death on 31 December 2021	170,000
Liability if Una gifts the villa to Won on 18 November 2016	(34,000)
Inheritance tax saved	136,000

Capital gains tax

Farmland situated in England

A gift of the farmland would result in a liability to capital gains tax as set out below. No gift relief would be available as the farmland is an investment (as opposed to a business asset), does not qualify for agricultural property relief, and the gift does not give rise to an immediate charge to inheritance tax. The farmland is not a qualifying asset for entrepreneurs' relief as it is not a business asset.

	£
Proceeds (market value)	900,000
Less cost	(720,000)
Gain	180,000
Capital gains tax @ 28% (Una is a higher rate taxpayer)	50,400

Villa situated in Soloria

A gift of the villa would result in a liability to UK capital gains tax as set out below. The villa is an investment and not a business asset, so no capital gains tax business reliefs would be available. There is no capital gains tax in Soloria.

	£
Proceeds (market value)	745,000
Less cost (probate value)	(600,000)
Gain	145,000
	£
Capital gains tax @ 28% (Una is a higher rate taxpayer)	40,600

Summary of capital taxes position

	Farmland £	Villa £
Inheritance tax – potential saving	64,960	136,000
Capital gains tax – liability	(50,400)	(40,600)
Net tax saving	14,560	95,400

Other tax implications in respect of the gift to Won

Inheritance tax

If Una were to die after 18 November 2022, there would be an additional 20% taper relief in the UK. If she were to survive the gift by seven years, there would be no UK inheritance tax in respect of the asset gifted and the inheritance tax nil rate band would be available against the death estate.

Stamp duty land tax

There is no charge to stamp duty land tax on a gift of land in England. The situation in Soloria would need to be investigated if a gift of the villa is proposed.

Financial implications in respect of the gift to Won

The potential gifts are income generating assets. Accordingly, Una should be aware that the gift will reduce her available income. The income in respect of the villa is subject to income tax in Soloria at the rate of 50%, so no UK income tax is payable due to double tax relief. The income in respect of the farmland is subject to UK income tax at a maximum rate of 40%.

The capital gains tax would be payable on 31 January 2018 (31 January following the end of the tax year in which the gift is made). This is at least four years prior to the eventual inheritance tax saving. Because there is a gift of land but gift relief is not available, it would be possible to pay the capital gains tax in ten equal annual instalments (provided Won continues to own the asset gifted), but interest would be charged on the balance outstanding.

(ii) **Payment of Alona's rent**

The payments will be exempt if they represent normal expenditure out of income. For this exemption to be available, Una would have to show that:

- Each gift is part of her normal expenditure.
- The gifts are made out of income rather than capital.
- Having made the gifts, she still has sufficient income to maintain her usual standard of living.

Una must be able to demonstrate that her annual income exceeds her normal expenditure by the annual rental cost of £450 x 12 = £5,400 (maximum – less if Alona's rent is only payable during university term-time).

(b)

Una's address

15 June 2016

Dear Una

Income received in respect of the luxury motor car

I set out below our advice in relation to the income received in respect of the luxury motor car.

I have considered the circumstances surrounding the rental income in respect of the car and concluded that the profits from the hiring of the car are liable to income tax. In determining the taxable profit, the income you have received can be reduced by the expenses relating to the running and maintenance of the car. We can assist you in determining the taxable profit.

The taxable profit must be reported to HM Revenue and Customs; failure to disclose the profit would amount to tax evasion, which is a criminal offence. In addition, you will appreciate that we would not wish to be associated with a client who has engaged in deliberate tax evasion, as this poses a threat to the fundamental principles of integrity and professional behaviour. Accordingly, we cannot continue to act for you unless you are willing to disclose the hiring activity to HM Revenue and Customs and to pay any ensuing tax liabilities. We are required to notify the tax authorities if we cease to act for you, although we would not provide them with any reason for our action.

HM Revenue and Customs will charge interest on any tax liabilities that are overdue. A penalty may also be charged in respect of the non-declaration of the income. The maximum penalty is 70% of the tax liability for a deliberate non-disclosure of income where there is no attempt to conceal it (for example, by submitting false evidence in support). This penalty may be reduced if the income is disclosed to the authorities at a time when there is no reason to believe that the non-disclosure is about to be discovered and full assistance is provided to the authorities to enable them to quantify the error. The minimum penalty in these circumstances is 20% of the tax liability.

Yours sincerely

Tax manager

17 Kantar (ATAX 12/14)

Text references. Inheritance tax exemptions and lifetime transfers are covered in Chapter 16. The basics of capital gains tax are dealt with in Chapter 11. Trading losses are the subject of Chapter 8. Self assessment for individuals is covered in Chapter 15. Ethics will be found in Chapter 30. Value added tax registration is dealt with in Chapter 28.

Top tips. In part (b)(i) there are a lot of figures involved so it was important to lay out your computations in an orderly manner so that the tax savings could be picked out easily when making the evaluation of which loss relief would be more beneficial.

Easy marks. There were some easy marks in part (a)(i) for describing the small gifts exemption. The ethical points in part (c) should have been well known. The registration requirements in part (d) were basic knowledge from F6.

Examiner's comments. Part (a) was in two parts. Both parts were answered reasonably well but it felt as though many candidates spent too much time on them. This may have been because it was the first question and thus time may not have appeared to be such a pressing issue. However, of course, any overruns on this part would still have caused candidates to run out of time later on in the exam. Part (a) was only worth 8 marks in total and so should have been completed in less than 15 minutes, but some candidates found the time to explain the meaning of potentially exempt transfers, the manner in which they are taxed and the other exemptions that may be available rather than simply addressing the requirements of this particular question part. Candidates will always benefit from answering the specific requirements of the question and from not digressing into other, irrelevant, areas. Part (a)(i) related to inheritance tax and concerned the small gifts exemption and potentially exempt transfers. Candidates' knowledge in this area was satisfactory. The only common error was the failure to identify the fall in value of the donor's estate as a result of the gift. Part (a)(ii) related to capital gains tax and concerned the disposal of a piece of land in two stages. The key issue here was the A/A+B calculation of the cost in respect of the first disposal. The majority of candidates knew that such a calculation was necessary but many did not know exactly how to perform it. In addition, a minority of candidates failed to recognise that the base cost of the whole of the land was its value at the time of the uncle's death.

Part (b)(i) related to a trading loss and required candidates to calculate the tax which would be saved in respect of the offset of the trading loss depending on how the loss was relieved. This part of the question was not tackled particularly well. Many candidates did not know the rules for the offset of trading losses well enough and were unable to determine an approach to answer the question efficiently. As always, it was necessary to think first and decide how to approach the question in order to prepare the required answer. With trading losses there are two main things that candidates need to know; 1) what the losses can be offset against and 2) when. Many candidates did not possess this precise knowledge and others treated the individual taxpayer as a company or made other fundamental errors. Many candidates also failed to make use of the information in the question. In particular, the tax liability for the tax year [2015/16] was given in the question but many candidates calculated it themselves, thus wasting time. A final problem was that some candidates were unwilling to commit themselves to an answer, such that they described some of the issues but did not prepare calculations. This made it difficult for them to score particularly well. Part (b)(ii) concerned payments on account under self-assessment and was not done well. The question required candidates to have a precise knowledge of the manner in which payments of tax under self-assessment are determined and to be able to apply those rules in a chronological manner to the facts of the question and the three tax years concerned. Many candidates had an awareness of the rules but their knowledge was somewhat vague and confused, such that they were unable to apply it to the facts. Some candidates tried to describe the system but this did not satisfy the requirement. Other candidates presented their answers in confusing ways without explaining which tax year and/or which payments they were referring to. For a candidate who knew the rules, this part of the question was not particularly challenging, although it did require thought and care. Unfortunately, very few candidates had sufficient precise knowledge to produce an acceptable answer.

Part (c) was answered well by the majority of candidates. However, the problem here was that many candidates wrote far too much. There were only four marks available, so four decent sentences were sufficient, yet many candidates wrote the best part of a page. Candidates should think before they write and decide on the points they intend to make. They should then make each point concisely, and they should make it only once.

Part (d) concerned VAT registration and the recovery of pre-registration input tax. Answers to this part of the question were generally satisfactory. Candidates' knowledge of the rules regarding VAT registration was generally sound, although some candidates displayed a tendency to write generally rather than to address the specifics of the question. In addition, candidates need to take care to be precise in their use of language and terminology. The historic test relates to supplies in the 'previous 12 months', and not the sales of 'the trading period', and HMRC must be notified 'within 30 days' as opposed to 'within a month'. Candidates' knowledge of the rules regarding the recovery of pre-registration input tax was not as strong as that relating to registration but was still generally of an acceptable standard.

Marking scheme

				Marks
(a)	(i)	Small gifts exemption	1½	
		Potentially exempt transfer	2½	
				4
	(ii)	Chargeable gain: gift 1 February 2016	2	
		Chargeable gain: sale 2 February 2016	1	
		Capital gains tax liability	1	
				4
(b)	(i)	Loss relieved as soon as possible		
		Income tax	1	
		Capital gains tax	3	
		Loss carried forward		
		Taxable incomes	2½	
		Tax liabilities and saving	2	
		£50,000 restriction	1	
		Evaluation	1	
		Explanatory notes	1½	
		Max		10
	(ii)	Payments required if loss carried forward		
		2015/16	2½	
		2016/17	1½	
		2017/18	2	
		Max		5
(c)		Implications for Kantar	2	
		Fundamental principles	1	
		Cease to act	2½	
		Max		4
(d)		When registration required	2	
		VAT incurred prior to registrar	2	
				4
Format and presentation			1	
Analysis			1	
Quality of explanations			1	
Quality of calculations			1	
				4
				35

Notes for meeting

(a) (i) **Inheritance tax**

Small gifts exemption

Outright gifts to individuals totalling £250 or less per donee in any one tax year are exempt. If gifts total more than £250 the whole amount is chargeable. Therefore the small gifts exemption does not apply to the gifts of £400 each to Kantar's nephews.

Potentially exempt transfer on 1 February 2016

	£
Value of the land prior to gift	290,000
Less value of land after gift	(170,000)
Diminution in value (transfer of value)	120,000
Less: annual exemption 2015/16	(3,000)
unused annual exemption 2014/15 b/f £[3,000 – (3 × £400)]	(1,800)
Potentially exempt transfer	115,200

(ii) **Capital gains tax liability for tax year 2015/16**

	£	£
1 February 2016 gift		
Proceeds (market value)	100,000	
Less: cost		
$£200,000 \times \dfrac{100,000}{100,000 + 170,000}$	(74,074)	
Gain		25,926
2 February 2016 sale		
Proceeds	170,000	
Less cost £(200,000 – 74,074)	(125,926)	
Gain		44,074
Chargeable gains		70,000
Less annual exempt amount		(11,100)
Taxable gains		58,900
Capital gains tax £58,900 × 28% (higher rate taxpayer)		16,492

Tutorial note

Rollover relief will not be available in respect of the chargeable gain on the sale of the land, as it is not a business asset.

(b) (i) **Budgeted trading loss for the year ended 31 March 2017**

1 *Loss relieved as soon as possible*

The trading loss can be relieved against general income in the tax year of the loss (2016/17) and the previous tax year (2015/16).

Kantar should not make a claim to relieve the loss in 2016/17 as his only income for this tax year is £5,000 property business income which will be covered by the personal allowance.

If Kantar makes a claim to relieve the loss in 2015/16, he cannot choose the amount of loss to relieve so the loss must be set against income which would be covered by the personal allowance. He would therefore set off £(57,000 + 5,000) = £62,000 of the loss against general income and the tax saving would be the whole tax liability for the tax year 2015/16 of £14,203.

The £50,000 relief cap does not apply to trading income of the same trade and is therefore not relevant to the claim for the tax year 2015/16.

Kantar may include a further claim to set the remaining loss of £(68,000 – 62,000) = £6,000 against his chargeable gains for the tax year 2015/16. Also, since Kantar has no taxable income following loss relief against general income, his basic rate band is now available to be set against the taxable gains. The capital gains tax saved is £4,859 as shown below.

	£
Chargeable gains (part (a)(ii))	70,000
Less loss relief	(6,000)
	64,000
Less annual exempt amount	(11,100)
Taxable gains	52,900
Capital gains tax	
£31,785 × 18%	5,721
£(52,900 – 31,785) = £21,115 × 28%	5,912
	11,633
Capital gains tax saving £(16,492 (part (a)(ii)) – 11,633)	4,859

The total tax saving would therefore be £(14,203 + 4,859) = £19,062

2   *Loss carried forward for future relief*

The loss would be set against Kantar's trading income for the tax year 2017/18. The tax saving would be £23,523 as shown below.

	Without loss relief	With loss relief
	£	£
Trading income 2017/18		
£(83,000 + 4,000)	87,000	87,000
Less trading loss brought forward		(68,000)
		19,000
Property business income	5,000	5,000
Net income	92,000	24,000
Less personal allowance	(10,600)	(10,600)
Taxable income	81,400	13,400
Income tax		
£31,785/£13,400 × 20%	6,357	2,680
£(81,400 – 31,785) = £49,615 × 40%	19,846	
	26,203	2,680
Income tax saving £(26,203 – 2,680)		23,523

Carrying forward the loss would therefore increase the tax saving. However, Kantar cannot be certain that he will make the budgeted profit in the year to 31 March 2018. The tax saving will also be delayed.

(ii)   **Future tax payments if loss carried forward**

	Notes	£
2015/16		
Balancing payment 31 January 2017		
Income tax £(14,203 – 8,827)	1	5,376
Capital gains tax (part (a)(ii))		16,492
		21,868

	Notes	£
2016/17		
Payments on account	2	0
Balancing payment		0
2017/18		
Payments on account	3	0
Balancing payment 31 January 2019 (part (b)(i)(2))		2,680

Notes

1 Kantar will have made payments on account equal to his tax liability for the previous tax year (2014/15).

2 Kantar should make a claim to reduce his payments on account to nil as he does not expect to have any tax liability for 2016/17.

3 Kantar will not have to make any payments on account for the tax year 2017/18 as he will not have a tax liability for the tax year 2016/17.

(c) **Reporting of chargeable gains**

Kantar may be liable to interest and penalties (based on potential lost revenue) if he does not report his chargeable gains to HM Revenue and Customs (HMRC).

The evasion or attempted evasion of tax by Kantar may also be the subject of criminal charges under both tax law and money laundering legislation. We may need to submit a report under the money laundering rules.

Our firm must not be associated with a client who has deliberately evaded tax as this is against the ACCA fundamental principles of integrity and professional behaviour.

We should not continue to act for Kantar if he does not agree to disclose the chargeable gains to HMRC. If he does not agree to disclosure, we are still under a professional duty to ensure that he understands the seriousness of offences against HMRC.

If we do cease to act for Kantar, we must inform HMRC of this cessation but not the reasons for it. We should advise Kantar that the notification that we are no longer acting for him may alert HMRC that tax irregularities have taken place and urge on Kantar the desirability of making a full disclosure.

(d) **Value added tax (VAT)**

Kantar will be liable to register for VAT if the value of his cumulative taxable supplies (excluding VAT) exceeds £82,000 in any 12 month period. At the end of every month he must therefore calculate his cumulative turnover of taxable supplies to date. Kantar is required to notify HMRC within 30 days of the end of the month in which the £82,000 limit is exceeded.

VAT incurred before registration can be treated as input tax and recovered from HMRC subject to certain conditions. For input tax on goods purchased prior to registration the following conditions apply:

- Acquired for the purposes of business carried on by Kantar at the time of supply
- Not supplied onwards or consumed before the date of registration
- Input tax incurred in the four years prior to the date of registration

For input tax on the supply of services prior to registration the following conditions apply.

- Supplied for the purposes of business carried on by Kantar at the time of supply
- Input tax incurred in the six months prior to the date of registration

Tutorial note

The recovery of input tax will reduce the expenses incurred by the business. It will also reduce the cost of the equipment purchased in the year ending 31 March 2017 for the purposes of capital allowances.

18 Kesme and Soba (ATAX 06/14)

Text references. Property income and the accrued income scheme is covered in Chapter 3 and taxable income in Chapter 1. Principal private residence relief is dealt with in Chapter 14. Overseas aspects of inheritance tax are covered in Chapter 18.

Top tips. In part (b) it would be useful to structure your answer using bullet points to make sure that you cover all the relevant issues.

Easy marks. There were easy marks in part (a) for a basic computation of taxable income. The rules about PPR relief and letting relief in part (b) should have been well known from F6.

Examiner's comments. Part (a) required an explanation of the availability and operation of rent-a-room relief together with a calculation of an individual's taxable income. The basics of rent-a-room relief were reasonably well-known by many candidates. However, a minority thought that the £4,250 could be deducted in addition to expenses incurred as opposed to instead of those expenses. Also, many candidates neglected to divide the £4,250 between the two owners of the property. Very few candidates mentioned the need to make an election for the relief to apply. The calculation of the individual's taxable income was done well by the majority of candidates. The interest arising in respect of the loan stock was not handled particularly well with the majority of candidates failing to recognise that the accrued income scheme applied, such that ten months of interest needed to be included.

Part (b) was more challenging. It required candidates to consider the effect of renting out part of the family home on the amount of the taxable capital gain on a future sale of the home. Almost all candidates realised that this required them to consider the principal private residence exemption but many were not sufficiently methodical in their approach. The main area of difficulty related to thinking about the whole of the period over which the property will have been owned as opposed to just the period during which the property will have been let. The period of ownership should be split into three parts: the period prior to letting (wholly exempt), the last 18 months of ownership (wholly exempt) and the period in between (70% exempt). Very few candidates addressed these three periods in a clear manner. There was then the need to consider the letting exemption. Most candidates recognised the need to refer to this exemption and their knowledge of it was satisfactory. However, a minority of candidates did not mention the exemption at all.

The final part of the question concerned inheritance tax and was done reasonably well. It required an explanation of the implications of electing to be treated as UK domiciled for the purposes of inheritance tax and a calculation of the residue of an estate. The explanation of the election required two main points to be made: the effect on the spouse exemption and the fact that overseas assets would become subject to UK inheritance tax. Many candidates identified both of these points, although a minority wrote about the remittance basis, which did not have any relevance here. The calculation aspect of the question was more challenging than the explanations and very few candidates did particularly well. The difficulty was that most candidates wanted to calculate an inheritance tax liability when what was required was a calculation of the residue. The residue was calculated by deducting the legacy to the daughter and the inheritance tax liability from the estate. So a calculation of the inheritance tax liability was a necessary step on the way but was not an end in itself. The calculation of the inheritance tax liability also required the gift to the daughter to be grossed up because the residue of the estate was exempt. Very few candidates identified this point but it was possible to score a very good mark without it.

Marking scheme

		Marks
(a)	Rent a room relief	
	Availability	1
	Operation	1½
	Claim	1½
	Pension income	1
	Property business income	½
	8% loan stock	2
	Personal allowance	½
		8

			Marks
(b)	Situation prior to letting rooms	1	
	Principal private residence exemption	3	
	Letting exemption	3	
		Max	6
(c)	Election to be treated as UK domiciled	2½	
	Value of residue		
	Calculation of amount received by Soba	1½	
	Inheritance tax liability	2	
			6
			20

(a)   Income tax

Availability and operation of rent a room relief

Rent a room relief is relevant because Kesme and Soba are letting furnished rooms in their main residence. The limit for each of them is £4,250/2 = £2,125.

Since gross rents exceed the limit, Kesme and Soba would be taxed under the normal property business income rules unless they elect for the 'alternative basis'. If they so elect, they will each be taxable on gross receipts less £2,125, with no deductions for expenses.

An election for the alternative basis must be made by 31 January 2018 (22 months after the end of the tax year 2015/16). The election will then continue to apply until it is withdrawn.

Tutorial note

The election would also cease to apply in the unlikely event that the gross annual rent fell below £4,250.

Taxable income for the tax year 2015/16

	£
State retirement pension	7,900
Pension from former employer	24,515
Property business income (W1)	5,075
8% loan stock interest (W2)	1,200
Net income	38,690
Less personal allowance	(10,600)
Taxable income	28,090

Workings

1   *Property business income*

	£
Income receivable £14,400/2	7,200
Less rent a room limit	(2,125)
Assessable income	5,075

2   *Loan stock interest*

	£
Interest received 31 May 2015	
£18,000 × 8% × 6/12	720
Accrued interest deemed received 30 September 2015	
£18,000 × 8% × 4/12	480
Interest assessable	1,200

Tutorial note

Kesme has sold the loan stock cum interest. Under the accrued income scheme, Kesme will be treated as having received interest for the period from 1 June 2015 to 30 September 2015.

(b)   **Capital gain on the eventual sale of the family home**

No chargeable gain arises on the sale of a house which has always been occupied by its owner due to the availability of principal private residence (PPR) relief. Therefore if the rooms were not rented out, no chargeable gain would arise on the eventual sale of the family home.

However, following the renting out of the furnished rooms, part of the property (30%) is no longer occupied by Kesme and Soba, so a chargeable gain may arise on the eventual sale. This chargeable gain will be calculated as follows:

- The initial gain is the excess of the sales proceeds over the original cost. This will then be reduced by PPR relief and the letting exemption.

- PPR relief is calculated by assuming that the gain has accrued evenly over the period of ownership from 1 July 1992 until the sale of the property. It exempts the total of the following:

    - 100% of the gain which accrued from 1 July 1992 until 5 April 2015 (ie the period up to the date on which the rooms were first rented out), and

    - 70% (the proportion of the property occupied by Kesme and Soba) of the gain which accrued from 6 April 2015 until the date 18 months before the date of sale, and

    - 100% of the gain which accrued during the last eighteen months of ownership.

- That part of the gain not covered by PPR relief (ie the 30% of the gain which accrued during the period from 6 April 2015 until the date eighteen months prior to the date of sale) is then reduced by letting relief. This is equal to the lowest of:

    - PPR relief as calculated above.
    - Gain attributable to the letting.
    - £40,000.

    The letting exemption cannot convert a gain into an allowable loss.

(c)   **Soba**

Election to be treated as UK domiciled

This election will remove the limit (equal to the nil band of £325,000) on the spouse exemption which would otherwise apply on transfers from Kesme to Soba.

However, it will also mean that any overseas assets owned by Soba will be subject to UK inheritance tax in the future as they will no longer be excluded property for inheritance tax purposes.

Tutorial note

The limit of £325,000 on the spouse exemption applies where the transferor spouse is UK domiciled and the transferee spouse is non-UK domiciled.

Value of the residue of the estate

Soba will receive the residue of the estate, ie the estate less the gift to the daughter and the inheritance tax on that gift. The inheritance tax is calculated as follows:

	£
£325,000 @ 0%	0
£ 45,000 @ 40/60	30,000
£370,000	30,000

The gross transfer is £(370,000 + 30,000) = £400,000.

The residue available to Soba is £(1,280,000 – 400,000) = £880,000.

Tutorial note

The inheritance tax due on the specific gift to the daughter will be paid out of the residue of the estate, such that it will be borne by Soba. Because the residue of the estate is exempt, due to the spouse exemption, the gift must be grossed up.

19 Pescara (ATAX 12/13)

Text references. Valuation of quoted shares for IHT purposes and the transfer of the nil rate band are covered in Chapter 17. Lifetime transfers of value are dealt with in Chapter 16. The basic chargeable gains computation, the annual exempt amount, rates of capital gains tax and the valuation of quoted shares for CGT purposes will be found in Chapter 11. Capital gains tax on disposals of shares, including takeovers, are covered in Chapter 12. EIS relief is covered in Chapter 2 and Chapter 13. Gifts with reservation of benefit are dealt with in Chapter 18.

Top tips. Where the nil rate band from a deceased spouse is transferred, account must be taken of the increase in the amount of the nil rate band between the date of death of the first spouse and the date of death of the second spouse.

Easy marks. There were some easy marks in part (a) for a basic inheritance tax computation on a potentially exempt transfer. The rules about gifts with reservation of benefit in part (c) should have been well known.

Examiner's comments. In part (a) the majority of candidates performed well and scored high marks. Less well-prepared candidates were unable to value the shares in Sepang plc and/or the amount of the nil rate band to be transferred from the donor's deceased husband. This was because they either did not know the rules or were unable to apply them to the facts in the question. Some candidates failed to identify that the husband's nil rate band was available for transfer.

Part (b) concerned capital gains tax and was in two parts; neither part was done particularly well.

Part (b)(i) required a calculation of the tax due on the sale of shares. The shares had been acquired via gift and had then been the subject of a share for share takeover and a bonus issue. Accordingly, the calculation of the base cost required a certain amount of work. It was first necessary to realise that, due to the fact that gift relief was not claimed on the original gift (the question stated that gift relief was not available), the base cost of the original shares was their market value [calculated for CGT purposes] at the time of the gift. Following the takeover, this original cost had to be split between the new shares and cash received by reference to the market value of the consideration. Finally, the bonus issue increased the number of shares but had no effect on the total base cost. A significant number of candidates lost marks here because they side-stepped the first two stages of this calculation by attributing a cost to the new shares equal to their market value at the time of the takeover. The majority of candidates had no problem with the bonus issue. When calculating the amount subject to capital gains tax it was necessary to deduct EIS deferral relief equal to the whole of the £50,000 invested in EIS shares. Many candidates confused this relief with the relief available in respect of income tax when EIS shares are acquired.

Part (b)(ii) required a statement of the capital gains tax implications of the future sale of the EIS shares. The first problem that some candidates had here was that they answered the question by reference to income tax rather than capital gains tax. Many of those who did address capital gains tax did not score as many marks as they might have done because they were not methodical in their approach. It was important to (briefly) consider four possible situations, i.e. sale of the shares at a profit or a loss both within and after the three-year period.

Part (c) was not done particularly well as those candidates who clearly had some knowledge did not pay sufficient attention to the requirement. The question asked how the gift would be treated for the purposes of calculating the inheritance tax due on death. This required consideration of the value to be used, whether or not the reservation was lifted prior to death and the relief available in order to avoid double taxation. Many candidates wrote more broadly about gifts with reservation, explaining the rationale behind the rules and the actions necessary in order for the reservation to be lifted. These generalisations did not score any marks.

Marking scheme

		Marks
(a)	Value of shares	2
	Annual exemptions	1
	Nil rate band	2½
	Inheritance tax liability	1½
		7

				Marks
(b)	(i)	Proceeds less cost	4	
		EIS deferral relief, annual exempt amount and liability	2	
				6
	(ii)	Zolder plc	1	
		EIS shares	3½	
		Max		3
(c)		Initial gift	1	
		Reservation lifted within seven years	1½	
		Reservation in place at death	1	
		Double taxation avoidance	1½	
		Max		4
				20

(a) **Marina – Inheritance tax payable in respect of the gift of the shares in Sepang plc**

	£
Value of shares: 375,000 × £1.86 (W1)	697,500
Less: annual exemption 2011/12	(3,000)
annual exemption 2010/11 b/f	(3,000)
Potentially exempt transfer now chargeable	691,500

	£
£476,667 (W2) @ 0%	0
£214,833 @ 40%	85,933
£691,500	85,933
Less taper relief (4 to 5 years) @ 40%	(34,373)
Death tax payable	51,560

Workings

1   *Value of shares in Sepang plc for IHT purposes as at 1 February 2012*

Quarter up £1.84 + ([1.96 – 1.84]/4)	£1.87
Average highest and lowest marked bargains £[1.80 + 1.92]/2)	£1.86
Lower of quarter up and average bargains	£1.86

2   *Nil rate band available*

	£	£
Nil rate band: Marina		325,000
Nil rate band: Galvez 2007/08	300,000	
Less legacies to Pescara/brother 2 × £80,000	(160,000)	
	140,000	
Increase pro-rata		
$\frac{£325,000}{£300,000} \times £140,000$		151,667
Total nil rate band available to Marina		476,667

(b) (i) **Pescara – Capital gains tax liability for the tax year 2016/17**

	£
Proceeds: sale of 1,000,000 shares in Zolder plc	445,000
Less cost (W)	(275,362)
Chargeable gain c/f	169,638

	£
Chargeable gain b/f	169,638
Less: EIS deferral relief	(50,000)
annual exempt amount	(11,100)
Taxable gain	108,538
Capital gains tax @ 28%	30,391

Workings

1   *Base cost of 1,000,000 shares in Zolder plc*

	Number	*Cost* £
Sepang plc shares – MV of gift 375,000 × £1.90 (W2)	375,000	712,500
Zolder plc shares		
Cost of new shares $\frac{£2}{£2+£0.30} \times £712,500$	750,000	619,565
Bonus issue 2 for 1	1,500,000	0
	2,250,000	619,565
Disposal $\frac{1,000,000}{2,250,000} \times £619,565$	(1,000,000)	(275,362)
C/f	1,250,000	344,203

2   *Value of shares in Sepang plc for CGT purposes as at 1 February 2012*

£1.84 + ([1.96 – 1.84]/2)   £1.90

(ii)   **Pescara – Capital gains tax implications of selling the EIS shares**

The gain deferred in respect of the sale of the shares in Zolder plc will be chargeable in the year the EIS shares are sold.

If the EIS shares are disposed of within the minimum holding period (usually three years from the date of issue), any gain on the EIS shares is computed in the normal way. If the shares are disposed of after the end of the minimum holding period, any gain is exempt from CGT.

If EIS shares are disposed of at a loss at any time, the loss is allowable but the acquisition cost of the shares is reduced by the amount of EIS income tax relief attributable to the shares which has not been withdrawn on sale.

(c)   **Pescara – Gift of a UK property**

The gift of a property will be a potentially exempt transfer (PET). The value of this PET will be the market value of the property at the time of the gift less any available annual exemptions.

The amount which will be subject to inheritance tax in respect of this gift with reservation depends on whether or not the reservation of benefit ceases before Pescara dies, for example if she stops using the property rent-free.

(i)   If the reservation ceases within the seven years before Pescara's death, then the gift is treated as a PET made at the time the reservation ceased. The charge is based on its value at that time. Annual exemptions cannot be used against such a PET.

(ii)   If the reservation still exists at the date of Pescara's death, the asset is included in her death estate at its value at that time (not its value at the date the gift was made).

Where Pescara dies within seven years of the original PET such that the gift is taxable as a PET when made, as well as taxed under (i) or (ii) above, it will be taxed either as a PET when made, or, under (i) or (ii), (but not both), whichever gives the higher total tax.

20 Mirtoon (ATAX 12/11)

Text references. Chargeable gains in outline are covered in Chapter 11 and Chapter 14 deals with principal private residence relief. Entrepreneurs' relief and gift relief are covered in Chapter 13. Trading losses are dealt with in Chapter 8, the basis period in Chapter 6, and the basic income tax computation in Chapter 1. VAT deregistration is covered in Chapter 28. Overseas aspects of income tax and capital gains are dealt with in Chapters 10 and 14 respectively. Associated operations and gifts with reservation of benefit will be found in Chapter 18.

Top tips. In scenario questions such as this, it is important to identify all the relevant information for each requirement which may appear in different parts of the question. For example, in this question, the overlap profits could have been overlooked as they were contained in the background information, whereas the remainder of the information about trading losses was in the extract from the email from Mirtoon.

Easy marks. The computations in this question were relatively uncomplicated. In part (b), the basic rules concerning gifts with reservation with benefit should have produced easy marks provided that your explanation was clear and succinct.

Examiner's comments. Part (a) concerned Mirtoon's financial position in view of his plans to sell his house, cease his business and leave the UK. It required a calculation of the total proceeds generated by the proposed transactions.

The sale of the house was handled well with almost all candidates identifying the availability of principal private residence relief and the need to restrict the relief to 80% of the gain arising. The crystallisation of the heldover gain in respect of the agricultural land (due to Mirtoon becoming non-resident), on the other hand, was spotted by only a small minority of candidates. However, this was an easy point to miss and it was possible to obtain a perfectly good mark without any reference to it.

The treatment of the losses arising on the cessation of the business was not handled well due to a lack of knowledge of the closing year rules. This meant that many candidates struggled to determine the assessment for the final years of trading. There were also a considerable number of candidates who erroneously treated the overlap profits brought forward as taxable profits in the final tax year as opposed to being part of the allowable loss. The unincorporated trader is examined with great regularity and candidates are likely to benefit from knowing, in particular, the opening and closing years rules.

A minority of candidates demonstrated a lack of precision when considering the tax due in respect of the sale of the house and the tax saving in respect of the offset of the trading losses. This lack of precision included a failure to take account of the capital losses brought forward and/or the annual exempt amount and the omission of the personal allowance from the income tax computations. It was important to consider the personal allowance as Mirtoon's income exceeded £100,000 such that the personal allowance was restricted.

Part (b) was in three parts and produced a wide variety of answers.

Part (i) concerned the VAT implications of Mirtoon ceasing to trade. This part was done reasonably well, although, perhaps not as well as expected. Some candidates made it hard for themselves by writing generally rather than addressing the facts of the question. In particular, many candidates wrote at length about the sale of a business as a going concern. However the question made it clear that the business was to cease with the assets then being sold. The vast majority of candidates identified the need to deregister. However, a considerably smaller number pointed out the possible need to account for output tax on business assets owned as at cessation.

Part (ii) concerned Mirtoon's liability to income tax and capital gains tax whilst living overseas. There were some good answers to this part but also two particular areas of confusion.

The first area of confusion related to the taxation of income where an individual is not resident in the UK. It needs to be recognised that where an individual is not resident in the UK, any foreign income will not be subject to UK income tax. Where many candidates went wrong was to imagine that the remittance basis was relevant here. This led candidates to write at length about the remittance basis thus wasting time.

The second area of confusion concerned the temporary non-resident rules. These rules relate to capital gains tax and cause gains that would otherwise not be taxable in the UK to be so taxable if the individual is non-UK resident for less than five years. However, a minority of candidates incorrectly treated these rules as an extension of the residency rules as they relate to income tax.

Part (iii) concerned two areas of inheritance tax; associated operations and gifts with reservation. The good news was that the vast majority of candidates knew all about gifts with reservation and answered this part of the question well. Knowledge of associated operations was less common but this was to be expected. The bad news, however, was that many candidates did not restrict their answers to the above two areas but wrote at length about inheritance tax generally. Candidates must take care in identifying what has been asked and try to avoid addressing other areas.

Marking scheme

					Marks
(a)	Sale of house				
		Capital gain		½	
		Principal private residence relief		1	
		Capital gains tax		1½	
	Agricultural land			2½	
	Trading losses				
		Loss available for relief		2	
		Tax relief		4	
	Total proceeds net of tax adjustments			2	
	Explanatory notes (1 mark each – maximum 4 marks)			4	
			Max		17
(b)	(i)	Requirement to deregister		1½	
		Output tax		2	
			Max		3
	(ii)	Status		2½	
		Income tax		1½	
		Capital gains tax		5	
			Max		7
	(iii)	Associated operations		2½	
		Gift with reservation		5	
			Max		6
Approach to problem solving				1	
Appropriate style and presentation				1	
Effectiveness of communication				1	
					3
					36

(a) Mirtoon's financial position

	£
Proceeds from sale of home	850,000
Capital gains tax in respect of sale of home (W1)	(6,200)
Capital gains tax in respect of agricultural land (W2)	(16,184)
Proceeds from sale of business assets	14,000
Income tax relief in respect of trading losses £(42,507 – 20,427)(W3)	22,080
Total after tax proceeds	863,696

Workings

1   *Capital gains tax in respect of the sale of the house*

	£
Sale proceeds	850,000
Less cost	(540,000)
Gain	310,000

	£
Capital gain in respect of business use £310,000 × 20% (N1)	62,000
Capital gains tax £62,000 × 10% (N2)	6,200

Notes

1   The capital gain on the disposal of an individual's principal private residence is exempt from tax. However, where part of the house has been used exclusively for business purposes an equal proportion of the gain is subject to tax.

2   The gain in respect of the business use of the house will qualify for entrepreneurs' relief. The relief is available because the house will be in use for the purposes of the business at the time at which the business ceases, the business has been owned for at least one year and the disposal will be within three years of the date of cessation. Accordingly, the rate of tax is 10%.

2   *Capital gains tax in respect of agricultural land*

	£
Chargeable gain held over subject to tax in 2016/17 (N1)	72,900
Less: capital losses brought forward (N2)	(4,000)
annual exempt amount (N2)	(11,100)
Gain	57,800
Capital gains tax £57,800 × 28% (N3)	16,184

Notes

1   Where an individual becomes non-resident within six years of receiving a gift in respect of which gift relief was claimed, the capital gain held over will become subject to capital gains tax immediately prior to his/her departure from the UK. Accordingly, the held over gain on the agricultural land will become chargeable in January 2017 and will be taxed in the year 2016/17.

2   The capital losses and the annual exempt amount can be deducted from Mirtoon's capital gains in the most tax-efficient manner. Accordingly, they will be deducted from gains that would otherwise be taxed at 28%.

3   The taxable interest income in 2016/17 together with the capital gains qualifying for entrepreneurs' relief will clearly exceed the basic rate band such that all other capital gains will be taxed at 28%.

3   *Income tax relief in respect of trading losses*

	£
Loss in the year ended 30 June 2016	20,000
Loss in the six months ending 31 December 2016	17,000
Overlap relief	7,600
Loss for the tax year 2016/17 (N1)	44,600

Income tax liability for 2015/16

	Original £	Loss relief £
Trading income	90,000	90,000
Interest income £25,728 × 100/80	32,160	32,160
Total income	122,160	122,160
Less loss relief against general income	–	(44,600)
Net income	122,160	77,560
Less personal allowance (N2)	–	(10,600)
Taxable income	122,160	66,960

Tax

	Original £	Loss relief £
Taxable income – no loss relief		
£31,785 × 20%	6,357	
£(122,160 – 31,785) = £90,375 × 40%	36,150	
Taxable income – after loss relief		
£31,785 × 20%		6,357
£(66,960 – 31,785) = £35,175 × 40%		14,070
Income tax liability	42,507	20,427

Notes

1   The basis period for 2016/17 runs from the end of the basis period for the previous tax year until the date of cessation, ie from 1 July 2015 until 31 December 2016. The loss will be increased by the unrelieved overlap profits.

2   An individual's personal allowance is reduced by £1 for every £2 by which adjusted net income exceeds £100,000. Accordingly, with adjusted net income of over £121,200, Mirtoon will have no personal allowance.

Tutorial note

The interest income does not fall within the starting rate limit. Accordingly, there is no need to distinguish between the trading income and the interest income when computing the income tax liability as the rates of income tax will be the same.

(b)

Firm's address

Mirtoon's address

9 December 2016

Dear Mirtoon

Departure from the UK

I set out below our advice in respect of the value added tax (VAT) consequences of your cessation of business and the tax implications of your departure from the UK.

(i)   **VAT on the cessation of your business**

You must notify HM Revenue and Customs of the cessation of your business within 30 days of your ceasing to make taxable supplies, ie by 30 January 2017. You may be charged a penalty if you fail to do so.

You should charge VAT on any machinery and inventory that you sell whilst still registered for VAT. When you deregister you will need to account for output tax on all business assets that you still own in respect of which you have previously recovered input tax. There is no need to account for this output tax if it is less than £1,000.

(ii)   **Liability to UK income tax and capital gains tax whilst living in Koro**

In 2016/17 you will be UK resident. This is because you do not meet any of the automatic overseas tests to be non-resident and you do meet one of the automatic UK tests of residence (being in the UK that year for 183 days or more). However, because you are leaving the UK to work full-time overseas, you are able to treat the year of departure as split into two parts, a UK part and an overseas part. You are treated as though you are non-UK resident during the overseas part (ie from 15 January to 5 April 2017). You will then be non-UK resident in the following tax years while you remain overseas.

Income tax

Generally, UK source income is subject to income tax regardless of the residence status of the individual. However, where you are non-UK resident in a tax year, your liability on your bank interest will be limited to the tax deducted at source. Further, by declaring your non-UK resident tax status to the bank you will be able to receive future interest gross, without deduction of tax such that you will not suffer any UK tax on your bank interest.

Whilst you are non-UK resident you will not be subject to UK income tax on any of your overseas income.

Capital gains tax

Generally, individuals who are not resident in the UK are not subject to UK capital gains tax. However, temporary non-residents who realise capital gains whilst non-UK resident, in respect of assets acquired when they were still UK resident, are subject to capital gains tax in the tax year when they become UK resident again.

You will be regarded as a temporary non-resident if you are not UK resident for less than five years. This is because you have been resident in the UK for at least four of the seven tax years prior to the tax year of departure from the UK.

Accordingly, if you become UK resident again before 15 January 2022, any gains you make whilst you were non-UK resident in respect of assets you owned when you ceased to be UK resident, for example your agricultural land, will be subject to UK tax on your return to the UK. If you did become UK resident in 2021/22, it may be possible to split that tax year into an overseas part and a UK part, as in the year of departure.

(iii)   **Inheritance tax planning**

I summarise below the inheritance tax anti-avoidance rules you will need to be aware of when we discuss your inheritance tax planning ideas.

Associated operations

A scheme involving a series of transactions that seeks to reduce the value of a gift may be caught by the rules relating to associated operations. The definition of associated operations is quite broad but may be summarised as:

*   Two or more operations which affect the same property.

*   Where one operation is carried out by reference to a second operation or in order to enable the second operation to be carried out.

Where the rules apply, the series of transactions will be regarded as a single gift at the time of the final transaction in the series such that the total value transferred will be subject to tax.

Gifts with reservation

A donor of a gift who retains some interest in the asset transferred may be caught by the rules concerning gifts with reservation. A gift with reservation occurs where:

*   Possession and enjoyment of the property is not genuinely obtained by the donee.
*   The property given is not enjoyed virtually to the entire exclusion of the donor.

A gift will not be treated as a gift with reservation where:

- The donor gives full consideration for the benefit retained.

- In respect of a gift of land, the donor is an elderly or infirm relative of the donee and, due to an unforeseeable change in circumstances, there is a need for a benefit to be provided to the donor in the form of reasonable care and maintenance.

Where the rules apply:

- If the reservation is removed in the seven years prior to the death of the donor, the asset will be treated as having been gifted at the time the reservation is removed.

- If the reservation is not removed prior to the donor's death, the asset will be included in the donor's death estate at its value as at the time of death.

Provisions exist to ensure that the gift of the asset is not taxed twice, for example, at the time of the original gift and again at the time of death.

Please do not hesitate to contact me if you require any further information.

Yours sincerely

Tax manager

21 Cada (ATAX 12/14)

Text references. The implications of lifetime transfers for inheritance tax are dealt with in Chapter 16. The death estate is covered in Chapter 17. The inheritance tax implications of altering dispositions made on death are dealt with in Chapter 18 and the capital gains aspects in Chapter 13. Capital losses are covered in Chapter 11 and negligible value claims in Chapter 14.

Top tips. In part (b) you can save some time by working out the original inheritance tax liability (based on the original gift to charity) and the reduced inheritance tax liability (based on the increased gift to charity) side by side.

Easy marks. There were some easy marks in part (a) for explaining taper relief. In part (d) the explanation of losses should have been straightforward.

Examiner's comments. Part (a) required candidates to explain the inheritance tax advantages that would have arisen if the deceased had made additional lifetime gifts. The first thing to note here was that this part of the question concerned inheritance tax and not capital gains tax. The question also stated that candidates should not consider lifetime exemptions, for example the annual exemption. Many candidates did not identify these important points and thus wrote about both of these areas rather than focussing on the question requirements. In addition, many candidates wrote at length about business property relief. This was not relevant because business property relief is available in respect of both lifetime gifts and the death estate and thus additional lifetime gifts by the deceased would not have resulted in additional relief. Other candidates were of the opinion that lifetime gifts will reduce the value of the death estate (true) and therefore reduce the inheritance tax due on death (not necessarily true). These candidates had failed to recognise the inheritance tax due in respect of potentially exempt transfers in the seven years prior to death (which these transfers inevitably would be due to the facts of the question). Most candidates would have benefited from reading the question more carefully (and, for example, ignoring the annual exemption) and thinking more (thus recognising that business property relief was not relevant) and then writing a shorter answer that may very well have scored more marks. Having said that, the majority of candidates correctly identified taper relief as an advantage of lifetime gifts and many explained the concept of value freezing. However, very few candidates were able to explain fall in value relief correctly.

Part (b) required candidates to calculate the increase in the legacy to charity that would be necessary for the reduced rate of inheritance tax to apply. Candidates appeared to be well-prepared for a question on this area of the syllabus and this part was answered particularly well with the exception of a very small minority who were simply not aware of the new rules regarding the 36% rate of tax.

Part (c) concerned the inheritance and capital gains tax advantages of varying the terms of the taxpayer's will and the procedures necessary to achieve a valid variation. The tax advantages are not obscure, but they do require some thought and they are not particularly easy to explain. Candidates would have benefited from slowing down and thinking about how best to express what they wanted to say rather than writing in the hope that the necessary words would eventually appear on the page. As always, candidates had to apply their knowledge to the facts in the question. As far as capital gains tax was concerned, many candidates knew that there was no capital gains tax on death but failed to think about the potentially undesirable implication of the proposed gift of the house and how that implication could be avoided. In respect of inheritance tax, many candidates saw that this was linked to generation skipping but mentioning the term 'generation skipping' was not in itself sufficient. Candidates had to explain that the variation would avoid the need for Raymer to make a potentially exempt transfer and therefore removed the possibility of such a transfer being chargeable to inheritance tax in the event that Raymer died within seven years of making the gift. The majority of candidates were able to explain the procedures necessary in order to achieve a valid variation of the terms of the will.

Part (d) was slightly more challenging and was, again, based on the specific facts of the question. It concerned capital gains tax and the beneficial actions that could have been taken in respect of the individual's shareholdings. Many candidates were unsure of the answer to this question despite having sufficient knowledge to deal with it. Unfortunately, instead of calmly thinking about it, they wrote about various aspects of capital gains tax, and inheritance tax, until they ran out of time. In particular, many candidates wrote about using any unused annual exempt amount despite being told in the question that the individual paid capital gains tax every year. The key issue here was that, because there is no capital gains tax on death, any unrealised losses in respect of shares worth less than cost are lost. Candidates simply had to point out, for example, that the quoted shares that were valued at less than cost at the time of death should have been sold prior to death in order to realise a loss that could then have been offset against chargeable gains.

Marking scheme

				Marks
(a)	Value of lifetime transfer		1	
	Relief for fall in value		1	
	Taper relief availability		1	
	Taper relief: effect		1½	
		Max		4
(b)	Original liability		2½	
	Revised gift to charity		2½	
	Net saving		1	
		Max		5
(c)	Additional gift to charity		1	
	House		3½	
	Procedure for variation		2	
		Max		6
(d)	No relief for losses accrued at death		1	
	Realisation of losses on FR plc shares		1	
	Negligible value claim on KZ Ltd shares		2	
	Use of losses		2	
		Max		5
				20

(a) Inheritance tax advantages of additional lifetime gifts

If Cada had made additional lifetime gifts of quoted shares between 1 December 2012 and her death, the transfers of value would have been based on the value of the quoted shares at the date of the gifts, rather than their value at the date of Cada's death. Therefore, although the transfers of value would be chargeable to inheritance tax because Cada died within seven years of making them, if the shares had increased in value between the lifetime transfers and her death that increase would not be subject to inheritance tax.

In addition, if the shares had fallen in value between the date the lifetime transfers and her death, fall in value relief could be claimed in computing the lifetime transfers of value chargeable at death.

Taper relief of 20% would also apply to the death tax on the additional gifts if they were made between 1 December 2012 and 20 November 2013 (three to four years before Cada's death) and to the extent that they exceeded the nil rate band available, taking into account transfers in the seven years before the additional gift.

(b) **Additional gift to charity**

	Original gift to charity £	Increased gift to charity £
Assets owned at death	1,000,000	1,000,000
Less: original gift to charity	(60,000)	
increased gift to charity		
£(1,000,000 – 220,000) × 10%	_____	(78,000)
Chargeable estate	940,000	922,000
Inheritance tax		
£220,000 × 0%	0	0
£(940,000 – 220,000) = £720,000 × 40%	288,000	
£(922,000 – 220,000) = £702,000 × 36%	_____	252,720
	288,000	252,720
Additional gift to charity £(78,000 – 60,000)		18,000
Reduction in inheritance tax £(288,000 – 252,720)		35,280

Tutorial note

There is a reduced rate of inheritance tax (36%, rather than 40%) available on the chargeable death estate if Cada gifts at least 10% of her net estate to charity. For the purpose of determining whether the 10% condition is met, the net estate is calculated as the assets owned at death as reduced by liabilities, exemptions, reliefs and the available nil rate band, but before the charitable legacy itself is deducted.

(c) **Variation of Cada's will**

Gift to charity: potential tax advantages

If Cada's will were varied to gift £78,000 to charity instead of £60,000, the inheritance tax liability on the estate would be reduced by £35,280 as shown above.

Gift of house by Raymer: potential tax advantages

Cada's will could be varied to give the house directly to Raymer's son who would take the house at the probate value of £500,000 for capital gains tax purposes. Raymer would not be treated as making a disposal for capital gains tax purposes by making the variation.

If the will is not varied in this way, Raymer would make a disposal of house on 1 July 2017 at its market value at that time and there will be a chargeable gain if this value exceeds the probate value of £500,000. Raymer would not be able to claim principal private residence relief, as she does not intend to live in the house, and gift relief would not available as the house is not a business asset nor is the gift a chargeable lifetime transfer for inheritance tax.

For inheritance tax, the variation would mean that the house is treated as being given to Raymer's son in Cada's will so would be chargeable to inheritance tax as part of the chargeable estate in the same way as if gifted to Raymer. Raymer would not be treated as making a transfer of value for inheritance tax purposes by making the variation.

If the will is not varied in this way, Raymer would make a potentially exempt transfer of the market value of the house on 1 July 2017 and this would become a chargeable transfer if she dies within seven years (ie on or before 30 June 2024).

Procedures

A written variation must be made by 19 November 2018 (two years after Cada's death) by Raymer and Yang as they are the persons who benefit under Cada's will and whose entitlements to property under the will are reduced by the variation.

As Raymer and Yang wish the relevant terms of the will to be treated as replaced by the terms of the variation for both inheritance tax and capital gains tax purposes, this must be stated in the variation.

Tutorial note

Yang's entitlement under Cada's will is reduced by the variation because the increased gift to charity must come from the remaining assets of Cada's estate which have been given to Yang. However, the value of Yang's entitlement will actually increase due to the reduction in inheritance tax.

(d) **Capital gains tax – Beneficial actions in respect of shareholdings**

The shares in Cada's estate will pass at probate value to Yang and the accrued losses up to the date of Cada's death will therefore not be available for relief.

The FR plc shares which are valued at less than cost could have been sold in the tax year of Cada's death, thus realising the loss on those shares. This loss could have been offset against chargeable gains in that tax year and then carried back against chargeable gains of the three tax years before death on a last in, first out (LIFO) basis.

A negligible value claim could have been made in respect of the KZ Ltd shares to treat them as sold, and immediately reacquired, for no value so realising the loss on those shares. The sale and reacquisition would have been treated as taking place when the claim was made, or at a specified earlier time. The earlier time could have been any time up to two years before the start of the tax year in which the claim was made. The loss would be relieved in a similar way to the loss on the FR plc shares.

22 Claudia

Text references. Chapter 5 covers employee shareholder shares. The seed enterprise investment scheme (SEIS) is dealt with in Chapter 2 and SEIS reinvestment relief is covered in Chapter 13.

Top tips. In part (a)(ii) the relevance of the shares being listed on the London Stock Exchange means that they are 'readily convertible assets'. You need to think what the significance of this is for tax purposes. In part (b)(ii), it is important to state that SEIS reinvestment relief exempts part of a gain rather than being a deferral relief (compare EIS deferral relief).

Marks

(a)	(i)	Employee shareholder definition	1½	
		Conditions – ½ each	3	
			Max	4
	(ii)	Income tax	1½	
		National insurance	1	
			Max	2
	(iii)	Sale to unconnected buyer	2	
		Sale to spouse	1	
		Takeover	1	
				4
(b)	(i)	Tax reducer		1
	(ii)	Matching gain with SEIS expenditure	1	
		50% of gain exempt	1	
				2
	(iii)	Gift to daughter	1½	
		Sale to unconnected buyer	2	
			Max	3
				16

(a) (i) An employee shareholder is an individual who works under an employee shareholder employment contract which provides for certain employment rights, such as unfair dismissal compensation and statutory redundancy pay, to be given up in exchange for shares in the employer company.

The following conditions must be met for Claudia to be an employee shareholder:

- Noble plc and Claudia must both agree that Claudia will be an employee shareholder.

- Noble plc must give Claudia a written statement of the particulars of her status as an employee shareholder.

- Noble plc must give Claudia fully paid up shares in that company, which must be worth at least £2,000.

- Claudia must not pay for the shares in any way other than giving up the employment rights.

- Claudia must obtain advice from a relevant independent adviser whose costs must be paid by Noble plc.

- Claudia must wait for seven days from the day after receiving the advice before accepting or rejecting employee shareholder status.

(ii) On the issue of the employee shareholder shares, Claudia is treated as receiving specific employment income which is equal to the value of the shares (£5,000) less a deemed payment of £2,000, giving a taxable amount of £3,000.

As the shares are listed on the London Stock Exchange, they are 'readily convertible assets' and so the taxable amount of £3,000 will also be subject to Class 1 National Insurance as earnings.

Tutorial note

The deemed payment applies because Claudia did not have a material interest ($\geq$25% of voting rights) in Noble plc at any time in the 12 months before the acquisition of the employee shareholder shares.

(iii) 1 Since, when the employee shareholder shares were acquired, their total value was £50,000 or less, any gain on their disposal by Claudia is exempt from capital gains tax. If a loss arises on the disposal of the employee shareholder shares, the loss will not be allowable.

2   If Claudia transfers the employee shareholder shares to her husband Nigel, the usual no gain, no loss rules will not apply and so the capital gains tax consequences will be the same as in 1 above.

3   If Nobel plc is taken over by Token plc, the usual paper for paper rules will not apply so there will be a disposal of the employee shareholder shares by Claudia and so the capital gains tax consequences will be the same as in 1 above.

Tutorial note

The normal share pooling and matching rules do not apply to employee shareholder shares. If Claudia had a mixture of employee shareholder shares and other shares in Noble plc, on a disposal of Noble plc shares, she could decide which of the shares disposed of are to be treated as employee shareholder shares.

(b)   (i)   Claudia can claim SEIS income tax relief of £60,000 × 50% = £30,000 in 2015/16 against her income tax liability.

(ii)   The gain of £42,000 made on the plot of land can be matched with that amount of SEIS expenditure since they are made the same tax year (2015/16). The maximum SEIS reinvestment relief is 50% of the amount of the gain matched with the SEIS expenditure (ie £21,000). This amount of the gain is then exempted from capital gains tax.

(iii)   1   If Claudia gives her shares in Petite Ltd to Joanne in 2017, all of the SEIS income tax relief of £30,000 will be withdrawn as this is a disposal not at arm's length within three years of issue.

All of the capital gains tax SEIS reinvestment relief in respect of those shares will also be withdrawn by a chargeable gain of £21,000 being treated as arising in 2015/16.

2   If Claudia sells her shares in Petite Ltd to an unconnected buyer in 2017, £45,000 × 50% = £22,500 of the SEIS income tax relief will be withdrawn as this is a disposal at arm's length within three years of issue. This is 22,500/30,000 × 100% = 75% of the SEIS income tax relief.

The capital gains tax SEIS reinvestment relief in respect of those shares will also be reduced by a chargeable gain of £21,000 × 75% = £15,750 being treated as arising in 2015/16.

23 Robert, Meredith and Adrian

Text references. Chapter 14 deals with overseas aspects of CGT including residential property owned by a non-UK resident. Chapter 15 covers penalties for non-compliance. Chapter 13 includes entrepreneurs' relief.

Top tips. All of these topics are new in FAs15 and are therefore very examinable. Note the different methods of calculating the post 5 April 2015 gain in part (a)(i).

			Marks
(a)	(i)	Default method gain	1
		Time apportionment gain	2½
		PPR relief	2½
			6
	(ii)	Business asset gift relief	1
		Available on gift to non-UK resident	1
			2
(b)		Normal penalty for error	2
		Offshore matter	1
		Further penalty	2
			5
(c)		Entrepreneurs' relief conditions	1
		Shop	½
		Goodwill	1
		CGT liability	2½
			5
			18

(a) **Robert**

(i) *Redacre*

Non-UK resident individuals are subject to capital gains tax on the disposal of interests in UK situated residential property. However, only the gain accruing since 6 April 2015 is chargeable. The default method of computing the gain on 5 October 2018 is as follows:

	£
Proceeds	450,000
Less market value at 5 April 2015	(325,000)
Gain	125,000

However, Robert can elect to use an alternative straight line time apportionment of the gain calculated under normal CGT rules over the whole period of ownership with the part accruing after 5 April 2015 being chargeable. This would result in the following gain:

	£
Proceeds	450,000
Less cost	(150,000)
Gain	300,000

Robert owned the house from 6 April 2005 to 5 October 2018 (thirteen and a half years). The period from 6 April 2015 to 5 October 2018 is three and a half years.

Post 5 April 2015 gain 3.5/13.5 × £300,000 — 77,778

Robert should therefore make an election to use the straight line time apportionment method.

Robert is also entitled to principal private residence (PPR) relief on Redacre since it had been his main residence. Only the period of ownership after 5 April 2015 has to be considered. However, as Robert is non-UK resident and does not stay overnight at the property for at least 90 days in any tax year, there is no actual occupation taken into account for any of the tax years after 5 April 2015. Nonetheless, Robert is entitled to treat the last 18 months of ownership as if it were a period of occupation. He is also entitled to the annual exempt amount.

Robert's taxable gain will therefore be:

	£
Gain before PPR relief	77,778
Less PPR relief 1.5/3.5	(33,333)
Gain after PPR relief	44,445
Less annual exempt amount	(11,100)
Taxable gain	33,345

(ii) *Bluesky*

This is a furnished holiday letting and so is a business asset for the purposes of gift relief.

Gift relief is available on a gift to Emily who is a non-UK resident person because the residential property remains within the charge to CGT.

Tutorial note

This is an exception to the usual rule that gift relief cannot be claimed where the donee is not UK resident.

(b) **Meredith**

As a UK resident, Meredith is taxable on her worldwide income including the income from the overseas assets. A penalty for error might be imposed on her if she submits an inaccurate return by making a deliberate error which results in an understatement of her tax liability. The amount of the penalty for error is based on the Potential Lost Revenue (PLR) to HMRC as a result of the error. For a deliberate, but not concealed, error the maximum penalty is 70% of PLR.

Since the error relates to an offshore matter, the penalty may be increased. The rate of this increased penalty is linked to how much information the territory, in which the assets are situated, shares with HMRC. The harder it is for HMRC to obtain information from the territory, the higher the penalty.

There is a further penalty which may be imposed where there is a relevant offshore asset move intended to prevent or delay HMRC from discovering a potential loss of revenue once a non-compliance penalty for deliberate failure has been imposed. A relevant offshore asset move includes one where an asset ceases to be situated in a territory which automatically shares information with HMRC and becomes situated in a territory which does not.

(c) **Adrian**

Entrepreneurs' relief is available where there is a material disposal of business assets which includes a disposal of the whole of a business which has been owned by the individual throughout the period of one year ending with the date of the disposal.

Therefore, the disposal of Adrian's business is a material disposal of business assets and qualifies for entrepreneurs' relief on the gain on the freehold shop (a relevant business asset). However, since the disposal of the goodwill is to a close company of which Adrian is a participator, the goodwill is not a relevant business asset.

Adrian's capital gains tax liability on the sale of his business to Better Ltd is therefore as follows:

	Gains £	CGT £
Gains qualifying for entrepreneurs' relief		
Gain on shop	50,000	
CGT @ 10%		5,000
Gains not qualifying for entrepreneurs' relief		
Gain on goodwill	42,000	
Less annual exempt amount (best use)	(11,100)	
Taxable gain	30,900	
CGT @ 28%		8,652
CGT liability		13,652

24 Klubb plc (ATAX 12/14)

Text references. Corporation tax administration is covered in Chapter 22. Share schemes are dealt with in Chapter 5. Controlled foreign companies are covered in Chapter 27.

Top tips. In part (c)(i), state the conditions for a controlled foreign company to exist and then apply them to the question. The key point is the residence of the individual shareholder.

Easy marks. There were easy marks in part (a) for basic corporation tax administration. The computation of the CFC charge in part (c)(ii) was also straightforward.

Examiner's comments. Part (a) concerned a company with a long period of account. Candidates were required to state when any corporation tax returns needed to be filed and explain any penalties for late filing. The first thing candidates had to point out was the need to split the long period of account into two accounting periods. Unfortunately, many candidates failed to identify this point. Candidates then had to know the filing dates and the penalty rules. However, many candidates wrote about the dates on which corporation tax has to be paid as opposed to the filing dates of the returns, such that they did not answer the requirement set.

Part (b) of the question was more substantial. It required a comparison of two tax-advantaged share schemes: a share incentive plan and a share option scheme, by reference to certain specified areas. It was very important to identify clearly the particular areas that needed to be addressed, and to stick to them. Failure to do this could result in irrelevant parts of an answer that would score no marks, despite being technically accurate. Unfortunately many candidates were insufficiently disciplined in their approach and regarded the question as being about the two share schemes generally as opposed to being about certain aspects of the two schemes. Generally, candidates' knowledge of this area was good with many candidates providing satisfactory answers. The candidates who did best were those who structured their answer in a very clear manner so that it was always clear which aspect of which scheme was being addressed. This clear structure enabled candidates to keep their answers relatively brief whilst addressing all of the precise requirements of the question. However, a minority of candidates appeared to be making up their answer as they went along, such that they were setting out each thought as it occurred to them. The problem with this approach was that some points were repeated, other points were made which were not relevant and some aspects of the requirement were omitted altogether. Most candidates knew that under a share incentive plan, shares need to be offered to, broadly, all employees whereas, under a company share option plan, the employer can choose certain employees to join the scheme. Candidates' knowledge of the number or value of shares that could be offered under each scheme was also satisfactory notwithstanding that some candidates confused the two schemes or confused the different categories of shares that can be offered under a share incentive plan. When it came to the tax implications of acquiring and selling the shares it was important for candidates to stick to the facts of the question. It was clear from the question how long the shares would be held for and when they would be sold. Accordingly, there was no need to address all of the different tax implications that could occur if the shares were sold at other times. Candidates who failed to realise this wasted time writing lengthy answers that were not addressing the requirements of the question. When explaining the tax implications, stronger candidates were clear as to which scheme they were writing about and which tax (income tax or capital gains tax) they were addressing. The answers of other candidates were more confused and used the general term 'tax' as opposed to the specific tax concerned.

Part c(i) was done reasonably well by many candidates. Candidates had two main problems when answering this first part of the question. First, they confused the definition of a controlled foreign company with the exemptions that are available. Secondly, there was a tendency to write about all of the available exemptions as opposed to the particular one in the question requirement; this resulted in irrelevant parts of answers. Part (c)(ii) required a calculation of a controlled foreign company charge. Candidates had to remember to exclude the gains from the calculation, bring in only 30% of the trading profits, and deduct an appropriate amount of creditable tax. Answers here were generally not as accurate as might have been hoped.

				Marks
(a)		Two accounting periods	1	
		Filing date	1	
		Penalty	2	
				4
(b)		Employees included	2	
		Number or value of shares acquired		
		SIP	4	
		CSOP	2	
		Tax implications of acquiring and selling shares		
		SIP	2	
		CSOP	2	
		Max		9
(c)	(i)	Status of Hartz Co	2½	
		Low profits exemption	2	
		Max		4
	(ii)	Profits apportioned	1½	
		Calculation of charge	1½	
				3
				20

(a) **Late submission of corporation tax returns**

There are two accounting periods within the long period of account. These are for the 12 month period ended 30 November 2014 and the four month period ended 31 March 2015.

As the relevant period of account is not more than 18 months long, the filing date for both periods is 12 months from the end of the period of account which is 31 March 2016.

There is a £100 penalty for a failure to submit each return on time, as each return is made within three months of the filing date.

The £100 penalty is increased to £500 when a return was late (or never submitted) for each of the preceding two accounting periods.

Tutorial note

It has been assumed that HM Revenue and Customs issued notices requiring the returns to be made before 1 January 2016 so that the later three-month filing date rule does not apply.

(b) **Comparison of share incentive plan (SIP) with company share option plan (CSOP)**

Employees

Klubb plc would need to offer all full and part-time employees the opportunity to participate in a SIP, although a minimum qualifying period of employment of up to 18 months may be specified.

All the employees and full-time directors of Klubb plc can participate in a CSOP, but the scheme need not be open to all of them. Klubb plc can therefore select the employees it wishes to include.

A CSOP is therefore more likely to achieve the flexibility that Klubb plc wants, rather than a SIP.

Number or value of shares which can be acquired by each plan member

In a SIP, employees would be given free shares in Klubb plc, which are held in the plan, up to the value of £3,600 each tax year. Employees must be awarded free shares on similar terms to all of the plan members. This means that any variation in the number of free shares must be made by reference to objective criteria, such as level of remuneration, length of service or hours worked. However, Klubb plc can also specify the award can be conditional on the meeting of performance targets (within rules prescribed in the legislation) but there can be no deliberate weighting of rewards in favour of directors and the more highly paid employees. Employees can also purchase partnership shares through deduction from pre-tax salary up to the lower of £1,800 and 10% of salary in any tax year. Klubb plc can also award matching shares free to employees who purchase partnership shares at a maximum ratio of 2:1.

In a CSOP employees can be granted options to buy shares in Klubb plc up to the value of £30,000 (at the date of grant). Subject to that maximum amount, Klubb plc can decide how many options to grant to each employee.

Again, a CSOP is therefore more likely to achieve the flexibility that Klubb plc wants, rather than a SIP.

Tax implications of acquiring and selling the shares

There are no income tax implications when shares are given to employees in a SIP. Since the shares will be held within the SIP for five years, there will be no income tax charge when the shares are taken out of the SIP. There will also be no charge to capital gains tax on shares taken out of the SIP and sold immediately because their base cost will be equal to their market value at the time they are withdrawn from the SIP.

There is no income tax on the grant of options in a CSOP, nor on the exercise of an option under a CSOP since it will be exercised between three and ten years after the grant, which is a condition for a CSOP. When the shares acquired under a CSOP are sold, any gain is subject to capital gains tax. The cost in the gain calculation is the option price paid by the employee to acquire the shares. It is a condition for a CSOP that the option price must not be less than their market value at the time of the grant of the option.

Therefore, there will be no charge to income tax on either the SIP or the CSOP, but capital gains tax may be payable on the disposal of shares acquired under a CSOP, but not on those acquired under a SIP.

Tutorial note

It was not necessary to make all of the above points in order to score full marks for this question.

(c)   (i)   **Status of Hartz Co and availability of low profits exemption**

A controlled foreign company is a company which is not resident in the UK but is controlled by persons resident in the UK.

Hartz Co is owned 30% by Klubb plc (UK resident), 45% by Kort Co (non-UK resident) and 25% by Mr Deck. Therefore, Hartz Co will be a CFC only if Mr Deck is UK resident.

The chargeable profits of Hartz Co will not be exempt from apportionment under either of the conditions for the low profits exemption. This is because its profits are more than £50,000, and although they are under £500,000, its non-trading profits (chargeable gains) exceed £50,000.

(ii)   **CFC charge for Klubb plc**

	£
Chargeable profits of Hartz Co	330,000
Apportioned to Klubb plc £330,000 × 30%	99,000
Tax on apportioned profits £99,000 × 20%	19,800
Less creditable tax £99,000 × 11%	(10,890)
CFC charge	8,910

Tutorial note

Chargeable gains are not part of chargeable profits for the purposes of the CFC charge so only the trading profits are included.

25 Sank Ltd and Kurt Ltd (ATAX 06/12)

Text references. Payment of corporation tax and administration are covered in Chapter 22. Capital allowances in general are dealt with in Chapter 7. The division of the annual investment allowance is covered in Chapter 26 and research and development expenditure in Chapter 20.

Top tips. Before choosing to do a two-part question such as this, you must be confident about being able to produce a reasonable answer to both parts.

Easy marks. In part (a), the computation of corporation tax should have been easy marks. In part (b), the availability of the annual investment allowance and the writing down allowance were straightforward, even if you did not know the detail about the restriction for related companies.

Examiner's comments. In part (a)(i), the payment of corporation tax appeared to be fairly straightforward but care was needed if sufficient marks were to be earned. It was not enough to state that the company would pay corporation tax quarterly because it was large. Candidates needed to explain how they knew this (ie by reference to its profits and the number of related 51% group companies). There was also a need to point out that the company paid was large in the previous accounting period. [Note: these comments have been amended by BPP to reflect terminology and rule changes since the question was originally set.] Weaker candidates confused quarterly accounting with the payments of income tax by individuals and thought that the payments were paid on account by reference to the liability for the previous year.

Part (a) (ii) required candidates to explain the validity of the compliance check enquiry 'in relation to the date on which (it)...... was raised'. Many candidates simply wrote about compliance check enquiries generally such that this part of the question was not answered well.

Most candidates produced reasonable answers to part (b), but many would have done better if they had simply read the question more carefully and identified the relevance of all of the information and slowed down. In particular, many candidates wrote about the basic rules at some length rather than thinking about the particular situation of the question.

The owner of the company concerned owned three other companies. This information was intended to elicit a discussion of the need to split the annual investment allowance between the companies. However, many candidates wrote instead about the unavailability of group relief. The question also pointed out that the relevant accounting period was only eight months. This meant that the annual investment allowance and the writing down allowance needed to be multiplied by 8/12. However, this point was missed by many candidates.

A significant number of candidates were of the opinion that, because the company was loss-making, it should not claim all of its capital allowances. It should be remembered that, where the annual investment allowance is concerned, failing to claim allowances in full will considerably slow down the time it takes for a tax deduction to be obtained for the cost incurred as, in the future, there will only be a 18% writing down allowance on a reducing balance basis. Accordingly, there needs to be a strong reason not to claim allowances in full. Such a reason might include the situation where there are insufficient profits in the group to relieve a company's losses in the current year and any losses carried forward are likely to be locked inside the company for a considerable period of time. In such a situation it may be worthwhile claiming reduced capital allowances in the current year in order to have increased capital allowances in future years that can then be group relieved.

The tax treatment of the expenditure on scientific research was explained well by the majority of candidates, many of whom were aware that there was a possibility of claiming a 14.5% repayment. However, very few candidates attempted to evaluate whether or not the repayment should be claimed.

			Marks	
(a)	(i)	Corporation tax	½	
		Why required to pay by instalments	3	
		Payments required	3	
		Payment already made	1½	
		Interest	1	
		Future payments	½	
				7
	(ii)	Deadlines	2½	
		Conclusion	1	
		Max		3
(b)		Equipment		
		Annual investment allowance	3	
		Writing down allowance	1	
		Scientific research		
		Tax deduction	1	
		Repayment	1	
		Evaluation	2	
				8
				18

(a) (i) Sank Ltd – increase in the budgeted corporation tax liability for the 11 months ended 30 September 2016

Sank Ltd's corporation tax liability for the period is expected to be £750,000 × 20% = £150,000.

It is required to pay its corporation tax liability for the period in instalments because it profits exceed the profit threshold of £(1,500,000/3 × 11/12) = £458,333 for the period and it was a large company in previous years.

The payments required are as follows.

14 May 2016	3/11 of the final liability for the period
14 August 2016	3/11 of the final liability for the period
14 November 2016	3/11 of the final liability for the period
14 January 2017	2/11 of the final liability for the period (balance)

A payment should have been made on 14 May 2016 of £640,000 × 20% × 3/11 = £34,909, based on the budget prepared on 31 March 2016. However, if the new figure of taxable total profits is correct, the payment required on that day was £750,000 × 20% × 3/11 = £40,909.

Interest will be charged from 14 May 2016 until the additional £(40,909 – 34,909) = £6,000 is paid. The total interest due will be calculated by HM Revenue and Customs, once the corporation tax return has been submitted.

Future payments, ie from 14 August 2016 onwards, should be based on the latest budgeted figures in order to minimise interest charges.

(ii) Sank Ltd – circumstances necessary for the notice of the compliance check to be regarded as valid

The deadline for raising a notice of the compliance check depends on when the corporation tax return was filed.

Where the return was filed on time (ie by 31 October 2014), the compliance check must be notified, at the latest, by 31 October 2015. Where the return was submitted late, the compliance check must be notified by the 31 January, 30 April, 31 July or 31 October next following the first anniversary of

the actual date of delivery of the return. Accordingly, a notice of a compliance check dated 31 May 2016 will only be valid if the corporation tax return was submitted after 30 April 2015.

(b)   **Kurt Ltd**

Machinery

A 100% annual investment allowance is available for expenditure on machinery up to a maximum of £500,000 for a 12-month period. The maximum amount available to Kurt Ltd for the period ended 31 March 2016 is therefore £500,000 × 8/12 = £333,333.

However, only one annual investment allowance is available to companies that are related to each other. The other companies controlled by Mr Quinn will be regarded as related to Kurt Ltd if they share premises or carry on similar activities. Mr Quinn can choose to allocate the allowance available to related companies in the most tax efficient manner.

The excess of the expenditure over the available annual investment allowance will be eligible for a writing down allowance of 18% × 8/12 = 12% in the period to 31 March 2016.

Scientific research

Kurt Ltd is a small enterprise for the purposes of research and development. Accordingly, the expenditure of £28,000 will result in tax deductions of £28,000 × 230% = £64,400.

Kurt Ltd can choose to claim a tax credit of 14.5% of the lower of its trading loss and £64,400. This relief is an alternative to carrying the loss forward against future profits of the same trade.

Kurt Ltd should consider claiming the 14.5% tax credit if cash flow is its main priority. Alternatively, if the company wishes to maximise the tax saved in respect of the expenditure, it should carry the loss forward; it will then save tax at a minimum rate of 20% (provided it succeeds in becoming profitable).

26 Opus Ltd group (ATAX 06/14)

Text references. Groups and consortia are the subject of Chapter 26. Chargeable gains for companies are covered in Chapter 21. Ethics are dealt with in Chapter 30.

Top tips. It is a good idea to ascertain the membership of the 75% group relief group and the 75% capital gains group before you start to work out how profits can be moved around each group.

Easy marks. There were easy marks in part (b) if you applied the test for the substantial shareholding exemption. The ethics in part (c) should have been well known.

Examiner's comments. Part (a) concerned relief for trading losses within the group. The question was all about identifying various individual points in respect of each of the companies. That's why the email from the manager suggested 'you should think carefully about the tax position of each company'. Akia Ltd, the loss-making company, had realised a chargeable gain against which the loss could be offset. There was also the possibility of carrying the loss back 12 months, although very few candidates identified this point. Once the position of Akia Ltd, the loss-making company, had been considered it was then necessary to consider the group and consortium position. The group position was handled well but many candidates failed to spot that because Venere Ltd was a 75% subsidiary of Jarrah Ltd, it could not be a consortium company. Ribe Ltd had trading losses brought forward. These could not be group relieved (because only current period losses can be group relieved) and therefore could only be used against that company's trading profits. However, a minority of candidates simply added the losses of Ribe Ltd to those of Akia Ltd and then addressed the total losses together. Finally, Binni Ltd was not a member of the group for the whole of the period so it was necessary to determine the maximum loss that could be surrendered to it by Akia Ltd. This is a straightforward point but it was missed by many candidates.

The second part of the question concerned the sale of shares by one of the group companies and the availability of the substantial shareholding exemption (SSE). This was not done well for two main reasons. First, many candidates failed to consider the SSE despite it being an important exemption at P6. There were follow through marks available for those who found themselves in this predicament but only if they answered the question set. Unfortunately, many candidates failed to do so. Two lessons may be learned from what happened here.

Firstly, it is always worth thinking about how to do a calculation in an efficient manner rather than to just immediately start it. Those candidates who thought it was necessary to calculate a chargeable gain on each of the possible disposal dates should have realised that the only difference was an increase in sales proceeds of £20,000. This would, of course, increase the gain by £20,000; there was no need to repeat the whole calculation to determine this. The second lesson is that you must answer the question set. Candidates were asked to consider on which of the two dates it would be more financially advantageous to sell the shares. This required candidates to consider the post-tax proceeds on each of the potential disposal dates, but the majority of candidates simply focussed on the amount of the chargeable gain.

The final part of the question concerned an error in a corporation tax return and the matters that needed to be considered in relation to the disclosure of the error to HM Revenue and Customs. This was a standard question and an opportunity for all candidates to earn some straightforward marks. Unfortunately, a minority of candidates decided to address the penalties aspect of the question in great detail without thinking about the other relevant issues. Stronger candidates recognised the need to consider the importance of disclosing the error from the point of view of tax evasion, money laundering and the acceptability of continuing to act for the company. These stronger candidates were able to score well on this part of the question.

Marking scheme

			Marks
(a)	Loss of Akia Ltd		
	Offset against total profits of Akia Ltd		
	Against own total profits	2	
	Against gain from Lido Ltd	2	
	Group relief		
	Members of group and consortium	2	
	Opus Ltd	2½	
	Binni Ltd	1½	
	Ribe Ltd	1	
	Loss carried forward	2	
	Loss of Ribe Ltd	1	
	Capital allowances	2	
		Max	14
(b)	Sale on 30 June 2016	1½	
	Sale on 30 April 2017	3	
	Comparison	1	
		Max	5
(c)	Interest on underpaid tax	2	
	Action required		
	Necessary to disclose	2	
	Implications of failure to disclose	3½	
		Max	6
			25

(a) **Trading losses of Akia Ltd and Ribe Ltd**

	Notes	£	£
Akia Ltd			
Trading loss for the year ended 31 March 2016			93,000
Offset of losses in Akia Ltd:			
Year ended 31 March 2016	1		(27,000)
Year ended 31 March 2015	2		Unknown
Group relief:	3		
Opus Ltd			
Trading profit		10,000	
Property business income		8,000	
Gain on shares in Venere Ltd	4	0	
			(18,000)
Binni Ltd	5		(31,000)
Ribe Ltd	6		0
Amount unrelieved	7		17,000
Ribe Ltd			
Trading loss b/f at 1 April 2015			68,000
Offset against trading profit y/e 31.3.16	6		(41,000)
Trading loss c/f at 31 March 2016			27,000

Notes

1   Lido Ltd is in a chargeable gains group with Akia Ltd. This is because Opus Ltd has a direct interest of at least 75% in Akia Ltd and has direct interest of at least 75% in Ribe Ltd which, in turn, has a direct interest of at least 75% in Lido Ltd and Opus Ltd has an effective interest in Lido Ltd of more than 50% (80% × 85% = 68%). The chargeable gain of £21,000 can therefore be transferred to Akia Ltd and added to its own gain of £6,000 to give total chargeable gains of £27,000.

2   Akia Ltd can offset its trading losses against its total profits (income and chargeable gains) of the loss making period and those of the previous 12 months. We therefore need to know the company's total profits for the year ended 31 March 2015.

3   Akia Ltd is in a 75% group relief group with Opus Ltd, Ribe Ltd and Binni Ltd. Lido Ltd is not in the group as the effective interest of Opus Ltd is less than 75%.

    Venere Ltd is not a consortium company because it is a 75% subsidiary of Jarrah Ltd.

4   The chargeable gain on the sale of shares in Venere Ltd is exempt under the substantial shareholding exemption. This is because Opus Ltd and Venere Ltd are trading companies and Opus Ltd owned at least 10% of the shares in Venere Ltd for a continuous period of at least 12 months in the two years prior to the disposal.

5   Binni Ltd joined the Opus Ltd group on 1 December 2015, such that it is in a group relief group with Akia Ltd for the four months from 1 December 2015 to 31 March 2016.

    The maximum loss which can be surrendered by Akia Ltd to Binni Ltd is the lower of:

    Loss of Akia Ltd for the overlapping period £93,000 × 4/12   £31,000

    Total profits of Binni Ltd for the overlapping period £78,000 × 4/10   £31,200

6   The trading losses brought forward in Ribe Ltd must be offset against the first available trading profits of the same trade. Therefore, the company has no profits which can be relieved through group relief.

    Ribe Ltd and Lido Ltd form a 75% group relief group. However, the remaining losses cannot be surrendered as group relief to Lido Ltd as only current period losses can be group relieved.

7   The use of losses carried forward in Akia Ltd will be delayed because the company is not expected to be profitable for some time. Akia Ltd can turn what would otherwise be trading losses *carried forward* into future *current period* trading losses (available for immediate relief via group relief) by not claiming capital allowances equal to its unrelieved current period trading loss.

Reducing the capital allowances would increase the tax written down value of the main pool and consequently the capital allowances and trading loss in future periods. The increased trading loss could then be group relieved.

Reducing the capital allowances would reduce the trading loss of Akia Ltd for the year ended 31 March 2016. This in turn would reduce the maximum loss which could be surrendered to Binni Ltd.

Tutorial note

The chargeable gain of Lido Ltd could alternatively be transferred to Opus Ltd or Ribe Ltd, rather than Akia Ltd, and be relieved with Akia Ltd's loss via group relief. It would not be beneficial to transfer the gain to Binni Ltd because of the restriction on the surrender of losses to that company.

(b)   **Sale of shares in Venere Ltd**

If the shares are sold on 30 June 2016, the chargeable gain arising will be exempt under the substantial shareholding exemption. This is because Opus Ltd would have owned at least 10% of the shares in Venere Ltd for a continuous period of at least 12 months (from 1 July 2014 to 30 September 2015) during the two years prior to the sale. Accordingly, the post-tax proceeds will be equal to the gross proceeds of £80,000.

If the shares are sold on 30 April 2017, there will not be a continuous 12 month period in the previous two years where Opus Ltd has owned at least 10% of the shares in Venere Ltd. Therefore, on the assumption that the shares are sold for £100,000, there will be a chargeable gain of £73,235 (W). This gain will be subject to corporation tax of £(73,235 × 20%) = £14,647. The post-tax proceeds will be £(100,000 – 14,647) = £85,353.

Therefore, while there may be a marginal increase in the post-tax proceeds from delaying the sale until after the results for the year ending 31 March 2017 are known, there is no guarantee that a higher level of sales proceeds will be achieved and there will be a significant delay in obtaining the sales proceeds. Also, these figures assume that any costs of sale will be the same at both dates, which may not be the case.

Working

		£
Proceeds		100,000
Less:	cost £65,000 × 50,000/170,000	(19,118)
	indexation allowance £19,118 × 0.400 (assumed)	(7,647)
Chargeable gain		73,235

(c)   **Error in the corporation tax return of Binni Ltd**

Interest on underpaid tax

Binni Ltd will be regarded as having underpaid corporation tax on each of the four payment dates for the year ended 31 May 2014. Accordingly, interest may be charged from 14 December 2013, 14 March 2014, 14 June 2014 and 14 September 2014 on any amounts of underpaid corporation tax.

Disclosure of the error

The directors of Binni Ltd must be advised to make full disclosure of the error or authorise our firm to make such disclosure, without delay. If they refuse, we can no longer act for the company. The directors should be advised of this, and also that we must inform HMRC that we have ceased to act for the client. We should not, however, advise HMRC of the error unless the directors consented to such disclosure.

Even if we cease to act for Binni Ltd, we are is still under a professional duty to ensure that the directors understand the seriousness of offences against HMRC, including the possibility of criminal prosecution.

Tax evasion may also constitute money laundering and we are also bound by legislation to report suspicions to the appropriate authority. Again, this may lead to criminal prosecution.

27 Helm Ltd group (ATAX 06/15)

Text references. Groups, including pre-entry losses, are the subject of Chapter 26. Chargeable gains for companies, including the substantial shareholding exemption and rollover relief, are covered in Chapter 21. Stamp duty land tax is covered in Chapter 19. The loan relationship rules are explained in Chapter 20 and deficits on non-trading loan relationships in Chapter 24. Ethics are dealt with in Chapter 30.

Top tips. It is very important to answer the question set and not give a lot of irrelevant detail which will waste time and not score marks.

Easy marks. There were some easy marks in part (a) for working out the degrouping charge gain and the gain on the sale of shares in Bar Ltd. The identification of the non-availability of rollover relief in part (c) was very easy.

Examiner's comments. Part (a) consisted of various aspects of corporation tax with some easy and some more challenging marks. Candidates who did well had a good knowledge of the subject and addressed all of the issues briefly rather than writing about a small number of issues in great detail. When calculating the gain on the sale of the shares in Bar Ltd, the majority of candidates recognised that here would be a degrouping charge and most candidates explained the reasons for the charge arising. However, a minority of candidates were unable to calculate the indexation allowance correctly and so failed to gain some of the available marks. Candidates who performed less well often confused the sale of shares with the sale of assets and calculated gains on the individual assets owned by the company. Candidates must take the time to ensure that they understand the transactions that have taken place in a scenario. It was then necessary to consider the availability of the substantial shareholding exemption. Most candidates knew that at least 10% of the company's shares needed to be owned for 12 months in the two years prior to the sale. However, fewer candidates pointed out that the companies needed to be trading companies. The final element, which was only picked up by a small number of candidates, was the fact that the ownership period was satisfied in this particular situation due to the trade of Bar Ltd having been owned by another group company, Aero Ltd, previously. The stamp duty land tax aspects of the question were not handled well with very few candidates recognising that the inter group exemption that was available when the trade and assets of Aero Ltd were transferred to Bar Ltd would be withdrawn due to the sale of Bar Ltd within three years.

Part (b) concerned the loan relationships rules and produced a great variety of answers. Those candidates with a good knowledge of the rules were able to present a brief, methodical answer that scored very well. Candidates who were less confident in this area did not pursue the question to its conclusion and therefore did not address the detail of the offset of non-trading loan relationship deficits. This made it difficult to pick up many marks.

Part (c) concerned rollover relief and the offset of capital losses within a capital gains group. Most candidates identified the fact that rollover relief was not available because the building had never been used in the company's trade. The problem was that many candidates described all of the rules relating to rollover relief in addition to making the one relevant point that was worth a mark. Performance in respect of capital losses was mixed. The majority of candidates knew that, in certain circumstances, capital losses can effectively be transferred between companies in capital gains groups. The problem was that this could not occur in this question because the capital losses concerned were pre-entry capital losses, such that their use was restricted. Many candidates did not identify this point but I suspect that they would have done if they had simply paused and thought before they started writing.

The final part of the question concerned the information required and the actions to be taken before becoming tax advisers to a new client. Many candidates did well here. Those who did not either did not have the necessary knowledge or did not make a sufficient number of points briefly, but instead wrote at length about a small number of matters.

			Marks
(a)	Chargeable gain on the sale of Bar Ltd		
	Calculations		
	Degrouping charge	2	
	Chargeable gain on sale of Bar Ltd	2½	
	Explanations	2	
	Substantial shareholding exemption	3	
	Stamp duty land tax	3	
	Max		11
(b)	Loan arrangement fee	1	
	Split of loan	1½	
	Tax treatment of costs	4	
	Max		5
(c)	Rollover relief	1	
	Capital losses	3	
			4
(d)	Information needed	3	
	Action to take	3	
	Max		5
			25

(a) **Sale of Bar Ltd**

Degrouping charge

The transfer of the building on 1 December 2014 by Aero Ltd to Bar Ltd was deemed to have be made for consideration such that Aero Ltd had neither a gain nor a loss (a 'no gain, no loss' disposal). This was because Aero Ltd and Bar Ltd were members of a chargeable gains group at that date since Helm Ltd owned at least 75% of the shares of both companies.

A degrouping charge arises because Bar Ltd left the chargeable gains group while it owned the building transferred to it by Aero Ltd on a no gain, no loss basis within the previous six years. Bar Ltd is treated as though it had, at the time of its acquisition of the building, sold and immediately reacquired it at its then market value.

The gain arising is therefore:

	£
Deemed proceeds (MV on 1 December 2014)	830,000
Less cost	(425,000)
	405,000
Less indexation allowance	
$\frac{257.5 - 149.1}{149.1}$ (0.727) × £425,000	(308,975)
Indexed gain	96,025

This gain is added to the sale proceeds received by Helm Ltd when computing the gain on sale of the shares in Bar Ltd.

Chargeable gain on sale of shares in Bar Ltd

	£
Proceeds	1,200,000
Degrouping charge gain (above)	96,025
	1,296,025
Less cost	(1,000,000)
	296,025
Less indexation allowance	(388)
$\dfrac{257.8 - 257.7}{257.7} \times £1,000,000$	
Indexed gain	295,637

Tutorial note

The indexation factor should not be rounded to three decimal places because the disposal is from a share pool.

Substantial shareholding exemption

There is an exemption from corporation tax on a gain arising when a trading company (Helm Ltd) disposes of a shareholding in another trading company (Bar Ltd) where the first company has held a substantial shareholding in the second company for certain period.

Helm Ltd has held a substantial shareholding in Bar Ltd because it held at least 10% of ordinary share capital of Bar Ltd. The 10% test must have been met for a continuous 12 month period during the two years preceding the disposal. Since Bar Ltd was only incorporated on 1 October 2014, this test is initially appears not to be met.

However, the twelve month period condition can also be satisfied by including a period during which assets, which are being used in its trade by Bar Ltd, were being used in the trade of another chargeable gains group company (Aero Ltd) and then transferred to Bar Ltd before the sale of its shares. Therefore the substantial shareholding exemption will apply to the sale of shares in Bar Ltd by Helm Ltd.

Stamp duty land tax (SDLT)

Relief from SDLT was given for the transfer of the building between Aero Ltd and Bar Ltd because at the date of the transfer they were members of a SDLT group since Helm Ltd had beneficial ownership of at least 75% of the ordinary share capital of both companies. However, the relief will be withdrawn because Bar Ltd leaves the group within three years of the transfer whilst still owning the building. Bar Ltd will therefore have to pay SDLT of £830,000 × 4% = £33,200.

(b) **Drill Ltd**

If the company is a borrower in a loan relationship, it will have loan relationship debits which include loan interest payable and incidental costs including those incurred in bringing a loan relationship into existence such as the loan arrangement fee.

If the loan relationship is for a trade purpose (trading loan relationship), any debits charged through its accounts are allowed as a trading expense and are therefore deductible in computing trading profits. If the loan relationship is for a non-trade purpose (non-trading loan relationship) non-trade debits must be netted off against non-trade credits such as the £50 bank interest received by Drill Ltd each year.

In this case, one-quarter of the building will be rented out as an investment so that one-quarter of the cost of the building (£1,200,000 × ¼ = £300,000) will be for non-trading purposes. Therefore £(300,000/1,350,000 × 100) = 22.2% of the loan will be a non-trading loan relationship and the remaining 77.8% will be a trading loan relationship which will be dealt with as described above.

There will be a deficit on the non-trading loan relationship which can be relieved as follows:

- Deducted from any profit of the same accounting period
- Surrendered for group relief
- Deducted from non-trading loan relationship credits in the previous twelve months
- Deducted from non trading profits of the company for succeeding accounting periods

(c) **Cog Ltd**

Replacement of business assets (rollover) relief

Rollover relief will not be available to relieve the chargeable gain arising of the sale of Cog Ltd's warehouse. This is because the warehouse was not a qualifying asset when it was sold since it was not used in the trade of Cog Ltd.

Drill Ltd's capital losses

In general, two members of a chargeable gains group, such as Drill Ltd and Cog Ltd, can elect to transfer all or part of a capital gain between them into order to utilise a brought forward capital loss.

However, Drill Ltd's capital losses are pre-entry capital losses since they were made before Drill Ltd joined the Helm Ltd group. These losses can therefore only be relieved against gains on assets which:

- Drill Ltd disposed of before joining the Helm Ltd group.
- Drill Ltd already owned when it joined the Helm Ltd group.
- Drill Ltd acquired after joining the Helm Ltd group from someone outside that group.

Therefore, Drill Ltd's capital losses cannot be transferred to Cog Ltd and used to relieve the chargeable gain on the sale of the warehouse.

(d) **Becoming tax advisors to Gomez and the Helm Ltd group**

Information required

- Gomez: independent evidence of identity (such as a passport, driving licence, HMRC document such as a notice of coding) and proof of address.

- Helm Ltd group: proof of incorporation of each company; primary business addresses and registered office; identifying members and directors of the companies; establishing the identities of those persons giving instructions on behalf of the companies and verifying that those persons are authorised to do so.

Actions to take

- Consider any threats to compliance with the fundamental principles of professional ethics (such as integrity and professional competence) which may arise by becoming tax advisers to Gomez and the Helm Ltd group.

- If any such threats are identified, determine whether safeguards can be implemented to reduce those threats to an acceptable level. If appropriate safeguards cannot be implemented, we should decline to act.

- Ascertain whether there are any professional or other reasons for not accepting the engagement, for example by direct communication with the existing accountant to establish the facts and circumstances behind the proposed change.

28 Bond Ltd group (ATAX 12/14)

Text references. Computation of taxable total profits and the patent box election are dealt with in Chapter 20. Losses are covered in Chapter 24. Capital allowances are the subject of Chapter 7 and the allocation of the annual investment allowance is dealt with in Chapter 26. Rollover relief for companies is covered in Chapter 21. Partial exemption and the capital goods scheme are dealt with in Chapter 29.

Top tips. In part (a), 11 marks were available for the written notes on the calculation of the corporation tax liability of Bond Ltd so it was important that you dealt with the matters raised in detail.

Easy marks. There were some easy marks in part (a) for explaining basic principles such as capital allowances in a short period of account, losses brought forward and rollover relief.

Examiner's comments. Part (a) required candidates to calculate the corporation tax liability of a company for a six-month accounting period and to include notes on various aspects of the computation. Almost all candidates identified that they were dealing with a six-month accounting period, but many of them did not recognise the areas where this point was relevant, ie the annual investment allowance and the rate of writing down allowance. It was stated in the question that the required notes represented approximately two thirds of the marks available and it was pleasing that most candidates picked up on this guidance and addressed all three areas on which notes were required in various levels of detail. The capital allowances were handled reasonably well with most candidates recognising the mistake the client had made. However, many candidates did not recognise that the expenditure that did not qualify for the additional investment allowance would qualify for writing down allowances. Of those that did, many forgot to reduce the rate of the writing down allowance by 6/12 to reflect the length of the accounting period. The use of the company's brought forward trading losses required candidates to consider two matters. First, had the company changed its trade? If it had, the losses brought forward could not be used in the future. Secondly, because there had been a change in ownership of the company, it was necessary to consider if there had been a major change in the nature or conduct of the trade. The company's trade continued to be the baking and selling of bread and baked products. However, the changes made to its products and customers were likely to represent a major change in the nature or conduct of the trade, such that the losses could not be carried forward beyond the date of the change of ownership of the company. The third area of explanatory notes concerned rollover relief. In order to score well here, candidates had to first be aware of the meaning of a qualifying business asset for the purposes of rollover relief and the qualifying period for reinvestment. Qualifying business assets include land and buildings and fixed plant and machinery used in the business. Most candidates were not sufficiently clear on these rules. The qualifying time period was identified by the majority of candidates. Candidates then had to consider the chargeable gains group aspects of rollover relief. A sizable minority of candidates did not consider this aspect and, of those who did, a minority thought that Madison Ltd, a 65% subsidiary, was a member of the gains group because the holding was more than 50%. However, the direct holding between each company in the group has to be at least 75%; it is any indirect holding between the principal company and a non-directly held subsidiary that has to be more than 50%. Finally, candidates had to point out that only part of the gain can be rolled over if only part of the sales proceeds are reinvested in qualifying replacement assets. Although many candidates were aware of this point, not all of them were able to calculate the amount of gain that could be rolled over given a specific level of reinvestment in the question.

Part (b) required candidates to write briefly about the patent box regime. This regime was introduced in Finance Act 2013 and so is fairly new. This aspect of the question was mainly knowledge-based. A minority of candidates were not aware of the regime and consequently did not score well. Those who knew about the regime scored well provided they took care to address the requirement and made separately identifiable points rather than repeating themselves. As always, time spent identifying relevant points before putting pen to paper was time well-spent.

Part (c) concerned the VAT capital goods scheme. Despite this being examined regularly, it was not tackled particularly well. Many candidates thought, incorrectly, that the scheme applies to plant and machinery generally. The way in which the scheme operates was also misunderstood by many candidates who were unable to explain the adjustments that would be made in future years. This aspect of VAT is not part of the Paper F6 (UK) syllabus and thus is new knowledge at P6 (UK). It should be regarded as an area that is likely to continue to be examined regularly in future Paper P6 (UK) exams.

		Marks
(a)	Corporation tax computation	
	Taxable total profits	2
	Corporation tax liability	½
	Capital allowances	
	Maximum AIA for short accounting period	1
	Group aspect	1
	Calculation of adjustment to capital allowances	1½
	Losses brought forward	
	Set against future profits of same trade	2
	Major change in the nature or conduct of trade	3
	Replacement of business assets relief	5
		16
(b)	Identification of each relevant point – one mark	
	Possible points include:	
	Availability of scheme	
	Election for treatment	
	Meaning of patent profits	
	10% rate	
	Phasing in of scheme	
		5
(c)	Building	
	Original recovery	1
	Capital goods scheme	1
	Example	2
	Machinery	1
	Max	4
		25

(a) **Bond Ltd – Corporation tax computation for the six months ended 30 September 2016**

	Notes	£
Tax adjusted trading income as previously calculated		470,000
Add: reduction in capital allowances		
£(285,000 – 253,150)	1	31,850
Less trading losses brought forward	2	(0)
Revised tax adjusted trading income		501,850
Chargeable gain	3	40,000
Taxable total profits		541,850
Corporation tax @ 20%		108,370

Notes

1   *Capital allowances*

The maximum annual investment allowance (AIA) for the six month period to 30 September 2016 is £500,000 × 6/12 = £250,000. Bond Ltd and Ungar Ltd are in a group and therefore are entitled to a single AIA between the group companies. Bond Ltd and Ungar Ltd can decide how to allocate the AIA between them and they should do so in the most beneficial way, taking into account the nature of the expenditure by each company (eg main pool, special rate pool).

Assuming that the AIA is wholly allocated to Bond Ltd, the capital allowances for the period are:

	AIA £	Main pool £	Allowances £
Additions qualifying for AIA	285,000		
AIA	(250,000)		250,000
Transfer to pool	35,000	35,000	
WDA @ 18% × 6/12		(3,150)	3,150
TWDV c/f		31,850	
Maximum capital allowances			253,150

2 *Trading losses brought forward*

Trading losses can be carried forward and deducted from income of the same trade in future accounting periods. Bond Ltd is carrying on the same trade before and after 1 April 2014 (baking and selling bread and other baked profits).

However, trading losses may be restricted where there is a change in ownership of a company and, for example, there has been a major change in the nature or conduct of the trade within three years after the change of ownership. This restriction will probably apply in the case of Bond Ltd as it previously only sold low cost products to schools, hospital and prisons but now 65% of its turnover and 90% of its profits relate to high quality products sold to supermarkets and independent retailers.

If the restriction applies, losses incurred before the change in ownership on 1 April 2014 cannot be carried forward against post acquisition profits. Therefore, the trading losses which arose up to 31 March 2014 cannot be set against the profits for the period ended 30 September 2016.

Tutorial note

If the restriction is relevant, it also applies to the two previous accounting periods ended 31 March 2015 and 31 March 2016. This means that it will be necessary to recalculate Bond Ltd's corporation tax liability for those periods.

3 *Rollover relief*

A gain on a qualifying business asset may be relieved where the proceeds on the disposal of that asset are matched with expenditure on another qualifying business asset under replacement of business assets (rollover) relief. The members of a chargeable gains group are treated as a single unit for the purpose of claiming such relief. Bond Ltd and Ungar Ltd are in a chargeable gains group because Bond Ltd owns at least 75% of Ungar Ltd. Madison Ltd is not in the chargeable gains group because Bond Ltd only owns 65% of that company.

Bond Ltd can therefore match its gain with acquisitions made by itself or by Ungar Ltd within the period starting 1 May 2015 and ending 30 April 2019. Full relief will be available if the expenditure is at least £350,000. Otherwise, there will be a chargeable gain equal to the amount of proceeds not reinvested, up to a maximum equal to the gain of £180,000.

The only qualifying acquisition about which there is information is the building acquired by Ungar Ltd on 1 July 2015 for £310,000. Rollover relief of £140,000 (£180,000 - £40,000) would be available on this acquisition as £(350,000 – 310,000) = £40,000 of the gain is left in charge.

Further relief may be available if there are more acquisitions of qualifying assets, for example if there are items of fixed plant within the purchases of plant and machinery made by Bond Ltd.

(b) **Ungar Ltd – Patent box election**

The patent box scheme could apply to Ungar Ltd as it has patent profits attributable to qualifying patents because it has carried on qualifying development in relation to the patents for new baking processes and techniques.

Ungar Ltd would need to make an election to HM Revenue and Customs for the patent box scheme to apply.

Patent profits within the patent box would include royalty income received directly from qualifying patents and a proportion of Ungar Ltd's profits in respect of the sale of products incorporating the use of those patents.

A reduced rate of corporation tax applies to profits within the patent box by deducting an amount from the company's taxable profits so that, when the corporation tax rate is applied to the reduced figure, the effective rate is 10% on the patent box profits.

In FY 2015, only 80% of the profits within the patent box are taxed at the effective 10% rate. In future years, this percentage will increase until all the profits within the patent box are taxed at an effective 10% rate.

(c) **Recovery of Value added tax (VAT) on assets acquired by Madison Ltd**

Building

The capital goods scheme will apply to the building because it cost £250,000 or more.

Madison Ltd will be able to recover (£400,000 × 20% = £80,000) × 80% = £64,000 on the building in the year ended 30 September 2017.

For each subsequent VAT year, during the recovery period of 10 years, an adjustment will be made to the VAT recovery. The adjustment is equal to the difference in percentage use between the first VAT year and the VAT year under review × 1/10 × the original input tax. For example, if the percentage in the year to 30 September 2018 is 75%, Madison Ltd would need to repay to HM Revenue and Customs:

((80% − 75%) = 5%) × 1/10 × £80,000 = £400.

Machinery

The capital goods scheme does not apply to machinery. Madison Ltd will be able to recover £300,000 × 20% × 80% = £48,000 on the machinery in the year ended 30 September 2017 and there will be no adjustment in later years.

29 Trifles Ltd (ATAX 12/10)

Text references. Repurchase of own shares is covered in Chapter 23 and close companies are dealt with in Chapter 25.

Top tips. If you are asked to compute tax on an extra amount of income, you should compute tax at the marginal rate on that extra income rather than produce a full income tax computation. Note the acceptable 'short cut' of computing higher rate tax on dividend income using the 25% rate.

Easy marks. The calculation of the capital receipt was relatively straightforward.

Examiner's comments. Part (a) required candidates to explain whether two of the conditions necessary to enable the amount received to be treated as capital were satisfied. Many candidates answered this part well but others, with similar knowledge levels, did not perform well because they failed to answer the question. Rather than addressing the two particular conditions set out in the question, this latter group attempted to address all of the conditions despite the majority of them being irrelevant.

Candidates had a good knowledge of the five-year rule and the 30% rule but were much less comfortable with the condition relating to the shareholder's interest in the company following the purchase. The rules require the shareholder's interest to be no more than 75% of the interest prior to the purchase – this is not the same as the shareholder selling 25% of his shares because the shares sold are cancelled thus reducing the number of issued shares.

Only a minority of candidates were aware that the ownership period of the husband could be added to that of the wife. Even fewer knew that the usual five-year ownership period is reduced to three where the shares are inherited.

Part (b) required calculations of the after tax proceeds depending on the tax treatment of the sum received. This part was answered well by the vast majority of candidates. The only point that many candidates missed was the availability of entrepreneurs' relief. It was particularly pleasing to see the majority of candidates correctly identify the after tax proceeds as the amount received less the tax liability (as opposed to the taxable amount less the tax liability).

The final part of the question was more difficult and, unsurprisingly, caused more problems. The question concerned the loan of a motorcycle to a shareholder in a close company who was not an employee. Candidates had no problem recognising that the company was a close company but many then decided that this was a loan to a participator as opposed to the loan of an asset.

Another relatively common error was to state, correctly, that the benefit would be treated as a distribution but to then give an incorrect tax rate of 40%. Candidates would benefit from slowing down and ensuring that they apply their basic tax knowledge correctly in the exam.

Marking scheme

			Marks
(a)	Victoria		
	Period of ownership	2½	
	Reduction in level of shareholding	½	
	Melba		
	Period of ownership	1	
	Reduction in level of shareholding	2½	
	Max		6
(b)	Capital receipt	4	
	Income receipt	2½	
	Max		6
(c)	Close company	1½	
	Melba		
	Recognition of distribution	1½	
	Supporting calculations	1½	
	Trifles Ltd	1	
	Max		5
			17

(a) **Purchase of own shares – conditions relating to period of ownership and reduction in level of shareholding**

Victoria

Victoria inherited the shares from her husband, Brownie. Accordingly, the required period of ownership in order for the capital treatment to apply is three years rather than the usual five years. Victoria is permitted to extend her period of ownership to include that of Brownie. Accordingly, her qualifying period is from 1 February 2013 until 28 February 2017 such that she satisfies the condition. Victoria is selling all of her shares and will therefore satisfy the condition relating to the reduction in the level of her shareholding.

Melba

Melba acquired the shares on 1 February 2009. Accordingly, she has owned them for more than five years such that she satisfies the condition for capital treatment.

After the purchase of Victoria's shares, Melba's 1,700 shares will represent 20% (1,700/(10,000 – 1,500)) of Trifles Ltd issued share capital. In order to satisfy the condition for capital treatment, her interest in the company after the purchase of her shares must be no more than 15% (20% × 75%). However, after the purchase of her shares she will own 1,250 shares (1,700 – 450) out of a total issued share capital of 8,050 shares (10,000 – 1,500 (Victoria) – 450 (Melba)) representing a 15.53% holding such that the condition is not satisfied.

(b)   **Victoria – after tax proceeds from the purchase of own shares**

Capital receipt

	£
Proceeds (1,500 × £30)	45,000
Less cost (probate value)	(16,000)
	29,000
Less capital loss brought forward	(3,300)
	25,700
Less annual exempt amount	(11,100)
Taxable gain	14,600
Capital gains tax @ 10% (entrepreneurs' relief rate)	1,460
	£
After tax proceeds £(45,000 – 1,460)	43,540

Income receipt

	£
Amount received (1,500 × £30)	45,000
Less original subscription price (1,500 × £2)	(3,000)
Distribution	42,000
Income tax @ 25% (N)	10,500
After tax proceeds £(45,000 – 10,500)	34,500

Note

This is the effective rate of income tax suffered by a higher rate taxpayer on a distribution, ie 100/90 × (32.5% – 10%).

Tutorial note

If the amount received is treated as income, Victoria will also realise a capital loss of £13,000. This is the excess of her cost (£16,000) over the original subscription price of the shares (£3,000).

(c)   **Tax implications of the loan of the motorcycle**

Trifles Ltd is a close company as it is controlled by five or fewer shareholders.

Melba

The loan of the motorcycle cannot give rise to an employment income benefit because Melba will not be a director or employee of Trifles Ltd. However, the provision of a benefit by a close company to a shareholder who is not a director or an employee is treated as a distribution. Melba will be treated as having received a distribution equal to the amount that would have been taxable as employment income had she been an employee, ie £1,440 (£9,000 × 20% – (12 × £30)). Income tax will be charged at 25% (N) on the £1,440, resulting in income tax payable of £360.

Note

This is the effective rate of income tax suffered by a higher rate taxpayer on a distribution, ie 100/90 × (32.5% – 10%).

Trifles Ltd

Trifles Ltd will not be able to claim capital allowances in respect of the motorcycle or a tax deduction in respect of its running costs.

30 Bamburg Ltd (ATAX 06/14)

Text references. The flat rate scheme for VAT is covered in Chapter 29. Capital allowances are covered in Chapter 7 and replacement of business assets relief in Chapter 13. The computation of income tax is dealt with in Chapter 1 and national insurance contributions on employment income in Chapter 4. Close companies are covered in Chapter 25.

Top tips. In part (c), don't forget to consider the national insurance implications of a loan benefit.

Easy marks. There were some marks each for describing the flat rate scheme in part (a). The rules on close companies in part (c) are frequently examined.

Examiner's comments. Part (a) concerned the VAT flat rate scheme. Candidates were required to explain whether or not a particular company could join the scheme and the matters that needed to be considered in order to determine whether or not it would be financially beneficial to do so. Almost all candidates realised that the ability of the company to join the scheme depended on its taxable supplies being below the limit of £150,000. However, a small minority did not apply their knowledge to the facts of the question where there was sufficient information to reach a conclusion in respect of the company concerned. The matters that needed to be considered in relation to the financial implications of joining the scheme were not handled particularly well with many candidates appearing to be somewhat confused as to the implications of joining the scheme. This was partly due to mixing up the flat rate scheme with other VAT special schemes and also due to a lack of methodical thought. In particular, candidates should have slowed down and tried to explain the payments made to HMRC under the existing arrangements and the payments that would be made under the flat rate scheme so that a comparison could be made.

In part (b), candidates were required to explain 'the tax and financial implications' of proposals to sell a machine and rent a replacement. When candidates read the model answer to this question they will realise that this was not a challenging requirement. However, very few candidates scored well. The problem here was that candidates started writing before they had identified the issues. As a consequence of this, most candidates addressed the chargeable gain point and very little else. This was unfortunate as the chargeable gain point was not as easy as it appeared, such that many candidates got it wrong. Other points that most candidates should have been well-equipped to tackle if they had thought to do so included: a balancing charge would arise, the inability to offset capital losses against trading profits and the rent representing a cost to the company that would reduce its taxable profits.

The final part of the question concerned the extraction of funds from the company by its owner, Charlotte, and was split into two sub-requirements. The first part required calculations of the cost to the company of providing Charlotte with post-tax income of £14,000. This was relatively challenging and was not done particularly well. Candidates needed to identify that Charlotte was a higher rate taxpayer and paying national insurance contributions at the margin at the rate of 2% in order to gross up the amount required at the appropriate rate. They then had to identify that the company would have to pay employer's national insurance contributions and that this would be a tax deductible expense for the purposes of corporation tax. A minority of candidates did not read the question carefully enough, such that they calculated the cost to Charlotte of being paid a bonus or a dividend of £14,000.

				Marks
(a)	Eligibility		1½	
	VAT due normally		1	
	VAT due under flat rate scheme		2½	
	Conclusion		1	
		Max		5
(b)	One mark for each relevant point			5
(c)	(i)	Payment of bonus	3½	
		Payment of dividend	2	
			Max	5
	(ii)	Charlotte	1½	
		Bamburg Ltd		
		Close company loan to participator	2½	
		Class 1A national insurance contribution	1	
		Exemption not applicable	1	
			Max	5
				20

(a) **Value added tax (VAT) flat rate scheme**

Bamburg Ltd will be permitted to join the flat rate scheme provided its taxable supplies for the next year are not expected to exceed £150,000. On the basis that its budgeted taxable supplies for the year ending 31 March 2017 are expected to be £114,000 (£120,000 – £6,000), it is likely that this condition will be satisfied.

Bamburg Ltd currently pays VAT to HM Revenue and Customs (HMRC) equal to the output tax on its standard rated sales less its recoverable input tax.

Under the flat rate scheme, the company would pay HMRC a fixed percentage of the total of its VAT inclusive sales. Exempt supplies are included in sales for this purpose. The percentage will depend on the particular business sector in which Bamburg Ltd operates.

Whether or not it is financially beneficial for Bamburg Ltd to join the flat rate scheme will depend on the percentage which it is required to use. However, the scheme is primarily intended to reduce administration and any financial benefit is unlikely to be significant.

(b) **Implications of selling the 'Cara' machine**

The balance on the main pool of Bamburg Ltd is nil. This means that the sale of the machine will result in a balancing charge equal to the sales proceeds received of £80,000 which will increase the taxable trade profit of Bamburg Ltd.

The 'Cara' machine is a depreciating asset for the purposes of replacement of business assets. Therefore the chargeable gain of £13,000 which was deferred in respect of the purchase of the 'Cara' machine will become chargeable when the machine is sold. This will increase the taxable total profit of Bamburg Ltd in the year of sale.

No allowable capital loss will arise on the sale of the machine because it qualified for capital allowances.

In summary, Bamburg Ltd will receive proceeds of £80,000 but will have to pay additional corporation tax of £(80,000 + 13,000) × 20% = £18,600.

Once the machine has been sold, Bamburg Ltd will have to pay rent in respect of the replacement machine. This represents an outflow of cash for the company, although it will be an allowable deduction when computing the company's taxable trading profit.

(c)   (i)   **Bamburg Ltd to make an additional payment to Charlotte of £14,000**

Payment of bonus

	£
Bonus required £(14,000/(100 − 42)%)	24,138
Employer's national insurance £24,138 × 13.8%	3,331
	27,469
Less reduction in corporation tax £27,469 × 20%	(5,494)
Total cost to Bamburg Ltd	21,975

Payment of dividend

Cash dividend £(14,000/(100 − 25)%)	£18,667

Tutorial notes

1   Charlotte's salary of £46,000 will mean that the bonus will be subject to income tax at 40% and national insurance contributions at 2%.

2   The effective rate of income tax suffered by a higher rate taxpayer on dividend income is 25% (100/90 × (32.5% − 10%)).

(ii)   **Tax implications of Bamburg Ltd making a loan of £14,000 to Charlotte**

Charlotte

The interest-free loan will result in an annual employment income benefit for Charlotte because she is an employee of Bamburg Ltd. The benefit will be £420 (£14,000 × 3%) on which Charlotte will have to pay income tax at 40%.

Bamburg Ltd

Bamburg Ltd is a close company as it is wholly owned and controlled by Charlotte. When a close company makes a loan to a participator (eg a shareholder), it must pay HMRC an amount equal to 25% of the loan, in this case £3,500. This will be payable at the same time as Bamburg Ltd's corporation tax liability by 1 January 2018.

Bamburg Ltd will also have to pay class 1A national insurance contributions of £(420 × 13.8%) = £58 in respect of the loan benefit. These contributions will be allowable when computing the company's taxable trading profits.

The payment to HMRC will be required even though the loan will be for less than £15,000. This is because Charlotte owns more than 5% of the company.

31 Liza (ATAX 06/13)

Text references. Chargeable gains for companies are covered in Chapter 21 with chargeable gains groups dealt with in Chapter 26. Capital allowances are the subject of Chapter 7. VAT groups are covered in Chapter 28.

Top tips. If you choose to answer this type of multiple topic question in the exam, it is important that you are confident that you can achieve reasonable marks on all parts.

Easy marks. The computation of the chargeable gain in part (a) should have yielded easy marks. Group registration for VAT (part (c)) is a standard exam topic.

Examiner's comments. Part (a)(i) required a calculation of the chargeable gain on the sale of a building and the correct treatment of the various expenses incurred in acquiring, enhancing and maintaining the property. This was a gentle introduction to the question and was done well. Part (a) (ii) concerned rollover relief and groups for the purposes of chargeable gains. It was done well by those candidates who knew the rules and who expressed themselves carefully. This part required candidates to know three things: that rollover relief can be claimed where one company in a gains group sells a qualifying business asset and another company in the group buys one, the definition of a gains group, and the time period in which a replacement asset needs to be purchased in order for rollover relief to be available. The majority of candidates knew the first and third points although a small minority failed to address the third point despite, probably, knowing the rule.

The difficulty came in dealing with the second point and the definition of a gains group where a minority of candidates revealed a level of confusion. This stemmed from a problem in distinguishing the 75% aspect of the rule from the 51% aspect and led to some candidates concluding erroneously that Vault Ltd and Bar Ltd were in a gains group. For there to be a chargeable gains group, the direct holding between each company in the chain must be at least 75%; if it isn't, the two companies cannot be in a group regardless of the level of the indirect holding. Part (a)(iii) concerned the amount that needed to be invested in order for the maximum amount of gain to be rolled over. This was the hardest part of the question and was not done particularly well. It required candidates to know the basic rule whereby the whole of the relevant proceeds has to be spent on replacement assets in order for the maximum gain to be rolled over, whilst recognising the relevance of the non-business use of both the asset sold and the asset acquired. Almost all candidates knew the basic rule but the majority struggled to apply it in these particular circumstances.

Part (b) concerned the availability of capital allowances in respect of electrical, water and heating systems acquired as part of a building and was done well.

Part (c) concerned VAT groups. The idea here was to test another aspect of groups in order to ensure that candidates appreciated the difference between a group for the purposes of VAT and one for the purposes of chargeable gains as tested in part (a). Candidates were also required to identify the advantages and disadvantages of registering as a group for the purposes of VAT. The majority of candidates made a reasonable job of discussing the advantages and disadvantages of registering as a VAT group and made a series of concise points. However, the definition of a group for the purposes of VAT was not handled particularly well. In particular, a sizable minority of candidates thought that the required holding was 75% as opposed to control. In addition, many candidates did not appreciate that control could be exercised by an individual, ie Liza, as well as by a company, such that all of the companies in the question were able to register as a single group. As always, a minority of candidates wrote in general terms, for example, about partial exemption, rather than addressing the specifics of the question, such that they wasted time.

Marking scheme

					Marks
(a)	(i)	Chargeable gain	Max		3
	(ii)	Chargeable gains group		2	
		Identification of relevant companies		1½	
		Qualifying period		1	
			Max		4
	(iii)	Amount relievable via rollover relief		2	
		Total acquisitions necessary		1	
		Further acquisitions necessary		1½	
			Max		4
(b)		Plant and machinery as integral feature		1	
		Special rate pool		½	
		Use of AIA		1	
			Max		2
(c)		Ability to register as a group		2	
		Discussion		6	
			Max		7
					20

(a) (i) **The chargeable gain on the sale of Building 1**

		£	£
Net sale proceeds			860,000
Less: purchase price		315,000	
legal fees		9,000	
work on roof to make fit for use		38,000	
			(362,000)
			498,000
Less indexation allowance			

$$\frac{260.8 - 224.1}{224.1} = 0.164 \times £362,000$$

	£
	(59,368)
Chargeable gain	438,632

Tutorial note

A deduction is available for the legal fees incurred in acquiring the building and the costs incurred shortly afterwards in order to make the building fit for use (see *Law Shipping Co Ltd v CIR 1923*). The cost of repainting the building would have been an allowable deduction in calculating the company's trading profits and would not be allowable when computing the chargeable gain.

(ii) **Acquisition of qualifying assets for the purposes of rollover relief**

The assets can be purchased by companies within the Bar Ltd chargeable gains group. A chargeable gains group consists of a principal company, Bar Ltd, its 75% subsidiaries, the 75% subsidiaries of those subsidiaries and so on. Bar Ltd must have an effective interest of more than 50% in all of the companies in the group. Accordingly, the only companies able to purchase qualifying replacement assets are Bar Ltd and Pommel Ltd. Ring Ltd is not a 75% subsidiary of Bar Ltd, such that it and Vault Ltd cannot be members of the Bar Ltd chargeable gains group. The Hoop Ltd group is a separate group.

The qualifying replacement assets must be purchased in the period from 1 June 2015 to 31 May 2019.

(iii) **The additional amount that would need to be spent on qualifying assets**

Bar Ltd owned the building from 1 June 2010 to 31 May 2016, a period of 72 months. The building was not used for trading purposes from 1 January 2012 to 30 June 2013, a period of 18 months. Accordingly, the building was used for the purposes of the trade for a period of 54 (72 – 18) months, such that only 54/72 of the gain can be relieved via rollover relief.

Therefore, qualifying business assets costing £645,000 (£860,000 × 54/72) will need to be acquired in order to relieve the whole of the gain qualifying for rollover relief.

Only two-thirds of the new building is to be used for trading purposes, such that only £480,000 (£720,000 × 2/3) of its cost will be a qualifying acquisition for the purposes of rollover relief. Accordingly, the additional amount that would need to be spent on qualifying acquisitions in order to relieve the whole of the gain that qualifies for rollover relief would be £165,000 (£645,000 – £480,000).

(b) **Capital allowances available in respect of the new building**

Electrical, water and heating systems qualify for plant and machinery capital allowances.

They are classified as integral features, such that they are included in the special rate pool where the writing down allowance is only 8%.

The annual investment allowance available to the Bar Ltd group should be set against these additions in priority to those assets which qualify for the 18% writing down allowance.

(c) **Group registration for the purposes of value added tax (VAT)**

The companies able to register as a group

Two or more companies may register as a group provided they are established in the UK, or have a fixed establishment in the UK, and they are controlled by the same person. The person can be an individual, a company, or a partnership. Accordingly, all of the companies in the Bar Ltd and Hoop Ltd groups can register as a single group for the purposes of VAT.

The potential advantages and disadvantages of registering as a group

The advantage of a group registration would be that there would be no need to charge VAT on the transactions between the group companies. This would reduce administration and improve the group's cash flow.

The group would have to appoint a representative member which would account for the group's VAT liability as if the group were a single entity. Consequently, there would be a need to collate information from all of the members of the group and to present it in a single VAT return. This may not be straightforward, depending on the accounting systems and procedures used by the various companies within the two separate groups.

Vault Ltd makes zero rated supplies and will therefore be in a repayment position, such that it can improve its cash flow by accounting for VAT on a monthly basis. However, if it were registered as part of a VAT group, it would not be able to do this as the group, as a single entity, is very unlikely to be in a regular repayment position. Accordingly, if a group registration is to be entered into, consideration should be given to excluding Vault Ltd from that registration.

Finally, it should be recognised that all of the companies within the group registration would have joint and several liability for the VAT due from the representative member. Liza, and the minority shareholders, should give careful consideration to the possible dangers of linking the two groups in such a manner.

32 Drake Ltd, Gosling plc and Mallard Ltd

Text references. Intangible assets and research and development relief are covered in Chapter 20. Disincorporation relief is dealt with in Chapter 21.

Top tips. The treatment of goodwill in part (a) is new in FAs15 and so is highly topical. Note the difference between the tax treatment of a credit on the disposal of goodwill (trading) and a debit on the sale of goodwill (non-trading). In part (b), don't forget to deduct the R&D expenditure as well as dealing with the additional elements which give extra relief.

Easy marks. In part (c), you should learn the conditions for disincorporation relief for easy marks.

Marking scheme

				Marks
(a)	No deduction for amortisation		1	
	Disposal of goodwill calculation		1	
	Tax treatment of credit		½	
	Tax treatment of debit		1½	
				4
(b)	(i)	Deduction relief		
		Deduct R&D expenditure	½	
		Additional deduction	1	
		Corporation tax	½	
				2

170   Answers

BPP LEARNING MEDIA

				Marks
(ii)	ATL relief			
	Add tax credit	1		
	Deduct R&D expenditure	½		
	Corporation tax	½		
	Deduct tax credit	1		
				3
(c) (i)	Going concern transfer to shareholder	1		
	All assets except cash	½		
	MV does not exceed £100,000 – information needed	1		
	Individuals and shares held at least 12 months	1		
	Dates	½		
				4
(ii)	Election by company and shareholder	1		
	Date for election	1		
				2
(iii)	Shop	1½		
	Goodwill	2		
		Max		3
(iv)	Motor car	1		
	Inventory	1		
				2
				20

(a) Drake Ltd

Whilst Drake Ltd owns the goodwill no tax deduction will be available for the amortisation of the goodwill so this must be added back in calculating the company's tax-adjusted trading profit.

On a disposal of the goodwill, a credit (profit) or debit (loss) must be calculated. This is the difference between the proceeds received and the original cost of the goodwill.

If there is a credit on the sale of the goodwill, this is taxable as trading income.

If there is a debit on the sale of the goodwill this is a non-trading debit. The non-trading debit can be set off against total profits in the same accounting period or a claim can be made for group relief. Any remaining debit is carried forward to the next accounting period as a non-trading debit of that period.

(b) Gosling plc – R&D reliefs

(i) *Deduction relief*

	£
Taxable total profit before R&D expenditure	4,500,000
Less R&D expenditure	(500,000)
R&D additional deduction £500,000 × 30%	(150,000)
Taxable total profit	3,850,000
Corporation tax payable £3,850,000 × 20%	770,000

(ii) *ATL tax credit*

	£
Taxable total profit before R&D expenditure	4,500,000
Add ATL credit £500,000 × 11%	55,000
Less R&D expenditure	(500,000)
Taxable total profit	4,055,000
Corporation tax £4,055,000 × 20%	811,000
Less ATL credit £500,000 × 11%	(55,000)
Corporation tax payable	756,000

(c)   **Mallard Ltd – Disincorporation relief**

   (i)   An election for disincorporation relief may be made where:

   1   The company is transferring its business as a going concern to an individual who is a shareholder.

   2   All of the assets of the business (except cash) are being transferred.

   3   Market value of the goodwill and land and buildings does not exceed £100,000 – further information is required to confirm whether this condition is met.

   4   The transfer is to individuals who have held shares in the company for at least 12 months prior to the transfer.

   5   The transfer will occur after 1 April 2013 but before 31 March 2018.

   (ii)   Mallard Ltd and Nathan must make a joint election for disincorporation relief.

   The election must be made within two years of the transfer to Nathan.

   (iii)   The freehold shop is deemed to have been disposed of by Mallard Ltd at the lower of market value and cost. Therefore no chargeable gain will arise. Nathan will acquire the shop at the deemed disposal value.

   The goodwill is deemed to have been disposed of at the lower of market value and tax written down value. Since the goodwill has been built up since incorporation (rather than being purchased), the tax written down value is nil and so the deemed proceeds are therefore nil. Therefore no profit will arise on disposal. Nathan will acquire the goodwill at nil value.

   (iv)   Motor car – since Mallard Ltd and Nathan are connected persons, an election can be made to transfer the motor car at its tax written down value.

   Inventory – since Mallard Ltd and Nathan are connected persons, an election can be made to transfer the inventory at the greater of original cost and transfer price.

33 Jerome (ATAX 06/12)

Text references. Value added tax on the incorporation of a business is covered in Chapter 30. Taxable benefits and expenses for employees are deal with in Chapter 4. Allowable expenses for business are covered in Chapter 6. Corporation tax payable is the subject of Chapter 22.

Top tips. It is important to state that the transfer of assets on incorporation will be a supply for VAT unless the conditions for transfer of the business as a going concern are satisfied.

Easy marks. The conditions for VAT TOGC in part (a) should have been well known. In part (b), the calculation of car and fuel benefits and the mileage allowance were straightforward.

Examiner's comments. In part (a), candidates first needed to recognise that the sale was a transfer of a business as a going concern such that VAT should not be charged. This was done well with the majority of candidates listing the conditions that needed to be satisfied. Candidates were then expected to realise that the building being sold was a commercial building that was less than three years old. Accordingly, VAT would need to be charged in respect of the building unless the purchaser made an election to tax the building at the time of purchase. Very few candidates identified this point.

Part (b) required calculations of the total tax cost for Tricycle Ltd and Jerome in relation to the lease of car. The car would be leased by Jerome, an employee of the company, or by Tricycle Ltd. This was a practical problem that was not particularly technically difficult but required care and thought in order to score well. It was not done as well as it should have been.

The point here was that Jerome owned Tricycle Ltd such that he was interested in the total tax cost to himself and the company in respect of each of the two options. Candidates needed to recognise that there were tax implications for both the employer, Tricycle Ltd, and the employee, Jerome, in each situation. For example, if Jerome leased the car, the payment of 50 pence per business mile was tax deductible for the company but resulted in taxable income for Jerome. There was also the need to consider national insurance contributions as well as income tax and corporation tax.

The main problem for candidates was a lack of exam technique. In particular, weaker candidates did not spend sufficient time thinking about the different tax implications for both parties in each situation but focussed on Jerome when he leased the car and on Tricycle Ltd when it leased the car.

Marking scheme

					Marks
(a)		Administration – one mark for relevant point	1		
		Charge VAT unless transfer of a going concern	1		
		Conditions (one mark each, maximum three marks)	3		
		Land and buildings	2½		
				Max	6
(b)	(i)	Motor car leased by Tricycle Ltd			
		Income tax payable by Jerome	2½		
		Net taxes saved by Tricycle Ltd	3		
		Net tax cost	½		
	(ii)	Motor car leased by Jerome			
		Total tax payable by Jerome	3		
		Net taxes saved by Tricycle Ltd	1½		
		Net tax saved	½		
				Max	10
(c)		Conditions – one mark each			2
					18

(a) **Value added tax (VAT) on the sale of the business**

HM Revenue and Customs should be notified of the sale of the business within 30 days.

Jerome's VAT registration will need to be cancelled unless it is to be taken over by Tricycle Ltd.

VAT must be charged on the sale of the business assets unless it qualifies as a transfer of a going concern. For the sale of the business to be regarded as a transfer of a going concern, the following conditions must be satisfied:

- The business must be a going concern.
- Tricycle Ltd must use the assets to carry on the same kind of business as that carried on by Jerome.
- Tricycle Ltd must be VAT registered or be required to be VAT registered as a result of the purchase (based on the turnover of the purchased business in the previous 12 months).
- There should be no significant break in trading before or after the purchase of the business.

Even if the transfer satisfies the above conditions, Jerome will need to charge VAT on the sale of the building as it is a commercial building that is less than three years old. The only exception to this is if Tricycle Ltd makes an election to tax the building at the time of purchase.

(b)   **Tax costs incurred in respect of the motor car**

(i)   **Motor car is leased by Tricycle Ltd**

Jerome

	£
Taxable benefit in respect of the private use of the motor car	
145 (rounded down) − 95 = 50 ÷ 5 =	
10% + 14% + 3% (diesel) = 27%	
27% × £31,000	8,370
Taxable benefit in respect of the private fuel	
27% × £22,100	5,967
	14,337
Income tax at 40% payable by Jerome	5,735

Tricycle Ltd

	Allowable expenses £	Tax £
Lease payments		
£4,400 × 85% (100% − 15%)	3,740	
Running costs	5,000	
Class 1A NICs £14,337 × 13.8%	1,979	1,979
	10,719	
Reduction in corporation tax £10,719 × 20%		(2,144)
Net taxes saved by Tricycle Ltd		(165)
Total tax cost £(5,735 − 165)		5,570

Tutorial notes

1   Jerome's salary of £48,000 per year exceeds the personal allowance plus the basic rate band, such that he will be a higher rate taxpayer.

2   15% of the lease payments will be disallowed because the CO_2 emissions of the car are above 130 g/km.

(ii)   **Motor car is leased by Jerome**

Jerome

	£
Taxable mileage allowance	
10,000 × (50 − 45)p	500
(14,000 − 10,000) × (50 − 25)p	1,000
	1,500
Income tax at 40% payable by Jerome	600
Class 1 NICs payable by Jerome	
14,000 × (50 − 45)p × 2%	14
Total tax payable by Jerome	614

Tricycle Ltd

	Allowable expenses £	Tax £
Mileage allowance paid 14,000 × 50p	7,000	
Class 1 NICs payable by Tricycle Ltd 14,000 × (50 – 45)p × 13.8%	$\underline{97}$ 7,097	97
Reduction in corporation tax £7,097 × 20%		(1,419)
Net taxes saved by Tricycle Ltd		(1,322)
Net taxes saved £(1,322 – 614)		708

Tutorial notes

1   The calculations reflect the tax implications of the two alternatives. Jerome controls the company such that the non-tax costs incurred (lease payments, running costs and mileage allowances) are going to be incurred regardless of who leases the car and are therefore only relevant to the extent that they increase or reduce a tax liability. However, Jerome may need to extract funds from the company in order to pay the costs relating to the motor car. This would give rise to further tax liabilities that would need to be considered.

2   Class 1 national insurance contributions are payable in respect of mileage allowances on the excess of the rate paid over the HMRC rate for up to 10,000 miles. Jerome's salary of £48,000 exceeds the upper earnings limit of £42,385 so the rate of Jerome's national insurance contributions will be 2%.

(c)   **Conditions for deduction of travel costs**

- The employee must be absent from the UK for a continuous period of at least 60 days for the purposes of performing the duties of his employment.
- The journey must be from the UK to the place where the employee is carrying out the duties of his employment.

Tutorial note

A deduction is only available for two outward and two return journeys by the same person(s) in the same tax year.

34 Spetz Ltd group (ATAX 12/13)

Text references. Value added tax partial exemption is dealt with in Chapter 29. Company residence is covered in Chapter 20 and double taxation relief and the exemption for overseas branches in Chapter 27.

Top tips. Remember to round up the percentage recovery for partial exemption to the nearest whole number.

Easy marks. The computation of corporation tax and double tax relief in part (b)(ii) was not particularly complicated. You might have guessed that travel for a private holiday in part (c) was not relevant for tax purposes.

Examiner's comments. Part (a) was done reasonably well by those candidates who had a working knowledge of the *de minimis* rules. A minority of candidates had very little awareness of the rules, such that their performance was poor. Candidates who did not have a precise knowledge of the rules were able to score reasonably well provided they satisfied the requirement and attempted to address all three *de minimis* tests.

Part (b)(i) required an explanation of how to determine whether or not the company was resident in the UK. This simply required a statement of the rules regarding country of incorporation and place of management and control but the majority of candidates were unable to state these fundamental rules.

Part (b)(ii) required an explanation of the company's corporation tax liability together with the advantages and disadvantages of making an election to exempt the profits of an overseas permanent establishment from UK tax. This was done well. The majority of candidates prepared a short accurate calculation and were able to state the particular disadvantages of making such an election.

Part (c) concerned the travel and subsistence costs of an employee seconded to work overseas. This was relatively tricky but was done reasonably well by those candidates who were methodical in their approach. In particular, candidates who did not necessarily know all of the detailed rules were still able to score an acceptable mark if they applied basic principles to all three elements of the question. Very few candidates identified that the overseas workplace would be a temporary workplace. In addition, a minority of candidates discussed the tax implications for the company rather than for the employee. Candidates must read the requirement for each question carefully and ensure that their answer is always focussed on satisfying that requirement.

Marking scheme

				Marks
(a)	Test 1		1	
	Test 2		1½	
	Input tax attributed to taxable supplies and unattributed input tax		1½	
	Test 3		1½	
	Adjustment and date		1½	
				7
(b)	(i)	Not incorporated in UK	1	
		Central management and control	2	
				3
	(ii)	Calculation of liability	1½	
		Taxation of worldwide profits	1	
		Discussion of election		
		Advantage	1½	
		Disadvantage	2	
		Max		5
(c)	Flights at start and end of contract		3	
	Return flight in February		1½	
	Laundry and telephone calls		2	
		Max		5
				20

(a)   **Novak Ltd – Value added tax (VAT) partial exemption annual adjustment**

Test 1 is not satisfied, as the total input tax exceeds an average of £625 per month (£625 × 12 = £7,500).

Test 2 is not satisfied, as the total input tax less that directly attributed to taxable supplies exceeds an average of £625 per month (£12,200 + £4,900 + £16,100 − £12,200 = £21,000, £21,000/12 = £1,750).

	£
Input tax attributable to taxable supplies	12,200
Unattributed input tax £16,100 × 74% (W1)	11,914
Recoverable input tax (W2)	24,114
Less input tax recovered on quarterly returns	(23,200)
Annual adjustment – additional input tax recoverable	914

The annual adjustment must be made on the final VAT return of the year, which is the return for the period ended 30 September 2016, or the first VAT return after the end of the year at the option of the company.

Workings

1   *Recoverable unattributed input tax*

$$\frac{£1,190,000}{£1,190,000 + £430,000} \times 100 = 73.4\%, \text{ rounded up to } 74\%.$$

2   *Recoverable input tax*

Exempt input tax of (£4,900 + £[16,100 − 11,914]) = £9,086 exceeds the Test 3 limit of £625 per month and is therefore irrecoverable.

(b)   (i)   **Residence status of Kraus Co**

A company is regarded as resident in the UK if it is incorporated in the UK or if its central management and control is exercised in the UK. Kraus Co was incorporated in the country of Mersano.

Accordingly, Kraus Co will only be resident in the UK if its central management and control is exercised in the UK. The central management and control of a company is usually regarded as being exercised in the place where the meetings of the board of directors are held.

(ii)   **Kraus Co**

UK resident companies are subject to corporation tax on their worldwide income.

	£
Corporation tax: £520,000 × 20%	104,000
Less: unilateral double taxation relief £520,000 × 17%	(88,400)
UK corporation tax liability	15,600

Tutorial note

The profits will be subject to tax because no election has been made to exempt the profits and losses of the overseas permanent establishment from UK corporation tax.

Election to exempt the overseas profits from UK tax

The advantage of making such an election would be that the profits made in Mersano would not be subject to UK corporation tax. Based on the current rates of corporation tax in the two countries, this would save corporation tax at the rate of (20% − 17%) = 3%.

When considering this election, it should be recognised that it is irrevocable and would apply to all future overseas permanent establishments of Kraus Co. Accordingly, there would be no relief in the UK for any losses incurred in the trade in Mersano in the future or for any other losses incurred in any additional overseas trades operated by Kraus Co.

(c)   **Meyer's secondment to Kraus Co**

The reimbursement of expenses by an employer represents taxable income for an employee. Accordingly, the cost of the flights at the start and end of the contract represents taxable income for Meyer. However, a deduction of an equal amount will be available because:

- It is necessary for Meyer to travel to Mersano in order to perform the duties of his employment.

- The workplace in Mersano is a temporary workplace (the secondment is for less than 24 months), so the travelling does not constitute ordinary commuting.

The cost of the return journey to the UK in February 2017 has no UK tax implications. Meyer will not be able to claim a tax deduction for the costs incurred because the journey is for a private purpose and he, rather than Spetz Ltd, will bear the cost.

The reimbursement of the cost of laundry and telephone calls home will be exempt from tax if less than £10 per night. If this limit is exceeded, the whole of the amount reimbursed will be subject to UK income tax.

Tutorial note

Credit was also available to candidates who focused their answers on the special rules relating to travel cost where duties are performed abroad.

35 Nocturne Ltd (ATAX 06/15)

Text references. Close companies are covered in Chapter 25 and capital allowances in Chapter 7. Chattels are dealt with in Chapter 14. Income tax computation is covered in Chapter 1. Value added tax partial exemption is dealt with in Chapter 29.

Top tips. Make sure you read the question carefully and do not jump to conclusions about what it is asking you!

Easy marks. There were some easy marks for applying the partial exemption tests in part (c).

Examiner's comments. Part (a) concerned two alternative ways in which a computer was to be provided to a shareholder who was not employed by the company. Despite knowing the relevant rules, candidates did not perform as well as they could have done in this part for two reasons. Firstly, they failed to consider all of the aspects of the situation and secondly, they did not answer the question set. Most candidates appreciated that the provision of the computer would give rise to a distribution but many failed to address the capital allowances position of the company. This was important because it differed in the two alternative situations. Similarly, many candidates failed to address the tax treatment of the loss on the transfer of the existing computer in the second alternative. Candidates will benefit if they think before they write and identify all the different aspects of the transaction. They should then address each of the aspects in a concise manner. The failure to answer the question set related to the need to determine the after-tax cost for the company. Most candidates focussed on the tax treatment for the individual, which meant that they missed out on some of the available marks.

Part (b) concerned Siglio, the company's managing director, who was going to borrow money from a bank and then lend it to the company. Many candidates provided unsatisfactory answers to this question part because they wanted the question to deal with a loan from a close company to a participator in that company – but it wasn't. It was also important to deal with the two loans separately. The loan to the company was a normal commercial loan. The company would obtain a tax deduction for the interest paid and Siglio would pay income tax on the interest income in the normal way. It was no more complicated than that. The loan from the bank to Siglio was more interesting in that it would be a qualifying loan, such that the interest paid by Siglio would be tax deductible. Some candidates were aware of this point but very few stated the detailed reasons for the tax deduction being available.

The final part of the question concerned VAT and was in two parts. Part (i) concerned the partial exemption *de minimis* tests. It was a straight forward test of the rules and was done well by those candidates who knew them. As always, it was important to read the question carefully and to address the requirement and nothing more; some candidates wasted time by addressing other aspects of VAT that were not required. Candidates should recognise that VAT is tested at every sitting and that the partial exemption rules are tested regularly. Part (ii) concerned the annual test for computing recoverable input tax and was not done well. The problem here was that the majority of candidates addressed the annual accounting scheme rather than the subject of the question. This was unfortunate and meant that very few candidates did well on this part of the question. Candidates should always try to be sure as to what the question is about; both parts of part (c) related to partial exemption.

Marking scheme

				Marks
(a)	Close company		1	
	Purchase of new computer for Jed		2½	
	Transfer of existing computer to Jed		3½	
	Conclusion		½	
		Max		7
(b)	Treatment of interest received		1½	
	Conditions for income tax deduction		2½	
	Conclusion		½	
		Max		4

				Marks
(c)	(i)	Test 1	2	
		Test 2	2	
		Conclusion	½	
		Max		4
	(ii)	Annual test		
		Conditions	2	
		Application to Nocturne Ltd	1	
		Implications	3	
		Max		5
				20

(a) Provision of laptop computer for Jed

Option 1: Purchase of new laptop computer

Nocturne Ltd is a close company because it is under the control of five or fewer shareholders (in this particular case it is controlled by any three out of its four shareholders) who are called 'participators'. Jed is a participator in Nocturne Ltd.

As Jed does not work for Nocturne Ltd, the provision of the laptop is not taxable under the benefits code, but since he is a participator of Nocturne Ltd he will treated as receiving a deemed distribution of the amount that would otherwise be taxed as a benefit (the use of asset benefit). No national insurance contributions are payable. Nocturne Ltd cannot deduct capital allowances on the new laptop.

Nocturne Ltd cannot deduct any further capital allowances on the old laptop because it already has a tax written value of nil.

Option 1 therefore has an after-tax cost to Nocturne Ltd of the cost of the laptop which is £1,800.

Option 2: Transfer of existing laptop computer

As Jed is a participator of Nocturne Ltd he will treated as receiving a deemed distribution of the amount that would otherwise be taxed as a benefit (the gift of asset benefit). No national insurance contributions are payable.

The transfer of the old laptop computer to Jed will result in a balancing charge of £150 (market value less tax written down value of pool) for Nocturne Ltd. This will result in additional corporation tax of £150 × 20% = £30.

The transfer of the old laptop will also be a disposal of a chattel by Nocturne Ltd but this is an exempt disposal as both cost and deemed proceeds are less than £6,000.

The new laptop will be eligible for capital allowances as it is to be used in Nocturne Ltd's business. The annual investment allowance will be available to cover the full amount of £1,800 and so there will be a corporation tax saving of £1,800 × 20% = £360 so the net cost of the new laptop will be £(1,800 − 360) = £1,440.

Option 2 therefore has an after-tax cost to Nocturne Ltd of £(30 + 1,440) = £1,470.

Conclusion

Option 2 is therefore the preferable option for Nocturne Ltd as it would result in a lower after-tax cost.

(b) Provision of loan finance by Siglio

Siglio will receive interest on the loan from Nocturne Ltd net of basic rate tax. The gross amount of interest will be taxable on Siglio as savings income at his marginal rate of tax with credit given for the tax deducted at source.

The money lent by the bank to Siglio is then lent by him to a close company (Nocturne Ltd) to be used wholly and exclusively for the purpose of its business. Interest paid on a loan taken out to make a loan to a close company can be deductible against income. To be deductible, when the interest is paid, Siglio either must hold some shares in Nocturne Ltd and work the greater part of his time in the actual management or conduct of the company (almost certainly the case since he is the managing director) or must have a material interest in Nocturne Ltd (ie hold more than 5% of the shares). So, in fact Siglio probably meets both of these alternative conditions.

The interest payable by Siglio on the loan from his bank is therefore deductible from Siglio's total income to compute his net income and he is thus given tax relief.

(c)   (i)   **Recoverable input VAT for the year ended 31 March 2016**

Test 1

All the input VAT is recoverable if the amount of input VAT relating to exempt supplies is small (*de minimis*). Under Test 1, the *de minimis* condition is satisfied if the total input VAT incurred is no more than £625 per month on average (£7,500 a year) and the value of exempt supplies is no more than 50% of all supplies.

As the total input VAT incurred by Nocturne Ltd for the year to 31 March 2016 is £(7,920 + 1,062 + 4,150) = £13,132, Test 1 is not satisfied even though the value of exempt supplies is only 14% of all supplies.

Test 2

Under Test 2, the de minimis condition is satisfied if the total input VAT incurred less input VAT directly attributed to taxable supplies is no more than £625 per month on average (£7,500 a year) and the value of exempt supplies is no more than 50% of the value of all supplies.

Test 2 is satisfied because the total input VAT incurred by Nocturne Ltd less input VAT directly attributed to taxable supplies is £(13,132 − 7,920) = £5,212 and the value of exempt supplies is 14%.

(ii)   **Annual test**

The annual test gives Nocturne Ltd the option of applying the *de minimis* test once a year rather than for every VAT return period.

To use the annual test, Nocturne Ltd must satisfy the following conditions:

- Have been *de minimis* in the previous partial exemption year;
- Will consistently apply the annual test throughout any given partial exemption year;
- Have reasonable grounds for not expecting to incur more than £1m input tax in its current partial exemption year.

As Nocturne Ltd was *de minimis* in the partial exemption year to 31 March 2016 and should satisfy the other conditions for the partial exemption year ended 31 March 2017, Nocturne Ltd can opt to treat itself as *de minimis* in that year.

This means that there will be provisional recovery of all input tax in the year which will give a cash flow benefit and an administrative time saving. The administrative time saving is particularly useful as the company's turnover and associated costs are expected to increase in the year ended 31 March 2017 so that Tests 1 and 2 may no longer be satisfied and the more complex Test 3 might otherwise have to be applied for each return period.

At the end of the year to 31 March 2017, Nocturne Ltd must review its status using the *de minimis* tests applied to the year as a whole. If one of the tests is failed, it must carry out an annual adjustment which will result in a repayment of part of the input VAT previously recovered in full.

36 Desiree (ATAX 06/10)

Text references. Basis of assessment for unincorporated businesses is covered in Chapter 6 and losses in Chapter 8. The basis of assessment for companies is covered in Chapter 20 and losses in Chapter 24. Registration for VAT is covered in Chapter 28.

Top tips. The trading loss for a tax year is usually simply the trading loss in the basis period for that tax year. However, if basis periods overlap, as in this question, then a loss in the overlap period is a trading loss for the earlier tax year only.

Easy marks. The basis of assessment for companies and sole traders should have produced easy marks.

Examiner's comments. The majority of candidates scored high marks in part (a)(i) although some had difficulty calculating the figure for the second tax year of an unincorporated business based on the first 12 months of trading. Those who did not do so well simply did not know the basic mechanical rules and either missed out this part of the question or tried to make it up. The opening and closing year's rules for unincorporated traders are examined regularly and candidates preparing for future sittings are likely to benefit from being able to handle them.

Part (a) (ii) was done well by almost all of the candidates who attempted it. In order to maximise marks here it was necessary to be precise in terms of language used. For example, it was not sufficient to state that losses can be carried forward against future profits. Instead, candidates needed to state that losses could be carried forward for offset against future profits of **the same trade**.

There was also a requirement to state which business structure would best satisfy the client's objectives. The mark available for this was missed by those candidates who had stopped thinking and were simply writing down everything they knew about loss relief.

The other difficulty which candidates had with this part of the question was a failure to recognise that not all possible loss reliefs were available due to the particular facts of the question. Candidates should ensure that they do not write at length about matters which are irrelevant.

In the final part of the question, many candidates let themselves down by not reading the question carefully such that they simply listed all the advantages and disadvantages they could think of without focusing on the word 'financial' or the particular facts surrounding the client. This meant that they missed the possibility of recovering pre-registration VAT, which was often the difference between an OK mark and a good mark.

Marking scheme

					Marks
(a)	(i)	Business is unincorporated			
		Application of opening year rules		2½	
		Losses counted once only		1	
		Business operated as a company		1	
			Max		4
	(ii)	Business is operated via a company		2½	
		Business is unincorporated			
		Reliefs available		2½	
		Application to Desiree's position		3	
	Conclusion			1	
			Max		8
(b)	Advantages				
		Recovery of input tax		1½	
		Pre-registration input tax		1½	
	Disadvantages			1½	
			Max		4
					16

(a)   (i)   **Taxable profit/allowable loss for each of the first three taxable periods**

Business is unincorporated

	Taxable profit £	Allowable loss £
2016/17		
1 September 2016 to 5 April 2017 (actual)		
Taxable profit	0	
Allowable loss £(46,000) × 7/10		32,200
2017/18		
1 September 2016 to 31 August 2017 (first 12 months)		
Taxable profit	0	
Loss of period ending 30 June 2017		46,000
Less loss allocated to 2016/17		(32,200)
Loss allocated to 2017/18		13,800
Profit of period 1 July 2017 to 31 August 2017		
£22,000 × 2/12		(3,667)
Loss 2017/18		10,133
2018/19		
1 July 2017 to 30 June 2018 (current year basis)		
Taxable profit	22,000	
Allowable loss		0

Business operated via a company

	Taxable profit £	Allowable loss £
10 month period ending 30 June 2017	0	46,000
Year ending 30 June 2018	22,000	0
Year ending 30 June 2019	64,000	0

(ii)   **Advice on whether or not the business should be incorporated**

Business is operated via a company

If the business is operated via a company, the loss of the period ending 30 June 2017 will be carried forward for offset against future trading profits of the same trade.

The earliest that any of the company's losses will be relieved is the year ending 30 June 2018 thus reducing the corporation tax payable on 1 April 2019. However, the tax savings will only arise if the budgeted profits are achieved. If the business does not achieve profitability the losses will be wasted.

Business is unincorporated

If the business is unincorporated, the loss in each of the two tax years can be offset against:

- The general income of the year of loss and/or the previous year

- The general income of the three years prior to the year of loss starting with the earliest of the three years

This enables Desiree to obtain immediate relief for the losses.

Desiree has employment income in 2016/17 of only £12,000 (£72,000 × 2/12) together with bank interest of less than £1,000. Most of this income will be covered by her personal allowance. Her general income in earlier years is her salary of £72,000 and the bank interest. Accordingly, she should offset the losses against the income of 2015/16 and earlier years rather than the income of 2016/17.

The loss of 2016/17 could be offset against the general income of 2015/16 (the previous year) or 2013/14 (the first of the three years prior to 2016/17) under early years loss relief.
The loss of 2017/18 could be offset against the general income of 2014/15 (the first of the three years prior to 2017/18) under early years loss relief.

This will obtain full relief for the losses mostly at the higher rate of tax.

Conclusion

Desiree's primary objective is the most beneficial use of the loss. She should run the business as an unincorporated sole trader in order to obtain relief for the losses as soon as possible.

(b)   **Financial advantages and disadvantages of Desiree registering voluntarily for VAT**

Advantages

Registering for VAT will enable the business to recover input tax, where possible, on expenses and capital expenditure. This will reduce the costs incurred by the business thus reducing its losses and its capital allowances.

The VAT incurred on the fees paid to the market research consultants in March 2016 can be recovered as pre-registration input tax. The payment in November 2015 is more than six months prior to registration and therefore the input tax in relation to it cannot be recovered.

Disadvantages

The business will have to charge its customers VAT at 20%. This will represent an increase in the prices charged to those customers who are unable to recover VAT, ie domestic customers and non-VAT registered business customers. Desiree may need to consider reducing prices in order to reduce the impact of the additional VAT on these customers.

37 Poblano (ATAX 06/10)

Text references. Employment income is covered in Chapter 4. The personal accountability of senior accounting officer of large company is described in Chapter 22. Inheritance tax on lifetime gifts is dealt with in Chapter 16 and on the death estate in Chapter 17. Trusts are described in Chapter 18 and trust income is covered in Chapter 3.

Top tips. You must attempt all the parts of a question if you are to be successful in the P6 examination.

Easy marks. The calculation of inheritance tax liabilities in part (c) was reasonably straightforward.

Examiner's comments. Part (a) concerned the implications of a change to an employee's location of work. On the whole this part of the question was done reasonably well. However, in order to score a high mark for this part it was necessary to focus on the client's financial position and calculate how much better or worse off he was going to be as a result of the change. This required candidates to think in terms of income and costs (with tax as a cost) and to recognise that costs that are not tax deductible are still costs and are therefore still relevant. This aspect of the question was not handled particularly well.

The calculation of the benefit in respect of the flat provided by the company was done well. However, the majority of candidates failed to recognise that the mileage allowance related to travel to and from work and was therefore taxable in full.

It was pleasing to note that fewer candidates than in the past provided lengthy explanations of what they were going to do before getting on and doing it. However, the question asked for an explanation of the tax treatment of two particular points; the receipt of the mileage allowance and the receipt of the rent. Many candidates failed to provide these explanations. Candidates must identify and carry out all of the tasks in the question in order to maximise their marks.

Part (b) concerned the rules in relation to senior accounting officers. The majority of candidates were not aware of them and, consequently, found it difficult to score well on this part of the question. Having said that, there were also marks available for pointing out that the client's error needed to be communicated to HMRC and for identifying the action necessary if the client was unwilling to make such disclosure. Accordingly, it was possible to score reasonably well in this part of the question without any knowledge of the senior accounting officer rules.

Part (c) of the question concerned inheritance tax and the advantages of lifetime giving. At first sight it was a daunting question requiring the consideration of three possible property values, two dates of death and a lifetime gift or gift via will; a total of 12 possible situations. However, there was guidance from the 'manager' as to where to start together with the reassurance that 'you should find that the calculations do not take too long'.

It was very pleasing to find that the majority of candidates had no problem with this part of the question and that their knowledge of the basic mechanics of inheritance tax was sound. Candidates benefited from thinking rather than writing such that they were then able to realise that, for example, with a lifetime gift, the only difference between the two possible dates of death was the availability of taper relief. The best answers were admirably short and to the point.

The one area where candidates could have done better was in identifying the possible gift with reservation. The failure by many candidates to do this indicates, yet again, that some candidates do not take enough care in identifying all that has been asked of them.

The final part of the question concerned the tax treatment of income received from a trust. This was a test of knowledge, as opposed to application of knowledge, and candidates should have scored well. However, the marks for this part were not as high as expected because candidates were not sufficiently careful in their approach. As always, the advice here is to stop and think. The question made it clear that the nature of the trust was not known and therefore candidates were expected to consider the income tax position of receipts from both an interest in possession trust and a discretionary trust. There was also the need to be specific and precise, as regards grossing up fractions and tax rates, rather than superficial and general in order to maximise the marks obtained.

			Marks
(a)	Salary less tax, national insurance contributions and motoring expenses	2	
	Living in the company flat		
	Tax on the benefit	2	
	Contribution	½	
	Additional salary required	1	
	Further information required	2	
	Staying with aunt in Manchester		
	Calculations	1½	
	Mileage allowance	1½	
	Rent paid to aunt	1½	
		Max	10
(b)	Senior accounting officer	3½	
	The need to disclose the errors	2½	
	The implications of non-disclosure	2	
		Max	7
(c)	Inheritance tax liabilities		
	Nil band	1	
	Lifetime gift		
	Value at time of gift and tax rate	1	
	Fall in value post gift	1	
	Taper relief	1	
	Gift via will	1½	
	Full set of outcomes	2	
	Conclusions (1 mark each, maximum 2 marks)	2	
	Gift with reservation	2½	
	Capital gains tax	1½	
		Max	12
(d)	Nature of the trust	2	
	Tax treatment – 2 × 2 marks	4	
			6
	Appropriate style and presentation	1	
	Effectiveness of communication	1	
			2
			37

Meeting notes

Date: 7 June 2016

Re: Poblano

(a)   **Working in Manchester – Poblano's financial position**

Living in the company flat

The calculations set out below are based on the information currently available.

	£
Additional salary	15,000
Less tax £15,000 × 40% (N1)	(6,000)
national insurance contributions £15,000 × 2%	(300)
petrol and depreciation £(1,400 + 1,500) (N2)	(2,900)
Additional salary after tax, NICs and motoring expenses	5,800
Less tax on benefit in respect of use of the flat (W) £17,100 × 40% (N1)	(6,840)
contributions by Poblano £200 × 12	(2,400)
Poblano would be worse off by	(3,440)
Additional salary required for Poblano not to be out of pocket £3,440/58%	5,931

Not living in the company flat

	£
Additional salary after tax, NICs and motoring expenses	5,800
Mileage allowance 9,200 × 50p	4,600
Tax and NICs on mileage allowance £4,600 × 42% (N3)	(1,932)
Rent £325 × 12 (N4)	(3,900)
Poblano would be better off by	4,568

Notes

1   The marginal tax rate would be 40% as Poblano's adjusted net income would remain below £100,000 and so there would be no reduction in his personal allowance. This assumes any benefits eg furniture provided at the flat (see below) do not cause this limit to be exceeded.

2   The depreciation is not an immediate cost but will increase the funds needed by Poblano to purchase his next car. Poblano will not be able to claim a tax deduction for the petrol costs as they relate to travelling to and from work and not to the performance of his duties.

3   The mileage allowance would be subject to tax and national insurance contributions as Poblano would be travelling to and from work and not in the performance of his duties. Manchester will not be a temporary workplace for Poblano because he expects to work there for more than two years.

4   Poblano's aunt will not be subject to income tax on the rent. This is because it will be in respect of a (presumably) furnished room in her house and the rent does not exceed £4,250 per year.

Further information required

The cost of the furniture provided in the flat – there will be an annual taxable benefit equal to 20% of the cost.

Any running costs (utilities and maintenance etc) in respect of the flat borne by Capsicum Ltd – there will be a taxable benefit equal to the costs incurred.

Any capital improvements made to the property before the start of the tax year for which the benefit is being calculated.

Working

Taxable benefit in respect of use of the flat

	£
Annual value	9,300
Additional benefit £(415,000 – 75,000) = £340,000 × 3%	10,200
Contribution to be made by Poblano	(2,400)
Taxable benefit	17,100

Note

The cost of £415,000 will be increased by any capital improvements made to the property before the start of the tax year for which the benefit is being calculated.

(b) **Financial accounting problems in Manchester**

Responsibilities of a senior accounting officer

The senior accounting officer of a qualifying company or group of companies are required to:

- Ensure that a company's accounting systems are adequate for the purposes of calculating the company's tax liabilities.

- Certify to HM Revenue and Customs that such accounting systems exist for each financial year.

- Notify HM Revenue and Customs of any inadequacies in the accounting systems.

These rules apply to a company, or a group of companies, with turnover (revenue) of more than £200 million and/or a balance sheet total of more than £2 billion. Penalties apply for non-compliance with the rules.

The senior accounting officer of Capsicum Ltd is the director or officer with overall responsibility for the company's financial accounting arrangements. This could be Poblano or another director within the group.

Errors in the corporation tax computation

We have submitted the corporation tax return of the subsidiary of Scoville plc. We cannot allow HM Revenue and Customs to continue to rely on it now that we know it contains errors.

The company must disclose the errors to HM Revenue and Customs or authorise us to do so. This can be done via an amendment to the corporation tax return as we are within 12 months of the filing date. Disclosure of the errors is likely to increase the company's tax liability. However, we cannot continue to act for the company unless this disclosure is made.

If the company refuses to disclose the errors we will advise HM Revenue and Customs that we no longer act for the company. We would not, however, provide any details of the errors in the financial statements.

Non-disclosure of the errors would also represent tax evasion by the company, which could result in criminal proceedings under both the tax and money laundering legislation.

(c) **Property in Chilaca**

Inheritance tax liabilities

Lifetime gift on 1 August 2016

Value at death (assumed) £	Death on 31 December 2018	£	Death on 31 December 2020 (N3)	£
450,000 (N1)	£(450,000 – 35,000) (N2) × 40%	166,000	£166,000 × 60%	99,600
600,000	£(600,000 – 35,000) × 40%	226,000	£226,000 × 60%	135,600
900,000	£(600,000 – 35,000) × 40%	226,000	£226,000 × 60%	135,600

Gift via will on 31 December 2018 or 31 December 2020 (N4)

Value at death (assumed) £		£
450,000	£(450,000 – 35,000) (N2) × 40%	166,000
600,000	£(600,000 – 35,000) × 40%	226,000
900,000	£(900,000 – 35,000) × 40%	346,000

Notes

1   When made the gift will be a potentially exempt transfer, thus, if the value of the property at the time of death is less than it was at the time of the gift, the inheritance tax payable will reflect the fall in value.

2   The nil band remaining following the gift into trust on 1 June 2015 will be £35,000 (£325,000 – £290,000).

3   31 December 2020 would be between four and five years after the gift such that 40% taper relief would be available. Accordingly, the liability will be 60% of the liability calculated in respect of death occurring on 31 December 2018.

4   The date of death will not affect the amount of inheritance tax due if the property is left in the will.

Inheritance tax liabilities – conclusions

If the property is gifted on 1 August 2016, the inheritance tax due on death will never be more than that due if the property is transferred via Paprikash's will, even if the value of the property falls prior to death.

Making a lifetime gift would turn out to be particularly beneficial if:

* The value of the property increases, as the tax would be based on the value as at 1 August 2016 rather than the value at the time of death.

* Paprikash survives the gift by more than three years such that taper relief would be available.

Gift with reservation

Once the property has been given to Poblano, the occasional use of it by Paprikash may result in the gift being treated as a gift with reservation. In these circumstances, the transactions would be subject to IHT in one of two ways. The first way would be for the gift to be ignored for inheritance tax purposes and the property included in Paprikash's death estate at its value at the time of death. The second way would be for the gift to be charged to IHT and the property not included in Paprikash's death estate. The treatment which gives the greater IHT liability will apply.

In order to ensure that the gift is effective for inheritance tax purposes Paprikash should have only minimal use of the property unless he pays Poblano a market rent.

Capital gains tax

If Paprikash is resident in the UK in the year in which he gives the property to Poblano, it will be necessary to calculate a capital gain on the gift of the property.

The gain would be the market value of the property less its cost. The gain, less any available annual exempt amount, would be taxed at 28%.

There would be no capital gains tax if the property were given to Poblano via Paprikash's will.

(d)   **Tax treatment of trust income received by Poblano's daughter**

The trust will be either an interest in possession trust or a discretionary trust. It will be an interest in possession trust if Piri has an absolute right to the income generated by the trust assets. It will be a discretionary trust if the trustees have the right to accumulate the income and pay it to Piri when they choose.

It is understood that the only income received by the trustees of the trust is dividend income.

Interest in possession trust

The income to which Piri is entitled must be grossed up at 100/90. Where the income falls into Piri's basic rate band (after calculating the tax on her salary) it will be taxed at 10%. The balance of the income will be taxed at 32.5%. There will be a 10% tax credit.

Discretionary trust

The income received must be grossed up at 100/55. Where the income falls into Piri's basic rate band it will be taxed at 20%. The balance of the income will be taxed at 40%. There will be a 45% tax credit.

38 Ziti (ATAX 06/14)

Text references. Trade profits are covered in Chapter 6 and capital allowances in Chapter 7. The income tax computation is dealt with in Chapter 1. Capital gains tax computations are covered in Chapter 11 and reliefs in Chapter 13. Value added tax on land and buildings is dealt with in Chapter 29 and the conditions for transfer of a going concern in Chapter 30. Inheritance tax on lifetime transfers is covered in Chapter 16 and business property relief in Chapter 17.

Top tips. It is important to adopt a methodical approach to questions where there are alternative dates for actions. First, work out the income tax position for a cessation on 31 January 2017 and, second, the position for a cessation on 30 April 2017. Then repeat for the capital gains tax disposals. As required in the question, finally bring the computations together in a summary.

Easy marks. There were some easy marks for basic income tax computations in part (a)(i) and inheritance tax computations in part (b).

Examiner's comments. Part (a)(i) was quite substantial and was worth 17 marks. Stronger candidates structured their answers in such a way that it was very clear which of the possible methods of disposal they were addressing and then dealt with the two methods one at a time. Weaker candidates did not spend sufficient time thinking about the facts of the question and simply dealt with a disposal without making it clear which of the possibilities they were considering. The income tax aspects of the disposal revolved around the closing year rules for the unincorporated trader. It was important to be able to identify the tax years of the proposed disposal and the basis of assessment for each of the relevant years. Many candidates did not have a clear understanding of these basic rules, such that they were not able to identify the relevant tax years or to accurately calculate the taxable profits for each of the relevant tax years. The trader had purchased equipment, which was then to be sold on the cessation of the business. Most candidates identified the annual investment allowance (AIA) but many then omitted to follow the story through to the disposal, such that the balancing charge was left out. In addition, weaker candidates prepared comprehensive (and time-consuming) calculations of capital allowances in order to arrive at an AIA of £6,000. The treatment of overlap profits, the personal allowance and the calculation of income tax was done well by the vast majority of candidates. The capital gains tax implications of the sale of the business were straightforward and were handled reasonably well. However, one common error was to treat the sale of the business as if it were a sale of a single asset as opposed to a sale of the individual assets of the business. Many candidates concluded that the capital gains tax implications were the same regardless of which of the methods of disposal took place. However, this was not the case because there was a disposal of goodwill only where the business was sold as a going concern. Finally, candidates were required to prepare a summary. In order to score the maximum three marks available, candidates had to include the trading income and the proceeds from the sale of the assets together with both the income tax and the capital gains tax. It was also important to exclude any non-cash items. Very few candidates managed to score all three marks; and many candidates failed to produce any sort of summary.

Part (a)(ii) concerned the VAT implications of the disposal. This was handled well by the majority of candidates with many candidates demonstrating a good knowledge of the various conditions necessary for a sale to be regarded as a transfer of a going concern.

Part (b) concerned the basic mechanics of inheritance tax; it was done well by many candidates. Almost all candidates identified the gift of the business as a potentially exempt transfer that would become chargeable following the death of the donor within seven years. They were also competent at dealing with the annual exemptions, the nil rate band (with one exception – see below), the tax rate and taper relief.

The one area where a lot of candidates did not perform as well was when it came to business property relief (BPR). To begin with, many candidates omitted BPR altogether. Those candidates who did include BPR in their answers often failed to realise that if the business was sold by Ziti (the donee) before the death of his father (the donor), BPR would not be available because the rules require the donee to own the assets gifted at the date of the donor's death. The point referred to above regarding the nil rate band relates to the relevance of the chargeable lifetime transfer (CLT) made by the donor of the business on 1 May 2008. It was thought by some candidates that this gift would have no effect on the nil rate band available as it was more than seven years prior to the death of the donor. However, because the CLT was made within seven years of the gift of the business on 1 July 2012, the nil rate band available when calculating the tax due in respect of the gift of the business has to be reduced by the amount of the CLT.

Marking scheme

					Marks
(a)	(i)	Income tax position			
		Cessation on 31 January 2017			
		Trading income	1		
		Capital allowances	1½		
		Overlap profits	½		
		Basis period	1		
		Income tax payable	1		
		Cessation on 30 April 2017			
		Basis period	1		
		Trading income	½		
		Capital allowances	1½		
		Overlap profits	½		
		Income tax payable	1		
		Capital gains tax position			
		Cessation on 31 January 2017			
		Capital gains	2		
		Capital gains tax	1		
		Availability of entrepreneurs' relief	1		
		Cessation on 30 April 2017			
		Capital gains	½		
		Capital gains tax	½		
		Availability of entrepreneurs' relief	1		
		Summary	3		
		Assumption	1		
				Max	17
	(ii)	Sale on 31 January 2017	1½		
		Sale on 30 April 2017			
		Charge VAT unless TOGC	1		
		TOGC conditions	3		
				Max	5
(b)		Death prior to disposal of business	2		
		Death post disposal of business			
		Value of transfer	1½		
		Annual exemptions	1		
		Business property relief not available	1½		
		Taper relief	1		
		Nil rate band available	1½		
		Inheritance tax liabilities	2		
				Max	9

		Marks
Approach to problem solving	1	
Clarity of calculations	1	
Effectiveness of communication	1	
Overall presentation	1	
		4
		35

Notes for meeting

Prepared by: Tax senior
Date: 6 June 2016
Subject: Ziti – sale of business and inheritance tax

(a) **Sale of business**

(i) **Post-tax income and sales proceeds**

Income tax position

Business cessation on 31 January 2017

Taxable trading profits

Y/e 30.4.16

	£
Profits 12 × £5,000	60,000
Less: annual investment allowance on equipment 1.8.15	(6,000)
Taxable trading profits	54,000

P/e 31.1.17

	£
Profits 9 × £5,000	45,000
Add balancing charge on equipment £(0 – 10,000)	10,000
Less overlap profit on commencement	(9,000)
Taxable trading profits	46,000

Income tax 2016/17

Final year of trading: basis period 1 May 2015 to 31 January 2017.

	£
Trading income £(54,000 + 46,000)/Net income	100,000
Less: personal allowance	(10,600)
Taxable income	89,400

	£
Income tax:	
£31,785 @ 20%	6,357
£57,615 @ 40%	23,046
Income tax liability	29,403

Business cessation on 30 April 2017

Taxable trading profits

Y/e 30.4.16

	£
As above	54,000

Y/e 30.4.17

	£
Profits 12 × £5,000	60,000
Add balancing charge on equipment £(0 – 10,000)	10,000
Less overlap profit on commencement	(9,000)
Taxable trading profits	61,000

Income tax 2016/17

Current year basis: basis period 1 May 2015 to 30 April 2016.

	£
Trading income/Net income	54,000
Less personal allowance	(10,600)
Taxable income	43,400

Income tax:	
£31,785 @ 20%	6,357
£11,615 @ 40%	4,646
Income tax liability	11,003

Income tax 2017/18

Final year of trading: basis period 1 May 2016 to 30 April 2017.

	£
Trading income/Net income	61,000
Less personal allowance	(10,600)
Taxable income	50,400

Income tax:	
£31,785 @ 20%	6,357
£18,615 @ 40%	7,446
Income tax liability	13,803

Capital gains tax position

Sale of assets on 31 January 2017

Capital gains tax 2016/17

	£
Building £(330,000 – 60,000(N1))	270,000
Equipment (N2)	0
Chargeable gains	270,000
Less: annual exempt amount	(11,100)
Taxable gains	258,900

Capital gains tax:	
£258,900 @ 10% (N3)	25,890

Notes

1   The base cost of the building for Ziti is the original cost for Ravi as gift relief was claimed on the disposal of the business assets from Ravi to Ziti.

2   All of the equipment has a market value and cost of £6,000 or less and so is exempt from capital gains tax.

3   Entrepreneurs' relief is available on the disposal of the assets because the business has been owned by Ziti throughout the period of one year ending with the date on which the business ceased to be carried on and the date of cessation is within three years before the date of the disposal.

Sale of business on 30 April 2017

Capital gains tax 2017/18

	£
Capital gains tax:	
On gains as above (N)	25,890
Goodwill £40,000 @ 10% (N)	4,000
Capital gains tax	29,890

Note

Entrepreneurs' relief is available as this is the disposal of whole or part of a business by Ziti who has owned the business throughout the period of one year ending with the date of the disposal. As with the building, the base cost of the goodwill for Ziti is the original cost to Ravi ie nil, because of gift relief on the disposal from Ravi to Ziti.

Summary of post-tax cash position

	Sale on 31.1.17 £	Sale on 30.4.17 £
Trading income £(60,000 + 45,000)	105,000	
Trading income £(60,000 + 60,000)		120,000
Equipment purchase 1 August 2015	(6,000)	(6,000)
Proceeds of sale:		
Goodwill	0	40,000
Building	330,000	330,000
Equipment	10,000	10,000
Less: income tax 2016/17	(29,403)	(11,003)
income tax 2017/18	0	(13,803)
capital gains tax 2016/17	(25,890)	0
capital gains tax 2017/18	0	(29,890)
	383,707	439,304

Conclusion

Delaying the sale until 30 April 2017 would be financially beneficial.

It would also delay the payment of some of the income tax and all of the capital gains tax by one year.

Assumptions

Ziti has not used his annual exempt amount for 2016/17 (for a sale on 31 January 2017) or 2017/18 (for a sale on 30 April 2017).

(ii) **Value added tax (VAT)**

Sale of assets on 31 January 2017

VAT @ 20% will need to be charged on the sale of the equipment.

The sale of the building will be exempt since it is more than three years old and the option to tax has not been exercised.

Sale of assets on 30 April 2017

VAT @ 20% will need to be charged on the sale of the equipment and the goodwill unless the sale qualifies as the transfer of a going concern.

The conditions for the transfer of assets not to be treated as a supply for VAT purposes and to be treated as a transfer of a going concern are:

- The assets are to be used purchaser in the same kind of business (whether or not as part of an existing business) as that carried on by Ziti, the business being transferred as a going concern.

- The purchaser is a taxable person when the transfer takes place or immediately becomes one as a result of the transfer.

- There is no significant break in the normal trading pattern before or immediately after the transfer.

As above, the sale of the building is exempt.

(b) **Inheritance tax**

Date of death	Notes	IHT liability £
7 June 2016 to 30 April 2017	1	0
1 May 2017 to 30 June 2017	2	48,480
1 July 2017 to 30 June 2018	3(i)	32,320
1 July 2018 to 30 June 2019	3(ii)	16,160

Notes

1 If Ravi dies whilst Ziti still owns the business, business property relief at 100% will apply on the value of the transfer. This is because the transfer was of an unincorporated trading business owned by Ravi for at least two years.

2 Business property relief will not apply as Ziti does not own the business when Ravi dies and he has not reinvested the whole of the proceeds in replacement business assets.

Taper relief applies as there are at least three years between the transfer and the death of Ravi.

The inheritance on the transfer is computed as follows:

	£	£	£
Transfer of value			
£(40,000 + 300,000 + 9,000)			349,000
Less: annual exemptions			
2012/13 and 2011/12 b/f			(6,000)
Chargeable transfer			343,000
Nil rate band at death of Ravi		325,000	
Transfer of value 1 May 2008	190,000		
Less: annual exemptions			
2008/09 and 2007/08 b/f	(6,000)		
		(184,000)	
Available nil rate band		141,000	
Inheritance tax:			
£141,000 @ 0%			0
£202,000 @ 40%			80,800
			80,800
Less: taper relief (4 to 5 years)			
£80,800 @ 40%			(32,320)
Inheritance tax liability			48,480

3 IHT liability after additional taper relief

(i) Taper relief of 60% (5 to 6 years) £(80,800 − 48,480)   32,320

(ii) Taper relief of 80% (6 to 7 years) £(80,800 − 64,640)   16,160

39 Dokham (ATAX 06/10)

Text references. Pensions are covered in Chapter 2 and the EMI scheme in Chapter 5. Lifetime transfers of value for IHT are dealt with in Chapter 16 and capital gains disposals in Chapter 11. Chargeable gains reliefs are covered in Chapter 13.

Top tips. Make sure that you make an attempt to answer all the requirements of the question. A good tip is to tick off each requirement after you have dealt with it in your answer.

Easy marks. There were some easy marks for basic points about inheritance tax and capital gains tax in part (b).

Examiner's comments. The pension scheme element of part (a) was not done particularly well. Candidates struggled in an attempt to produce detailed calculations when a few well chosen sentences would have been much more efficient. Many candidates failed to consider national insurance contributions and there was particular confusion in relation to the employer's contributions to the pension scheme with many candidates deducting the contributions from the employee's salary.

The main problem here was an inability to set down a clear explanation of the rules. Before starting to write an answer, candidates should be willing to stop and think in order to plan what they want to say. Also, as, part of their preparation for the exam, candidates should practise explaining the tax implications of transactions in writing in order to improve their ability to get to the point in a clear and precise manner.

A small minority of candidates failed to address the three additional questions raised by the client in respect of pension scheme benefits. This was a shame as there were some relatively straightforward marks available here.

The enterprise management incentive scheme element of part (a) again required candidates to address particular points as opposed to writing generally. Although many candidates were aware that there was a maximum value to the options granted under such a scheme, not all of them applied the rule to the facts of the question in terms of the restriction on the number of share options granted by the company. A significant number of candidates confused the enterprise management incentive scheme with the enterprise investment scheme.

Part (b) was done well by many candidates. Those who did not do so well were often too superficial in their explanations; the question required candidates to 'explain in detail'. Also, weaker candidates failed to consider the capital gains tax implications of the gifts and/or the possibility of the exemption in respect of normal expenditure out of income being available in relation to inheritance tax. Of those who did address capital gains tax, many thought, incorrectly, that gift relief would be available in respect of the proposed gift of quoted shares.

Marking scheme

			Marks
(a)	Additional pension contributions		
	Income tax	2½	
	National insurance contributions	1	
	Benefits from pension scheme	2	
	Enterprise management incentive scheme		
	Maximum number of shares	1½	
	Exercise of option	1½	
	Sale of shares	2	
	Max		9
(b)	One-off gift of cash		
	Potentially exempt transfer	1	
	Death within 7 years	2	
	Taper relief	1	
	Payment of tax	1	
	Capital gains tax	½	
	One-off gift of shares		
	Inheritance tax	½	
	Capital gains tax	1	

		Marks
Series of gifts		
Exemption for normal expenditure out of income	1	
Able to maintain standard of living	1	
If exemption does not apply	½	
Max		7
		16

(a) **The information requested by Dokham**

Additional salary instead of pension contributions

There are no tax implications for you when Criollo plc makes contributions into your personal pension scheme.

If you received additional salary instead, your taxable income would increase by £8,000 resulting in additional tax of £3,200 (£8,000 × 40%). However, you would pay the additional pension contributions net of 20% income tax (saving you £1,600) and, as a result of the pension contributions, £8,000 of your taxable income would be taxed at 20% rather than 40% (saving you a further £1,600).

Accordingly, the effective income tax implications of the two alternatives are the same.

However, you would have to pay additional national insurance contributions of £160 (£8,000 × 2%) if Criollo plc paid you additional salary of £8,000.

Benefits from the pension scheme

You cannot receive any benefits from the pension scheme until you are 55 (unless you are incapacitated by ill health).

Once you are 55 you can start to receive benefits from the pension scheme and one way to do this is under flexible access drawdown. You can take a tax-free lump sum of up to 25% of the pension fund. The rest of the pension fund can then be reinvested to give taxable pension income as required.

The number of shares within the enterprise management incentive (EMI) scheme

The value of shares over which you can be granted options within the EMI scheme rules is restricted to £250,000. This rule results in a maximum number of shares of 26,233 (£250,000/£9.53) at the current share price of £9.53. Accordingly, it appears that Criollo plc is intending to grant you an option in respect of the maximum possible number of shares whilst allowing for a small increase in the company's share price between now and when the option is granted to you.

Exercise of option and sale of shares

When you exercise the option and purchase shares in Criollo plc you will be liable to income tax and national insurance on the amount by which the value of the shares at the time the option is granted exceeds the price you pay for the shares, ie £13,878 (26,185 × (£9.53 − £9)). When you sell the shares, the excess of the sale proceeds over the amount paid for them plus the amount charged to income tax, ie £249,543 ((26,185 × £9) + £13,878) less your capital gains tax annual exempt amount (currently £11,100) if available, will be taxable. The rate of tax will be 10% since a claim for entrepreneurs' relief can be made, provided you wait at least a year between being granted the options and selling the shares.

Tutorial note

Entrepreneurs' relief applies to shares acquired under an EMI option if the option was granted at least one year prior to the date of disposal of the shares and the individual was an officer or an employee of the trading company throughout that one year period. There is no minimum ownership period for the shares themselves nor a minimum percentage shareholding.

(b) **The tax implications of Virginia contributing towards the children's school fees**

One-off gift to Dokham of cash of £54,000

The gift will be a potentially exempt transfer for the purposes of inheritance tax. There will be no inheritance tax liability if Virginia survives the gift for seven years.

If Virginia were to die within seven years of the gift inheritance tax would be charged at 40% on the excess of the gift over the available nil rate band. The available nil rate band is the nil rate band (currently £325,000) as reduced by chargeable transfers in the seven years prior to the gift. Chargeable transfers include, broadly, transfers into trust in the seven years prior to the gift and transfers to individuals prior to the gift that take place within the seven years prior to death.

Any inheritance tax due in respect of the gift will be reduced by 20% if Virginia survives the gift for three years and by a further 20% for each additional year she survives.

Any tax due will be payable by Dokham within six months of the end of the month of death.

There is no liability to capital gains tax on a gift of cash.

One-off gift to Dokham of quoted shares worth £54,000

The inheritance tax implications are the same as for the one-off cash gift of £54,000.

However, Virginia will be subject to capital gains tax at 28% on the excess of the value of the shares over the price she paid for them.

Tutorial note

Gift relief would not be available on the gift of the shares as Panatella plc is a quoted company and Virginia owns less than 5% of the company.

Gift to Dokham of cash of £8,000 every year for the next seven years

Virginia should argue that this series of gifts represents normal expenditure out of her income such that each gift is an exempt transfer for the purposes of inheritance tax. For this exemption to be available, Virginia would have to show that:

- Each gift is part of her normal expenditure.
- The gifts are made out of income rather than capital.
- Having made the gifts, she still has sufficient income to maintain her usual standard of living.

Virginia's taxable income of more than £120,000 per year would help to support this argument.

If the exemption in respect of normal expenditure out of income is not applicable, each gift of £8,000 would be a potentially exempt transfer and the inheritance tax implications of each gift would be the same as for the one-off cash gift of £54,000. Again, there will be no liability to capital gains tax on these cash gifts.

40 King (ATAX 06/15)

Text references. The calculation of chargeable gains and liability to capital gains tax is covered in Chapter 11. Gift relief is dealt with in Chapter 13. Inheritance tax on lifetime transfers is covered in Chapter 16. Income tax on trusts is dealt with in Chapter 3. Associated operations are covered in Chapter 18 and related property valuation in Chapter 17.

Top tips. In part (a) it is important to think through what is meant by post-tax proceeds. You need to separate out the calculation of the capital gains tax for each share and then deduct this tax from the proceeds of each share to work out the net proceeds of sale. Then it is a simple matter to work out how many shares need to be sold to produce total net proceeds of £30,000.

Easy marks. There were some easy marks in part (b)(i) for explaining basic inheritance tax concepts.

Part (a) required candidates to calculate the number of shares that needed to be sold in order to realise post-tax proceeds of £30,000. This was done relatively well by the majority of candidates, although only a minority of candidates managed to arrive at the correct answer. A minority of candidates did not know how to solve this problem and simply calculated a tax liability based on an assumed number of shares sold. For those candidates who could see what needed to be done, the main mistake that was made in arriving at post-tax proceeds was to deduct the tax liability from the gain as opposed to from the sale proceeds.

Part (b) concerned the transfer of assets to a trust and was in two parts. Part (i) required candidates to advise on the capital gains tax and inheritance tax implications of the transfer of the assets. This was a straightforward requirement where candidates simply needed to know the basic rules and to be organised and methodical. For example, it was important to deal with the two taxes separately and not at the same time. The capital gains tax implications were done well with most candidates recognising that gift relief was available because the gift was immediately chargeable to inheritance tax. The only common mistake was a failure to point out that cash is an exempt asset for the purposes of capital gains tax. The inheritance tax implications were also handled reasonably well although some candidates were unable to follow through the position in relation to the availability of the annual exemptions. Also, many candidates reduced the available nil rate band due to the gift to the daughter on 1 June 2015. This was incorrect because the gift to the daughter was a potentially exempt transfer that will only become subject to inheritance tax if the donor dies within seven years. Therefore it has no effect on the nil rate band whilst the donor is alive. Part (ii) concerned the income tax position of the life tenant of the trust. This was done well by those candidates who knew the rules. The only difficulty here was to ensure that the answer given was comprehensive and referred to the need to gross up the income, the rate of tax and the availability of the tax credit.

The final part of the question concerned inheritance tax and, in particular, related property and associated operations. This was a challenging part of the question but there were plenty of accessible marks for those candidates who were willing to be brave and to simply apply their knowledge to the facts. It was therefore important that candidates did not simply decide that they had not learnt the rules relating to associated operations, such that they were unable to answer the question. Basic knowledge of inheritance tax, including the need to take account of related property, went a long way towards obtaining reasonable marks here.

Marking scheme

					Marks
(a)		Calculation of number of shares			3
(b)	(i)	Capital gains tax		4	
		Inheritance tax		3	
			Max		6
	(ii)	Life tenant entitled to income		1	
		10% notional tax credit		1	
		No additional tax payable, with reasons		2½	
			Max		4
(c)		Explanation of associated operations		1	
		Application to gift of flat		1½	
		Implication (value with vacant possession)		1	
		Increase in inheritance tax liability		4½	
			Max		7
					20

(a) **Minimum number of Wye Ltd shares to be sold to generate £30,000 after-tax**

Each share will be sold for £45 and so will result in a gain of £(45 – 5) = £40.

King has already used his annual exempt amount for 2016/17 so the full gain will be taxable.

King will pay tax at 28% on the gain since his income exceeds the basic rate threshold. The tax per share sold is therefore £40 × 28% = £11.20.

The after-tax proceeds for each share is therefore £(45 − 11.20) = £33.80.

King will therefore have to sell £(30,000/33.80) = 888 shares to generate total after-tax proceeds of £30,000.

Tutorial note: alternative algebraic calculation

Let x be the number of shares to be sold.

$45x − ([45 − 5]x × 28\%) = 30,000$

$45x − 11.2x = 30,000$

$33.8x = 30,000$

$x = 888$ (rounded up)

(b)　(i)　**Gifts into interest in possession trust**

Capital gains tax (CGT)

Cash is an exempt asset for CGT and so there are no CGT implications of the gift of £30,000 to the trust.

There will be disposal at market value of the cottage in Newtown on its transfer to the trust, probably resulting in a chargeable gain. Gift relief will be available to defer this gain because the transfer is subject to an immediate inheritance tax (IHT) charge as it is a chargeable lifetime transfer as a gift to a trust. King alone (without the trustees) can elect within four years after the end of the tax year of the transfer (by 5 April 2021 as the disposal is in 2016/17) for gift relief to apply. The full gain can be deferred since there is no consideration for the transfer.

Inheritance tax (IHT)

The transfer of the cash and the cottage to the trust will be a transfer of value for IHT of £(30,000 + 315,000) = £345,000.

The annual exemption for 2016/17 of £3,000 is available. The annual exemption for 2015/16 has already been used against the transfer of value to Florentyna on 1 June 2015. The net chargeable lifetime transfer is therefore £(345,000 − 3,000) = £342,000.

The available nil rate band is £325,000 since there are no chargeable lifetime transfers in the seven years prior to this transfer. The lifetime IHT payable by King is therefore £(342,000 − 325,000) = £17,000 × 20/80 = £4,250.

Tutorial note

The potentially exempt transfer to Florentyna is treated as exempt during King's lifetime and so has no effect on the nil rate band while King is alive.

(ii)　**Income tax payable by Florentyna on trust income**

Since Florentyna is the life tenant of the trust, she is entitled to receive all the income of the trust during her lifetime.

The only income is dividend income from the quoted shares and so it will be received by Florentyna with a notional 10% tax credit. Since Florentyna is a basic rate taxpayer on this income (her earnings will use up her personal allowance), she will have no further income tax to pay on this income since the tax credit will cover her basic rate liability.

(c)　**Gift of flat in Unicity**

Associated operations for IHT are broadly defined as:

- Two or more operations which affect the same property.
- Any two or more operations, where one is effected with reference to the other(s).

Where the rules apply, the series of transactions will be regarded as a single gift at the time of the final transaction in the series so that the total value transferred will be subject to tax.

The flat gifted to Axel is subject to a pre-existing rental agreement between King and Joy, as original owners of the property, and Axel's daughter as tenant. Because of this agreement, there is no right to vacant possession of the flat and so its value is reduced. The creation of the rental agreement and subsequent gift of the property may therefore be associated operations. If this is the case, the rental agreement with Axel's daughter and the transfer of the property to Axel will be a single transaction for IHT so that the transfer of the flat will be valued on a vacant possession basis, even though the rental agreement was made on a commercial basis.

If the associated operations rules do not apply, the transfer of value will be the greater of the stand alone value of a 75% share of the flat without vacant possession (£160,000) and the related property valuation since King and his wife jointly own the flat. The related property valuation is:

$$\frac{160,000}{160,000+40,000} \times £250,000 \qquad\qquad \underline{£200,000}$$

The related property valuation therefore applies.

If the associated operations rules do apply, the transfer of value will be greater of the stand alone value of a 75% share of the flat with vacant possession (£220,000) and the related property valuation of:

$$\frac{220,000}{220,000+60,000} \times £340,000 \qquad\qquad \underline{£267,143}$$

Again, the related property valuation therefore applies.

The increase in the value of the transfer if the associated operation rules apply is therefore £(267,143 – 200,000) = $\underline{£67,143}$.

If King dies on 1 May 2018, the potentially exempt transfer will become chargeable. The annual exemptions for 2015/16 and 2016/17 have already been used and King's nil rate band will have used up by his previous lifetime transfers. The additional IHT payable if the associated operations rules apply is therefore £67,143 × 40% = $\underline{£26,857}$.

41 Robusto Ltd (ATAX 12/10)

Marking scheme

			Marks
(a)	Partial exemption position	2	
	Cognac Ltd	1	
	Fonseca Inc	3	
	Pisco	2	
	Maximum salary	2½	
	Max		9
(b)	One mark for each contractual arrangement		3
(c)	Implications for Robusto Ltd and Cognac Ltd		
	Tax treatment of the fee	1	
	Additional implications for Cognac Ltd		
	Personal service company rules apply	½	
	Deemed salary payment	2½	
	Robusto Ltd's preference		
	Employer's class 1 NIC	1	
	Comparison with Cognac Ltd	1	
	Max		5
			17

(a) **Market analysis services**

Cheapest provider

Robusto Ltd is partially exempt for the purposes of value added tax (VAT) and can only recover 75% (W) of its input VAT. Accordingly, purchasing the services from Cognac Ltd would result in irrecoverable VAT that would increase the overall cost of the services.

	£
Fee excluding VAT	28,500
Irrecoverable VAT (£28,500 × 20% × 25%)	1,425
	29,925

Purchasing the services from Fonseca Inc would cause a similar problem. International services provided by one business to another are treated as supplied in the country where the customer carries on its business. Accordingly, the services would be treated as supplied in the UK. Robusto Ltd would have to apply the reverse charge procedure and account for output tax at the rate of 20%. It could then recover 75% of the VAT as input tax in the normal way. Fonseca Inc has quoted a higher fee than Cognac Ltd and therefore the total cost including irrecoverable VAT would also be higher.

Pisco is not registered for VAT and therefore the total cost would be the fee of £29,500, which would appear to be the cheapest option.

However, it should be borne in mind that Pisco will need to register for VAT if, as a result of the supply of the market analysis services to Robusto Ltd, its total supplies in a 12-month period exceed the registration limit of £82,000. If this were to occur, it would then become more expensive than Cognac Ltd.

Tutorial note

Robusto Ltd will obtain a tax deduction for the cost incurred but, since this will be the case in each situation, this will not affect the decision as to which is the cheapest supplier of the services.

Working

Proportion of recoverable input tax

	£
Standard rated supplies	850,000
Zero rated supplies	120,000
	970,000
Exempt supplies	330,000
Total supplies	1,300,000

Recoverable input tax – £970,000/£1,300,000 rounded up	75%

Maximum salary

The cost of taking on an employee to carry out the analysis will include the employer's class 1 national insurance contributions. The salary (y) that would result in a total cost of £29,500 is calculated below.

$$y + ((y - £8,112) \times 13.8\%) = £29,500$$
$$y + 0.138y - (£8,112 \times 13.8\%) = £29,500$$
$$1.138\ y - £1,119 = £29,500$$
$$1.138\ y = £29,500 + £1,119 = £30,619$$
$$y = £30,619/1.138$$
$$y = £26,906$$

Tutorial note

Proof of maximum salary

	£
Salary	26,906
Class 1 national insurance contributions ((£26,906 - £8,112) × 13.8%)	2,594
Total cost	29,500

(b)   **Contractual arrangements that would indicate an employer/employee relationship**

Any THREE of the following:

- Any necessary equipment or tools to be provided by Robusto Ltd.
- Robusto Ltd to have control over when and how the work is to be carried out by Pisco.
- Pisco is not permitted to provide a substitute to carry out the work.
- No obligation for Pisco to correct any unsatisfactory work at his own expense.
- The right to dismiss Pisco before the contract has been completed.

Tutorial note

Other contractual arrangements that would indicate an employer/employee relationship would include rewarding Pisco by reference to time spent rather than work done or provision for payments to be made in respect of illness or holidays. However, it is clear from the question that Pisco would charge a fixed fee for the work so it would not be possible for the contract to include such terms.

(c)   **Employer/employee relationship between Robusto Ltd and the individual carrying out the services**

Tax implications for Robusto Ltd and Cognac Ltd

The fee, including the irrecoverable VAT, will be tax deductible for Robusto Ltd.

The fee, net of VAT, will be taxable trading income for Cognac Ltd.

The contract between Robusto Ltd and Cognac Ltd would be a relevant engagement for the purposes of the personal service company rules and thus:

- Cognac Ltd will be deemed to have made a salary payment to Offley on 5 April each year based on the amounts it has received in respect of all such relevant engagements less certain allowable deductions.
- Cognac Ltd will have to pay employers' class 1 national insurance contributions in respect of the payment and deduct PAYE and employees' class 1 national insurance contributions from the payment.
- The deemed salary payment, together with the employers' national insurance contributions, will be deductible when calculating Cognac Ltd's taxable trading profits.

Robusto Ltd's preference

If HM Revenue and Customs could successfully argue that the relationship between Robusto Ltd and Pisco is one of employer and employee, Robusto Ltd would be required to pay employers' class 1 national insurance contributions on behalf of Pisco. This would increase the cost of the services to Robusto Ltd.

If the services are purchased from Cognac Ltd there is no effect on Robusto Ltd because the national insurance contributions are borne by Cognac Ltd under the personal service companies rules as set out above.

Accordingly, Robusto Ltd might prefer to offer the contract to Cognac Ltd rather than to Pisco.

42 FL Partnership (ATAX 12/13)

Text references. Ethics are covered in Chapter 30. Capital allowances are dealt with in Chapter 7. Inheritance tax basic principles are covered in Chapter 16, reliefs in Chapter 17 and trusts in Chapter 18. Capital gains tax principles will be found in Chapter 11 and reliefs in Chapter 13.

Top tips. Did you remember to include a summary of your calculations and a statement of the key issues in part (b)(iii)? These were awarded four valuable marks.

Easy marks. You should have been able to obtain some easy marks in part (a) for common-sense points. In part (b) there were some easy marks for basic computations. Make sure you get the easy mark for format and presentation!

Examiner's comments. Part (a) should have been straightforward but, on the whole, it was not done particularly well. The main problem was a lack of thought before answering the question. The question asked for the information required before becoming advisers to the partners but a significant number of candidates listed the information they would need in order to be able to give advice to them once they had become clients (including personal details, information in respect of prior years and so on). Candidates will always benefit from reading the requirement carefully and thinking before they begin to write their answers. It is important to think about the specifics of the situation, for example, the fact that the partners required sophisticated and specialised tax planning work, such that the firm needed to be sure that it had staff with sufficient knowledge and competence.

Part (b)(i) was reasonably straightforward and again, on the whole, it was not done well. The answer should have explained how the balancing adjustment would be calculated and explained why the assets could not be transferred at tax written down value. However, many answers included detailed calculations of capital allowances over many years (despite the fact that the question did not include the information necessary to prepare such calculations) or tried to explain everything about capital allowances, very little of which was relevant to this particular question. A short thoughtful answer was able to score three marks whereas many answers covering more than a page only scored a single mark.

Part (b)(ii) mainly required an explanation of the calculation of an inheritance tax liability. This was done very well by most candidates. However, performance in respect of the availability of capital gains tax gift relief was not quite as strong; candidates must learn when the various capital gains tax reliefs are available. Gift relief is available where a transfer is immediately subject to inheritance tax regardless of the nature of the assets disposed of.

Part (b)(iii) was the more demanding part of this question and was not done well. It was important that candidates approached the question methodically. There was to be a sale of the business followed by a gift of shares and subsequent sales of shares in the future. The question stated that incorporation relief was available on the sale of the business. Candidates needed to calculate the tax that would be charged in respect of these transactions both with and without incorporation relief and then make some sensible comments regarding their findings. The first thing to note is that many candidates did not have a thorough attempt at this part of the question. Many answers were very short, despite the number of marks available, and some candidates omitted it altogether. Other candidates avoided producing calculations and simply wrote about the issues in general terms which was never going to be particularly successful. In addition, most candidates who attempted the question did not give it sufficient thought before starting their answers. As a result, many answers were confused and did not cover sufficient ground to score well. In particular, it was often not obvious which aspect of the question was being addressed and the summary of calculations and statement of key issues required by the question were often missing. Finally, many candidates addressed inheritance tax in this part of the question, which was not required and, therefore, could not score any marks.

In addition to the general problems regarding the approach to the question, there were two specific technical problems. Firstly, the majority of candidates tried to calculate the gain on the disposal of the business by reference to the total value of the assets sold as opposed to calculating the gain on each individual chargeable asset. There was only one chargeable asset in the question, goodwill, so all that was needed was the gain on the goodwill. Secondly, many candidates then struggled with the calculation of incorporation relief and its effect on the base cost of the shares.

The general impression was that many candidates had not practised sufficient past exam questions, such that they were unable to plan their approach to a question of this type and then to carry that plan out.

Marks were available for professional skills in this question. In order to earn these marks candidates had to provide a suitable amount of appropriate narrative, calculations that were clear and logical and sensible analysis in relation to the position of Lauda in an appropriately formatted memorandum. On the whole, the performance of candidates in this area was good with the majority of candidates producing a memorandum in a style that was easy to follow.

Marking scheme

				Marks
(a)	Information required	1		
	Contact existing tax adviser	1		
	Fundamental principles	1		
	Competence	1		
	Conflict of interest	2		
			Max	5
(b)	(i) Allowances available	1½		
	Calculation of balancing adjustment	2		
	Consideration of transfer at tax written down value	1½		
				5
	(ii) Inheritance tax			
	Tax may be payable at time of gift	1		
	Business property relief	1½		
	Valuation and exemptions	1½		
	Inheritance tax and due date	3		
	Capital gains tax: gift relief	1½		
			Max	7
	(iii) Capital gains tax on sale of business	1½		
	With incorporation relief			
	Incorporation relief	1½		
	Capital gains tax and due date	1		
	Capital gains tax on gift of shares	2		
	Capital gains tax and due date	1		
	Without incorporation relief			
	Capital gains tax on sale of business	1		
	Capital gains tax on gift of shares	1½		
	Explanations	4		
	Summary and key issues	4		
			Max	14
Format and presentation		1		
Analysis		1		
Quality of explanations and calculations		2		
				4
				35

(a) **Becoming tax advisers to Farina and Lauda**

Information required in respect of Farina and Lauda

- Independent evidence of their identities (eg passport)
- Proof of their addresses

Action to be taken by the firm

- The firm should contact the existing tax advisers of Farina and Lauda. This is to ensure that there has been no action by either Farina or Lauda which would preclude the acceptance of the appointment on ethical grounds.

- The firm should consider whether becoming tax advisers to Farina and Lauda would create any threats to compliance with the fundamental principles of professional ethics. Where such threats exist, the appointment should not be accepted unless the threats can be reduced to an acceptable level via the implementation of safeguards.

- With this in mind, the firm must ensure that its engagement team possesses the necessary skills to carry out the sophisticated tax planning required by Farina and Lauda.

- In addition, it is possible that providing advice to Farina and Lauda on the sale of their business could give rise to a conflict of interest, as a course of action (for example, the timing of the sale) which is beneficial for one of them may not be beneficial for the other. The firm should obtain permission from both Farina and Lauda to act for both of them and should consider using separate engagement teams.

(b)
To:	The files
From:	Tax senior
Date:	6 December 2016
Subject:	The FL Partnership

The purpose of this memorandum is to advise Farina and Lauda, the partners in the FL Partnership, on the sale of the business to JH plc and on the proposed disposals of shares in JH plc in the future.

(i) Capital allowances of the FL Partnership for its final trading period

There will be no annual investment allowance, first year allowances or writing down allowances in the period in which the partnership business ceases. Instead, there will be a balancing adjustment which will either be a balancing allowance or a balancing charge.

The balancing adjustment will be calculated as follows:

	£
Tax written down value brought forward at the start of the period	X
Add additions in the period	X
Less disposals during the period at the lower of cost and sales proceeds	(X)
	X
Less proceeds on the sale of the equipment on 1 March 2017	(150,000)
Balancing allowance/(balancing charge)	X/(X)

It is not possible for an election to be made to transfer the equipment to JH plc at its tax written down value because Farina and Lauda will not be connected with JH plc as they will not control the company.

(ii) Farina

(1) Inheritance tax

The gift of the JH plc shares to the trustees will be a chargeable lifetime transfer, so inheritance tax may be due at the time of the gift. Business property relief will not be available as JH plc is a quoted company and Farina will not be a controlling shareholder.

The shares will be valued at £4 per share, such that the value of the gift will be 15,000 × £4 = £60,000. This will be reduced by the annual exemptions for the tax year 2017/18 and also for the tax year 2016/17 if they have not been used against any other gifts. The annual exemption is £3,000.

The transfer must be grossed up because the tax will be paid by Farina so the tax is 20/80 of the net chargeable transfer in excess of the available nil rate band. The available nil rate band will be £325,000 as reduced by any chargeable transfers made by Farina in the previous seven years.

Any inheritance tax due will be payable on 30 April 2018.

(2)   *Capital gains tax gift relief*

Gift relief will be available in respect of the transfer of the shares to the trustees because, as noted above, the transfer is immediately subject to inheritance tax. For the same reason, gift relief will also be available in respect of any subsequent transfers of shares from the trustees to the beneficiaries as there will be exit charges for inheritance tax on these transfers.

(iii)   **Lauda**

The sale of the business will result in a chargeable gain in respect of the goodwill. The gain, equal to the market value of the goodwill of £1,300,000, will be split equally between Farina and Lauda. Lauda's chargeable gain will therefore be £650,000. As all of the equipment qualified for capital allowances, no capital losses will arise on its disposal.

With incorporation relief

Sale of business on 1 March 2017

	£
Chargeable gain on the sale of the goodwill	650,000
Less incorporation relief £650,000 × $\frac{£600,000}{£740,000}$ (N1)	(527,027)
Chargeable gain after incorporation relief	122,973
Capital gains tax @ 10% (N2)	12,297

The tax will be payable on 31 January 2018.

Shares in JH plc – Lauda's base cost

	£
Market value of shares received 200,000 × £3	600,000
Less incorporation relief	(527,027)
Base cost	72,973

Gift of 40,000 shares on 1 June 2018 (N3)

	£
Deemed proceeds (market value) 40,000 × £5	200,000
Less cost £72,973 × $\frac{40,000}{200,000}$	(14,595)
Chargeable gain	185,405
Capital gains tax @ 28% (N4)	51,913

The tax will be payable on 31 January 2020.

Notes

1   The relief is restricted by reference to the value of the shares divided by the value of the total consideration received. Lauda will receive a total of £740,000, consisting of cash of £140,000 and shares worth 200,000 × £3 = £600,000.

2   Capital gains tax will be charged at 10% because entrepreneurs' relief will be available. This relief is available because the business is to be sold as a going concern and has been owned for at least a year. It is assumed that Lauda has not exceeded the lifetime limit of £10,000,000 and will claim this relief. The restriction for goodwill does not apply because JH plc is not a close company.

3   Gift relief will not be available in respect of this gift because the shares are quoted and Lauda will hold 200,000/8,400,000 = 2.38% of the shares which is less than 5% of the company so it is not Lauda's personal company.

4   Capital gains tax will be charged at 28% because Lauda pays income tax at the additional rate and so has used up her basic rate band. Entrepreneurs' relief will not be available because Lauda will hold less than 5% of JH plc.

Tutorial note

In order for entrepreneurs' relief to be available in respect of the gift of the shares, Lauda would also need to be an officer or employee of JH plc.

Without incorporation relief

Sale of business on 1 March 2017

	£
Chargeable gain on the sale of the goodwill	650,000
Capital gains tax @ 10% (N2 above)	65,000

The tax will be payable on 31 January 2018.

Shares in JH plc – Lauda's base cost

	£
Market value of shares received 200,000 × £3	600,000

Gift of 40,000 shares on 1 June 2018 (N3 above)

	£
Deemed proceeds (market value) 40,000 × £5	200,000
Less cost £600,000 × $\dfrac{40,000}{200,000}$	(120,000)
Chargeable gain	80,000
Capital gains tax @ 28% (N4 above)	22,400

The tax will be payable on 31 January 2020.

Summary

	With incorporation relief	Without incorporation relief
	£	£
Capital gains tax on sale of business	12,297	65,000
Capital gains tax on gift of shares 1 June 2018	51,913	22,400
	64,210	87,400

Effect of incorporation relief on base cost of shares

	With incorporation relief	Without incorporation relief
	£	£
Base cost	72,973	600,000
Less used on gift of shares 1 June 2018	(14,595)	(120,000)
	58,378	480,000
Increase in gain on eventual disposal of shares if incorporation relief applies £(480,000 – 58,378)		421,622
Increase in capital gains tax £421,622 @ 28%		118,054

Key issues

If Lauda were to disclaim incorporation relief, she would have higher initial capital gains tax liabilities.

However, disclaiming incorporation relief will result in a higher base cost in the shares, such that on a sale of the shares in the future, there will be tax savings which will exceed the increased initial liability.

Tutorial notes

1   Incorporation relief reduces the capital gains tax payable on the sale of the business and the gift of the shares by £23,190 (£87,400 − £64,210). When this amount is deducted from the additional tax due because of the reduced base cost, we arrive at an overall increase in the capital gains tax liability of £94,864 (£118,054 − £23,190).

   This overall increase in the capital gains tax liability is simply the tax on the deferred gain of £527,027 at 28% in the future rather than at 10%, due to the availability of entrepreneurs' relief, now: £527,027 × 18% (28% − 10%) = £94,865 (and a rounding difference of £1).

2   Capital gains tax gift relief in respect of gifts of business assets will not be available on the sale of the business to JH plc, because Farina and Lauda are not gifting the business to the company. They are selling the business for market value, which is received in the form of cash and shares.

Mock exams

ACCA Professional Paper P6 – Options Module

Advanced Taxation (UK)

Mock Examination 1

Question Paper	
Time allowed	**3 hours 15 minutes**
This paper is divided into two sections	
Section A	**BOTH questions are compulsory questions and MUST be attempted**
Section B	**TWO questions ONLY to be attempted**

DO NOT OPEN THIS PAPER UNTIL YOU ARE READY TO START UNDER EXAMINATION CONDITIONS

SECTION A: BOTH questions are compulsory and MUST be attempted

1 Calisia (ATAX 06/11)

68 mins

Your manager has sent you an email with two attachments in respect of a new client called Calisia. The first attachment is an extract from a letter from Calisia, in which she has asked the firm to consider how she can increase the income of her daughter, Farfisa, and to review her own inheritance tax position.

The second attachment is a schedule setting out what your manager wants you to do in order to prepare for a meeting with Calisia.

Attachment 1 – Extract from letter from Calisia

(a) **Farfisa – Additional income**

My daughter, Farfisa, will leave home and start her first job on 1 October 2016 in London. She will be working for Jelmini Ltd and will be paid a salary of £27,500 (gross) per year. Jelmini Ltd will also provide Farfisa with an interest free loan of £2,700 in order for her to purchase suitable business clothing. The loan is to be repaid on 30 September 2018.

We have estimated that Farfisa's expenses will be £2,500 per month (of which £550 will be rent) so her salary after tax will be insufficient. At present Farfisa has no other income so I have identified three possible transfers of capital that I could make to her in order to generate the income she requires.

(i) **Gift of shares quoted on UK stock exchange**

I would give Farfisa sufficient quoted shares to generate the additional income she requires. On average the quoted shares would generate dividends equal to 4% of their current market value. It can be assumed that, on average, the capital gain arising on the quoted shares will equal a quarter of their market value. I do not hold more than 1% of the share capital of any quoted company.

(ii) **Sale of investment property followed by gift of proceeds**

I own a two-bedroom investment property situated in London. I bought it in 2004 for £90,000 and it is now worth £270,000. I have always rented it out to tourists such that it qualifies as commercially let furnished holiday accommodation.

I would give Farfisa the net proceeds of the sale after paying any tax and other costs. Farfisa would place the cash on bank deposit; I estimate that the deposit would earn interest at 3% (gross). Farfisa would only spend the interest, not the capital, so I would then give Farfisa quoted shares to generate the remainder of the additional income she requires as in (i) above.

(iii) **Gift of investment property**

Under this option, instead of selling the property, I would give it to Farfisa who would then receive the annual rental income, after all allowable expenses, of £5,100. Again, I would then give Farfisa quoted shares to generate the remainder of the additional income she requires as in (i) above.

(b) **Calisia – Inheritance tax**

I would like to discuss my inheritance tax position with you so that I can understand the amount of tax that would be payable if I were to die now. I set out below the assets I own together with their current market values. I have not included my home as I assume that it is not subject to inheritance tax. I have never made any lifetime gifts and neither did my husband before he died. I intend to leave £150,000 to the Fairness for All political party when I die and the rest of my estate to Farfisa.

	£
Investment property in London	260,000
Investment property in Sakura	380,000
Share (25%) in the 'Therson Partnership'	700,000
Building used by the 'Therson Partnership'	440,000
Shares quoted on the UK stock exchange	1,300,000
Art and antiques	200,000
Motor cars	100,000
Cash and other possessions	320,000

Attachment 2 – Schedule from your manager

(a) **Farfisa – Additional income**

During the meeting I only want to focus on any immediate tax liabilities as opposed to liabilities that may or may not arise in the future.

Prepare notes, with supporting calculations, showing Calisia's capital gains tax liability in respect of:

- Each of the three possibilities identified by her.

- A fourth possibility (which I expect to be more tax efficient) whereby Calisia gifts the property to Farfisa who then lives in it. Any shortfall in income could then be satisfied by renting out the second bedroom. You should include a calculation of the minimum monthly rent that would need to be charged in order to provide sufficient income for Farfisa.

Start by calculating the excess of Farfisa's budgeted expenditure over her salary after all taxes for a 12-month period. This will enable you to determine the value of shares she will need to be given under each of the possibilities in order to provide her with the income she needs. Remember to take into account any income tax due on the income received by Farfisa when calculating the income she will retain in respect of the assets transferred.

Conclude with a summary, showing the capital gains tax payable in respect of each of the four alternatives.

Please include a note of the stamp duty or stamp duty land tax implications of each proposal.

You should assume the following:

- A sale or gift of the investment property will result in legal fees of £6,000.
- There will be no disposal costs in relation to any gift of shares.
- All claims and elections necessary to reduce immediate tax liabilities will be made.

Further information

Calisia and Farfisa are resident in the UK.

Calisia is a higher rate taxpayer who makes sufficient capital gains every year to utilise her annual exempt amount.

Calisia has not made a claim for entrepreneurs' relief in the past.

(b) **Calisia – Inheritance tax**

Calisia is domiciled in the UK and has not made any lifetime gifts. I want you to prepare a comprehensive explanation of how Calisia's inheritance tax liability would be calculated if she were to die today. Please try to identify all of the issues that are relevant to Calisia's situation together with any matters that need to be confirmed with her in order for reliefs and/or exemptions to be available. I do not want you to perform any calculations as we do not have sufficient information at present.

Further information

Calisia's husband died in 2006. He had not made any lifetime gifts and he left the whole of his estate, consisting principally of quoted shares and UK property, to Calisia.

Required

(a)   **Farfisa – Additional income**

        Prepare the notes and supporting calculations as set out in the schedule from your manager.   **(21 marks)**

(b)   **Calisia – Inheritance tax**

        Prepare the explanation as set out in the schedule from your manager.   **(10 marks)**

Professional marks will be awarded in this question for the effectiveness with which the information is communicated and the extent to which the calculations are approached in a logical manner.   **(4 marks)**

(Total = 35 marks)

You should assume that the tax rates and allowances of the tax year 2015/16 will continue to apply for the foreseeable future.

2 Petzold (ATAX 06/11)

Your manager has sent you an email concerning a client, Petzold. An extract from the email together with two schedules of information from Petzold are set out below.

Email from your manager

Petzold has owned 100% of the ordinary share capital of Glenz Ltd for many years. Glenz Ltd is a profitable trading company that provides Petzold with the majority of his income. However, the company is currently suffering from a short-term cash flow problem.

Glenz Ltd has owned 100% of the ordinary share capital of Clementi Ltd for many years. Clementi Ltd has owned three wholly owned trading subsidiaries for many years.

I want you to draft a letter to Petzold from me that deals with the following issues.

(a)   **Glenz Ltd – Payments to the tax authorities**

    (i)   Calculations of the payments that will be made by Glenz Ltd to the tax authorities in respect of the three months ended 30 June 2016 and the equivalent figure for the three months ended 30 September 2016 based on the company's budgeted figures as set out in Schedule 1 from Petzold.

        Petzold is only interested in those payments which affect the company's cash flow position. Accordingly, as the annual salaries shown represent the gross salaries earned there is no need to calculate the income tax or employees' national insurance contributions payable in respect of them.

        Glenz Ltd is partially exempt for the purposes of value added tax (VAT) and was unable to recover all of its input tax in the year ending 31 March 2016.

        Please provide explanations of the amount of input tax recoverable by Glenz Ltd but do not include any other narrative.

    (ii)   Petzold's calculation of the company's corporation tax liability for the year ending 31 March 2016 is correct (see Schedule 1) but I would like you to explain how the tax is payable.

(b)   **Glenz Ltd – cash flow**

    (i)   The implications of the following suggestions from Petzold to improve the company's cash flow position.

        –   Paying Glenz Ltd's VAT liabilities in respect of the quarters ending 30 June 2016 and 30 September 2016 late. Glenz Ltd's previous four VAT returns have been submitted on time with the exception of the return for the three months ended 30 June 2015.

        –   The retention by Glenz Ltd of a refund of corporation tax of £21,000 that it received from HM Revenue and Customs in May 2016. Petzold has not been able to identify any reason for this refund.

    (ii)   I have suggested to Petzold that Glenz Ltd could improve its cash flow position by selling its warehouse and then renting it back. I have agreed to provide him with a summary of the corporation tax implications of this proposal together with supporting calculations.

        The summary should include a detailed explanation of how the chargeable gain arising on the sale of the warehouse could be relieved via rollover relief into a new warehouse.

        You should assume that any sale of the warehouse will take place on 1 July 2016 and that rent will be paid from that date. Base your calculations on the figures provided by Petzold in Schedule 2.

        I do not want you to address the VAT or the stamp duty land tax implications of this proposal.

Tax manager

Schedules provided by Petzold

Schedule 1

Glenz Ltd – Budgeted figures

	Three months ending 30 June 2016 £	Three months ending 30 Sept. 2016 £
Sales revenue – Standard rated (excluding VAT)	360,000	365,000
Sales revenue – Exempt	24,500	23,400
Input tax:		
Attributable to taxable supplies	40,000	42,000
Attributable to exempt supplies	950	2,200
Non-attributable	800	1,500
Total	41,750	45,700

Total annual salaries for the company's eight full-time employees – £332,000
Corporation tax liability for the year ended 31 March 2016 £383,500 × 20% = £76,700

Schedule 2

The warehouse

Cost (1 February 2006)	£180,000
Current market value	£330,000
Estimated commercial annual rent payable to the new owner	£22,000

Required

Prepare the letter to Petzold requested in the email from your manager. The following marks are available.

(a) Glenz Ltd – Payments to the tax authorities **(11 marks)**
(b) Glenz Ltd – Cash flow **(14 marks)**

Note. The following figures from the Retail Prices Index should be used.

February 2006   194.2
July 2016   261.5 (assumed)

You should assume that the tax rates and allowances of the tax year 2015/16 and the Financial Year 2015 will continue to apply for the foreseeable future.

(Total = 25 marks)

SECTION B: TWO questions ONLY to be attempted

3 Pita plc (ATAX 06/14)   39 mins

Your firm has been asked to provide advice to Pita plc in respect of providing employees with financial assistance with childcare and encouraging them to work from home, the establishment of an enterprise management incentive scheme, and a redundancy package provided to an employee.

Pita plc:

- Is a UK resident company which trades in the UK and is quoted on the UK Stock Exchange.
- Has an issued share capital of 10,000,000 irredeemable £1 ordinary shares.
- Has gross assets of £24,000,000 and 180 employees.

Issues – Pita plc:

- Intends to provide assistance with childcare to employees and to encourage them to work from home.
- Intends to establish an enterprise management incentive (EMI) scheme for nine key employees.
- Has provided a redundancy package to Narn, an employee.

Financial assistance with childcare and encouraging working from home:

- Pita plc will provide employees with vouchers to purchase £42 of childcare per child per week.
- The vouchers will cost Pita plc 95 pence for each £1 of childcare purchased.
- Pita plc will pay employees an extra £3 per day when they work from home.
- The payments are intended to cover the additional household costs of working from home.

The EMI scheme:

- The scheme would reward seven full-time and two part-time key employees.
- Each key employee will be granted an option to acquire 10,000 shares at £1.75 per share.
- The options will be exercised in six years' time when the shares are expected to be worth £5 each.
- An ordinary share in Pita plc is expected to be worth £2 when the options are granted.

Redundancy package provided to Narn on 31 March 2016:

- Statutory redundancy of £8,100 paid on 31 March 2016.
- An additional payment of £26,000 made on 31 March 2016.
- Continued use of her company car until 30 September 2016.
- Pita plc paid £18,400 for Narn's diesel powered car; it had a list price of £19,500.
- The car has CO_2 emissions of 119 grams per kilometre.

Required

(a) Explain whether or not the planned financial assistance with childcare and encouragement to work from home will give rise to taxable employment income for the employees.   **(6 marks)**

(b) (i)   Explain, with reference to the information provided, whether or not Pita plc is a qualifying company for the purpose of the enterprise management incentive (EMI) scheme and if it is able to make the scheme available to just the nine key employees.   **(4 marks)**

     (ii) On the assumption that an EMI scheme is established, explain the income tax and capital gains tax implications for the employees in respect of the grant and exercise of the options and the sale of the shares, including the availability of entrepreneurs' relief.   **(5 marks)**

(c) Explain, with supporting calculations, the taxable amounts arising in respect of the redundancy package provided to Narn.   **(5 marks)**

(Total = 20 marks)

4 Capstan (ATAX 06/11)   39 mins

Capstan requires advice on the transfer of a property to a trust, the sale of shares in respect of which relief has been received under the Enterprise Investment Scheme (EIS), and the sale of shares and qualifying corporate bonds following a takeover.

The following information was obtained from a meeting with Capstan.

Capstan:

- Expects to have taxable income in the tax year 2016/17 of £80,000.
- Transferred a UK property to a discretionary trust on 1 May 2016.
- Plans to sell ordinary shares in Agraffe Ltd and loan stock and ordinary shares in Pinblock plc.
- Will make all available claims to reduce the tax due in respect of his planned disposals.
- Entrepreneurs' relief is not available in respect of any of these disposals.

Transfer of a UK property to a discretionary trust:

- Capstan acquired the property in May 2008 for £285,000.
- The market value of the property on 1 May 2016 was £425,000.
- Capstan had used the property as a second home throughout his period of ownership.
- Capstan will pay any inheritance tax due on the gift of the property to the trust.

Sale of ordinary shares in Agraffe Ltd:

- Capstan subscribed for 18,000 shares in Agraffe Ltd for £32,000 on 1 February 2014.
- He obtained EIS relief of £9,600 against his income tax liability.
- Capstan intends to sell all of the shares for £20,000 on 1 July 2016.
- Capstan will relieve the loss arising on the shares in the most tax efficient manner.

Sale of loan stock and ordinary shares in Pinblock plc:

- Capstan will sell £8,000 7% Pinblock plc non-convertible loan stock for £10,600.
- Capstan will also sell 12,000 shares in Pinblock plc for £69,000.
- The sales will take place on 1 August 2016.

Capstan's acquisition of loan stock and ordinary shares in Pinblock plc:

- Capstan purchased 15,000 shares in Wippen plc for £26,000 on 1 May 2009.

- Pinblock plc acquired 100% of the ordinary share capital of Wippen plc on 1 October 2012.

- The takeover was for *bona fide* commercial reasons and was not for the avoidance of tax.

- Capstan received £8,000 Pinblock plc non-convertible loan stock (a qualifying corporate bond) and 20,000 ordinary shares in Pinblock plc in exchange for his shares in Wippen plc.

- The loan stock and the shares were worth £9,000 and £40,000 respectively as at 1 October 2012.

Required

(a)   Set out, together with supporting calculations, the inheritance tax and capital gains tax implications of the transfer of the UK property to the trust and the date(s) on which any tax due will be payable.   **(7 marks)**

(b)   Explain, with supporting calculations, in connection with the sale of shares in Agraffe Ltd:

- The tax implications of selling them on 1 July 2016
- Any advantages and disadvantages to Capstan of delaying the sale   **(8 marks)**

(c)   Calculate Capstan's taxable capital gains for the tax year 2016/17.   **(5 marks)**

Note. In parts (a) and (b) you should clearly state any assumptions you have made together with any additional information that you would need to confirm with Capstan before finalising your calculations.

You should assume that the tax rates and allowances of the tax year 2015/16 will continue to apply for the foreseeable future.

(Total = 20 marks)

5 Loriod plc group (ATAX 06/11)   39 mins

The Loriod plc group intends to acquire an overseas business. It requires advice on the relief available in respect of any initial losses made by the business, the use of foreign tax credits, and transfer pricing. The following information has been obtained from the management of the Loriod plc group.

Loriod plc group:

- Loriod plc is a UK resident trading company.
- Loriod plc has a large number of wholly-owned UK resident trading subsidiary companies.
- Elivar Ltd, one of the Loriod plc group subsidiaries, is to acquire the 'Frager' business.
- The purchase of the 'Frager' business will follow either Strategy A or Strategy B.

Elivar Ltd:

- Makes qualifying charitable donations of £2,000 each year.
- Has taxable total profits of approximately £90,000 per year.

The 'Frager' business:

- Is carried on in the country of Kuwata and is owned by Syme Inc, a company resident in Kuwata.
- Manufactures components used by Elivar Ltd and other Loriod plc group companies.
- Carries on the same trade as Elivar Ltd.
- Is expected to make a loss in the year following its acquisition by Elivar Ltd.
- Is expected to have taxable profits of £120,000 per year following the year of acquisition.

Strategy A:

- Elivar Ltd will purchase the trade and all of the assets of Syme Inc such that Elivar Ltd will be carrying on the 'Frager' business through a permanent establishment in Kuwata.
- The permanent establishment will be controlled from the UK.

Strategy B:

- Elivar Ltd will purchase the whole of the share capital of Syme Inc such that Syme Inc will be a subsidiary of Elivar Ltd resident in Kuwata.
- It has been determined that no charge would arise within the controlled foreign company (CFC) regime in respect of Syme Inc.

The tax system in the country of Kuwata:

- Is broadly the same as that in the UK with a corporation tax rate of 17%
- Trading losses may only be utilised by companies resident in Kuwata.
- Kuwata is not a member of the European Union and there is no double tax treaty between the UK and Kuwata.

Required

(a) Provide a detailed explanation of the relief available in respect of the expected loss to be made by the 'Frager' business depending on whether the purchase follows Strategy A or Strategy B.   **(8 marks)**

(b) For this part of the question it should be assumed that the purchase has followed Strategy A, the 'Frager' business is now profitable and that no election has been made in respect of the profits of the business.

Explain, with supporting calculations, how to determine the maximum loss that can be surrendered to Elivar Ltd by the Loriod plc group companies if relief in respect of the tax suffered in Kuwata is not to be wasted.

(6 marks)

(c) For this part of the question it should be assumed that the purchase has followed Strategy B.

Explain the effect of the prices charged by the subsidiary in Kuwata to other companies in the Loriod plc group on the total tax paid by the group and the implications of the transfer pricing legislation.   **(6 marks)**

You should assume that the tax rates and allowances of the Financial Year 2015 will continue to apply for the foreseeable future.

(Total = 20 marks)

Answers

DO NOT TURN THIS PAGE UNTIL YOU HAVE
COMPLETED THE MOCK EXAM

A plan of attack

What's the worst thing you could be doing right now if this was the actual exam paper? Wondering how to celebrate the end of the exam in about three hours time? Panicking, flapping and generally getting in a right old state?

Well, they're all pretty bad, so turn back to the paper and let's sort out a **plan of attack**!

First things first

Look through the paper and work out which optional questions to do and the order in which to attack the questions. You've got **two options**. Option 1 is the option recommended by BPP.

Option 1 (if you're thinking 'Help!')

If you're a bit worried about the paper, do the questions in the order of how well you think you can answer them. If you find the questions in Section B less daunting than the compulsory questions in Section A start with Section B. Remember you only need to do two of the three questions in Section B; you may find it easier if you start by deciding which question you will not do and put a line through it.

- **Question 3** is about employment benefits, Enterprise Management Incentives and redundancy payments.
- **Question 4** requires a knowledge of capital gains tax and inheritance tax.
- **Question 5** is a corporate tax question about groups and overseas aspects.

Do not spend longer than the allocated time on Section B. When you've spent the allocated time on **two** of the three questions in Section B turn to the longer questions in Section A. Read these questions through thoroughly before you launch into them. Once you start make sure you allocate your time to the parts within the questions according to the marks available and that, where possible, you attempt the easy marks first.

Lastly, what you mustn't forget is that you have to **answer both questions in Section A and TWO in Section B**.

Option 2 (if you're thinking 'It's a doddle')

It never pays to be overconfident but if you're not quaking in your shoes about the exam then **turn straight to the compulsory questions** in Section A.

Once you've done these questions, move to Section B. The question you attempt first really depends on what you are most confident at. You then have to select one of the two remaining questions. If you are undecided look at the requirements. It maybe easier to obtain more marks if these are broken down into several smaller parts.

No matter how many times we remind you....

Always, always **allocate your time** according to the marks for the question in total and then according to the parts of the question. And **always, always follow the requirements** exactly. Question 1 part (a), for example, asks you to conclude with a summary showing the capital gains tax payable in respect of four alternatives.

You've got spare time at the end of the exam.....?

If you have allocated your time properly then you **shouldn't have time on your hands** at the end of the exam. But if you find yourself with five or ten minutes to spare, check over your work to make sure that you have answered all the requirements of the questions and all parts of all requirements.

Forget about it!

And don't worry if you found the paper difficult. More than likely other candidates will too. If this were the real thing you would need to **forget** the exam the minute you leave the exam hall and **think about the next one**. Or, if it's the last one, **celebrate**!

1 Calisia (ATAX 06/11)

Text references. Principles of income tax are covered in Chapter 1. Property income is dealt with in Chapter 3. Employment income is dealt with in Chapter 4. Chargeable gains are covered in Chapter 11. Reliefs are in Chapter 13. Stamp duty and stamp duty land tax will be found in Chapter 19. Inheritance tax is covered in Chapters 16 to 18.

Top tips. It was very important in part (a) to deal with each of the situations in turn and then to compare the capital gains tax payable at the end. There was a big hint that the fourth scenario should have given the least capital gains tax payable!

Easy marks. The inheritance tax aspects of this question were relatively straightforward and should have yielded easy marks. As usual, easy marks could also be obtained for professional skills such as using appropriate language and style.

Examiner's comments. Part (a) was for 21 marks. With a question part of this size it was important for candidates to be clear as to what they had been asked to do and how they were going to do it. It was very pleasing to see the majority of candidates taking a well-structured approach to this question and addressing all of the alternatives in a consistent manner. There were some very good answers to this question with some candidates scoring full marks.

The question centred on capital gains business reliefs and the taxation of various sources of income. The income tax elements were done well but candidates' knowledge of business reliefs was often not as good as it could have been. However, there was a clear indication that candidates were taking the right approach to capital gains tax in that they were considering the availability of reliefs every time a gain arose. This was very good to see and it now remains for candidates to improve their knowledge of the conditions that must be satisfied for the reliefs to be available.

The first task was to calculate the amount of additional income required by the client's daughter, Farfisa. This was a relatively simple task and many candidates scored full marks. Other candidates failed to identify that the proposed loan was for less than £10,000 such that it was an exempt benefit or were not careful enough in distinguishing taxable income (income less personal allowance) from post-tax income (income less tax).

Under the first alternative the income was to be provided via a transfer of quoted shares. The majority of candidates were happy calculating the number of shares to be transferred but many failed to consider how the dividends would be taxed in the hands of Farfisa. Those who did address this point often considered the rate of tax but not the credit. The point that needed to be identified was that there would be no tax to pay on the dividend income because, as Farfisa would be a basic rate taxpayer, the tax liability would be covered by the tax credit.

Under the first alternative candidates then had to calculate the capital gain on the proposed gift of the shares. This is where some candidates began to have problems as they thought that gift relief would be available. However, the relief was not available because the shares were quoted and Calisia did not own at least 5% of the voting rights.

Under the second alternative candidates had to calculate the capital gains on the proposed sale of a building that was rented out as qualifying furnished holiday accommodation. Calculating the gain was simple; but again there was the need to consider the availability of business reliefs. Many candidates failed to realise that entrepreneurs' relief would be available such that tax would only be taxed at 10%. A minority of candidates also had the problem here of distinguishing a taxable gain (proceeds less cost) from post-tax proceeds (proceeds less tax).

Under the third and fourth alternatives the rental property was to be gifted rather than sold. Candidates had to identify that gift relief would be available under both alternatives. It was then necessary to consider how the rental income received by Farfisa in respect of the property would be taxed. Under the third alternative the income would be simply be taxed at 20%. But under the fourth alternative rent a room relief would be available. These points were identified by the vast majority of candidates.

Candidates were also asked to consider stamp duty and stamp duty land tax and to prepare a summary of the capital gains tax liabilities under each of the alternatives. A minority of candidates did not carry out one or both of these tasks thus sacrificing some fairly easy marks.

Part (b) required candidates to prepare a comprehensive explanation of how Calisia's inheritance tax liability would be calculated; this was done well by many candidates.

This question was fairly unstructured such that candidates had to think and impose their own structure in order to maximise their marks. Candidates who failed to do this often repeated themselves, did not cover sufficient aspects of the question and included material in their answers which was irrelevant. In particular, some candidates wasted time by writing about inheritance tax in general terms, including giving general advice on inheritance tax planning, or by preparing computations when they were told not to.

Candidates' knowledge of inheritance tax was often very good. The link between domicile and the taxation of overseas assets, the transfer of the husband's nil rate band, the treatment of the donation to the political party and the taxation of the client's home were identified and understood by the majority of candidates.

Business property relief was often explained well although, as always, there was a small minority of candidates who confused reliefs available in respect of capital gains tax with those available in respect of inheritance tax. It was important to provide some detail here (the requirement was for a comprehensive explanation) so a statement that 'business property relief would be available' was, despite being true, insufficient to score. Candidates needed to address the assets that would qualify for the relief, the qualifying ownership period and the rate of relief; many candidates did not address as much as they could have.

In respect of the property situated overseas, the marks available for explaining the relief in respect of tax suffered overseas were missed by many candidates. Other marks that were often missed included the deduction available for the costs of administering the property situated overseas, the treatment of Calisia's home, the deduction available in respect of funeral costs and the need for the political party to qualify in order for the donation to be exempt.

Marking scheme

			Marks
(a)	Calculation of additional income required	3½	
	Gift of shares		
	Tax on dividends	1½	
	Capital gains tax	3½	
	Sale of investment property followed by gift of proceeds		
	Capital gains on investment property	2½	
	Farfisa's income position	3½	
	Capital gains tax on transfer of shares	1½	
	Gift of investment property – rented out by Farfisa		
	Gift relief available	1	
	Farfisa's income position	2	
	Capital gains tax on transfer of shares	1	
	Gift of investment property – to be lived in by Farfisa	2½	
	Summary of capital gains tax payable	1	
	Stamp duty and stamp duty land tax	2	
	Max		21
(b)	Relevance of domicile	1	
	Calisia's home subject to tax	½	
	Business property relief	4	
	Cost of administering the property in Sakura	1	
	Political party	1½	
	Funeral costs	½	
	Nil rate bands	1½	
	Tax and double tax relief	2	
	Max		10
Appropriate style and presentation		1	
Effectiveness of communication		2	
Approach to problem solving		1	
			4
			35

Prepared by A. N. Taxadviser

Date   6 June 2016

Subject   Farfisa – Additional income

               Calisia – Inheritance tax

(a)   **Farfisa – Additional income**

        Additional income required

	£
Salary	27,500
Less: Income tax £(£27,500 – 10,600) × 20%	(3,380)
Class 1 national insurance contributions £(£27,500 – 8,060) × 12%	(2,333)
Income receivable from Jelmini Ltd	21,787
Less estimated expenditure £2,500 × 12	(30,000)
Additional income required	(8,213)

        The interest free loan will not result in a tax liability because it is for less than £10,000.

(i)   **Gift of shares quoted on UK stock exchange**

        If Farfisa were to be given shares resulting in dividend income of £8,213, her taxable income would remain below the higher rate threshold of £31,785 as set out below. There would be no income tax to pay on the dividend income as the tax liability will be covered by the 10% tax credit.

	£
Salary	27,500
Dividend income £8,213 × 100/90	9,126
Less: personal allowance	(10,600)
Taxable income	26,026

        Accordingly, with a yield of 4%, Farfisa would need to own shares valued at £205,325 (£8,213/4%).

        The gift would give rise to a capital gain calculated by reference to market value. Holdings in quoted companies do not qualify for gift relief, except in the case of an individual's personal trading company in which they own at least 5% of the voting rights.

        Calisia has estimated that the gain on the shares will be one quarter of their market value, ie £51,331 (£205,325 × ¼).

        Calisia is a higher rate taxpayer who uses her annual exempt amount every year. Accordingly, her capital gains tax liability would be £14,373 (£51,331 × 28%).

        Stamp duty is charged on the amount of consideration paid. Accordingly, there would be no stamp duty on a gift of quoted shares.

(ii)   **Sale of investment property followed by gift of proceeds**

	£
Proceeds	270,000
Less: disposal costs	(6,000)
cost	(90,000)
Chargeable gain	174,000

        Entrepreneurs' relief is available in respect of capital gains on furnished holiday accommodation. Accordingly, capital gains tax of £17,400 (£174,000 × 10%) would be due.

        The gift of cash to Farfisa would be £246,600 (£270,000 – £6,000 – £17,400). This would give rise to gross interest of £7,398 (£246,600 × 3%).

Farfisa's taxable income would remain below the higher rate threshold of £31,785 as set out below. Accordingly, the interest income would be taxed at 20% and Farfisa's after-tax income would be £5,918 (£7,398 × 80%).

	£
Salary	27,500
Interest income	7,398
Less personal allowance	(10,600)
Taxable income	24,298

In addition to the interest income, Farfisa would require after-tax dividend income of £2,295 (£8,213 – £5,918) in order to meet her budgeted expenditure. There would be no income tax to pay on this dividend income as her taxable income will clearly still remain below the higher rate threshold (£31,785 – £24,298 = £7,487) such that the tax liability will be covered by the 10% tax credit.

Calisia's capital gains tax liability on the gift of the shares would be £4,016 (£2,295/4% × ¼ × 28%).

Calisia will not be liable to stamp duty land tax on the sale of the property as this would be payable by the purchaser of the property.

There would be no stamp duty on the gift of the shares.

(iii) **Gift of investment property – rented out by Farfisa**

The property qualifies as commercially let furnished holiday accommodation. Accordingly, gift relief would be available in respect of the capital gain and no capital gains tax would be payable. Farfisa would pay tax on the rental income at 20%. Accordingly, her rental income, after tax, would be £4,080 (£5,100 × 80%).

In addition to the rental income, Farfisa would require after-tax dividend income of £4,133 (£8,213 – £4,080) in order to meet her budgeted expenditure. There would be no income tax to pay on this dividend income as her taxable income will clearly still remain below the higher rate threshold such that the tax liability will be covered by the 10% tax credit.

Calisia's capital gains tax liability on the gift of the shares will be £7,233 (£4,133/4% × ¼ × 28%).

Stamp duty and stamp duty land tax is charged on the amount of consideration paid. Accordingly, there would be no duty on either of the gifts.

(iv) **Gift of investment property – lived in by Farfisa**

If Farfisa were to live in the investment property she would not have to pay the rent of £550 per month. Also, she could rent out the spare room to generate additional income. Provided the room is furnished and the rent does not exceed £4,250, the rental income would not be subject to income tax.

As above in (iii), gift relief would be available in respect of the gain on the property.

	£
Additional income required	8,213
Less rental expenditure no longer incurred £(550 × 12)	(6,600)
	1,613
Minimum monthly rent required in respect of spare room £(1,613/12)	134

There would be no stamp duty land tax on the gift of the property.

Summary

Capital gains tax payable by Calisia under each alternative:

(i) £14,373
(ii) £21,416 (£17,400 + £4,016)
(iii) £7,233
(iv) Nil

(b)   **Calisia – Inheritance tax**

Explanation of inheritance tax liability on death

The amount subject to inheritance tax on Calisia's death (her taxable estate) will be the value of all of the assets she owns when she dies, including her home and any assets situated overseas (because she is domiciled in the UK) less certain deductions.

The following amounts will be deducted from the value of her assets in arriving at her taxable estate.

–   The interest in the 'Therson Partnership' will be 100% relieved by business property relief provided the partnership carries on a qualifying business; this excludes dealing in securities and shares or land and buildings and the making or holding of investments. Calisia's share of the value of the partnership assets not used wholly or mainly for business purposes (ie investments) will not qualify for this relief.

–   The building used by the 'Therson Partnership' will be 50% relieved by business property relief provided it is used wholly or mainly for the purposes of a qualifying business carried on by the partnership.

–   Calisia will need to satisfy the minimum qualifying ownership period of two years in respect of her interest in the partnership and the building used by the partnership in order for business property relief to be available.

–   The cost of administering or realising the property in the country of Sakura up to a maximum of 5% of the property's value will be deducted from the property's value.

–   The legacy to the Fairness for All political party will be deducted only if it is a qualifying political party. A qualifying political party is one which has two elected members in the House of Commons or one member and at least 150,000 votes at the last general election.

–   Liabilities due at the time of death, reasonable funeral costs including the cost of a tombstone are also deductible.

Because Calisia has made no lifetime gifts, there will be no tax on the first £325,000 (the nil rate band) of her estate. An additional deduction of £325,000 will also be available in respect of her husband's nil rate band as it was not used on his death.

Tax will be charged at 40% on the taxable estate.

Any inheritance tax suffered in the country of Sakura will be deducted from the UK inheritance tax liability up to a maximum of the UK inheritance tax on the Sakuran property. The UK inheritance tax on the Sakuran property will be calculated by determining the percentage, by reference to the market values, of Calisia's assets represented by the Sakuran property and applying that percentage to the total inheritance tax due.

Confirmations required

For business property relief, as set out above, to be available the following matters need to be confirmed:

–   The partnership carries on a qualifying business.
–   Calisia satisfies the minimum qualifying ownership period.

2 Petzold (ATAX 06/11)

Text references. VAT is covered in Chapters 28 and 29. Employer's national insurance is dealt with in Chapter 4. Calculation of corporation tax is covered in Chapter 22. Ethical issues are in Chapter 30. Chargeable gains for companies are covered in Chapter 21.

Top tips. Don't neglect ethical aspects of taxation practice in your preparation for the P6 exam – this topic is often examined.

Easy marks. There were some easy marks for basic computations related to national insurance computations, corporation tax and chargeable gains.

Examiner's comments. Part (a) concerned value added tax (VAT), corporation tax and national insurance. Candidates' performance was pretty mixed with some very good scripts, some very poor ones and a range in between.

The VAT element required calculations and explanations of the company's VAT liabilities for two quarters. This was done well by those candidates who knew how to do it but, unfortunately, many candidates had little more than an awareness of the rules and did not know how to apply them to the facts. There are always a reasonable number of marks in the exam relating to VAT and changes introduced by the latest Finance Act are often examined so it should not have been surprising to see partial exemption being tested. (**BPP note.** This comment relates to the situation when this question was originally set in June 2011 but has been retained as an important point for students to note about the examination of the most recent Finance Act.)

The national insurance element was straightforward and done well by those who attempted it. The problem was that many candidates did not identify the need to carry out the calculations despite the clues in the question.

Part (b) concerned the company's cash flow position in relation to VAT, the treatment of a refund of corporation tax and the sale and leaseback of a warehouse.

The VAT element concerned the default surcharge penalty. Just as with the VAT element of part (a), it was done very well by those who knew the rules and (inevitably) considerably less well by those who did not. As noted above, candidates would do well to recognise that VAT features in every exam.

The client was proposing to retain a recently received tax refund despite not knowing what it was for. Candidates were expected to recognise that this was not acceptable behaviour and the vast majority were able to do so. However, a minority of candidates did not do much more than that such that they failed to explain the implications of not returning the money in relation to both the client and its advisers.

The implications of the sale and leaseback were covered well by many candidates. Candidates had to slow down and think in order to provide sufficient information. The question asked for a 'detailed explanation' of relief of the gain via rollover relief. This required candidates to consider the period in which the replacement assets needed to be acquired, the implications of reinvesting some, rather than all, of the proceeds and the manner in which the relief would be given. Very few candidates addressed all of these matters but it is likely that the vast majority of candidates knew something about all of them. When asked to write in detail, candidates must plan their answers such that they cover all of the relevant issues.

Marks

(a) VAT

Three months ending 30 June 2016	3
Three months ending 30 September 2016	3½
Employer's national insurance contributions	3
Corporation tax	
Explanations of payment	3½
Max	**11**

(b) Late payment of VAT

Explanation	3½
Calculations	1½
Retention of the tax refund	4
Sale of the warehouse	
Chargeable gain	1½
Rollover relief and time period	1½
Proceeds not reinvested	1½
Manner of relief	1
Treatment of rent	1
Max	**14**
	25

Firm's address

Petzold's address

6 June 2016

Dear Petzold

Glenz Ltd

I set out below the information you require to assist you in dealing with the company's cash flow problems.

(a) **Glenz Ltd – Payments to the tax authorities**

The payments that will be made by Glenz Ltd to the tax authorities in respect of the two, three-month periods ending 30 June 2016 and 30 September 2016 are calculated at appendix 1. The calculations are based on the budgeted figures provided by the company. In summary, the following payments will be due:

	Three months ending 30 June 2016 £	Three months ending 30 September 2016 £
Value added tax (VAT)	30,250	29,590
Employer's national insurance contributions	7,215	9,215
Corporation tax instalment (if required – see explanation)	19,175	19,175

Glenz Ltd's corporation tax liability for the year ended 31 March 2016 has been correctly calculated as £383,500 × 20% = £76,700. However, it is necessary to consider whether this amount should have been paid by instalments if Glenz Ltd is a large company. The profits threshold of £1,500,000 must be divided by five because Glenz Ltd had four other related 51% group companies at the end of the previous accounting period, since Glenz Ltd directly or indirectly owned more than 50% of the ordinary shares of each company. This reduces the profits threshold to £300,000 (£1,500,000/5) which is less than the profits of £383,500. Glenz Ltd is therefore a large company in the year to 31 March 2016.

If Glenz Ltd was not a large company in the year to 31 March 2015, it will not have to pay corporation tax in instalments for the year to 31 March 2016 and so the corporation tax of £76,700 will be due on 1 January 2017.

However, if Glenz Ltd was a large company in the year to 31 March 2015, it should have paid its corporation tax for the year to 31 March 2016 by instalments of £76,700/4 = £19,175 on 14 October 2015, 14 January 2016, 14 April 2016 and 14 July 2016. Interest is payable on late paid instalments.

(b) **Glenz Ltd – Cash flow**

(i) *Your proposals to improve the company's cash flow position*

Late payment of VAT

When the company submitted its return late for the three months ended 30 June 2015 it would have received a surcharge liability notice.

A late payment of VAT in respect of one of the subsequent four quarters will result in a penalty of 2% of the VAT payable and an extension of the 12-month surcharge period. Accordingly, if Glenz Ltd's payment for the three months ending 30 June 2016 is made late, there will be a penalty of £605 (£30,250 × 2%).

The penalty for a second late payment within the surcharge period is 5% of the VAT payable. Accordingly, there will be a further penalty of £1,479 (£29,590 × 5%) if the payment for the three months ending 30 September 2016 is also late and the surcharge period will be extended again to include the following four quarters, ie to 30 September 2017.

The surcharge liability period will only end when four consecutive quarterly returns have been submitted on time and any VAT due has been paid on time. The penalties for a third and subsequent defaults are 10% and 15% respectively of the VAT payable.

Retention of the tax refund

I suggest that we carry out a review of the company's tax affairs in order to identify the reason for the tax refund. If, as you suspect, it is an error it should be repaid immediately. You may well be committing a civil and/or a criminal offence if you fail to return the money in these circumstances. Immediate voluntary disclosure is advisable in order to minimise any interest and penalties that may otherwise become payable.

In addition, unless you return the money, we would have to consider ceasing to act as your advisers. In these circumstances we are required to notify the tax authorities that we no longer act for you, although we would not provide them with any reason for our action.

(ii) *Sale of warehouse*

Chargeable gain

The chargeable gain on the sale of the warehouse would be £87,540 (appendix 2). This would be subject to corporation tax in the year ending 31 March 2017 unless it is relieved via rollover relief.

Rollover relief would be available if a new warehouse was purchased for use in the business within the period beginning one year prior to the sale and ending three years after the sale.

In order for the whole of the gain to be relieved you would need to reinvest the whole of the sale proceeds the new warehouse. Otherwise, there would be a chargeable gain equal to the amount of proceeds not reinvested subject to a maximum of £87,540.

The gain relieved is deducted from the cost of the new warehouse. This will increase the gain on a future disposal of the new warehouse.

Rent paid

The rent paid following the sale of the warehouse would be a tax-deductible expense when calculating the company's corporation tax liability. Accordingly, there would be a tax deduction in the year ending 31 March 2017 of £16,500 (£22,000 × 9/12).

Please contact me if you require any further information.

Yours sincerely

Tax Manager

Appendix 1

Glenz Ltd – Payment to the tax authorities

Value added tax (VAT)

Glenz Ltd does not satisfy the partial exemption annual test as it was unable to recover all of its input tax in the year ended 31 March 2016. However, it can still provisionally recover all of its input tax in any quarter of the current year in which it passes the *de minimis* test.

	Three months ending 30 June 2016 £
Output tax £360,000 × 20%	72,000
Recoverable input tax £(40,000 + 950 + 800) (N2)	(41,750)
Amount payable to HMRC	30,250

	Three months ending 30 September 2016 £
Output tax £365,000 × 20%	73,000
Recoverable input tax	
Attributable to taxable supplies	(42,000)
Non-attributable £1,500 × 94% (N3,4,5)	(1,410)
Amount payable to HMRC	29,590

Notes

1   Partial exemption simplified test 1 is clearly not satisfied in either quarter, as total input tax incurred exceeds £625 per month on average.

2   Partial exemption simplified test 2 will be satisfied in the quarter ending 30 June 2016 because:

Total input tax less that directly attributable to taxable supplies does not exceed £625 per month on average ((£41,750 – £40,000)/3 = £583); and

The value of exempt supplies does not exceed 50% of the value of all supplies (£24,500/(£360,000 + £24,500) = 6.4%).

Accordingly, Glenz Ltd can provisionally recover all of its input tax.

3   Partial exemption simplified test 2 will not be satisfied in the quarter ending 30 September 2016 because:

Total input tax less that directly attributable to taxable supplies exceeds £625 per month on average ((£45,700 – £42,000)/3 = £1,233).

4   Exempt input tax of £2,290 (£2,200 + (£1,500 – (£1,500 × 94% (N5)))) exceeds £625 per month (main test) and is therefore not *de minimis*.

5   Glenz Ltd's taxable supplies represent 93.97% (£365,000/(£365,000 + £23,400)) of its total supplies. This figure is rounded up to 94% for the purpose of calculating recoverable input tax.

Employer's Class 1 national insurance contributions

	£
Average annual liability per employee £((332,000/8) − 8,112) × 13.8%	4,608
Quarterly liability for eight employees £4,608 × 3/12 × 8	9,215

The employment allowance of £2,000 will be set against the liability for the quarter ended 30 June 2016 so the liability for this quarter will be £7,215.

Appendix 2

Chargeable gain on sale of warehouse

	£
Proceeds	330,000
Less: cost	(180,000)
indexation allowance £180,000 × 0.347 ((261.5 − 194.2)/194.2)	(62,460)
Chargeable gain	87,540

3 Pita plc (ATAX 06/14)

Text references. Taxable and exempt benefits are covered in Chapter 4. Share schemes and lump sum payments are covered in Chapter 5.

Top tips. Make sure that you attempt all parts of a multi-part question such as this. Use the allocated marks to guide your answer. For example, you should not have spent more than 11 minutes answering part (a).

Easy marks. There were some easy marks for describing the benefits in part (a) and the rules on lump sum payment in part (c) should have been well-known.

Examiner's comments. Part (a) tested the provision of vouchers to purchase childcare and payments made to employees when they work from home. The taxation of vouchers to be used for the purchase of childcare was tackled well by the majority of candidates. The majority of candidates were aware that an exemption was available in respect of the provision of such vouchers, with many knowing that the amounts of the exemption depend on the employee's marginal rate of tax. The rules regarding the ability of an employer to make tax-free payments to employees who work from home were not as well known, such that very few candidates scored well on this aspect of the question.

Part (b) tested various aspects of the enterprise management incentive (EMI) scheme and was split into two sub-requirements. The first part concerned the ability of the company concerned to establish such a scheme and to make it available to nine key employees. This part of the question was done reasonably well. The majority of candidates knew that there were conditions relating to the number of employees and the gross assets of the company, although not all knew the precise detail of the conditions. Most candidates were also aware that it is acceptable for an EMI scheme to be provided to key employees (rather than to all of a company's employees) but many did not realise that part-time employees are not permitted to be members of such a scheme. The second part related to the tax implications of the grant and exercise of the share options and the sale of the shares. This was arguably a more difficult requirement and was not done particularly well. As always, those candidates who adopted a methodical approach and dealt with the grant, exercise and sale as three separate issues did better than those who tried to address everything at once. Candidates will almost always benefit from starting a new paragraph for each new issue that needs to be addressed.

The final part of the question concerned a redundancy package to be received by an employee of the company. The package consisted of a payment of statutory redundancy, an additional payment and the provision of a company car after the employment ceased. All three matters were handled well by many candidates with most candidates demonstrating awareness of the £30,000 exemption. The one area where almost all candidates could have improved their performance was the additional payment. The question was deliberately silent as to the reason for and the nature of the payment. It was up to candidates to raise the matter as to whether or not the payment was for work carried out or a restriction to be placed on the employee's future working activities, such that it would be taxable in full.

Marks

(a)	Vouchers to purchase childcare		
	Taxable employment income	1	
	Availability of exemption	1	
	Amount of exemption	2	
	Payments for working from home	2½	
	Max		6
(b)	(i) Qualifying company	3	
	Qualifying employees	2	
	Max		4
	(ii) Grant of options	1	
	Exercise of options	1½	
	Sale of shares	3	
	Max		5
(c)	Statutory redundancy	1	
	Additional payment	3	
	Continued use of car	2	
	Max		5
			20

(a) **Financial assistance with childcare and encouraging working from home**

Vouchers to purchase childcare

The general rule is that the employee is taxed on the cost to the employer of providing the voucher rather than the childcare that is purchased by the voucher.

However, a certain amount of this childcare is tax free if the employer provides childcare vouchers to pay an approved childcarer. The childcare vouchers must usually be available to all employees.

A £55 per week limit applies to basic rate employees who receive childcare vouchers giving tax relief of £11 per week. Higher and additional rate employees can receive vouchers tax-free up to £28 per week and £25 per week respectively, giving them the same amount of tax relief. Whether an employee is considered basic rate, higher rate or additional rate for these purposes is determined by the level of the employee's employment income only (and not other income).

Payments for working from home

Employer contributions towards additional household costs incurred by an employee who works wholly or partly at home may be exempt.

Payments up to £4 per week (or £18 per month for monthly paid employees) may be made without supporting evidence. Payments in excess of that amount require supporting evidence that the payment is wholly in respect of additional household expenses.

Tutorial note

Credit was available for identifying the exemption limits in respect of the vouchers and home working payments but it was possible to score full marks without this knowledge.

(b) (i) **Ability to establish an enterprise management incentive (EMI) scheme**

Pita plc is a qualifying company for the purposes of the EMI scheme because it has:

- Gross assets of no more than £30 million.
- Fewer than 250 full-time employees.
- A permanent establishment in the UK.

Under the EMI scheme rules, Pita plc is allowed to make the scheme available to just its nine key employees. However, the two part-time key employees cannot join the scheme unless they work for Pita plc for at least 25 hours per week or, if lower, 75% of their working time.

Tutorial notes

1   The following conditions would also be relevant but the information necessary to address them was not provided in the question.

 - An employee owning 30% or more of the company's ordinary shares would not be permitted to join the scheme.

 - Pita plc must carry on a qualifying trade and must not be controlled by another company.

2   The answer does not include the need for the shares to be fully paid up irredeemable ordinary shares as the requirement refers to the conditions relating to the company and the employees, and not to the shares.

(ii)   **Income tax and capital gains tax implications for the employees**

There will be no income tax on the grant of the share options.

The options are to be exercised within ten years of the date on which they were granted. Therefore income tax will only be charged on the excess of the market value of the shares at the time the options were granted over the price paid on exercise which is £(2.00 – 1.75) = £0.25 per share.

When the shares are sold, there will be a capital gain per share equal to the excess of the sales proceeds over the market value at the time the options were granted, which is £(5.00 – 2.00) = £3.00 per share.

On a disposal of EMI shares in Pita plc, entrepreneurs' relief will be available if:

 - Pita plc was a trading company throughout the year prior to the disposal.
 - The shareholder was employed by the company throughout the year prior to disposal.
 - The options were granted at least one year prior to the date of the disposal of the shares.

Tutorial note

There is no requirement for the individual to own at least 5% of the shares in the company where the shares are EMI shares.

(c)   **Redundancy package for Narn**

The statutory redundancy payment is covered by the £30,000 exemption which is available in respect of termination payments which are not in respect of services provided by the employee.

The additional amount of £26,000 will be taxable in full if:

 - Narn was contractually entitled to receive it, for example a terminal bonus in respect of work done by Narn or a payment in lieu of notice.

 - Narn's agreed to limit his future conduct or activities in return for the payment (a restrictive covenant).

If the payment is not taxable in full, £(30,000 – 8,100) = £21,900 will be exempt and the balance of £4,100 will be taxable.

The continued use of the company car will result in a taxable benefit in the tax year 2016/17 after Narn has left the company. The benefit will be (6/12 × £19,500 × 21% (14% + ((115 – 95)/5)% + 3%)) = £2,047.

4 Capstan (ATAX 06/11)

Text references. Lifetime transfers for IHT are covered in Chapter 16. The enterprise investment scheme is dealt with in Chapter 2. The CGT aspects of shares and securities are covered in Chapter 12.

Top tips. The P6 exam is not just about technical tax knowledge. When thinking about advantages and disadvantages which might arise on delaying the sale of the shares in Agraffe Ltd, don't forget about practical and commercial aspects that might be important to the client.

Easy marks. The inheritance tax calculation was very straightforward. The sale of the loan stock after a takeover should also have given easy marks.

Examiner's comments. Part (a) required candidates to consider both the capital gains tax and inheritance tax implications of the transfer of a property to a discretionary trust. The inheritance tax implications were addressed very well by all but a tiny minority of candidates. The only common error was a failure to set out any assumptions made as required by the note to the question.

The capital gains tax element of this part was not answered well. The problem here was that most candidates did not think; instead they simply deducted the cost from the proceeds and addressed rates of tax. Some candidates then realised that gift relief was available and that, per the question, all available claims would be made. As a result, although they had wasted some time, they were still able to score full marks. Other candidates, however, did not address the gift relief point and consequently did not score any marks for the capital gains tax element of the question.

Part (b) concerned the sale of shares in respect of which EIS relief had been claimed. Almost all candidates identified the claw back of the relief if the shares were sold within three years of the acquisition. However, many stated that the whole of the relief obtained would be withdrawn as opposed to a proportion of it.

The implications of delaying the sale were not identified particularly well. Many candidates simply stated the opposite of what they had already written, ie that the relief obtained would not be withdrawn if the shares were held for three years. More thoughtful candidates considered other matters and recognised that delaying the sale delayed the receipt of the sales proceeds and that the value of the shares might change (for the better or the worse).

The final part of the question concerned the sale of shares and qualifying corporate bonds that had been acquired following a paper for paper exchange. This part was done well by those candidates who knew how to handle this type of transaction.

The first task was to recognise that the cost of the original shares needed to be apportioned between the new shares and the corporate bonds. Many candidates knew what they were doing here and were on the way to doing well in this part of the question.

However, there was often confusion as to the treatment of the sale of the corporate bonds. Many candidates who knew that corporate bonds are exempt from capital gains tax went on to calculate a gain on the sale and include it in the taxable capital gains for the year. Also, many candidates were not able to identify the gain on the original shares that was frozen at the time of the paper for paper exchange and then charged when the corporate bonds were sold.

Marking scheme

			Marks
(a)	Inheritance tax		
	Explanations and assumptions	3½	
	Calculations	2	
	Capital gains tax	1½	
			7
(b)	Withdrawal of EIS relief	2	
	Loss on sale	1½	
	Offset of loss	1	
	Advantage of delay	2	
	Disadvantages of delay	2	
	Max		8

(c)	Sale of loan stock		3½
	Gain on sale of shares		1
	Annual exempt amount		½
			5
			20

(a) Transfer of a UK property to a discretionary trust

Inheritance tax

A lifetime transfer to any form of trust is immediately chargeable to inheritance tax.

	£
Market value of property	425,000
Less: AE 2016/17	(3,000)
AE 2015/16 b/f	(3,000)
Net transfer of value (Capstan pays IHT)	419,000

			£
IHT	£325,000	× 0% =	Nil
	£ 94,000	× 20/80 =	23,500
	£419,000		23,500

The gross transfer of value for accumulation is £(419,000 + 23,500) = £442,500.

Check

			£
IHT	£325,000	× 0% =	Nil
	£117,500	× 20% =	23,500
	£442,500		23,500

It has been assumed that:

- Capstan has made no other transfers of value in 2015/16 or in 2016/17 prior to 1 May 2016 such that there are two annual exemptions available.

- Capstan has made no chargeable lifetime transfers in the seven years prior to 1 May 2016 such that the whole of the nil rate band is available.

Since the transfer took place between 6 April and 30 September 2016, the tax will be due on 30 April 2017. Inheritance tax on land and buildings can be paid by instalments but not where the tax is being paid by the donor.

Capital gains tax

Gift relief will be available on the transfer because the gift is immediately chargeable to inheritance tax. Accordingly, there will be no capital gains tax liability in respect of the transfer.

(b) Agraffe Ltd

A sale on 1 July 2016 will result in a withdrawal of the EIS income tax relief as the shares will have been held for less than three years. On the assumption that the sale is a bargain at arm's length the withdrawal of relief will be £(20,000/32,000) × £9,600 = £6,000.

There will also be a loss on the sale of the shares. However, when calculating the loss, the allowable cost of the shares will be reduced by the EIS relief obtained.

	£
Proceeds	20,000
Less cost £(32,000 – (9,600 – 6,000))	(28,400)
Allowable loss	(8,400)

Capstan can offset the loss against his general income of 2016/17 and/or 2015/16 because the shares qualified for EIS relief.

This is advantageous as Capstan will save income tax at 40% (he is a higher rate taxpayer) rather than capital gains tax at 28%.

There would be no withdrawal of EIS relief if Capstan were to sell the shares after 1 February 2017 as he would then have held them for three years. However, this would reduce the allowable loss on the sale by £6,000 (because the allowable cost would be £6,000 less) such that the tax saved via the offset of the loss would be reduced by £2,400 (40% × £6,000). The overall saving to Capstan would be £3,600 (£6,000 – £2,400).

The disadvantages of delaying the sale are that the receipt of the sales proceeds will be delayed and that the value of the shares could continue to fall such that Capstan's financial loss would increase.

(c) **Capstan's taxable capital gains for the tax year 2016/17**

	£
Gain arising on sale of Pinblock plc loan stock (W1)	4,224
Gain arising on sale of the shares in Pinblock plc (W2)	56,265
	60,489
Less annual exempt amount	(11,100)
Taxable gains	49,389

Tutorial note

Candidates who assumed in their answer to part (b) above that the loss arising on the sale of the shares in Agraffe Ltd would be set off against Capstan's capital gains were given full credit in this part of the question.

Workings

1 *Capital gain arising on sale of loan stock*

The profit on the sale of the 7% Pinblock plc non-convertible loan stock will not be subject to capital gains tax because qualifying corporate bonds are exempt assets.

However, a gain will have arisen when the shares in Wippen plc were exchanged for the loan stock. This gain will become chargeable on the sale of the loan stock.

	£
Market value of loan stock on 1 October 2012	9,000
Less cost £(26,000 × (9,000/(9,000 + 40,000)))	(4,776)
Chargeable gain	4,224

2 *Capital gain arising on the sale of shares in Pinblock plc*

	£
Proceeds	69,000
Less cost 12,000/20,000 × £(26,000 × (40,000/(9,000 + 40,000)))	(12,735)
Chargeable gain	56,265

5 Loriod plc group (ATAX 06/11)

Text references. Overseas aspects of corporation tax are covered in Chapter 27. Transfer pricing is dealt with in Chapter 20.

Top tips. Read the question carefully. For example, in part (c), you are told to consider the position for transfer pricing if Strategy B is adopted. (You might like to think why the question directs you to do this.)

Easy marks. There were some easy marks in this question for basic comparisons between permanent establishments and subsidiaries, and transfer pricing.

Examiner's comments. Part (a) required candidates to explain the relief available in respect of the expected loss to be made by the business depending on whether it was established as a branch or a subsidiary of the UK company. This was an area where candidates had a certain amount of knowledge but, on the whole, did not score as well as they could have done because they wrote generally about branch versus subsidiary as opposed to addressing the particular facts and requirements of this question.

In particular, despite being asked to address loss relief, many candidates wrote about the taxation of profits. Many of those who did address losses did not address them as precisely as they could have done in the context of the question such that they did not consider the relevance of the tax rates provided.

Part (b) concerned group relief and the preservation of double tax relief. It required technical knowledge that almost all candidates had regarding double tax relief being the lower of the UK tax and the overseas tax on the overseas income. However, it also required candidates to be able to work out how to ensure that sufficient overseas profits remained within the charge to tax such that relief in respect of the overseas tax was not wasted. This task was carried out elegantly by a minority of candidates but the majority struggled with the problem. Credit was available for approaching the question by reference to double tax relief but many candidates simply stated that group relief was restricted to the lower of the losses available and the profits subject to tax.

The final part of the question concerned transfer pricing and was done reasonably well by many candidates who had a good knowledge of the transfer pricing rules. However, only a small minority made reference to the relevance of the size of the companies in determining whether or not the rules would apply or to the possibility of reaching an agreement with HM Revenue and Customs.

The question also required candidates to explain how the prices charged between the group companies would affect the total tax paid by the group. In order to do this, candidates had to focus on the difference between the tax rate in the UK and that in Kuwata and the possibility of group profits being taxed at the lower rate. It was important here to address the situation from a group perspective rather than that of a particular company. However, the majority of candidates did not address this element of the question.

Marking scheme

			Marks
(a)	Use of permanent establishment	4	
	Use of subsidiary	3	
	Comparison	1	
			8
(b)	Explanations		
	Double taxation relief	2	
	UK tax on overseas profits	2	
	Calculations	2	
			6
(c)	Impact of prices on total tax paid by the group	2	
	Transfer pricing		
	Why the rules apply	2	
	Application of the rules	1½	
	HMRC confirmation of pricing arrangements	1	
	Max		6
			20

(a) **The relief available in respect of the expected loss**

Strategy A – Elivar Ltd purchases the trade and all of the assets of Syme Inc

The business in Kuwata would be an overseas permanent establishment of Elivar Ltd. The permanent establishment would be an extension of Elivar Ltd. Accordingly, because the overseas operations are to be controlled from the UK, the loss made in the year following the acquisition will be offset in calculating Elivar Ltd's trading income. If Elivar Ltd makes a trading loss, the overseas losses can be included in a group relief surrender to other group companies. Any unrelieved losses will be carried forward for relief against future profits of the same trade. The relief of the overseas losses will save UK corporation tax at 20%.

Strategy B – Elivar Ltd purchases the share capital of Syme Inc

Syme Inc would be a subsidiary of Elivar Ltd resident in Kuwata. It would be a separate legal entity and its losses would be subject to the tax regime of Kuwata. This will save tax in Kuwata at only 17% as opposed to the 20% relief available under strategy A. However, it may be possible for the loss generated by the 'Frager' business to be carried back for relief in earlier years in Kuwata if strategy B is adopted.

(b) ### Strategy A – 'Frager' business operated via a permanent establishment

Maximum loss to be surrendered to Elivar Ltd

The tax suffered in Kuwata of £20,400 (£120,000 × 17%) can be offset against the corporation tax liability of Elivar Ltd up to a maximum of the UK tax on the overseas income. Accordingly, in order not to waste double tax relief, the UK tax on the overseas profits must be at least £20,400.

In determining the UK tax on the profits of Elivar Ltd, the company can choose to offset the qualifying charitable donations and the group relief in the most tax efficient manner. Accordingly, the qualifying charitable donations and the group relief will be deducted first from the UK profits, reducing them to zero. It should then be used to reduce the overseas profits to the amount that results in the UK corporation tax being equal to the tax suffered in Kuwata.

The overseas profits in respect of the permanent establishment should not be reduced below £102,000 (£20,400/20%).

The maximum loss that should be surrendered to Elivar Ltd is set out below.

	£
In respect of:	
UK profits less qualifying charitable donations £(90,000 – 2,000)	88,000
Overseas profits £(120,000 – 102,000)	18,000
Maximum loss to be surrendered to Elivar Ltd	106,000

(c) ### Strategy B – 'Frager' business operated via a subsidiary

Transfer pricing

The rate of corporation tax in Kuwata is lower than that in the UK. Accordingly, the total tax paid by the group will be reduced if more of the group's profits are generated in Kuwata. This could be achieved by increasing the prices charged by the subsidiary in Kuwata.

The transfer pricing rules will apply to transactions between Elivar Ltd and its subsidiary in Kuwata because Elivar Ltd controls the subsidiary. The exemption for small and medium sized enterprises is unlikely to be available, regardless of the size of the Loriod plc group, as there is no double tax treaty between the UK and Kuwata.

Any reduction in Elivar Ltd's profits caused by paying inflated prices to the subsidiary in Kuwata would be regarded as a potential tax advantage. The transfer pricing rules would counteract such an advantage by requiring Elivar Ltd to calculate its taxable profits as if it had been charged arm's length prices by its overseas subsidiary.

Elivar Ltd could approach HMRC for confirmation that its pricing arrangements with its overseas subsidiary are acceptable in order to remove uncertainty in this area.

ACCA Professional Paper P6 – Options Module

Advanced Taxation (UK)

Mock Examination 2

Question Paper	
Time allowed	**3 hours 15 minutes**
This paper is divided into two sections	
Section A	**BOTH questions are compulsory questions and MUST be attempted**
Section B	**TWO questions ONLY to be attempted**

DO NOT OPEN THIS PAPER UNTIL YOU ARE READY TO START UNDER EXAMINATION CONDITIONS

SECTION A: BOTH questions are compulsory and MUST be attempted

1 Flame plc group (ATAX 12/12)

63 mins

Your manager has had a meeting with Gordon, the Group Finance Director of the Flame plc group of companies. Flame plc is quoted on the UK Stock Exchange. An extract from the memorandum prepared by your manager after the meeting, together with an email from him detailing the tasks for you to perform, is set out below.

Extract from the memorandum prepared by your manager

Background

Flame plc is a UK resident company, which has annual taxable profits of more than £200,000. It owns the whole of the ordinary share capital of Inferno Ltd, Bon Ltd and six other companies. All of the companies in the Flame plc group are UK resident companies with a 31 March year end.

Flame plc – sale of Inferno Ltd

Flame plc purchased the whole of the ordinary share capital of Inferno Ltd on 1 March 2012 for £600,000. The value of Inferno Ltd has increased and Gordon has decided to sell the company. For the purposes of our work, we are to assume that the sale will take place on 1 January 2017. The budgeted taxable profits of Inferno Ltd for the nine months ending 31 December 2016 are £160,000.

The sale will be carried out in one of two ways:

(i)   A sale by Flame plc of the whole of the ordinary share capital of Inferno Ltd for £1 million; or

(ii)   A sale by Inferno Ltd of its trade and assets for their market value

Gordon needs to know the tax cost for the Flame plc group of each of these options to help him in his negotiations.

Inferno Ltd owns the following assets.

	Note	Cost £	Current market value £
Equipment	1,3	100,000	60,000
Milling machine	2,3	95,000	80,000
Goodwill	4	Nil	530,000
Building – business premises	5	300,000	490,000

Notes

1   No item of equipment will be sold for more than cost.

2   The milling machine is an item of fixed plant and machinery that was purchased on 1 June 2013. Inferno Ltd claimed rollover relief in respect of the purchase of this machine to defer a chargeable gain of £8,500 made on 1 May 2012.

3   Capital allowances have been claimed in respect of the equipment and the milling machine. The tax written down value of the main pool of Inferno Ltd as at 1 April 2016 was zero. There have been no additions or disposals since that date.

4   The goodwill has been generated internally by Inferno Ltd since it began trading on 1 May 2007.

5   Inferno Ltd purchased the building from Flame plc on 15 March 2012 for its market value at that time of £300,000. Flame plc had purchased the building on 1 January 2008 for £240,000.

Flame plc – employee share scheme

Gordon is planning to introduce a share option scheme in order to reward the senior managers of Flame plc.

Email from your manager

(a)   I want you to draft a report to the Group Finance Director that addresses the following:

(i)   **Flame plc – sale of Inferno Ltd**

The tax cost of each of the two possible ways of carrying out the sale. Please note that I have already considered the availability of the substantial shareholding exemption and concluded that it will not be available in respect of the sale of Inferno Ltd because the Flame plc group is not a trading group.

The report should include concise explanations of matters where the calculations are not self-explanatory.

(ii)   **Flame plc – employee share scheme**

- The tax advantages for the employees of introducing a Schedule 4 company share option plan (CSOP) as opposed to a non-tax advantaged share option scheme.

- Why a CSOP would be a suitable tax advantaged scheme for Gordon to choose.

- The restrictions within the CSOP rules in respect of the following:

    - The number of share options that can be granted to each employee.
    - The price at which the shares can be sold to the employees.

(iii)   **Bon Ltd – the grant of a lease**

The value added tax (VAT) implications for the lessee if Bon Ltd were to opt to tax the building prior to granting the lease.

(b)   **Bon Ltd – refund of corporation tax**

Prepare a summary of the actions that we should take and any matters of which Bon Ltd should be aware in respect of the refund of corporation tax.

Tax manager

Required

(a)   Draft the report to the Group Finance Director requested in the email from your manager. The following marks are available.

(i)   Flame plc – sale of Inferno Ltd

Notes for part (a)(i)

1   For guidance, approximately equal marks are available for calculations and explanations.

2   The following indexation factors should be used, where necessary.

January 2008 to March 2012   0.148
January 2008 to January 2017   0.256 (assumed)
March 2012 to January 2017   0.095 (assumed)   **(15 marks)**

(ii)   Flame plc – employee share scheme   **(8 marks)**

(iii)   Bon Ltd – the grant of a lease   **(3 marks)**

Professional marks will be awarded in part (a) for the overall presentation of the report, the provision of relevant advice and the effectiveness with which the information is communicated.   **(4 marks)**

(b)   Prepare the summary requested in the email from your manager.   **(5 marks)**

(Total = 35 marks)

2 Dana (ATAX 12/12)

Your manager has received a letter from Dana, a new client of your firm. Extracts from the letter and from an email from your manager are set out below.

Extract from the letter from Dana

Relief available in respect of a trading loss

I resigned from my job on 31 December 2013, having earned an annual salary of £40,000 for the previous three years. I spent the whole of 2014 planning my new business and began trading on 1 January 2015. The business was profitable initially but I made a loss in the year ended 30 September 2016.

The results of the business have been:

Period ended 30 September 2015 – a profit of £14,900.
Year ended 30 September 2016 – a loss of £30,000.

I own a number of rental properties that are let on long-term tenancies. On 1 February 2016, I sold one of these properties for £310,000. I paid £250,000 for this property on 1 December 2014.

My taxable property business profits in recent tax years have been:

	£
2012/13	13,520
2013/14	15,085
2014/15	27,410
2015/16	33,385
2016/17 (estimated)	43,985

Please let me know how much tax I can save by relieving my trading loss for the year ended 30 September 2016.

Transfer of a rental property to a trust on 1 September 2016

On 1 September 2016, I transferred a rental property worth £270,000 to a trust for the benefit of my brother's children. I assume that there will be no tax liabilities for me or the trustees in respect of this gift. I also transferred a rental property to a trust in December 2011 and I am sure that no tax was paid in respect of that gift. I have never made any other gifts apart from gifts of cash to members of my family; none of these gifts exceeded £2,000.

Email from your manager

Dana is unmarried and has no children. She is resident and domiciled in the UK.

I have just spoken to Dana and she has provided me with the following additional information.

- Dana received a bonus of £2,000 from her employer when she left her job in December 2013. The bonus was to thank her for all of the work she had done over the years.

- The results Dana has provided in respect of her unincorporated business have been adjusted for tax purposes but do not take account of expenditure she incurred during 2014. During that year, Dana spent £1,400 on petrol as she travelled around the UK visiting potential customers.

Dana had no income or capital gains in the tax years concerned other than those referred to in her letter and in the additional information set out above.

Work required:

Please prepare the following for me for my next meeting with Dana.

(a) **Relief available in respect of the trading loss**

A reasoned explanation, with supporting calculations, of the most tax efficient manner in which Dana's trading loss can be relieved, together with a calculation of the total tax relief obtained by following the most tax efficient strategy. I want you to consider all of the ways in which Dana could relieve the loss with the exception of carry forward for relief in the future. You should assume that gift relief will be claimed in respect of the transfer of the rental property to the trust on 1 September 2016 when carrying out this work.

Your explanation should include:

- A brief summary of the other reliefs available for relieving the loss, together with your reasons for rejecting them
- The implications of the additional information provided by Dana

(b) **Transfer of the rental property to the trust on 1 September 2016**

    (i) *Capital gains tax*

    An explanation as to whether or not gift relief is available in respect of the transfer of the rental property on 1 September 2016 and, on the assumption that it is available, the action required in order to submit a valid claim.

    (ii) *Inheritance tax*

    In relation to Dana's gifts prior to 1 September 2016:

- A list of the precise information we need to request from Dana in order to enable us to determine whether the gifts to her family members were exempt and to calculate the inheritance tax due on the transfer to the trust on 1 September 2016
- An explanation of why the information is required

Tax manager

Required

Carry out the work required as requested in the email from your manager. The following marks are available.

(a) Relief available in respect of the trading loss.

In respect of part (a) of this question you should:

1   Ignore national insurance contributions.
2   Assume that the tax rates and allowances for the tax year 2015/16 apply to all years.   **(18 marks)**

(b) Transfer of the rental property to the trust on 1 September 2016.

    (i)   Capital gains tax   **(2 marks)**
    (ii)   Inheritance tax   **(5 marks)**

    (Total = 25 marks)

3 Banger Ltd and Candle Ltd (ATAX 12/12)   36 mins

Banger Ltd and Candle Ltd are two unrelated companies.

The management of Banger Ltd requires advice on the implications for one of the company's shareholders of the use of a motor car owned by the company and the proposed liquidation of the company.

The management of Candle Ltd has asked for a calculation of the company's corporation tax liability. Candle Ltd is an investment holding company.

(a)   **Banger Ltd:**

- Banger Ltd is a UK resident trading company.
- Sixty-five per cent of the company's share capital is owned by its managing director, Katherine.
- The remaining shares are owned by a number of individuals who do not work for the company.
- None of the shares has been acquired under the Enterprise Management Investment scheme.

Motor car provided to minority shareholder throughout the year ended 31 March 2016:

- Banger Ltd paid £17,400 for the motor car, which had a list price when new of £22,900.
- The car has a petrol engine and has CO_2 emissions of 117 grams per kilometre.

Liquidation of Banger Ltd:

- It is intended that a liquidator will be appointed on 31 January 2017 to wind up the company.

Distributions of company assets to shareholders being considered by Banger Ltd:

- A total distribution of £280,000 in cash to the shareholders prior to 31 January 2017
- The distribution of a building with a market value of £720,000 to Katherine after 31 January 2017

Required

(i)   Explain, with supporting calculations, the amount of the minority shareholder's taxable income in respect of the use of the motor car.   **(3 marks)**

(ii)   Explain in detail the tax implications for Banger Ltd, the minority shareholders and Katherine of the distributions that the company is considering.   **(7 marks)**

(b)   **Candle Ltd:**

- Is a UK resident investment holding company

The results of Candle Ltd for the year ended 31 March 2016:

	£
Interest receivable	41,100
Chargeable gains realised in the country of Sisaria, net of 18% Sisarian tax	15,580
Chargeable gains realised in the UK, excluding the sale of shares in Rockette plc	83,700
Fees charged by a financial institution in respect of an issue of loan stock	14,000
Interest payable on loan stock	52,900
General expenses of management	38,300

Sale of shares in Rockette plc on 1 January 2016:

- Candle Ltd purchased a 2.2% holding of the shares in Rockette plc for £31,400 in 2002.
- Piro plc acquired 100% of the ordinary share capital of Rockette plc on 1 January 2016.
- Candle Ltd received shares in Piro plc worth £147,100 and cash of £7,200 in exchange for its shares in Rockette plc.
- Piro plc's acquisition of Rockette plc was a commercial transaction and was not part of a scheme to avoid tax.
- The relevant indexation factor is 0.497.

Required

Calculate the corporation tax liability of Candle Ltd for the year ended 31 March 2016, giving explanations of your treatment of the disposal of the shares in Rockette plc. You should assume that Candle Ltd will claim all reliefs available to reduce its tax liability and you should state any further assumptions you consider necessary.

(10 marks)

(Total = 20 marks)

4 Ash (ATAX 12/12)   36 mins

Ash requires a calculation of his capital gains tax liability for the tax year 2015/16, together with advice in connection with entrepreneurs' relief, registration for the purposes of value added tax (VAT) and the payment of income tax.

Ash:

- Is resident in the UK.

- Had taxable income of £29,000 in the tax year 2015/16.

- Was the owner and managing director of Lava Ltd until 1 May 2015, when he resigned and sold the company.

- Is a partner in the Vulcan Partnership.

Ash – disposals of capital assets in the tax year 2015/16:

- The sale of the shares in Lava Ltd resulted in a capital gain of £235,000, which qualified for entrepreneurs' relief.

- Ash assigned a 37-year lease on a property for £110,000 on 1 May 2015.

- Ash sold two acres of land on 1 October 2015 for £30,000.

- Ash sold quoted shares and made a capital loss of £17,300 on 1 November 2015.

The lease:

- The lease was previously assigned to Ash for £31,800 when it had 46 years remaining.
- The property has always been used by Lava Ltd for trading purposes.
- Lava Ltd paid Ash rent, equivalent to 40% of the market rate, in respect of the use of the property.

The sale of the two acres of land:

- Ash purchased eight acres of land for £27,400 on 1 June 2007.
- Ash sold six acres of the land for £42,000 on 1 August 2010.
- The remaining two acres of land were worth £18,000 on 1 August 2010.

Vulcan Partnership (Vulcan):

- Has a 31 March year end.

- Has monthly turnover of: Standard-rated supplies £400
                              Exempt supplies   £200
                              Zero-rated supplies   £5,600

- Its turnover is expected to increase slightly in 2017.

- None of its customers is registered for the purposes of VAT.

- Ash expects to receive less profit from Vulcan for the tax year 2016/17 than he did in 2015/16.

Required

(a) (i) State the conditions that must be satisfied for Ash's assignment of the lease to be an associated disposal for the purposes of entrepreneurs' relief. **(3 marks)**

(ii) Calculate Ash's capital gains tax liability for the tax year 2015/16 on the assumption that the assignment of the lease does qualify as an associated disposal and that entrepreneurs' relief will be claimed where possible.

Note. The following lease percentages should be used, where necessary.

37 years 93.497
46 years 98.490 **(7 marks)**

(b) Discuss in detail whether the Vulcan Partnership may be required to register for value added tax (VAT) and the advantages and disadvantages for the business of registration. **(7 marks)**

(c) Set out the matters that Ash should consider when deciding whether or not to make a claim to reduce the payment on account of income tax due on 31 January 2017. **(3 marks)**

(Total = 20 marks)

5 Cuthbert (ATAX 12/12)

36 mins

Cuthbert requires advice on the tax implications of the payment of capital gains tax by instalments and an error he has made in an income tax return. He has also requested calculations in respect of the inheritance tax payable on the death of his uncle, Pugh.

Cuthbert:

- Is resident and domiciled in the UK.
- Intends to give a building to his brother on 1 March 2017.
- Made an error in his income tax return for the tax year 2014/15.

Cuthbert – proposed gift of a building to his brother on 1 March 2017:

- The building is currently let to long-term tenants and has a market value of £460,000.

Cuthbert – error in his income tax return for the tax year 2014/15:

- HM Revenue and Customs have written to Cuthbert in respect of his income tax return.
- HM Revenue and Customs are claiming that Cuthbert has under-declared his UK property income.

Pugh – valuation of assets owned at death on 1 February 2016:

	£
Home in the UK	720,000
Vintage motor cars located in the country of Camberia	490,000
Quoted shares (holdings of less than 1%) registered in Camberia	330,000
Cash held in bank accounts in the UK	45,000

Pugh – UK inheritance tax liability:

- Was calculated on the basis that Pugh was domiciled in the country of Camberia and that he had made no lifetime gifts
- Was paid on time

Pugh – information discovered after the payment of the UK inheritance tax:

- Pugh had been domiciled in the UK since 1 January 2006.
- Pugh had made a gift of UK quoted shares (all holdings of less than 1%) to a trust on 10 March 2009.
- The quoted shares were worth £322,400 and Pugh paid the UK inheritance tax due.

The system of inheritance tax in the country of Camberia:

- There is no nil rate band and the rate of inheritance tax is 25%.

- Inheritance tax is only charged on the value of land and buildings and quoted shares owned at the time of death and located in Camberia.

- There is no double tax treaty between the UK and Camberia.

Required

(a) Explain whether or not the capital gains tax due on the proposed gift of the building could be paid by instalments and the matters that Cuthbert would need to be aware of in respect of this method of payment.

(6 marks)

(b) Explain how any penalty would be calculated if it is determined that Cuthbert made a careless error when completing his 2014/15 tax return. **(4 marks)**

(c) Calculate the UK inheritance tax liability in respect of Pugh's estate following the discovery of the additional information, together with the interest on overdue tax that will be payable if the inheritance tax is paid on 1 January 2017. **(10 marks)**

(Total = 20 marks)

Answers

DO NOT TURN THIS PAGE UNTIL YOU HAVE
COMPLETED THE MOCK EXAM

A plan of attack

What's the worst thing you could be doing right now if this was the actual exam paper? Wondering how to celebrate the end of the exam in about three hours time? Panicking, flapping and generally getting in a right old state?

Well, they're all pretty bad, so turn back to the paper and let's sort out a **plan of attack**!

First things first

Look through the paper and work out which optional questions to do and the order in which to attack the questions. You've got **two options**. Option 1 is the option recommended by BPP.

Option 1 (if you're thinking 'Help!')

If you're a bit worried about the paper, do the questions in the order of how well you think you can answer them. If you find the questions in Section B less daunting than the compulsory questions in Section A start with Section B. Remember you only need to do two of the three questions in Section B; you may find it easier if you start by deciding which question you will not do and put a line through it.

- **Question 3** deals with close companies, liquidations and overseas aspects of corporation tax.

- **Question 4** is about entrepreneurs' relief, leases and part disposals for CGT, VAT registration and income tax payments on account.

- **Question 5** concerns payment of CGT, income tax errors and inheritance tax.

Do not spend longer than the allocated time on Section B. When you've spent the allocated time on **two** of the three questions in Section B turn to the longer questions in Section A. Read these questions through thoroughly before you launch into them. Once you start make sure you allocate your time to the parts within the questions according to the marks available and that, where possible, you attempt the easy marks first.

Lastly, what you mustn't forget is that you have to **answer both questions in Section A and TWO in Section B**.

Option 2 (if you're thinking 'It's a doddle')

It never pays to be overconfident but if you're not quaking in your shoes about the exam then **turn straight to the compulsory questions** in Section A.

Once you've done these questions, move to Section B.

- The question you attempt first really depends on what you are most confident at.
- You then have to select one of the two remaining questions. If you are undecided look at the requirements. It maybe easier to obtain more marks if these are broken down into several smaller parts.

No matter how many times we remind you....

Always, always **allocate your time** according to the marks for the question in total and then according to the parts of the question. And **always, always follow the requirements** exactly.

You've got spare time at the end of the exam.....?

If you have allocated your time properly then you **shouldn't have time on your hands** at the end of the exam. But if you find yourself with five or ten minutes to spare, check over your work to make sure that you have answered all the requirements of the questions and all parts of all requirements.

Forget about it!

And don't worry if you found the paper difficult. More than likely other candidates will too. If this were the real thing you would need to **forget** the exam the minute you leave the exam hall and **think about the next one**. Or, if it's the last one, **celebrate**!

1 Flame plc group (ATAX 12/12)

Text references. Chargeable gains for companies are covered in Chapter 21 and the degrouping charge in Chapter 26. Capital allowances are dealt with in Chapter 7 and the calculation of taxable total profits in Chapter 20. Corporation tax liability is in Chapter 22. Company share option plans are covered in Chapter 5. VAT on land and buildings will be found in Chapter 29. Ethics is covered in Chapter 30, which also has a section on approaching questions on the impact of taxes.

Top tips. There was a key piece of information in the email from the manager concerning the substantial shareholding exemption. This emphasises the need to read the whole question before starting your answer – don't expect all the information you need to be in one place in the question.

Easy marks. The capital allowances and gains calculations in section (a) were straightforward. The ethical matters in section (b) should have been well-known.

Examiner's comments. Answers to part (a)(i) varied in quality quite considerably. There were many candidates who clearly understood the two alternatives and the related tax implications whilst weaker candidates were unsure of the precise nature of the transactions and the related tax implications, such that they produced confused answers. A small minority of candidates treated the companies as individuals.

The sale of Inferno Ltd had two main implications; a chargeable gain on the sale of the shares and a degrouping charge. The chargeable gain was worth one mark. However, it took some candidates half a page or more to calculate and write about this gain in order to score that mark. This was most likely because it was the first thing they did in the exam and there were still almost three hours to go, such that the pressure was not yet on. Candidates must approach every mark in the exam in the same way and get on with it. There is no time to dither when there is so much to do.

Frustratingly, it was not uncommon for some candidates to only score half a mark for this gain because they based the indexation allowance on the unindexed gain rather than the cost. This may have been a lack of concentration rather than a lack of knowledge but the half mark was still lost.

It was stated in the question that the substantial shareholding exemption was not available. Many candidates simply included a statement to that effect in their report and earned a mark. However, a small minority of candidates wasted time writing at length about the exemption rather than getting on with the question.

The degrouping charge was done well on the whole. Those candidates who did not do so well were divided into two groups. The first group missed the degrouping charge altogether. This was perhaps due to a lack of knowledge but, in view of the fact that degrouping charges are examined regularly, was more likely due to a lack of thought. Candidates must give themselves time in the exam to think about issues before they start writing; it is difficult to successfully think of one issue whilst writing about a different one.

The second group of candidates knew that there would be a degrouping charge somewhere in the answer and earned most of the marks available for saying why and for calculating it. However, they did not know which of the two possible transactions would give rise to the charge and either put it into the wrong section of the report or put it into both sections. This was not particularly costly, but would have been in a different question which was only concerned with one of these two transactions. Candidates must know their stuff; degrouping charges only occur on the sale of a company, ie on the sale of shares, and not on the sale of assets.

The sale by Inferno Ltd of its trade and assets was not done particularly well. A small minority of candidates treated the disposal as the disposal of a single asset by adding up all of the proceeds and then deducting the total cost. Even those candidates who knew that each asset had to be handled separately failed to apply basic rules concerning capital allowances and chargeable gains.

Capital allowances were handled particularly poorly with very few candidates identifying that where the tax written down value is zero, any sale of machinery must result in a balancing charge. In addition, most candidates calculated capital losses on the sale of the machinery, thus failing to recognise that, due to the claiming of capital allowances, no capital losses would be available. Finally, only a minority of candidates identified that the deferred gain of £8,500 would crystallise on the sale of the milling machine; most candidates thought, incorrectly, that the gain would be deducted from the asset's base cost. A final thought on part (a) (i) relates to the narrative provided by candidates in their reports. The question required candidates to include concise explanations of matters where the calculations were not self-explanatory. On the whole this was done well. Most candidates kept their answers brief and very few fell into trap of writing down everything they knew about the broad technical areas relating to the question.

Part (a) (ii) concerned a Schedule 4 company share option plan. This was a straightforward question that tested candidates' knowledge of a particular share scheme. In order to do well, candidates needed to slow down for a moment and make sure that they were about to write about the correct scheme. They then needed to ensure that they addressed all of the issues set out in the question. The majority of candidates did both of these things and therefore scored well.

In part (b), candidates needed to realise that this refund had been received some time ago and that, if it had been paid in error, it had to be returned to HM Revenue and Customs. Most candidates recognised this situation and were able to list the actions that the firm needed to take and the matters that needed to be drawn to the attention of Bon Ltd.

Marking scheme

				Marks
(a)	(i)	*Sale of share capital*		
		Calculations		
		Gain (including degrouping charge)	2	
		Corporation tax	½	
		Narrative – one mark for each relevant point	5	
		Sale of trade and assets		
		Calculations		
		Equipment and milling machine	2	
		Goodwill	½	
		Premises	1½	
		Liability	½	
		Narrative – one mark for each relevant point	3	
				15
	(ii)	*Advantages*		
		Timing	2½	
		Taxes	3½	
		Suitability of CSOP	1	
		Restrictions	2	
		Max		8
	(iii)	Nature of supply	1	
		Recoverable input tax	2	
				3
		Format and presentation	1	
		Analysis	2	
		Quality of calculations and explanations	1	
				4
(b)		The need to repay the tax	3	
		Ceasing to act	3	
		Max		5
				35

(a) (i) **Flame plc – sale of Inferno Ltd**

Sale by Flame plc of the whole of the ordinary share capital of Inferno Ltd for £1 million

A sale of the share capital will result in a liability to corporation tax calculated as follows:

	£	£
Proceeds on sale of shares		1,000,000
Degrouping charge – deemed sale proceeds		
Market value of the premises at 15 March 2012	300,000	
Less: cost of premises 1 January 2008	(240,000)	
indexation allowance £240,000 × 0.148	(35,520)	
		24,480
Total sale proceeds		1,024,480
Less: cost of shares in Inferno Ltd 1 March 2012		(600,000)
indexation allowance £600,000 × 0.095		(57,000)
Chargeable gain		367,480
Corporation tax £367,480 @ 20%		73,496

Due to the unavailability of the substantial shareholding exemption, the sale of Inferno Ltd will result in a gain chargeable to corporation tax.

A degrouping charge will arise in respect of the building because it was transferred at no gain, no loss (Flame plc and Inferno Ltd are members of a capital gains group) within the six years prior to the sale of Inferno Ltd. Inferno Ltd will be regarded as having sold the building at the time of the no gain, no loss transfer for its market value at that time. In the computation of the degrouping charge, Inferno Ltd's base cost in the building, resulting from the no gain, no loss transfer, is the original cost to Flame plc plus indexation allowance up to 15 March 2012, the date Inferno Ltd purchased the building. The degrouping charge will increase the sales proceeds on the disposal of Inferno Ltd.

Sale by Inferno Ltd of its trade and assets for their market value

A sale of the trade and assets will result in a liability to corporation tax calculated as follows:

	£	£
Balancing charge on sale of equipment and milling machine £([60,000 + 80,000] – 0)		140,000
Profit on sale of goodwill £(530,000 – 0)		530,000
Additional trading profits		670,000
Crystallisation of gain deferred on milling machine		8,500

Chargeable gain on sale of premises

	£	£	
Proceeds		490,000	
Cost	240,000		
Indexation allowance to March 2012 £240,000 × 0.148	35,520		
Indexed cost: no gain/no loss transfer		(275,520)	
Indexation allowance to January 2017 £275,520 × 0.095		(26,174)	
			188,306
Taxable profits			866,806
Corporation tax £866,806 @ 20%			173,361

The excess of the sales proceeds (market value) of the equipment and the milling machine over the balance on the main pool will result in a taxable balancing charge.

The goodwill is a trading asset so the profit on its sale will be additional trading income.

When a rollover relief claim has been made in respect of the purchase of a depreciating asset, as in the case of the milling machine, the deferred gain crystallises on the sale of that replacement asset.

The equipment and the milling machine are to be sold for less than cost. However, no capital loss will arise because capital allowances have been claimed.

As noted above, Inferno Ltd's base cost in the building is the original price paid by Flame plc plus indexation allowance up to March 2012.

(ii) **Flame plc – employee share scheme**

The tax advantages of a Schedule 4 company share option plan (CSOP) over a non-tax advantaged scheme

- With a CSOP, there would be no income tax or national insurance contributions liability on the grant or exercise of the option, provided it is exercised between three and ten years after it is granted. Under a non-tax advantaged scheme, there would be a liability when the option is exercised.

- With a CSOP, the whole of the employee's profit on the shares will be subject to capital gains tax when the shares are sold. Under a non-tax advantaged scheme, the excess of the market value of the shares at the time the option is exercised over the amount paid by the employee for the shares will be taxable as specific employment income and so subject to income tax and national insurance contributions in the year the option is exercised; any subsequent increase in the value of the shares will be subject to capital gains tax when the shares are sold.

  The advantages of a charge to capital gains tax over charges to income tax and national insurance contributions are the availability of the annual exempt amount and the lower tax rates.

Suitability of a CSOP

Gordon wants to use the scheme to reward the company's senior managers as opposed to all of the company's staff. Accordingly, he needs to use a scheme that allows him to choose which employees are able to join. The two tax advantaged schemes that allow this are the CSOP and the enterprise management incentive scheme.

Restrictions

- The value of shares in respect of which an employee holds options cannot exceed £30,000.

- The exercise price of the shares must not be less than the value of the shares at the time of the grant of the option.

(iii) **Bon Ltd – the grant of a lease**

If Bon Ltd were to opt to tax the building, the proposed granting of the lease would be a standard rated supply rather than an exempt supply, so Bon Ltd would have to charge value added tax (VAT) on the rent. A lessee that was registered for VAT and making wholly taxable supplies would be able to recover all of the VAT charged. However, some or all of the VAT would be a cost for a lessee that was not registered or one that was partially exempt and not within the *de minimis* limits.

(b) **Refund of corporation tax**

We should review the tax affairs of Bon Ltd in order to identify the reason for the tax refund.

If, as would appear likely, it is an error on the part of HM Revenue and Customs (HMRC), we should inform Bon Ltd that it should be repaid immediately. Failure to return the money in these circumstances may be a civil and/or criminal offence.

We should advise Bon Ltd to disclose the matter to HMRC immediately in order to minimise any interest and penalties that might otherwise become payable.

In addition, unless the money is returned, we would have to consider ceasing to act as advisers to Bon Ltd. In these circumstances, we are required to notify the tax authorities that we no longer act for the company, although we would not provide them with any reason for our action. We should also consider whether or not we are required to make a report under the money laundering rules.

2 Dana (ATAX 12/12)

Text references. Trading losses for individuals are covered in Chapter 8 and the income tax computation in Chapter 1. Employment income generally is covered in Chapter 4 and terminal bonuses are dealt with in Chapter 5. Pre-trading expenditure and the basis of assessment for trading profits are covered in Chapter 6. Gift relief for capital gains tax is one of the topics in Chapter 13. Inheritance tax on lifetime transfers will be found in Chapter 16.

Top tips. When thinking about the use of trade loss relief, the three key aspects are the rate of relief, the timing of the relief and the loss of personal allowances.

Easy marks. Nearly all of the marks in this question were for knowledge from F6. You should have been able to gain easy marks for working out the trading profit for the period to 30 September 2015 and the opening years assessments in part (a). The technical information in part (b) was not difficult but you needed to keep your answer succinct and to the points required.

Examiner's comments. In part (a), the first task was to determine the trading profit/loss for each of the tax years. This required candidates to deduct the pre-trading expenditure from the profit of the first trading period and then to apply the opening years rules. They also needed to know that losses are only recognised once in the opening years. The treatment of the pre-trading expenditure was done well by only a minority of candidates. Other candidates either missed it out altogether or deducted it from the taxable profit for the tax year 2014/15 rather than the profit of the first trading period. The opening year rules and the treatment of the loss within those rules were done well by the majority of candidates. This was a significant improvement over the performance in recent exams.

Once the profits and losses had been determined, candidates needed to consider the reliefs available in respect of the loss. There were two aspects to this. First, candidates needed to know all of the available reliefs for the losses. This was done very well by the vast majority of candidates.

Secondly, candidates needed to compare the different reliefs and then calculate the total tax relief obtained by the most efficient strategy. Performance of this second task was mixed with some candidates calmly and efficiently calculating the tax due before and after claiming relief in order to determine the tax saving, whilst others wrote about how to do it in general terms without actually doing it. This is perhaps a confidence issue; candidates should ensure that they have practised as many questions as possible prior to sitting the exam and, once in the exam, should have the self-belief to address the figures and come up with specific advice.

Part (b)(i) concerned the availability of gift relief on the transfer of a rental property to a trust and was not done particularly well. The issue here was that gift relief would be available because the transfer was immediately subject to inheritance tax. This is true regardless of the nature of the asset, such that those candidates who focussed on whether or not the property was a business asset had missed the point. This was not too great a problem as there were only two marks available. However, a minority of candidates made things worse by ignoring the fact that this question part needed to be answered in approximately 4 minutes and wrote about gift relief at length, thus wasting time.

Part (b)(ii) concerned Dana's inheritance tax position. Those candidates who made a genuine attempt to answer the question here did well. The technical issues in this question were:

* The transfer of the rental property in December 2011 was a chargeable lifetime transfer, such that we needed a value for the property in order to determine the nil band available for the transfer in September 2016.

* The gifts of cash to family members were potentially exempt transfers, such that they would not affect the nil band whilst Dana is alive.

* The cash gifts may be exempt depending on the amount given, the date of the gift and the reason for the gift. Exempt gifts would not use Dana's annual exemptions, such that they may be available for relief against the transfer to the trust.

This question was different from past inheritance tax questions and required some thought before it could be answered. It was not technically difficult but required candidates to address the specific question; the minority of candidates who wrote about inheritance tax in general terms and ignored the specifics of the question did poorly, as did those who tried to calculate inheritance tax liabilities. Some candidates let themselves down by writing that they needed 'the details of the gifts' without specifying what those details were and why they needed them.

			Marks
(a)	Identification of years in which relief available	4	
	Employment income	1	
	Trading income	4	
	Income taxable at the higher rate	4	
	Capital gains taxable at the higher rate	1½	
	Tax savings	5	
	Notes in respect of additional information	2	
	Max		18
(b)	(i) Capital gains tax		2
	(ii) *Inheritance tax*		
	Gift in December 2011	1½	
	Gifts to family members		
	Information required	1½	
	Relevance of information	3	
	Max		5
			25

(a) **Relief available in respect of trading loss**

A trading loss for tax purposes of £22,500 (W2) has arisen in the tax year 2016/17.

It can be relieved against Dana's total general income of 2016/17, the year of the loss, and/or 2015/16.

Alternatively, because the loss has arisen in one of the first four tax years of trading, it can be relieved against Dana's total general income of the three years prior to the year of the loss starting with the earliest year, ie 2013/14.

The income taxable at the higher rate in each of the tax years is set out below.

	2013/14 £	2014/15 £	2015/16 £	2016/17 £
Employment income (W1)	32,000	0	0	0
Trading income (W2)	0	4,500	6,000	0
Property business income	15,085	27,410	33,385	43,985
Less personal allowance	(10,600)	(10,600)	(10,600)	(10,600)
Taxable income	36,485	21,310	28,785	33,385
Less basic rate band	(31,785)	(31,785)	(31,785)	(31,785)
Income taxable at higher rate/(basic rate band remaining)	4,700	(10,475)	(3,000)	1,600
Taxable gain: £([310,000 − 250,000] − 11,100)			48,900	
Gains taxable at the higher rate			45,900	

The claims against general income are 'all or nothing' claims. This means that the trading loss will be offset in full in one of 2013/14 or 2015/16 or 2016/17, depending on which relief is claimed. Because an early years trading loss relief claim would relieve the loss in full in 2013/14, it is not possible to relieve the loss in 2014/15.

The year with the most income taxable at the higher rate is 2013/14. Relieving the loss of £22,500 in that year would save income tax as follows:

	£
£4,700 × 40%	1,880
£(22,500 – 4,700) = £17,800 × 20%	3,560
Tax saving	5,440

Relieving the loss in 2016/17 would clearly save less tax, as there is less income taxable at the higher rate in that year than there is in 2013/14.

There is no income taxable at the higher rate in 2015/16 but there is a capital gain. Relieving the loss against the general income in the basic rate band would allow an equivalent amount of the capital gain to be taxed in the basic rate band rather than the higher rate band.

Accordingly, relieving the loss in 2015/16 would save tax as follows:

	£
Income tax	
£22,500 × 20%	4,500
Capital gains tax	
£22,500 × (28% – 18%)	2,250
Tax saving	6,750

The most beneficial claim is to relieve the loss in 2015/16 in order to save tax of £6,750.

Notes in respect of the additional information provided by Dana

- The bonus is in respect of work carried out by Dana for her employer. Accordingly, it is taxable in full in the year of receipt.

- The cost of travelling around the UK in 2014 would have been allowable had it been incurred after Dana began to trade. Accordingly, because it was incurred in the seven years prior to commencing to trade, it is treated as if it had been incurred on the first day of trading.

Workings

1   *Employment income in 2013/14*

	£
Salary for nine months £40,000 × 9/12	30,000
Bonus	2,000
	32,000

2   *Trading income*

	£
2014/15 (1 January 2015 to 5 April 2015)	
£13,500 (W3) × 3/9	4,500
2015/16 (1 January 2015 to 31 December 2015)	
£13,500 – 7,500 (£30,000 × 3/12)	6,000
2016/17 (Year ended 30 September 2016)	
Loss £(30,000 – 7,500)	(22,500)

The trading loss of £7,500 deducted in arriving at the taxable profit for the tax year 2015/16 is excluded from the loss available for relief in respect of the tax year 2016/17.

3   *Trading profit for the nine months ended 30 September 2015*

	£
Original figure	14,900
Less pre-trading expenditure	(1,400)
	13,500

(b) **Transfer of the rental property to the trust on 1 September 2016**

(i) *Capital gains tax*

Dana can claim gift relief in respect of the transfer of the property to the trustees because a lifetime transfer to any trust is a chargeable lifetime transfer for inheritance tax. The election must be signed by Dana and submitted by 5 April 2021 (ie four years after the end of the tax year in which the gift was made).

(ii) *Inheritance tax*

Information required in respect of the transfer to the trust in December 2011

- The value of the property at the time of the gift: the gift in December 2011 is within the seven-year period prior to the gift on 1 September 2016, and so will reduce the nil rate band available for the latter gift.

Information required in respect of the gifts to family members

- Date, value, recipient and occasion of each gift: this information is required in order to determine whether the gifts to family members are exempt or not. This will affect the annual exemptions available in respect of each of the gifts to the trusts

In addition to the annual exemption, the following lifetime gifts are exempt:

- Gifts of less than £250 in total to any individual in a tax year
- Gifts of no more than £1,000, made on the occasion of a marriage or civil partnership
- Normal (regular) gifts made out of income that do not affect Dana's standard of living

3 Banger Ltd and Candle Ltd (ATAX 12/12)

Text references. Close companies and investment holding companies are covered in Chapter 25. Liquidations are dealt with in Chapter 23. Chargeable gains for companies is the topic of Chapter 21 and overseas aspects are covered in Chapter 27.

Top tips. In part (a)(ii), it was important that you dealt with the tax implications for the company and then for the shareholders (which include Katherine who will receive both cash and the building).

Easy marks. The treatment of close companies is often examined and there should have been easy marks on the use of the motor car in part (a)(i). The double taxation relief in part (b) was straightforward.

Examiner's comments. Part (a)(i) required candidates to explain the taxable income arising out of the use by a minority shareholder of a car owned by the company. Almost all candidates were able to calculate the benefit in respect of the use of the car but not all of them realised that this would be taxed as a distribution rather than employment income. Many of those who knew this point still failed to earn full marks because they did not state the reasons for this treatment; those reasons being that the company is a close company and that the individual is not an employee.

Part (a)(ii) concerned the treatment of company distributions before and after the appointment of a liquidator. Performance in this part of the question was mixed. Those candidates who did not do well either did not know the rules or were not careful enough in addressing the requirements. A lack of knowledge of the rules was unfortunate and not something that could easily be rectified in the exam room. Failure to address the requirements carefully was a greater shame as potentially easy marks were lost. The requirement asked for the tax implications for 'Banger Ltd, the minority shareholders and Katherine'. Most candidates dealt with the minority shareholders and Katherine but many omitted the implications for Banger Ltd. Candidates should always read the requirement carefully and identify all of the tasks. It would have been helpful then to use sub-headings for each of the three aspects of the requirement to ensure that all of the aspects of the requirement were addressed.

Part (b) required candidates to calculate the corporation tax liability of Candle Ltd. On the whole, this part was done quite well by many candidates.

The two more difficult areas of this part of the question concerned loan relationships and a share for share disposal. The loan relationships issue was not done well. The vast majority of candidates failed to apply the basic rules such that they did not offset the amounts in order to arrive at a deficit on non-trading loan relationships. This was not a difficult or obscure matter; it simply felt as though candidates were not giving themselves the time to think before answering the question.

The share for share disposal was identified by the vast majority of candidates who went on to point out that no chargeable gain would arise in respect of the shares. There was then a further mark for recognising that there would also be no gain in respect of the cash received as it amounted to less than 5% of the total consideration received. This point was picked up by only a small number of candidates.

Marking scheme

				Marks
(a)	(i)	Explanation	2	
		Calculations	1½	
		Max		3
	(ii)	*Banger Ltd*	2½	
		Shareholders	1½	
		Katherine		
		Capital gain	1½	
		Taxation	2½	
		Max		7

		Marks
(b)	*Taxable total profits*		
	Loan relationships	3½	
	Chargeable gains	1½	
	Sale of shares in Rockette plc	½	
	Management expenses	½	
	Corporation tax liability		
	Corporation tax	½	
	Double taxation relief	1	
	Explanations	3	
	Max		10
			20

(a) **Banger Ltd**

(i) **Minority shareholder's taxable income in respect of the use of the motor car**

The minority shareholder is not employed by Banger Ltd. Accordingly, because Banger Ltd is a close company (it is controlled by Katherine), the use of the motor car will be treated as a distribution. The distribution will equal the amount that would have been taxable as employment income in respect of the motor car:

Amount by which CO_2 emissions exceed base level: (115 (rounded down) − 95) = 20 ÷ 5 = 4

Add to 14% = 18%.

The car benefit is therefore £22,900 (list price) × 18% = £4,122.

The taxable income will be the distribution multiplied by 100/90, ie £4,122 × 100/90 = £4,580.

(ii) **The tax implications of the distributions being considered**

Banger Ltd

The distribution of cash will be a normal dividend with no tax implications for Banger Ltd.

The distribution of the building is a dividend in specie and therefore a deemed disposal of the building by Banger Ltd at market value. This will result in a chargeable gain or allowable loss equal to the market value of the building less its cost. Indexation allowance will be deducted from any chargeable gain arising.

The shareholders

- The distribution of cash to all the shareholders

  The distribution of cash is to be made prior to the appointment of the liquidator and will therefore be taxed as a normal dividend. It will be grossed up at 100/90 and subject to income tax at 10%, 32.5% and 37.5%, depending on the income tax position of the individual shareholders. A 10% tax credit will be available.

- The distribution of the building to Katherine

  The distribution is to be made after the appointment of the liquidator and will therefore be taxed as a capital receipt in relation to Katherine's shares. The market value of the building will be treated as the sales proceeds of Katherine's shares in Banger Ltd from which the base cost (or part of the base cost if there are to be further distributions to Katherine) will be deducted in order to calculate the capital gain.

  The gain will be taxable at 18% and/or 28% depending on Katherine's tax position or, alternatively, at 10% where entrepreneurs' relief is available. Banger Ltd is a trading company. Accordingly, entrepreneurs' relief will be available, provided that Katherine has owned at least 5% of the ordinary share capital and can exercise at least 5% of the voting rights in the company by virtue of that holding of shares, and has been an officer or employee of Banger Ltd. Both these conditions must have been satisfied throughout the period of one year ending with the date of disposal (ie the date of the distribution).

BPP LEARNING MEDIA

Mock exam 2: answers   265

(b) **Candle Ltd – Corporation tax liability for the year ended 31 March 2016**

	Total £	UK £	Non-UK £
Chargeable gain realised in Sisaria			
£15,580 × 100/82	19,000		19,000
Chargeable gains realised in the UK	83,700	83,700	
Sale of shares in Rockette plc (N)	0	0	
	102,700	83,700	19,000
Less deficit on non-trading loan			
relationship (W1)	(25,800)	(25,800)	
general expenses of			
management	(38,300)	(38,300)	
Taxable total profits	38,600	19,600	19,000
Corporation tax @ 20%	7,720	3,920	3,800
Less double taxation relief (W2)	(3,420)		(3,420)
	4,300	3,920	380

Note

The acquisition of the shares in Rockette plc by Piro plc was a qualifying 'paper for paper' takeover because Piro plc acquired more than 25% of Rockette plc and the acquisition was a commercial transaction that did not have the avoidance of tax as one of its main purposes. Accordingly, no gain arose in respect of the shares in Piro plc received by Candle Ltd.

In addition, no gain arose in respect of the cash received because the cash represented less than 5% of the value of the total consideration received:

	£
Value of shares received in Piro plc	147,100
Cash received	7,200
Total value received	154,300

The cash received is $\dfrac{7,200}{154,300} \times 100 = 4.67\%$ of the total consideration.

Workings

1 *Deficit on non-trading loan relationship*

	£
Interest receivable	41,100
Less: interest payable	(52,900)
fees charged by financial institution	(14,000)
Net deficit	(25,800)

It has been assumed that the company has chosen to offset the deficit against its current period profits.

2 *Double taxation relief*

Lower of:

UK tax	£3,800
Overseas tax £(19,000 – 15,580)	£3,420
ie £3,420	

4 Ash (ATAX 12/12)

Text references. Entrepreneurs' relief is covered in Chapter 13. Leases are dealt with in Chapter 14 and part disposals in Chapter 11. VAT registration is covered in Chapter 28. Payments on account are covered in Chapter 15.

Top tips. Although P6 is not primarily a computational exam, it is important to set out the computations you do produce in a way that is easy for marking. Look at the layout of the division of gains between those on which entrepreneurs' relief can be claimed and those on which it could not be claimed.

Easy marks. There were some easy marks in part (a) for basic capital gains computations. Even if you did not know the detail of the rules about leases, you could have guessed how to deal with the cost from the lease percentages given in the question. There were also some easy marks for explaining VAT registration – remember that the limits are in the Tax Tables.

Examiner's comments. Part (a)(i) required a statement of the conditions necessary for the disposal of an asset to be an associated disposal for the purposes of entrepreneurs' relief and was not done well. This is not an area of the syllabus that one would expect to see examined regularly and many candidates will have known immediately on reading the requirement that they did not know the answer. However, the sensible approach would then have been to write a very brief answer with some sensible comments on entrepreneurs' relief. It was pretty likely that this would then score one of the three marks available.

Part (a) (ii) was more straightforward and required candidates to calculate a capital gains tax liability. In order to do so, candidates had to know how to calculate a gain on the assignment of a lease and on the disposal of a remaining piece of land following an earlier part disposal. Entrepreneurs' relief was available in respect of some of the gains and there was also a capital loss and the annual exempt amount that needed to be offset correctly.

In general this question was done well by many candidates. There was no problem in deciding what needed to be done, so those candidates who did poorly simply did not have sufficient knowledge of the rules.

Part (b) concerned registration for the purposes of VAT. The majority of the question was done very well including, in particular, the advantages and disadvantages of registering for VAT. However, some candidates' answers lacked precision when it came to the circumstances where compulsory registration is required in that taxable supplies were not clearly defined and/or the 12-month period was not clearly stated. Other candidates wasted time by writing far too much on the recovery of input tax. The one area where performance was not good was the exceptions to the need to register, which were only referred to by a very small number of candidates.

The final part of the question concerned the matters to consider when making a claim to reduce a payment on account of income tax. This was an area that candidates would have been familiar with but it approached it from a slightly unusual angle: it was not done well. Candidates needed to use their common sense as much as anything else here and to recognise that the claim would need to be made before the end of the tax year. This in turn meant that the tax liability would need to be estimated and that interest would be payable if the final liability turned out to be more than the estimated liability. Making these two points would have scored two of the three marks available for this part of the question.

Marking scheme

				Marks
(a)	(i)	Conditions – 1 mark each		3
	(ii)	*Taxable gains*		
		Assignment of lease	2½	
		Sale of land	2	
		Other matters	1½	
		Capital gains tax	1½	
		Max		7

(b)	Requirement to register	1½		
	Exceptions	2		
	Advantages	2		
	Disadvantages	2		
	Max		7	
(c)	Context	1½		
	Circumstances in which a claim can be made	2		
	Interest and penalties	1½		
	Max		3	
			20	

(a) (i) **The availability of entrepreneurs' relief in respect of the assignment of the lease**

The following conditions must be satisfied in order for the assignment of the lease to qualify as an associated disposal so entrepreneurs' relief will be available.

- Ash's disposal of the shares in Lava Ltd (the main disposal) must qualify for entrepreneurs' relief.

- The lease of the building must have been owned by Ash and the building used for the purposes of the business of Lava Ltd for at least one year.

- Ash must have sold the shares in Lava Ltd and the lease as part of a withdrawal from participating in the business of Lava Ltd.

(ii) **Ash – capital gains tax (CGT) liability for the tax year 2015/16**

	Entrepreneurs' relief available £	Entrepreneurs' relief not available £
Gain on sale of shares	235,000	
Gain on assignment of lease £79,812 (W1) × 60:40	47,887	31,925
Gain on sale of land (W2)		21,780
Loss on sale of quoted shares (best use)		(17,300)
		36,405
Annual exempt amount		(11,100)
	282,887	25,305
CGT @ 10%/28%	28,289	7,085
Total CGT liability £(28,289 + 7,085)		35,374

Workings

1 *Gain on the assignment of the lease*

	£
Proceeds	110,000
Less cost £31,800 × $\frac{93.497}{98.490}$	(30,188)
Gain	79,812

2 *Gain on the sale of the land*

	£
Proceeds	30,000
Less cost £27,400 − £(27,400 × $\frac{42,000}{42,000+18,000}$)	(8,220)
Gain	21,780

Tutorial notes

1   Entrepreneurs' relief in respect of the lease will be restricted to 60% (100% – 40%) of the gain, due to the rent charged by Ash to Lava Ltd.

2   Ash's taxable income is less than his basic rate limit. However, the gains qualifying for entrepreneurs' relief use up the remainder of the basic rate band so all of the non-qualifying gains are taxed at 28%.

(b)   **Vulcan Partnership (Vulcan) – Value added tax (VAT) registration**

Whether or not Vulcan may be required to register

Subject to the exceptions noted below, Vulcan will be required to register for VAT once its cumulative taxable supplies (those that are standard rated or zero rated) in a 12-month period exceed £82,000.

However, Vulcan will not be required to register if HM Revenue and Customs are satisfied that its total supplies for the following 12 months will be less than £80,000.

Vulcan could request to be exempt from registration because only a small proportion of its supplies are standard rated. This exemption will be available provided it would normally be in a repayment position if registered.

Advantages of registration

Vulcan will be able to recover all of its input tax if the amount relating to exempt supplies is de minimis under the partial exemption rules. Where Vulcan does not satisfy one of the de minimis tests, it will still be able to recover the majority of its input tax.

Registration may give the impression of Vulcan being a substantial business.

Disadvantages of registration

Registration will add to the amount of work required to administer the business. In addition, Vulcan may be subject to financial penalties if it fails to comply with the obligations imposed by the VAT regime.

The partnership's customers would be unable to recover any output tax charged by the partnership as they are not registered for VAT. Accordingly, the prices charged to the small proportion of customers purchasing standard rated items would increase unless Vulcan decides to reduce its profit in respect of these sales.

(c)   **Payment on account on 31 January 2017**

The payment on account due on 31 January 2017 is the first payment in respect of Ash's income tax payable (income tax liability as reduced by tax deducted at source) for 2016/17. The payment due is half of the income tax payable for 2015/16 unless Ash makes a claim to reduce the payment.

Ash can make a claim to reduce the payment if he expects the amount payable for 2016/17 to be less than that for 2015/16. The income tax payable for 2016/17 is likely to be less than that for 2015/16 due, principally, to Ash receiving less profit from Vulcan.

Ash will need to estimate his income tax payable for 2016/17 in order to decide whether or not to reduce the payment on account. Ash will be charged interest if the payment on account is reduced to an amount that is less than half of the final agreed amount payable for 2016/17. In addition, a penalty may be charged if Ash is fraudulent or negligent when he makes the claim to reduce the payment.

5 Cuthbert (ATAX 12/12)

Text references. Payment of CGT and income tax errors are covered in Chapter 15. Inheritance tax on lifetime transfers is dealt with in Chapter 16, the death estate in Chapter 17 and overseas aspects in Chapter 18.

Top tips. Make sure you read the question thoroughly and use all the information you are given to formulate your answer. For example, in part (c) you were told that the original computation of inheritance tax was based on the donor being non-UK domiciled and having made no lifetime gifts. This made a significant difference to the death estate tax computation.

Easy marks. The computation of inheritance tax in part (c), even with the overseas aspects, was straightforward.

Examiner's comments. Part (a) required detailed knowledge of the payment of capital gains tax by instalments. It was the most difficult part of the question and was not done well. The fundamental problem here was that candidates simply did not know the rules, such that they had very little to say. The smart candidates kept their answers brief and moved on to the easier marks in part (b) and, particularly, part (c).

Part (b) concerned the penalty for making a careless error in a tax return. The question stated that the error was careless but many candidates described the full range of penalties available for all error types thus wasting time. Having said that, candidates' performance in this part of the question was good with the exception of the meaning of potentially lost revenue (PLR), the figure on which the penalty would be based. PLR is the additional tax due following the correction of the error and not the amount of the undeclared income.

Part (c) required calculations of inheritance tax and was done well. Almost all candidates understood the relevance of the taxpayer being UK domiciled rather than non-UK domiciled and most candidates handled the chargeable lifetime transfer correctly.

There were two common areas where marks were lost. First, many candidates omitted to calculate the original inheritance tax liability that would have been paid before the additional information was discovered. This calculation was necessary in order to calculate the tax underpaid. Secondly, many candidates were not sure of the due date for inheritance tax or, if they knew the six-month rule, they did not know how to apply the rule to the facts.

A minority of candidates did not know the mechanics of inheritance tax particularly well. As a result, they did not deal with the nil rate band correctly or they included the chargeable lifetime transfer in the death estate. Other errors involved applying capital gains tax exemptions to inheritance tax and failing to calculate an estate rate in order to justify the double tax relief available.

			Marks
(a)	*Payment of capital gains tax by instalments*		
	Availability of payment by instalments	1½	
	Availability of gift relief	1½	
	Matters that Cuthbert would need to be aware of		
	Need for election	1½	
	Payment and interest	2	
	Subsequent sale of asset	1	
		Max	6
(b)	Maximum penalty	1½	
	Disclosure	1½	
	Minimum penalty	1½	
		Max	4

			Marks
(c)	Gift in seven years prior to death	2½	
	Death estate – if UK domiciled		
	Assets in UK	1	
	Assets in Camberia	1½	
	Nil rate band	1	
	Inheritance tax and double tax relief	2½	
	Death estate - if non-UK domiciled	1	
	Interest on underpayment	1½	
	Max		10
			20

(a) **Payment of capital gains tax (CGT) by instalments**

Availability

Payment of CGT by instalments is available in respect of gifts of certain assets, including land (this term includes buildings), where gift relief is not available. Gift relief will not be available in respect of the gift of the building as the building is not used in a business and is let to a long-term tenant so it cannot be a furnished holiday letting.

Matters that Cuthbert would need to be aware of

It is necessary to make an election to pay by instalments before the date that the CGT is normally due (ie 31 January 2018). There will be ten annual instalments beginning on 31 January 2018. Interest will be charged on the outstanding balance of the tax liability.

Cuthbert will be required to pay all of the remaining instalments immediately if the property is sold because Cuthbert and his brother are connected persons for the purposes of CGT.

(b) **The penalty due in respect of a careless error in Cuthbert's tax return**

The maximum penalty for a careless error is 30% of the potential lost revenue. The potential lost revenue in this case is the additional tax due following the correction of the error.

The penalty may be reduced depending on the level of disclosure Cuthbert provides to HM Revenue and Customs (HMRC) in terms of telling them about the error, providing them with assistance in quantifying it and allowing them access to his records.

Any disclosure provided by Cuthbert will be regarded as prompted, rather than unprompted, because Cuthbert is aware that HMRC suspect that an error has been made. The minimum penalty in these circumstances is 15% of the potential lost revenue.

(c) **Pugh – UK inheritance tax (IHT) liability**

Gift in the seven years prior to death

There would be no further tax due in respect of the gift on 10 March 2009 as the gross transfer of £317,500 (W1) is covered by the nil rate band of £325,000. However, the tax already paid will not be repaid.

Death estate

Pugh was UK domiciled and will therefore be subject to IHT on his Camberian assets as well as his UK assets.

	£	£
Home in the UK		720,000
Cash held in bank accounts in the UK		45,000
Vintage motor cars located in Camberia		490,000
Quoted shares registered in Camberia		330,000
		1,585,000
Nil rate band available		
Nil rate band at death	325,000	
Less transfer in previous seven years (W1)	(317,500)	
		(7,500)
Amount chargeable to inheritance tax @ 40%		1,577,500
Inheritance tax @ 40%		631,000
Less double taxation relief (W2)		(82,500)
Inheritance tax payable		548,500

The additional IHT due is £(548,500 – 176,000 (W3)) = £372,500.

Interest of £(372,500 × 3% × 4/12) = £3,725 will be charged in respect of the period from 31 August 2016 (six months after the end of the month of death) until the tax is paid on 1 January 2017.

Workings

1   *Gift in the seven years prior to death*

	£
Value transferred	322,400
Less annual exemptions 2008/09 and 2007/08 b/f	(6,000)
Net chargeable transfer of value	316,400
Less nil rate band in 2008/09	(312,000)
Amount chargeable to inheritance tax	4,400
Inheritance tax × 20/80	1,100
Gross chargeable transfer tax £(316,400 + 1,100)	317,500

2   *Double taxation relief*

Average rate of inheritance tax is $\frac{631,000}{1,585,000} \times 100 = 39.811\%$

This is clearly more than the Camberian inheritance tax rate of 25% and so double taxation relief is limited to the Camberian tax paid which was £330,000 × 25% = £82,500.

3   *Original calculation of IHT liability*

	£
Home in the UK	720,000
Cash held in bank accounts in the UK	45,000
	765,000
Nil rate band at death	(325,000)
Amount chargeable to inheritance tax @ 40%	440,000
Inheritance tax @ 40%	176,000

Tutorial note

Business property relief is not available in respect of quoted shares unless the donor controls the company.

ACCA Professional Paper P6 – Options Module

Advanced Taxation (UK)

Mock Examination 3 (ACCA September/December 2015 exam)

Question Paper	
Time allowed	3 hours 15 minutes
This paper is divided into two sections	
Section A	BOTH questions are compulsory questions and MUST be attempted
Section B	TWO questions ONLY to be attempted

DO NOT OPEN THIS PAPER UNTIL YOU ARE READY TO START UNDER EXAMINATION CONDITIONS

SECTION A: BOTH questions are compulsory and MUST be attempted

1 Jonny (ATAX 09/15)

63 mins

Your manager has had a meeting with Jonny who is establishing a new business. An extract from an email from your manager, a schedule and a computation are set out below.

Extract from the email from your manager

Jonny's new business will begin trading on 1 November 2016. Jonny will use an inheritance he received following the death of his mother to finance this new venture.

We have been asked to advise Jonny on his business and his inheritance. Some of the work has already been done; I want you to complete it.

Please prepare a memorandum for Jonny's client file addressing the following issues:

(a)   **Unincorporated business**

I attach a schedule which sets out Jonny's recent employment income and his plans for the new business. I think you will find it useful to read the schedule before you go through the rest of this email.

You should assume that Jonny does not have any other sources of income or any taxable gains in any of the relevant tax years.

(i)   **Jonny's post-tax income**

Jonny has asked for an approximation of his post-tax income position for the first two trading periods. I want you to prepare calculations in order to complete the following table, assuming that any available trading loss reliefs will be claimed in the most beneficial manner. You should include explanations of the options available to relieve the loss, clearly identifying the method which will maximise the tax saved (you do not need to consider carrying the loss forward).

Table to be completed

	Strong Demand £	Weak demand £
Aggregate budgeted net profit of the first two trading periods	39,200	2,800
Aggregate income tax (payable)/refundable in respect of the profit/loss for the first two tax years	?	?
Budgeted post-tax income	?	?

Include a brief explanation as to why these calculations are only an approximation of Jonny's budgeted post-tax income.

(ii)   **Salesmen**

Jonny intends to hire two salesmen to get the business started. Their proposed contractual arrangements are as set out in the attached schedule.

Explain which of the proposed contractual arrangements with the salesmen indicate that they would be self-employed and state any changes which should be made to the other arrangements in order to maximise the likelihood of the salesmen being treated as self-employed.

(iii)   **New contracts for the business**

Jonny is hoping to obtain contracts with local educational establishments and has asked us to help. One of our clients is a college and an ex-client of ours provided services to a number of schools and colleges. Accordingly, we have knowledge and experience in this area.

Explain the extent to which it is acceptable for us to use the knowledge we have gained in respect of our existing client and ex-client to assist Jonny.

(b)   **Jonny's inheritance from his mother**

Jonny's mother died on 31 July 2016. She left the whole of her estate, with the exception of a gift to charity, to Jonny. I attach a computation of the inheritance tax due; this was prepared by a junior member of staff and has not yet been reviewed. I can confirm, however, that all of the arithmetic, dates and valuations are correct. In addition, there were no other lifetime gifts, and none of the assets qualified for business property relief.

I want you to review the computation and identify any errors. You should explain each of the errors you find and calculate the value of the inheritance which Jonny will receive after inheritance tax has been paid.

Tax manager

Schedule – Employment income and plans for the new business

Jonny's income

Jonny worked full-time for many years until 30 June 2014 earning a salary of £6,000 per calendar month. From 1 July 2014, he worked part-time earning a salary of £2,000 per calendar month until he ceased employment on 31 March 2016.

Two budgets have been prepared for Jonny's business based on customer demand being either strong or weak. You should assume that no tax adjustments are required to Jonny's budgeted profit/loss figures for the first two trading periods.

For strong demand, the taxable trading profit for the first two tax years has been computed; these figures are correct and you do not need to check them. You will, however, need to calculate the equivalent figures for weak demand.

	Strong Demand £	Weak demand £
Budgeted net profit/(loss):		
Eight months ending 30 June 2017	9,200	(15,200)
Year ending 30 June 2018	30,000	18,000
Aggregate budgeted net profit of the first two trading periods	39,200	2,800
Taxable trading profit/(loss):		
2016/17	5,750	?
2017/18	19,200	?

Salesmen

Jonny is proposing to enter into the following contractual arrangements with two part-time salesmen:

•   They will work on Tuesday and Wednesday mornings each week for a two-month period.

•   They will be paid a fee of £300 for each new sales contract obtained. No other payments will be made.

•   They will use their own cars.

•   Jonny will lend each of them a laptop computer.

Computation – Inheritance tax payable on the death of Jonny's mother

Mother's lifetime gift		
		£
1 June 2012 – Gift of cash to Jonny		30,000

Mother's chargeable estate at death on 31 July 2016

	£	£
Freehold property – Mother's home		530,000
UK quoted shares		400,000
Chattels – furniture, paintings and jewellery	40,000	
Less items individually worth less than £6,000	(25,000)	
		15,000
Cash		20,000
		965,000
Less gift to charity		(70,000)
Annual exemption		(3,000)
Chargeable estate		892,000
Less nil rate band	325,000	
Gift in the seven years prior to death (£30,000 – £6,000)	(24,000)	
		(301,000)
		591,000
Inheritance tax (£591,000 × 40%)		236,400

Required

Prepare the memorandum as requested in the email from your manager. The following marks are available:

(a) **Unincorporated business:**

    (i)   Jonny's post-tax income. **(15 marks)**

    (ii)   Salesmen. **(4 marks)**

    (iii) New contracts for the business. **(5 marks)**

(b) **Jonny's inheritance from his mother.** **(7 marks)**

    Professional marks will be awarded for following the manager's instructions, the clarity of the explanations and calculations, problem solving, and the overall presentation of the memorandum. **(4 marks)**

Notes

1. Assume that the tax rates and allowances for the tax year 2015/16 apply to all tax years.
2. Ignore national insurance contributions throughout this question.

(Total = 35 marks)

2 Christina (ATAX 09/15)

Your manager has received a letter from Christina. Christina is the managing director of Sprint Ltd and owns the whole of that company's ordinary share capital. Sprint Ltd is a client of your firm. Extracts from the letter from Christina and an email from your manager are set out below.

Extract from the letter from Christina

I intend to purchase the whole of the ordinary share capital of Iron Ltd on 1 November 2016. My company, Sprint Ltd, purchases components from Iron Ltd, so the two companies will fit together well. I hope to increase the value of Iron Ltd over the next three to five years and then to sell it at a profit.

I need your advice on the following matters:

Corporation tax payable

Iron Ltd has not been managed particularly well. It has had significant bad debts and, as a result, is in need of more cash. To help determine its financial requirements, I need to know how much corporation tax Iron Ltd will have to pay in respect of its results for the 16-month period ending 30 June 2017. Iron Ltd's tax adjusted trading income for this period is budgeted to be only £30,000. In fact, if we discover further problems, it is quite possible that Iron Ltd will make a trading loss for this period; but please base your calculations on the budgeted profit figure of £30,000.

Iron Ltd has no income other than trading income. Following the acquisition, Iron Ltd will sell a small industrial building for £160,000 and an item of fixed machinery for £14,000 on 1 December 2016. The industrial building and the item of fixed machinery were both purchased on 1 June 2013 for £100,000 and £13,500 respectively. At that time, rollover relief of £31,800 was claimed against the acquisition of the industrial building and £3,200 against the acquisition of the item of fixed machinery.

Ownership of Iron Ltd

I need to decide whether I should purchase the shares in Iron Ltd personally or whether the shares should be purchased by Sprint Ltd. I will be the managing director of Iron Ltd regardless of who purchases the shares.

My preference would be to own Iron Ltd personally. However, I would be interested to learn of any advantages to the company being owned by Sprint Ltd. When Iron Ltd is eventually sold, I intend to use the proceeds to purchase a holiday home in Italy.

Value added tax (VAT)

Iron Ltd is not registered for the purposes of VAT. The current management of the company has told me that the level of bad debts is keeping the company's cash receipts in a 12-month period below the registration limit of £82,000. However, I suspect that when I have the opportunity to look at the figures in more detail, it will become apparent that the company should be registered.

Extract from the email from your manager

Additional information

1.   Sprint Ltd owns the whole of the ordinary share capital of Olympic Ltd. Both these companies are profitable and prepare accounts to 30 June each year. Both companies are registered for the purposes of VAT.

2.   Sprint Ltd, Olympic Ltd and Iron Ltd are all UK resident trading companies.

3.   Sprint Ltd will sell a warehouse on 1 February 2017. This will result in a capital loss of £38,000.

4.   Iron Ltd currently makes up its accounts to 28 February each year. Following its acquisition, however, its next set of accounts will be for the 16 months ending 30 June 2017.

5.   Iron Ltd currently has no related 51% group companies.

Please carry out the work set out below.

There will be quite a few points to draw to Christina's attention, so keep each one fairly brief.

(a) **Iron Ltd – Corporation tax payable**

Assuming the entire ordinary share capital of Iron Ltd is purchased by Christina personally on 1 November 2016, calculate the corporation tax payable by Iron Ltd in respect of the 16-month period ending 30 June 2017, and state when this tax will be due for payment.

(b) **Ownership of Iron Ltd**

Explain the tax matters which Christina needs to be aware of in order to decide whether the ordinary share capital of Iron Ltd should be purchased by herself, personally, or by Sprint Ltd. You should assume that Iron Ltd will be required to register for VAT. You should consider the tax implications of both:

- The ownership of Iron Ltd.
- The eventual sale of Iron Ltd (by either Christina or Sprint Ltd).

You should recognise that, regardless of who purchases and subsequently sells Iron Ltd, Christina intends to use the proceeds for personal purposes and that she is a higher rate taxpayer.

(c) **VAT registration**

Set out the matters which Christina should be aware of in relation to the need for Iron Ltd to register for VAT and the implications for that company of registering late.

Tax manager

Required

Carry out the work required as requested in the email from your manager. The following marks are available:

(a) **Iron Ltd – Corporation tax payable.**

Note: The following figures from the Retail Prices Index should be used, where necessary.

June 2013	249.7
December 2016	263.4

(9 marks)

(b) **Ownership of Iron Ltd.** **(13 marks)**

(c) **Value added tax (VAT) registration.** **(3 marks)**

(Total = 25 marks)

SECTION B: TWO questions ONLY to be attempted

3 Cinnabar Ltd (ATAX 09/15)   36 mins

Cinnabar Ltd requires advice on the corporation tax treatment of expenditure on research and development, the sale of an intangible asset, and a proposed sale of shares. Cinnabar Ltd has also requested advice on the potential to claim relief for losses incurred in a new joint venture.

Cinnabar Ltd:

- Is a UK resident trading company.

- Has one wholly-owned UK subsidiary, Lapis Ltd.

- Is a small enterprise for the purposes of research and development expenditure.

- Prepares accounts to 31 March each year.

- Expects to pay corporation tax by instalments for all relevant accounting periods.

- Intends to enter into a joint venture with another UK company, Amber Ltd. This joint venture will be undertaken by a newly incorporated company, Beryl Ltd.

Research and development expenditure – year ended 31 March 2016:

- The expenditure on research and development activities was made up as follows:

	£
Computer hardware	44,000
Software and consumables	18,000
Staff costs	136,000
Rent	30,000
	228,000

- The staff costs include a fee of £10,000 paid to an external contractor, who was provided by an unconnected company.

- The remainder of the staff costs relates to Cinnabar Ltd's employees, who are wholly engaged in research and development activities.

- The rent is an appropriate allocation of the rent payable for Cinnabar Ltd's premises for the year.

Sale of an intangible asset to Lapis Ltd:

- The intangible asset was acquired by Cinnabar Ltd in May 2011 for £82,000.

- The asset was sold to Lapis Ltd on 1 November 2015 for its market value on that date of £72,000, when its tax written down value was £65,600.

Sale of shares in Garnet Ltd:

- Cinnabar Ltd acquired a 12% shareholding in Garnet Ltd, a UK resident trading company, in July 2010 for £120,000.

- Cinnabar Ltd sold one third of this shareholding on 20 October 2015.

- Cinnabar Ltd intends to sell the remaining two thirds of this shareholding on 30 November 2016 for £148,000.

- It would be possible to bring forward this sale to October 2016 if it is beneficial to do so.

Beryl Ltd:

- Will be incorporated in the UK and will commence trading on 1 January 2017.
- Is anticipated to generate a trading loss of £80,000 in its first accounting period ending 31 December 2017.
- Will have no sources of income other than trading income.

Alternative capital structures for Beryl Ltd:

- Two alternative structures have been proposed for the shareholdings in Beryl Ltd:

    – **Structure 1**: 76% of the shares in Beryl Ltd will be held by Amber Ltd, with the remaining 24% held by Cinnabar Ltd.

    – **Structure 2**: 70% of the shares will be held by Amber Ltd, 24% by Cinnabar Ltd and the remaining 6% held personally by Mr Varis, the managing director of Amber Ltd.

Required

(a) (i) Explain, with supporting calculations, the treatment for corporation tax purposes of the items included in Cinnabar Ltd's research and development expenditure for the year ended 31 March 2016.

(5 marks)

(ii) Explain the corporation tax implications for Cinnabar Ltd of the sale of the intangible asset to Lapis Ltd. **(2 marks)**

(b) Calculate the after-tax proceeds which would be received on the proposed sale of the Garnet Ltd shares on 30 November 2016 and explain the potential advantage of bringing forward this sale to October 2016.

Note: The following indexation factor should be used where necessary:

July 2010 - November 2016 – 0.1762 **(5 marks)**

(c) Explain, with supporting calculations, the extent to which Cinnabar Ltd can claim relief for Beryl Ltd's trading loss under each of the proposed alternative capital structures. **(8 marks)**

(Total = 20 marks)

4 Hyssop Ltd (ATAX 12/15)   36 mins

Hyssop Ltd wishes to provide assistance with home to work travel costs for Corin, who is an employee, and also requires advice on the corporation tax implications of the purchase of a short lease and the value added tax (VAT) implications of the sale of a warehouse.

Hyssop Ltd:

- Is a UK resident trading company.
- Prepares accounts to 31 December each year.
- Is registered for VAT.
- Leased a factory on 1 February 2016.

Corin:

- Is resident and domiciled in the UK.
- Is an employee of Hyssop Ltd, who works only at the company's head office.
- Earns an annual salary of £55,000 from Hyssop Ltd and has no other source of income.

Hyssop Ltd – assistance with home to work travel costs:

- Hyssop Ltd is considering two alternatives to provide assistance with Corin's home to work travel costs.

    ### Alternative 1 – provision of a motorcycle:

    - Hyssop Ltd will provide Corin with a leased motorcycle for travelling from home to work.

    - Provision of the leased motorcycle, including fuel, will cost Hyssop Ltd £3,160 per annum. This will give rise to an annual taxable benefit of £3,160 for Corin.

    - Corin will incur no additional travel or parking costs in respect of his home to work travel.

    ### Alternative 2 – payment towards the cost of driving and provision of parking place:

    - Hyssop Ltd will reimburse Corin for the cost of driving his own car to work up to an amount of £2,240 each year.

    - Corin estimates that his annual cost for driving from home to work is £2,820.

    - Additionally, Hyssop Ltd will pay AB Parking Ltd £920 per year for a car parking space for Corin near the head office.

Acquisition of a factory:

- Hyssop Ltd acquired a 40-year lease on a factory on 1 February 2016 for which it paid a premium of £260,000.

- The factory is used in Hyssop Ltd's trade.

Disposal of a warehouse:

- Hyssop Ltd has agreed to sell a warehouse on 31 December 2016 for £315,000, which will give rise to a chargeable gain of £16,520.

- Hyssop Ltd had purchased the warehouse when it was newly constructed on 1 January 2013 for £270,000 (excluding VAT).

- The warehouse was used by Hyssop Ltd in its trade until 31 December 2015, since when it has been rented to an unconnected party.

- Until 1 January 2016, Hyssop Ltd made only standard-rated supplies for VAT purposes.

- Hyssop Ltd has not opted to tax the warehouse for VAT purposes.

- The capital goods scheme for VAT applies to the warehouse.

Required

Note: You should ignore value added tax (VAT) for parts (a) and (b).

(a) Explain, with the aid of calculations, which of the two alternatives for providing financial assistance for home to work travel is most cost efficient for:

   (i)   Corin. **(5 marks)**

   (ii) Hyssop Ltd. **(3 marks)**

(b) Explain, with the aid of calculations, the corporation tax implications for Hyssop Ltd of the acquisition of the leasehold premises on 1 February 2016, in relation to the company's tax adjusted trading profits for the year ended 31 December 2016 and its ability to roll over the gain on the sale of the warehouse.

(8 marks)

(c) Explain, with the aid of calculations, the VAT implications of the disposal of the warehouse on 31 December 2016. **(4 marks)**

(Total = 20 marks)

5 Stellar and Maris (ATAX 12/15)

36 mins

Your firm has been asked to provide advice to two unrelated clients, Stella and Maris. Stella requires advice on the tax implications of making an increased contribution to her personal pension scheme. Maris requires advice regarding the lump sum payment she has received from her pension scheme and the inheritance tax exemptions available on her proposed lifetime gifts.

(a) **Stella:**

- Is resident and domiciled in the UK.
- Receives a gross salary of £80,000 each year.
- Has income from a portfolio of unfurnished properties, totalling £92,000 in the tax year 2016/17.
- Has no other source of taxable income.
- Wishes to make an increased contribution to her personal pension scheme in the tax year 2016/17.

Personal pension scheme contributions:

- Stella has contributed £40,000 (gross) to her personal pension scheme in August of each of the four tax years 2012/13, 2013/14, 2014/15 and 2015/16.

- Stella wishes to make an increased contribution of £90,000 (gross) in the tax year 2016/17.

Required

Calculate Stella's income after tax and pension contributions for the tax year 2016/17 if she does pay £90,000 (gross) into her personal pension scheme. **(10 marks)**

(b) **Maris:**

- Is resident and domiciled in the UK and is widowed.

- Has three married children and five grandchildren under the age of 12.

- Attained the age of 68 on 30 January 2016 and decided to vest her pension benefits on that date.

- Wishes to make regular gifts to her family in order to reduce inheritance tax on her death.

Personal pension fund:

- Maris had a money purchase pension scheme which was valued at £1,550,000 on 30 January 2016.

- Maris followed advice to reinvest £937,500 of the fund to provide taxable pension income for the future and to take the remainder of the fund as a lump sum.

- Maris does not understand why the amount of cash she received as the lump sum was £447,500.

Assets and income:

- In addition to pension income and savings income totalling around £60,000, Maris receives dividends from shareholdings in quoted companies of around £45,000 each year.

- The shareholdings in quoted companies are currently valued at £980,000.

- Maris wishes to gift some of the shares or the dividend income to her children and grandchildren on their birthdays each year.

- Maris already makes gifts each year to use her annual exemption for inheritance tax purposes.

Required

(i)   Explain how the cash of £447,500 received by Maris as a lump sum from her pension scheme was calculated.   **(4 marks)**

(ii)   Advise Maris of TWO relevant exemptions from inheritance tax which she will be able to use when making the birthday gifts, together with any conditions she will need to comply with in order to obtain them.   **(6 marks)**

(Total = 20 marks)

Answers

DO NOT TURN THIS PAGE UNTIL YOU HAVE
COMPLETED THE MOCK EXAM

A plan of attack

What's the worst thing you could be doing right now if this was the actual exam paper? Wondering how to celebrate the end of the exam in about three hours time? Panicking, flapping and generally getting in a right old state?

Well, they're all pretty bad, so turn back to the paper and let's sort out a **plan of attack**!

First things first

Look through the paper and work out which optional questions to do and the order in which to attack the questions. You've got **two options**. Option 1 is the option recommended by BPP.

Option 1 (if you're thinking 'Help!')

If you're a bit worried about the paper, do the questions in the order of how well you think you can answer them. If you find the questions in Section B less daunting than the compulsory questions in Section A start with Section B. Remember you only need to do two of the three questions in Section B; you may find it easier if you start by deciding which question you will not do and put a line through it.

- **Question 3** is a corporation tax question dealing with research and development expenditure, intangible assets, chargeable gains for companies, and group and consortium relief.

- **Question 4** involved considering the tax implications for an employee and an employer of alternative home to work travel costs, corporation tax implications of acquiring a short lease and value added tax on the disposal of a building.

- **Question 5** covers two pension issues which were contributions to a personal pension scheme and receiving a lump sum from a money purchase scheme. It also dealt with inheritance tax exemptions.

Do not spend longer than the allocated time on Section B. When you've spent the allocated time on **two** of the three questions in Section B turn to the longer questions in Section A. Read these questions through thoroughly before you launch into them. Once you start make sure you allocate your time to the parts within the questions according to the marks available and that, where possible, you attempt the easy marks first.

Lastly, what you mustn't forget is that you have to **answer both questions in Section A and TWO in Section B**. Do not miss out more than one question in Section B and do not waste time answering three questions in Section B or you will seriously affect your chance of passing the exam.

Option 2 (if you're thinking 'It's a doddle')

It never pays to be overconfident but if you're not quaking in your shoes about the exam then **turn straight to the compulsory questions** in Section A.

Once you've done these questions, move to Section B.

- The question you attempt first really depends on what you are most confident at.

- You then have to select one of the two remaining questions. If you are undecided look at the requirements. It maybe easier to obtain more marks if these are broken down into several smaller parts.

No matter how many times we remind you....

Always, always **allocate your time** according to the marks for the question in total and then according to the parts of the question. And **always, always follow the requirements** exactly. For example, in Question 1(a)(i) you were required to produce calculations of Jonny's post-tax income, not just his income tax position.

The examiner has commented that **some candidates write about general issues that relate to the facts of the question but have not been asked for**. This occurs particularly in the Section A questions. It can sometimes look to be a way of avoiding having to get to grips with the requirements or perhaps it is a form of 'warming up' but, either way, **it creates unnecessary time pressure**.

You've got spare time at the end of the exam.....?

If you have allocated your time properly then you **shouldn't have time on your hands** at the end of the exam. But if you find yourself with five or ten minutes to spare, check over your work to make sure you've answered all the requirements.

Forget about it!

And don't worry if you found the paper difficult. More than likely other candidates will too. If this were the real thing you would need to **forget** the exam the minute you leave the exam hall and **think about the next one**. Or, if it's the last one, **celebrate**!

1 Jonny (ATAX 09/15)

Text references. The basics of income tax computation are dealt with in Chapter 1. Trade profits (including basis periods on commencement) are covered in Chapter 6 and trading losses in Chapter 8. Tests of employment versus self employment are dealt with in Chapter 4. Ethics are covered in Chapter 30. The death estate and the reduced rate of inheritance tax are dealt with in Chapter 17.

Top tips. In part (a)(i) you were required to work out Jonny's post-tax income. You need to adopt a logical approach to this requirement. First, you need to work out what is the profit or loss for each tax year if demand is weak. Then you need to consider how this will be taxed (if a profit) or relieved (if a loss). You should have been able to spot that early years trading loss relief was available. Next work out how much income tax is payable or repayable. This will then enable you to work out the post-tax income position using the pro forma given in the question.

Easy marks. There were some easy marks for identifying the factors which would indicate self-employment in part (a)(ii). The ethical issues in part (a)(iii) should have been well known.

Examiner's comments. A small number of candidates achieved full, or nearly full marks for part (a)(i) but a significant minority made no or very little attempt to address this part of this question, suggesting a lack of preparation for this type of question. Unincorporated business are tested in every paper, and questions frequently demand consideration of basis periods and/or relief for trading losses, so question practice on these areas should always form an important part of all candidates' preparation for this exam. Relief for trading losses is a technically demanding area, which requires accurate knowledge of what reliefs are available in which situations, and the precise rules or conditions in each case. Many candidates confined themselves to discussing just one method of loss relief, whereas careful reading of the question indicated that there were different options available and a decision was to be made regarding the optimum method of relief, thereby suggesting that more than one method of relief was available. It appeared that many candidates would have benefited from pausing and thinking more before they started to write. It is important in a question dealing with relief for losses that a well-considered and logical approach is taken. Weaker candidates prepared detailed income tax computations for several tax years in the apparent hope that this would eventually lead to being able to determine the rate of tax paid in each year, and an ability to calculate the tax refund suggested by the question. The problem with this approach was that it was very time consuming and tended to produce redundant information as tax years were included for which it was not possible to offset the loss. Candidates should be advised to consider first of all the tax years in which they believe loss relief is available, before launching into a series of detailed computations for which there are no marks available.

Part (a)(ii) concerned the employment status of two part-time salesmen and was done extremely well. The majority of candidates were able to identify which of the specific contractual arrangements given in the question concerning the work to be done by the salesmen indicated self-employment and any changes required to the other arrangements in order to maximise the likelihood of the salesmen being treated as self-employed. Many candidates gave the impression of being very confident with this topic, and happy to write at length about the different arrangements, giving the impression that they may well have exceeded the four marks worth of time which should have been allocated to this part. Candidates should always take note of the number of marks available for each question part and resist the temptation to elaborate unnecessarily on areas with which they are very comfortable.

Part (a)(iii) covered the ethical issue of confidentiality in relation to using knowledge and experience gained from dealing with both current and ex-clients to assist a new client. This part was done very well by the vast majority of candidates, with many scoring full marks. It was pleasing to see that most candidates related well to the specific client and the facts given in the scenario.

Part (b) of this question required candidates to identify errors in an inheritance tax computation on a death estate, and to calculate the amount to be received by the sole beneficiary of the estate, after the correct inheritance tax had been paid. Performance on this part of the question was mixed, with a disappointing number of candidates believing that the capital gains tax exemption for chattels with a value below £6,000 also applies to inheritance tax, and that inheritance tax annual exemptions are available against assets in the death estate. These are fundamental errors which candidates at P6 should not be making. Candidates should ensure that they are able to identify and apply correctly the different exemptions available for capital gains tax and inheritance tax as these are tested on a very regular basis. In order to calculate the correct amount of inheritance tax to be paid after correcting the errors found, the majority of candidates rewrote the entire death estate. This succeeded in gaining the relevant marks, but was probably fairly time-consuming, and candidates are encouraged to try and adopt a more efficient approach, focusing on the effect of correcting the error on the value of the chargeable estate as this would save time. Questions at P6 frequently ask for a calculation of after-tax proceeds – here, the amount receivable by the sole beneficiary of the estate. Candidates need to think more carefully about the starting point for this type of calculation. Here, it wasn't the value of the chargeable estate, as this includes a deduction for the nil rate band. Candidates needed to identify the actual value which would be received prior to making this deduction. Failure to identify the correct starting point is a common error.

Marking scheme

					Marks
(a)	(i)	Taxable trading profit/(loss) for weak demand		3	
		Income tax payable or refundable			
		Strong demand		2	
		Weak demand		2	
		Advice on use of loss			
		Options available		3	
		Recommendation		3	
		Summary		1	
		Calculation only an approximation		2	
			Max		15
	(ii)	One mark for each relevant point	Max		4
	(iii)	One mark for each relevant point			5
(b)		Identification of errors		4½	
		Calculations			
		Inheritance tax liability		2	
		Inheritance received by Jonny		1½	
			Max		7
Followed instructions				1	
Clarity of explanation and instructions				1	
Problem solving				1	
Overall presentation				1	
					4
					35

Memorandum

To	The files
Prepared by	Tax senior
Date	10 September 2016
Subject	Jonny – New business
	Inheritance tax
	Other matters

(a) **Unincorporated business**

(i) **Jonny's post-tax income**

Weak demand – taxable trading profit/(loss) for the first two tax years

	£	£
2016/17 (1 November 2016 to 5 April 2017)		
Loss (£15,200 × 5/8)		(9,500)
2017/18 (1 November 2016 to 31 October 2017)		
1 November 2016 to 30 June 2017		
Loss	(15,200)	
Less recognised in 2016/17	9,500	
		(5,700)
1 July 2017 to 31 October 2017		
Profit (£18,000 × 4/12)		6,000
Profit		300

Total income tax payable/refundable

	Note	2016/17 £	2017/18 £	Total £
Strong demand				
Taxable trading profit		5,750	19,200	
Income tax (payable)/refundable	1, 2	Nil	(1,720)	(1,720)
Weak demand				
Taxable trading profit/(loss)		(9,500)	300	
Income tax (payable)/refundable	3, 4	3,800	Nil	3,800

Notes

1. Strong demand – 2016/17

   The taxable trading income will be covered by the personal allowance.

2. Strong demand – 2017/18

   The tax liability will be £1,720 ((£19,200 - £10,600) × 20%).

3. Weak demand – 2016/17

   The taxable trading income will be nil, such that the tax liability will be nil.

   The loss of £9,500 can be offset against:

   (i) Total income of 2016/17 and/or 2015/16.

   In 2016/17, Jonny will have no taxable income.

   In 2015/16, Jonny had employment income of £24,000 (12 × £2,000), such that he was a basic rate taxpayer.

   Or

   (ii) Total income of 2013/14, 2014/15 and 2015/16 in that order.

   In 2013/14, Jonny had employment income of £72,000 (12 × £6,000), such that he had more than £9,500 of income taxable at the higher rate.

   The loss should therefore be offset in 2013/14, resulting in a tax refund of £3,800 (£9,500 × 40%).

4. Weak demand – 2017/18

The taxable trading income will be covered by the personal allowance.

Post-tax income position

	Strong £	Weak £
Aggregate budgeted net profit of the first two trading periods (per email)	39,200	2,800
Aggregate income tax (payable)/refundable for the first two tax years	(1,720)	3,800
Budgeted post-tax income	37,480	6,600

These post-tax income figures are an approximation because the total income arises in a period of 20 months (1 November 2016 to 30 June 2018), whereas the total income tax payable is in respect of only 17 months (five months in 2016/17 and the whole of 2017/18).

(ii) **Salesmen**

Proposed contractual arrangements indicating self-employed status

- The salesmen will be paid a fee by reference to the work they do. This will enable them to earn more by working more efficiently and effectively.

- The salesmen will not be paid sick pay or holiday pay; such payments would be indicative of employed status.

- The salesmen will be required to use their own cars.

Suggested changes in order to maximise the likelihood of the salesmen being treated as self-employed

- It would be helpful if the salesmen were able to work on the days they choose rather than being required to work on specific days.

- The salesmen should be required to provide their own laptop computer rather than borrowing one from Jonny.

Tutorial note

The period for which the salesmen will work is not a relevant factor in determining their status. However, the longer they are appointed for, the more likely it is that the factors indicating employment (for example, the degree of control over the worker) will be present.

(iii) **New contracts for the business**

- ACCA's Code of Ethics and Conduct includes confidentiality as one of the fundamental principles of ethics on which we should base our professional behaviour.

- Where we have acquired confidential information as a result of our professional and business relationships, we are obliged to refrain from using it to our own advantage or to the advantage of third parties.

- This principle of confidentiality applies to both ex-clients and continuing clients.

- As a result of this, we should not use any confidential information relating to our existing clients or ex-clients to assist Jonny.

- We are permitted to use the experience and expertise we have gained from advising our clients.

(b) **Jonny's inheritance from his mother**

Errors identified

1. Chattels (for example, furniture, paintings and jewellery) with a value of less than £6,000 are not exempt for the purposes of inheritance tax (although they are exempt for the purposes of capital gains tax).

2. The annual exemption is not available in respect of transfers on death.

3. The reduced rate of inheritance tax of 36% will apply. This is because:

- The chargeable estate, before deduction of the charitable donation but after deduction of the nil rate band, is £689,000 (£619,000 (£591,000 + £25,000 + £3,000) + £70,000).

- The gift to the charity of £70,000 is more than 10% of this amount.

Value of inheritance receivable by Jonny

	£
Chargeable estate per draft computation	892,000
No exemption for chattels valued at less than £6,000	25,000
No annual exemption	3,000
	920,000
Less nil rate band	(301,000)
	619,000
Inheritance tax at 36%	222,840
Assets inherited by Jonny	
(£530,000 + £400,000 + £40,000 + £20,000 – £70,000)	920,000
Less inheritance tax payable	(222,840)
Inheritance receivable by Jonny	697,160

2 Christina (ATAX 09/15)

Text references. Chapter 20 covers the computation of taxable total profits and Chapter 22 deals with the computation of corporation tax. Chargeable gains for companies is the subject of Chapter 21. Groups are dealt with in Chapter 26. Registration issues for value added tax are dealt with in Chapter 28. Reliefs for chargeable gains are covered in Chapter 13. Computation of income tax is covered in Chapter 1.

Top tips. It is really important to comply with the requirements of the question. For example, you were told to keep your points to be made to Christina brief. This should have alerted you to the fact that there were a relatively small number of marks for each point and that you should make your points clearly and concisely.

Easy marks. Stating the dates for payment of corporation tax in part (a) should have been easy marks if you realised that there were two accounting periods in the long period of account. There were also some easy marks for basic chargeable gains computations in the same part.

Examiner's comments. Part (a) required a calculation of the corporation tax payable for a company in respect of a 16-month set of accounts, including consideration of two asset disposals where rollover relief had been claimed previously. It was surprising, and indeed disappointing, to see that the majority of candidates calculated the corporation tax payable for the 16-month period as a whole, rather than recognising the need to split this into two separate accounting periods, the first covering the first 12 months and the second covering the remaining four months. Candidates are reminded that a good level of familiarity with the F6 (UK) syllabus is required for P6; it is not enough to just focus on the new areas, candidates must ensure that they are also confident in dealing with more basic issues. The majority of candidates recognised that the sale of the two business assets would cause the gain rolled over on the acquisition of these assets to become chargeable. However, the different treatments in respect of the depreciating asset (fixed machinery) and non-depreciating asset (building) was identified by only a small number of candidates.

Part (b) was the largest part of the question. It required a comparison of the tax implications of a company being acquired by an individual as opposed to by another company. Candidates who did well had a good knowledge of the subject, adopted a sensible, logical approach and addressed all of the issues briefly, as instructed in the question. Weaker candidates fell down in at least one of these areas. The adoption of a logical approach in this sort of question requiring a comparison of two alternatives can save considerable confusion and avoid wasting time due to needless repetition. Candidates should pause and think before they start writing. Dealing fully with the implications of one of the alternatives first, and then the other, tended to provide a much clearer answer than those who adopted a less logical approach, apparently writing points as they occurred to them, without making it clear which alternative they were dealing with, constantly swapping between the two, and leading to a confusing answer. Candidates should avoid repetition, including making the same point from different angles. An example in this case would be where a candidate has stated that if the company is acquired by another company, they would form a group for group relief purposes. Stating separately at a later point that if acquired by an individual there will not be a group for group relief purposes, scored no additional marks.

Part (c) concerned the often-tested area of registration for VAT, an area which the vast majority of candidates are very technically comfortable with. However, all but a handful failed to read the question in sufficient detail, and provided a very detailed account of the tests applied to determine whether compulsory registration is required, but this did not address the question and wasted a good deal of time. Where the subject coverage is very familiar it is particularly important to understand the context in which it is being tested. In this case, the key issue was recognition that monitoring the level of cash receipts is not relevant, it is the level of taxable supplies, ie the invoiced value of taxable sales which is relevant.

		Marks
(a)	Trading income	1
	Chargeable gains	
	Industrial building	2
	Machinery	1½
	Crystallisation of deferred gain	1
	Chargeable gains in correct period	½
	Corporation tax payable	1½
	Due dates	1½
		9
(b)	Ongoing	
	Group relief	2
	Relief for capital losses	2
	Rollover relief	1
	No gain, no loss transfers	1
	Annual investment allowance	1
	Related 51% group companies	1
	VAT group registration	2
	Sale of Iron Ltd	
	Sprint Ltd owns Iron Ltd	3½
	Christina owns Iron Ltd	2
	Max	**13**
(c)	Taxable supplies as monitoring basis	1
	Implications of late registration	2½
	Max	**3**
		25

(a) Iron Ltd – corporation tax payable for the period ending 30 June 2017

	Year ending 28 February 2017 £	4 months ending 30 June 2017 £
Trading income		
£30,000 × 12/16	22,500	
£30,000 × 4/16		7,500
Chargeable gains (below)		
Industrial building	88,049	
Fixed machinery	0	
Crystallisation of deferred gain re sale of fixed machinery	3,200	
Taxable total profits	113,749	7,500
Corporation tax payable		
£113,749/£7,500 × 20%	22,750	1,500
Due date	1 December 2017	1 April 2018

Tutorial note

If Christina owns Iron Ltd it will not be a related 51% group company with Sprint Ltd or Olympic Ltd. The profit threshold, for determining whether Iron Ltd is a large company for payment of corporation tax by instalments, will therefore be £1,500,000 for the year ending 28 February 2017 and 4/12 x £1,500,000 = £500,000 for the four months to 30 June 2017. Therefore, Iron Ltd does not have to pay its corporation tax by instalments.

Chargeable gains

	Industrial building £	Fixed machinery £
Proceeds	160,000	14,000
Less: Cost (£100,000 – £31,800)	(68,200)	(13,500)
Indexation allowance (June 2013 to December 2016)		
(0.055 (263.4 – 249.7)/249.7) × £68,200)	(3,751)	
(0.055 × £13,500 – but restricted because indexation allowance cannot create a loss)		(500)
Chargeable gain	88,049	0

(b) **Ownership of Iron Ltd**

Ongoing ownership of Iron Ltd

Corporation tax

It would be advantageous for Sprint Ltd, rather than Christina, to purchase Iron Ltd for the following reasons.

- It is possible that Iron Ltd will make a trade loss for the period ending 30 June 2017. If this were to occur, a proportion of the loss could be surrendered by way of group relief to Sprint Ltd and/or Olympic Ltd and be deducted in arriving at the taxable total profits of the recipient company. Whilst all three companies remain in the group, group relief would also be available between them in respect of any losses in future periods.

- Iron Ltd will join Sprint Ltd's capital gains group on 1 November 2016. The capital loss to be made by Sprint Ltd on the sale of the warehouse could therefore be relieved against the chargeable gains to be realised by Iron Ltd on the sale of the industrial building and the fixed machinery. This would reduce the corporation tax liability of Iron Ltd by £7,600 (£38,000 × 20%).

- A gain made by one of the companies in the group on the disposal of a qualifying business asset (land, buildings or fixed machinery used in the business) could be deferred if a qualifying business asset is purchased by any other company in the group during the qualifying period.

- Any future transfers of assets from one group company to another would take place on a no gain, no loss basis.

There is a possible disadvantage in Iron Ltd joining the Sprint Ltd group of companies in relation to capital allowances. The annual investment allowance will be split between the three companies if they are members of a group, whereas an additional full annual investment allowance would be available to Iron Ltd if Christina were to own Iron Ltd personally (unless Iron Ltd were to share premises or carry on activities similar to those of Sprint Ltd or Olympic Ltd).

There is another possible disadvantage as Iron Ltd would become a related 51% group company with Sprint Ltd and Olympic Ltd. The profit threshold for determining whether any of the companies are large for payment of corporation tax by instalments, would then be reduced in future accounting periods.

Value added tax (VAT)

It may be beneficial for Sprint Ltd and Iron Ltd (and possibly Olympic Ltd) to register as a group for the purposes of VAT. This is because it would remove the need for Iron Ltd to charge VAT on the sales it makes to Sprint Ltd. This will, however, be possible regardless of who owns Iron Ltd because Christina will have effective control of all three companies in both situations.

Sale of Iron Ltd

Sprint Ltd owns Iron Ltd

Any chargeable gain (or loss) on the sale of the shares will be exempt due to the substantial shareholding exemption (SSE). This exemption will be available because Sprint Ltd will have owned at least 10% of the ordinary share capital of Iron Ltd for more than a year and both companies are trading companies.

Although the existence of the SSE would appear to be a significant advantage, it should be recognised that the proceeds of sale will then need to be transferred to Christina. This could be carried out via, for example, the payment of a dividend to Christina. As Christina is a higher rate taxpayer, she would have an income tax liability of 25% or even 30·55% of the dividend received.

Tutorial notes

1   The rate of income tax payable by a higher rate taxpayer on dividend income is 25% (100/90 x (32·5% – 10%)). However, the dividend could cause Christina to become an additional rate taxpayer; the rate of income tax payable by an additional rate taxpayer on dividend income is 30·55% (100/90 x (37·5% – 10%)).

2   Credit was also available for reference to other ways in which the proceeds of sale could be transferred to Christina, for example, via the payment of a bonus.

Christina owns Iron Ltd personally

On a sale by Christina of the shares in Iron Ltd, there will be a chargeable gain equal to the excess of the sales proceeds over the price paid for the shares. This gain, after the deduction of any annual exempt amount not used against any other gains, will be subject to capital gains tax at 10% due to the availability of entrepreneurs' relief.

Entrepreneurs' relief will be available because Iron Ltd is a trading company and Christina will have owned at least 5% of its shares for more than a year, and Christina will be a director of Iron Ltd.

Tutorial note

It can be seen from the marking guide that it was not necessary to make all of the above points in order to score full marks.

(c)   **VAT registration**

Iron Ltd should be monitoring the level of its taxable supplies (excluding sales of capital assets), as opposed to its cash receipts, in order to determine when it needs to register for VAT.

The implications of registering late are:

●   Iron Ltd will be required to account for output tax on the sales it has made after the date on which it should have been registered. This will be a cost to Iron Ltd unless it is able to recover the VAT from its customers.

●   A penalty may be charged for failing to register by the appropriate date. This penalty would be a percentage of the potential lost revenue where the percentage depends on the reason for the late registration.

●   Interest may be charged in respect of the VAT paid late.

BPP
LEARNING MEDIA

3 Cinnabar Ltd (ATAX 09/15)

Text references. Research and development expenditure is dealt with in Chapter 20. Intra-group transfers of intangible assets are covered in Chapter 26. Chargeable gains for companies are the subject of Chapter 21. Groups and consortia are covered in Chapter 26.

Top tips. Whenever you see the disposal of shares in a company by another company, consider whether the substantial shareholding exemption applies (unless you are specifically told otherwise).

Easy marks. There were some easy marks for computing the gain in part (b). The fact that the date of disposal was important should have led you to consider the conditions for substantial shareholding exemption.

Examiner's comments. The first part required an explanation of the tax relief available for a small company in respect of expenditure on research and development. The majority of students were aware that directly related revenue expenditure qualifies for an additional [130]% deduction, but were rather vague in their explanations as to why items were or were not included. A small minority wasted time by discussing the tax credit which could be obtained in respect of a loss created by the enhanced deduction, despite there being no mention of a loss in the question, nor sufficient information to be able to calculate one. The first of the two assets sold was an intangible asset, which was sold to a wholly-owned subsidiary. Intangible assets are examined fairly frequently at P6, so candidates need to be aware of their tax treatment as trading assets, rather than capital assets, for companies, which will give rise to a balancing charge or allowance on sale, rather than a capital gain or loss. In the case of a transfer between two companies in a 75% group, the asset will be transferred at its written down value, thereby giving rise to neither profit nor loss. Interestingly, the majority of candidates identified one or other of these points, but very few identified both.

The second asset disposal related to shares in an unquoted trading company. This was the sale of an 8% shareholding in a company following a sale of 4% the previous year. In any question regarding the sale of shares in one company by another, candidates should automatically consider the application of the substantial shareholding exemption (SSE). This is an area where it is very important to know the precise conditions, to be able to state definitively whether or not the exemption applies, and the reasons why, or why not. In this case the timing of the disposal was critical; bringing the date of disposal forward would mean that the requirement to hold at least 10% of the shares for a continuous 12 month period in the two years prior to sale would be satisfied, whereas this would not be the case if the disposal was delayed. An ability to advise on the timing of transactions in respect of all taxes is an important skill at P6.

The final part of this question concerned a proposed joint venture between two companies, where two alternative group structures were being considered. The new company to be set up would be loss-making initially. The key issue here was to be able to differentiate between a group for group relief purposes (which requires one company to have a minimum 75% holding in another) and a consortium (which is formed where two or more companies hold a minimum of 75% between them in a third company, each with at least 5%, but none holding 75% or more on their own). It was disappointing to see that a good number of candidates were unclear on these definitions, thereby producing incorrect answers and scoring few marks. However, well-prepared candidates who were able to make this distinction tended to go on and score well in respect of the way in which the new company's trading losses could be relieved.

				Marks
(a)	(i)	Computer hardware – 100% capital allowance	1	
		Revenue expenditure qualifying for additional deduction	3½	
		Calculation of total deduction	1	
		Max		5
	(ii)	Intra-group disposal of intangible asset		2
(b)		After-tax proceeds	2	
		Advantage of disposal in October	3	
				5
(c)		Structure 1	2	
		Structure 2 – Consortium	2	
		Relief available	5½	
		Max		8
				20

(a)   (i)   **Research and development expenditure**

The computer hardware qualifies for a 100% capital allowance as capital expenditure on an asset related to research and development.

As Cinnabar Ltd is a small enterprise for research and development purposes, the revenue expenditure which is directly related to undertaking research and development activities qualifies for an additional 130% deduction in calculating its taxable trading income. This additional deduction applies to the software and consumables and the staff costs. However, as the external contractor is provided by an unconnected company, only £6,500 (65% of the £10,000 fee) will qualify for this additional deduction.

The rent payable is not a qualifying category of expense, so is not eligible for the additional deduction.

The total deduction from taxable trading profit for the year ended 31 March 2016 is therefore 423,650 (£228,000 + 130% × £(18,000 + 126,000 + 6,500)).

(ii)   **Intra-group transfer of an intangible asset**

As Cinnabar Ltd owns more than 75% of Lapis Ltd, the intangible asset will be treated for corporation tax purposes as having been transferred intra group at its tax written down value, thereby giving rise to neither profit nor loss in Cinnabar Ltd's corporation tax computation.

(b)   **Disposal of Garnet Ltd shares**

A chargeable gain will arise on the proposed disposal in November 2016, calculated as follows:

	£
Sale proceeds	148,000
Less: Cost £120,000 × 2/3	(80,000)
Indexation allowance 0.1762 × £80,000	(14,096)
Chargeable gain	53,904
Corporation tax payable (£53,904 × 20%)	10,781
After-tax proceeds (£148,000 – £10,781)	137,219

The substantial shareholding exemption would not be available in respect of a disposal in November 2016. This is because Cinnabar Ltd's shareholding was reduced to 8% following the disposal on 20 October 2015 and consequently it has not held at least 10% of the shares in Garnet Ltd for a continuous 12-month period in the two years prior to disposal.

As Cinnabar Ltd held 12% of the shares prior to the first disposal on 20 October 2015, the sale should be brought forward to a date prior to 20 October 2016 in order for the substantial shareholding exemption to apply to the sale. In this case, Cinnabar Ltd's corporation tax liability in relation to the disposal of these shares will be reduced to nil.

Tutorial note

The shares in Garnet Ltd are in the FA 1985 share pool. Accordingly, the indexation factor is not rounded to three decimal places.

(c) **Loss relief implications of the alternative structures**

Structure 1:

Under this structure, Amber Ltd will own more than 75% of the shares in Beryl Ltd, so Beryl Ltd will be in a group with Amber Ltd for the purposes of group relief for trading losses. Accordingly, none of Beryl Ltd's trading loss will be available for surrender to Cinnabar Ltd.

Structure 2:

Under this structure, Beryl Ltd will be a consortium-owned company, with Amber Ltd and Cinnabar Ltd as the consortium members. This is because each of the companies owns at least 5% of the shares in Beryl Ltd, and together they hold at least 75% of the shares.

Beryl Ltd's trading loss for the year ending 31 December 2017 may be surrendered to the consortium members according to their respective shareholdings. Cinnabar Ltd may therefore claim a maximum of £19,200 (24% of Beryl Ltd's loss of £80,000) in respect of this year. Relief will be taken against Cinnabar Ltd's taxable total profits for the corresponding accounting period(s).

As Cinnabar Ltd prepares accounts to 31 March annually, the maximum loss which can be claimed for relief in the year ending 31 March 2017 will be the lower of £4,800 (3/12ths of the available loss of £19,200) and 3/12ths of Cinnabar Ltd's taxable total profit for the year ending 31 March 2017. Similarly, the maximum loss which can be claimed for relief in the year ending 31 March 2018 is the lower of £14,400 (9/12ths of £19,200) and 9/12ths of Cinnabar Ltd's taxable total profit for the year ending 31 March 2018.

Cinnabar Ltd expects to pay corporation tax by instalments, so as it has one related 51% group (Lapis Ltd), its taxable total profit must exceed the profit threshold of £750,000 (£1,500,000/2). Therefore, the loss relief must be the lower figure for each 12-month period, which will be £4,800 in the year ending 31 March 2017 and £14,400 in the year ending 31 March 2018.

4 Hyssop Ltd (ATAX 12/15)

Text references. Employment income is covered in Chapter 4. Property income is dealt with in Chapter 3. Chargeable gains for companies is covered in Chapter 21. Value added tax on land and buildings and the capital goods scheme are dealt with in Chapter 29.

Top tips. In part (a), make sure you follow the requirements and deal first with Corin's position for both alternatives and then with Hyssop Ltd's position for both alternatives, rather than all the tax implications for each alternative. Don't forget that both employers and employees are liable for Class 1 national insurance contributions, but only employers pay Class 1A contributions.

Easy marks. There were some easy marks for dealing with the premium on the acquisition of the short lease in part (b).

Examiner's comments. The first part required candidates to consider two possible ways in which an employer could provide financial assistance to an employee in respect of home to work travel and to advise on the most cost efficient method. Although this was, arguably, very straightforward, it was not easy to get right. As always, those candidates who thought before writing did considerably better than those who simply wrote. In particular, they recognised the importance of national insurance contributions. Most candidates identified the income tax and corporation tax implications of the two alternatives. The one point that many missed out on was the fact that the provision of a parking space is an exempt benefit. The problems related to the national insurance position. Some candidates missed this out completely. Others were simply not orderly enough, such that they did not earn as many marks as they could have done. Candidates needed to recognise that the provision of a motorcycle to an employee would result in a liability to Class 1A national insurance contributions for the employer but no liability to national insurance contributions for the employee. Whereas, making a payment towards an employee's driving costs would result in a liability to Class 1 national insurance contributions for both the employer and the employee. Many candidates wrote about the statutory mileage rates, but these are only relevant where payments are in respect of journeys made when carrying out employment duties, which was not the case here.

The second part of the question concerned a premium paid in respect of a lease and the availability of rollover relief. This part was not done particularly well. There were two distinct aspects to this part of the question. The first concerned the tax deduction available in respect of the premium paid. Most candidates were able to make a start on this but very few made it to the end. The first task was to determine the amount of the premium that would be taxed on the landlord as income. This amount was then divided by the number of years of the lease in order to determine the annual deduction. The deduction in the current period was then 11/12 of the annual deduction because the lease was entered into when there were eleven months of the accounting period remaining. The second part of the question concerned the availability of rollover relief. Most candidates knew the basics of rollover relief. However, they did not score as well as they could have done for two reasons:

- The asset sold had not been used for the purposes of the trade for the whole of the period of ownership. As a result, although rollover relief was available, only the business-use proportion of the gain could be relieved and only that proportion of the proceeds needed to be reinvested in qualifying business assets.

- They failed to realise that the lease was a depreciating asset for the purposes of rollover relief, such that the gain would be deferred until the earliest of the date of disposal of the lease, the date the leased building ceased to be used in the business and ten years after the acquisition of the lease.

The final part of the question concerned the capital goods scheme for VAT and was not done particularly well. The capital goods scheme is not easy to explain and many candidates were unable to organise their thoughts and provide a coherent explanation of the implications of the disposal of a building. Candidates would help themselves if they told the story from the beginning.

- The first point to make was that the input tax on the purchase of the building would have been recovered in full.

- It was then necessary to recognise that the sale of the building would be an exempt supply.

- As a result of the exempt supply, there will be deemed to be 0% taxable use of the building for the remainder of the 10-year adjustment period resulting in a repayment of VAT to HMRC.

BPP
LEARNING MEDIA

				Marks
(a)	(i)	Cost of motor cycle	1½	
		Cost of driving costs reimbursement	3	
		Conclusion	½	
				5
	(ii)	Cost of provision of motorcycle	1½	
		Cost of driving costs reimbursement	1	
		All costs deductible for corporation tax	½	
		Conclusion	½	
		Max		3
(b)		Deduction:		
		Available against taxable trading income	1	
		Amount	3	
		Deferral relief available	3	
		Date gain crystallises	2	
		Max		8
(c)		Disposal exempt	1½	
		Initial reclaim	1	
		Repayment of VAT reclaimed previously y/e 31 December 2016	2	
		Max		4
				20

(a)   **Assistance with home to work travel costs for Corin**

(i)   **Cost to Corin**

Alternative 1 – Provision of a motorcycle

Corin is a higher rate taxpayer, so will pay income tax at 40% on the annual taxable benefit. This will be £1,264 (£3,160 × 40%).

Corin will have no national insurance liability in respect of this benefit, so the total cost to him is £1,264.

Alternative 2 – Payment towards the cost of driving and provision of parking place

Provision of a parking place at or near an employee's normal place of work is an exempt benefit for income tax.

Corin will pay income tax at 40% on the cash received as reimbursement of his driving costs, together with Class 1 national insurance contributions at 2%. This will give rise to a total tax cost of £941 (£2,240 × 42%).

The additional driving costs not reimbursed are £580 (£2,820 – £2,240). The total cost to Corin of this option is therefore £1,521 (£941 + £580).

The most cost efficient option for Corin is therefore provision of the motorcycle.

Tutorial note

The statutory mileage rates are not relevant in this case as the driving costs are not related to journeys made in the course of Corin carrying out his duties of employment.

(ii) **Cost to Hyssop Ltd**

Alternative 1 – Provision of a motorcycle

Hyssop Ltd will have to pay Class 1A national insurance contributions of £436 (£3,160 × 13.8%) in respect of the provision of the motorcycle. The total cost to Hyssop Ltd is therefore £3,596 (£3,160 + £436).

Alternative 2 – Payment towards the cost of driving and provision of parking place

As the provision of the parking place is an exempt benefit for income tax, there will be no Class 1A liability for Hyssop Ltd.

Hyssop Ltd will have a Class 1 national insurance liability in respect of the reimbursement of driving costs. This will be £309 (£2,240 × 13.8%).

The total cost to Hyssop Ltd is therefore £3,469 (£2,240 + £309 + £920).

The most cost efficient option for Hyssop Ltd is therefore the payment towards the cost of driving and provision of the parking place.

Hyssop Ltd will be able to deduct all the costs for corporation tax purposes under both options.

Tutorial note

As the amounts are deductible for corporation tax purposes under both options, there is no need to calculate the after-tax cost to Hyssop Ltd.

(b) **Corporation tax implications of the acquisition of the 40-year lease**

As Hyssop Ltd has paid a premium on the grant of a short lease on a property which is going to be used in its trade, a deduction is available for each year of the lease in calculating Hyssop Ltd's taxable trading income.

The annual deduction is calculated a $\dfrac{\text{Amount of premium taxed as income on the landlord}}{\text{Number of years of the lease}}$

The amount of the premium which is taxed as income on the landlord is £57,200 (£260,000 − (£260,000 × (40 − 1) × 2%)).

The annual deduction available to Hyssop Ltd is £1,430 (£57,200/40).

As the lease was only acquired on 1 February 2016, the deduction available in the year ended 31 December 2016 is restricted to £1,311 (£1,430 × 11/12).

The factory is used in Hyssop Ltd's trade, so the lease is a qualifying business asset, and it was acquired within the 12 months before the disposal of the warehouse. Therefore the full business use element of the gain arising may be deferred to the extent that the proceeds relating to the business use of the warehouse have been reinvested in the lease.

The warehouse will have been owned by Hyssop Ltd for four years (1 January 2013 to 31 December 2016).

The warehouse has been used by Hyssop Ltd in its trade for three years (1 January 2013 to 31 December 2015).

The proceeds relating to the business use element of the gain are £236,250 (75% × £315,000). This is less than the £260,000 premium reinvested in the acquisition of the lease, therefore the full 75% of the chargeable gain relating to the business use of the warehouse can be deferred against the acquisition of the lease. Accordingly, £12,390 (£16,520 × 75%) may be deferred.

The lease is for less than 60 years and so is a wasting asset for capital gains purposes. Accordingly, the gain will be deferred until the earliest of:

- The date of disposal of the lease
- The date the leased factory ceases to be used in Hyssop Ltd's business
- 1 February 2026 (ten years after the acquisition of the lease).

The remaining gain of £4,130 (£16,520 × 25%), relating to the non-business use, will be included in Hyssop Ltd's corporation tax computation for the year ending 31 December 2016.

(c) **Value added tax (VAT) implications of the disposal of the warehouse**

At the date of sale, the warehouse is more than three years old. Accordingly, because Hyssop Ltd has not opted to tax it, the disposal will be exempt from VAT.

As the warehouse was newly constructed when it was purchased, VAT of £54,000 (£270,000 × 20%) would have been charged and, as the warehouse was used in its standard-rated business, this would have been wholly reclaimed by Hyssop Ltd in the year ended 31 December 2013.

As the disposal is exempt from VAT, VAT will have to be repaid to HM Revenue and Customs (HMRC) as the warehouse is deemed to have 0% taxable use for the remainder of the ten-year adjustment period under the capital goods scheme. The amount of £32,400 (£54,000 × 6/10 × (100% − 0%)) will be repayable to HMRC as a result of the disposal.

Tutorial note

A further £5,400 (£54,000 × 1/10 × (100% − 0%)) will also be repayable to HMRC in respect of the year ending 31 December 2016 as the warehouse has been rented out throughout this year, with no option to tax.

5 Stella and Maris (ATAX 12/15)

Text references. The income tax computation is dealt with in Chapter 1. Pensions are covered in Chapter 2. Inheritance tax exemptions are dealt with in Chapter 16.

Top tips. In part (a) you need to consider the impact of the pension contribution on the personal allowance. You also need to think about how the basic rate and higher rate limits are increased.

Easy marks. There were some easy marks in part (a) for a basic income tax computation. The inheritance tax exemptions in part (b)(ii) should have been well known.

Examiner's comments. Part (a) required a calculation of an individual's income after the deduction of tax and pension contributions. In order to do this well, candidates had to pay attention to detail and to think before writing. This part of the question was done reasonably well. The question highlighted the following technical issues.

- In order to determine any reduction in the level of the personal allowance, it is necessary to compare adjusted net income (income after deduction of qualifying pension contributions) with the £100,000.

- The basic and higher rate bands must be extended by the gross amount of the qualifying pension contributions.

- There were excess contributions made. This required consideration of the contributions made and the annual allowance for the current year and the three preceding years.

Well-prepared candidates dealt with all three of these issues accurately. A final technical point, that was missed by the majority of candidates, was the need to consider relevant earnings in order to determine qualifying pension contributions.

[Part b(i) has been rewritten and the examiner's comments are no longer relevant.]

Part (b)(ii), the final part of the question, required candidates to identify two inheritance tax exemptions that were relevant to the facts given (other than the annual exemption). This was not a difficult requirement, but most candidates did not perform as well as they could have done because they started to write before they had identified the two exemptions. Many candidates wrote about potentially exempt transfers and the fact that no tax would be due if the donor survived the gift for seven years, which is nothing to do with exemptions. However, there were some satisfactory answers to this part. The two exemptions that candidates were expected to write about were the small gifts exemption and the exemption in respect of regular gifts out of income. These exemptions then needed to be addressed in relation to the particular gifts referred to in the question (cash or shares) and not to gifts generally. The conditions relating to the small gifts exemption are very easy to state but those relating to regular gifts out of income require more care if marks are to be maximised.

			Marks
(a)	Qualifying pension contributions	1½	
	Taxable income	2	
	Excess pension contribution	3	
	Income tax liability	2½	
	Net income after tax and pension contributions	2	
	Max		10
(b) (i)	Tax free amount	1½	
	Taxed amount	2½	
			4
(ii)	Small gift exemption	3	
	Exemption for normal expenditure out of income	4	
	Max		6
			20

(a) Stella – Income after tax and pension contributions 2016/17

	£
Employment income	80,000
Property income	92,000
Net income	172,000
Less personal allowance (W1)	(10,600)
Taxable income	161,400

Income tax liability: (W2)

	£
£111,785 × 20%	22,357
£49,615 × 40%	19,846
£161,400	42,203
Add additional charge: £30,000 × 40% (W3)	12,000
Income tax liability	54,203

Income after tax and pension contributions is £43,797 (£172,000 – £54,203 – £74,000) (W4).

W1: Personal allowance

The pension contributions qualifying for tax relief cannot exceed Stella's net relevant earnings, which are £80,000.

Adjusted net income is £92,000 (£172,000 – 80,000). Therefore there is no restriction of the personal allowance.

W2: Extending the basic and higher rate bands

The basic rate band is extended to £111,785 (£31,785 + £80,000).

The higher rate band is extended to £230,000 (£150,000 + £80,000).

W3: Excess contributions

	£
Annual allowance for 2016/17	40,000
Unused annual allowance for three previous tax years:	
2013/14 (£50,000 – £40,000)	10,000
2014/15 (£40,000 – £40,000)	0
2015/16 (£40,000 – £40,000)	0
Maximum gross pension contribution in 2016/17	50,000

Excess pension contribution is £30,000 (£80,000 – £50,000).

W4: Pension contributions paid

The amount actually paid in respect of the pension contribution by Stella is £74,000 (£64,000 (£80,000 × 80%) + £10,000).

(b) (i) **Maris – Maximum receivable as a lump sum**

The value of Maris's pension fund exceeds the lifetime allowance of £1,250,000.

The maximum lump sum which she could take tax-free was restricted to £312,500 (25% × £1,250,000).

The excess of the fund over the lifetime allowance was also taken as a lump sum, subject to an income tax charge at 55% on the value of this excess. Maris therefore received an additional £135,000 (45% × (£1,550,000 – £1,250,000)).

Maris's total receipt was therefore £447,500 (£312,500 + £135,000).

Tutorial note

The amount reinvested of £937,500 was equal to the remainder of the lifetime allowance (£1,250,000 – £312,500) after taking the tax-free lump sum.

(ii) **Inheritance tax – Lifetime exemptions available**

Small gift exemption

Maris can make exempt gifts valued at up to £250 each tax year to any number of recipients. If the total value of the gifts to any one recipient exceeds £250, the full value of the gifts will be taxable. The gifts can comprise either cash or shares.

Exemption for normal expenditure out of income

The following conditions must be satisfied for the gifts to be exempt:

- The gift is made as part of Maris's normal expenditure. As she is intending to make regular gifts to her family on their birthdays, she should be able to establish a regular pattern of giving.

- The gift is made out of income, not capital. Maris must therefore give cash, not part of her shareholdings.

- Maris is left with sufficient income to maintain her usual standard of living. As she appears to have fairly significant pension and savings income this condition should be satisfied.

There is no monetary limit on the amount of this exemption.

Tax tables

SUPPLEMENTARY INSTRUCTIONS

1. You should assume that the tax rates and allowances for the tax year 2015/16 and for the financial year to 31 March 2016 will continue to apply for the foreseeable future unless you are instructed otherwise.

2. Calculations and workings need only be made to the nearest £.

3. All apportionments may be made to the nearest month.

4. All workings should be shown.

TAX RATES AND ALLOWANCES

The following tax rates and allowances are to be used in answering the questions.

Income tax

		Normal rates	Dividend rates
Basic rate	£1 – £31,785	20%	10%
Higher rate	£31,785 – £150,000	40%	32.5%
Additional rate	£150,001 and over	45%	37.5%

A starting rate of 0% applies to savings income where it falls within the first £5,000 of taxable income.

Personal allowance

	£
Personal allowance	10,600
Transferable amount	1,060
Income limit	100,000

Residence status

Days in UK	Previously resident	Not previously resident
Less than 16	Automatically not resident	Automatically not resident
16 to 45	Resident if 4 UK ties (or more)	Automatically not resident
46 to 90	Resident if 3 UK ties (or more)	Resident if 4 UK ties
91 to 120	Resident if 2 UK ties (or more)	Resident if 3 UK ties (or more)
121 to 182	Resident if 1 UK tie (or more)	Resident if 2 UK ties (or more)
183 or more	Automatically resident	Automatically resident

Remittance basis charge

UK resident for:	Charge
7 out of the last 9 years	£30,000
12 out of the last 14 years	£60,000
17 out of the last 20 years	£90,000

Child benefit income tax charge

Where income is between £50,000 and £60,000, the charge is 1% of the amount of child benefit received for every £100 of income over £50,000.

Car benefit percentage

The base level of CO_2 emissions is 95 grams per kilometre.

The percentage rates applying to petrol cars with CO_2 emissions up to this level are:

50 grams or less per kilometre	5%
51 grams to 75 grams per kilometre	9%
76 grams to 94 grams per kilometre	13%
95 grams per kilometre	14%

Car fuel benefit

The base figure for calculating the car fuel benefit is £22,100.

Individual savings accounts (ISAs)

The overall investment limit is £15,240.

Pension scheme limits

Annual allowance	– 2014/15 and 2015/16	£40,000
	– 2012/13 and 2013/14	£50,000
Lifetime allowance		£1,250,000
The maximum contribution that can qualify for tax relief without any earnings		£3,600

Authorised mileage allowances: cars

Up to 10,000 miles	45p
Over 10,000 miles	25p

Capital allowances: rates of allowance

Plant and machinery

Main pool	18%
Special rate pool	8%

Motor cars

CO_2 emissions up to 75 grams per kilometre	100%
CO_2 emissions between 76 and 130 grams per kilometre	18%
CO_2 emissions over 130 grams per kilometre	8%

Annual investment allowance

Rate of allowance	100%
Expenditure limit	£500,000

Cap on income tax reliefs

Unless otherwise restricted, reliefs are capped at the higher of £50,000 or 25% of income.

Corporation tax

Rate of tax	20%
Profit threshold	£1,500,000

Patent box – deduction from net patent profit

Net patent profit x ((main rate – 10%)/main rate)

Value Added Tax (VAT)

Standard rate	20%
Registration limit	£82,000
Deregistration limit	£80,000

Inheritance tax: nil rate bands and tax rates

	£
6 April 2015 to 5 April 2016	325,000
6 April 2014 to 5 April 2015	325,000
6 April 2013 to 5 April 2014	325,000
6 April 2012 to 5 April 2013	325,000
6 April 2011 to 5 April 2012	325,000
6 April 2010 to 5 April 2011	325,000
6 April 2009 to 5 April 2010	325,000
6 April 2008 to 5 April 2009	312,000
6 April 2007 to 5 April 2008	300,000
6 April 2006 to 5 April 2007	285,000
6 April 2005 to 5 April 2006	275,000
6 April 2004 to 5 April 2005	263,000
6 April 2003 to 5 April 2004	255,000
6 April 2002 to 5 April 2003	250,000
6 April 2001 to 5 April 2002	242,000

Excess	Death rate	40%
	Lifetime rate	20%

Inheritance tax: taper relief

Years before death	Percentage reduction
Over 3 but less than 4 years	20%
Over 4 but less than 5 years	40%
Over 5 but less than 6 years	60%
Over 6 but less than 7 years	80%

Capital gains tax

Rates of tax	Lower rate	18%
	Higher rate	28%

Annual exempt amount	£11,100

Entrepreneurs' relief	Lifetime limit	£10,000,000
	Rate of tax	10%

National insurance contributions(not contracted out rates)

Class 1 employee	£1 – £8,060 per year	Nil
	£8,061– £42,385 per year	12%
	£42,386 and above per year	2%
Class 1 employer	£1 – £8,112 per year	Nil
	£8,113 and above per year	13.8%
	Employment allowance	£2,000
Class 1A		13.8%
Class 2	£2.80 per week	
	Small profits threshold	£5,965
Class 4	£1 – £8,060 per year	Nil
	£8,061 – £42,385 per year	9%
	£42,386 and above per year	2%

Rates of interest (assumed)

Official rate of interest	3%
Rate of interest on underpaid tax	3%
Rate of interest on overpaid tax	0.5%

Stamp Duty Land Tax

Non-residential properties	Rate
£150,000 or less	Nil
£150,001 to £250,000	1%
£250,001 to £500,000	3%
£500,001 and above	4%

Residential properties	
£125,000 or less	0%
£125,001 to £250,000	2%
£250,001 to £925,000	5%
£925,001 to £1,500,000	10%
£1,500,001 and above	12%

Stamp duty

Shares	0.5%

Review Form – Paper P6 Advanced Taxation (UK) (02/16)

Name: _____   Address: _____

_____

_____

How have you used this Kit?
(Tick one box only)

☐ On its own (book only)

☐ On a BPP in-centre course_____

☐ On a BPP online course

☐ On a course with another college

☐ Other _____

Why did you decide to purchase this Kit?
(Tick one box only)

☐ Have used the complimentary Study Text

☐ Have used other BPP products in the past

☐ Recommendation by friend/colleague

☐ Recommendation by a lecturer at college

☐ Saw advertising

☐ Other _____

During the past six months do you recall seeing/receiving any of the following?
(Tick as many boxes as are relevant)

☐ Our advertisement in *Student Accountant*

☐ Our advertisement in *Pass*

☐ Our advertisement in *PQ*

☐ Our brochure with a letter through the post

☐ Our website www.bpp.com

Which (if any) aspects of our advertising do you find useful?
(Tick as many boxes as are relevant)

☐ Prices and publication dates of new editions

☐ Information on product content

☐ Facility to order books

☐ None of the above

Which BPP products have you used?

Study Text	☐	*Passcards*	☐
Kit	☑	*Other*	☐

Your ratings, comments and suggestions would be appreciated on the following areas.

	Very useful	Useful	Not useful
Passing P6	☐	☐	☐
Questions	☐	☐	☐
Top Tips etc in answers	☐	☐	☐
Content and structure of answers	☐	☐	☐
Mock exam answers	☐	☐	☐

Overall opinion of this Kit	Excellent ☐	Good ☐	Adequate ☐	Poor ☐

Do you intend to continue using BPP products?   Yes ☐   No ☐

The BPP author of this edition can be emailed at: accaqueries@bpp.com

Please return this form to: Head of ACCA & FIA Programmes, BPP Learning Media Ltd, FREEPOST, London, W12 8AA

Review Form (continued)

TELL US WHAT YOU THINK

Please note any further comments and suggestions/errors below.